R

4-

HAUNTING
LEGACY

HAUNTING LEGACY

VIETNAM AND THE AMERICAN PRESIDENCY FROM FORD TO OBAMA

MARVIN KALB
DEBORAH KALB

BROOKINGS INSTITUTION PRESS
Washington, D.C.

Copyright © 2011
Marvin Kalb and Deborah Kalb

All rights reserved. No part of this publication may be reproduced or transmitted in any form or by any means without permission in writing from the Brookings Institution Press, 1775 Massachusetts Avenue, N.W., Washington, DC 20036, www.brookings.edu.

Library of Congress Cataloging-in-Publication data

Kalb, Marvin L.
  Haunting legacy : Vietnam and the American presidency from Ford to Obama / Marvin Kalb and Deborah Kalb.
    p.   cm.
  Includes bibliographical references and index.
  Summary: "Examines how presidential decision making has been influenced by America's defeat in the Vietnam war, studying presidents Ford, Carter, Reagan, George H. W. Bush, Clinton, George W. Bush, and Obama and how they have approached key decisions regarding conflicts while in office"—Provided by publisher.
  ISBN 978-0-8157-2131-4 (cloth : alk. paper)
  1. Presidents—United States—Decision making—History—20th century.
2. Presidents—United States—Decision making—History—21st century. 3. Vietnam War, 1961–1975—Influence. 4. United States—Military policy. 5. United States—Foreign relations—1945–1989. 6. United States—Foreign relations—1989– 7. United States—Politics and government—1945–1989. 8. United States—Politics and government—1989– I. Kalb, Deborah. II. Title.
  JK511.K35 2011
  973.92—dc22   2011013090

9 8 7 6 5 4 3 2 1

Printed on acid-free paper

Typeset in Minion

Composition by Cynthia Stock
Silver Spring, Maryland

Printed by R. R. Donnelley
Harrisonburg, Virginia

To Bernard Kalb

inspiring example, indefatigable editor,
curious, honest, and courageous journalist, who,
like so many others, covered the Vietnam War
and has lived ever since with its haunting memories

Contents

Acknowledgments

FIRST AND FOREMOST, our thanks go to four very special researchers and colleagues: Ilana Weinberg, who was present at the creation, helping with basic research, typing transcripts of many interviews, and organizing files; Sacha Evans, who took on Ilana's responsibilities with a smooth competence that was truly remarkable; Emma Zayer, who, like Ilana and Sacha, was a graduate of the George Washington University, dedicated to a career in journalism, smart, helpful, and efficient; and finally Joanna Margueritte, daughter of a French journalist based in Poland, who was educated in France and Germany, speaks four languages and has now decided to pursue a doctorate in photographic journalism at the University of Maryland. All four researchers threw themselves into the project with energy, a strong desire to learn, and a charm that softened even the occasional academic grouch. We're not sure we could have done it without them.

By transcribing many, many interviews, often under tight deadlines, Patti Pancoe, Gayane Manukyan, and Haykuhi Sekhposyan performed an invaluable service, and we thank them for their help.

A number of academic institutions and Washington think tanks were especially helpful, too, providing a stimulating intellectual environment essential for the completion of a book project that took more than five years. They were Harvard's Shorenstein Center on the Press, Politics and Public Policy at the Kennedy School; the Johns Hopkins School for Advanced International Studies; the Brookings Institution, especially its legendary lunchtime cafeteria, where every table hosts a serious seminar on issues from the morning newspapers; the Carnegie Endowment for International Peace, like Brookings, home to valuable research and exchanges of ideas and information; the United States Institute of Peace, a truly extraordinary institution devoted to peace making, a most worthy goal in our treacherous world; the Center for the National Interest, where lunches are the place for enlightening conversation about foreign policy questions; and, finally, the Global Media Institute at George Washington University's School of Media and Public Affairs, where one always enjoys the warm collegiality of friends and scholars. To have a desk, an office, or access to any of these institutions was a privilege.

We wish to offer special thanks to the late Walter Shorenstein, who inspired an academic discipline in press/politics and a pattern of generosity that was truly extraordinary. We miss him. His son, Doug Shorenstein, has picked up the banner and cause of the Shorenstein Center and carries it proudly. For maintaining the high quality of the center's work, Director Alex Jones has everyone's gratitude.

We are also grateful to Strobe Talbott and Stephen Hess of the Brookings Institution: Strobe for the winning environment he has created; Steve for his warm friendship, companionship, and scholarship. Richard Solomon and Tara Sonenshine of the United States Institute of Peace were cooperative, understanding, and tremendously helpful. Bless them both. Dimitri Simes and Paul Saunders of the Center for the National Interest could not have been more collegial. Michael Freedman of GW's Global Media Institute, and his colleagues Heather Date, Meaghan Calnan, and Lindsay Underwood, did more to advance this project than they realized, sometimes by doing no more than listening. Bill McCarren of the National Press Club, which cohosts *The Kalb Report* program, showed a remarkable calm in the chaos of contemporary journalism.

They all provided a home away from home.

Presidential libraries were an invaluable source of information. In almost all of them, the librarians were cooperative and knowledgeable. Several kept sending documents to us months after our initial request for help.

We interviewed dozens of senior officials from many different countries as well as former and current officials of the last seven presidencies. Many spoke on the record and they are quoted throughout the book, but many more chose to speak on background, still loyal to their earlier pledges of secrecy or concerned about offending or embarrassing colleagues. Very few spoke off the record.

Journalists were a special source. We loved them all. Most were generous, helpful, sharing firsthand impressions and information about the presidents and White House officials whom they covered. Journalists write and broadcast the first draft of history, operating in the worlds of politics, wars, and natural disasters. Many have shown extraordinary courage, skill, and a fearless determination to get their story—and get it right.

We reserved a special corner in our research for the officials, scholars, and journalists who had discovered the special qualities of Vietnam before, during, and after the war. Once touched by the country and the people, many remained students of Vietnam and tried never to forget the lessons of this lost war, always eager, in smaller circles as the years passed, to reminisce about a friend or a battle or a blunder. We benefited greatly from long conversations with many of them, including Stanley Karnow, whose *Vietnam: A History* still stands as a classic in an ever-widening field of study. What university today does not offer courses on the Vietnam War and depend on the works of, among others, Neil Sheehan, William Prochnau, and John Prados? Their books set the stage for what was to become the focus of this book, the haunting legacy of Vietnam whenever a president had to decide whether to send troops to fight.

We also benefited greatly from the cooperation of the gifted and professional staff of the Brookings Institution Press. Robert Faherty was first to spot the appeal and importance of *Haunting Legacy*. He has our eternal gratitude. His colleagues, including Chris Kelaher, Janet Walker, Venka Macintyre, Melissa McConnell, Natalie Fullenkamp, Erin Wiringi, Larry Converse, and Susan Woollen, richly deserve a heartfelt embrace for helping us through the process of contemporary publishing.

And then there were personal friends and colleagues, who listened, even laughed, made a suggestion or two or three, and seemed always to realize that all they had to do was be there—and they were: Dan Schorr, Hal Sonnenfeldt, Andy Glass, Arnaud deBorchgrave, Walter Reich, Elizabeth Drew, Ted Koppel, Garry Mitchell, and many others.

Finally, we thank those who make life worth living. Not for the first time, Madeleine G. Kalb has helped turn an idea for a book into a realistic project. Her keen editorial judgments and constant encouragement were not only welcome, they were essential. David Levitt and Jeremy Levitt were, as always, helpful and encouraging, David especially in finding televised reports concerning Vietnam. Aaron Kalb Levitt made the authors laugh through the long journey of researching, editing, and writing. He was an essential spark in the creative process. Estelle Levine lit a fire under us, knowing always when to say the uplifting word. Judith Kalb, Alexander Ogden, and Eloise Rose Kalb Ogden were loving and supportive. Bernard and Phyllis Kalb often made the difference, far more than they realized.

Marvin now cherishes this moment to extend special thanks to Deborah, and Deborah to Marvin. They made quite a team.

Introduction

No event in American history is more misunderstood than the Vietnam War. It was misreported then, and it is misremembered now.

—RICHARD NIXON, *No More Vietnams*, 1994

THE VIETNAM WAR ended on April 30, 1975. For the first time in American history, the United States lost: not to another superpower, which would have been bad enough, but to a small country in Southeast Asia. "A raggedy-ass little fourth-rate country," Lyndon Johnson said dismissively.

It was a humiliating experience for a nation proud of its history of freedom, economic opportunity, and military power. A certain mood of boundless self-confidence seemed to settle into a deepening self-doubt, as though the United States, having suffered its first defeat, had reached a tipping point in its distinguished history. Still a superpower, the United States went on to win the cold war; but the one battle of the war that it did lose, in Vietnam, had a disproportionate, powerful impact on American presidents, politics, and policy.

No doubt, a hundred years from now, historians will look back on this period and wonder why—given that the United States won the big war—its loss in the comparative backwater of Vietnam had so huge and lingering an impact on policymakers. Americans had enjoyed a feeling of limitless opportunity. No challenge seemed insurmountable, no war unwinnable. Even during the Tet offensive in January 1968, arguably the turning point in the Vietnam War, Secretary of State Dean Rusk pressed his thumb on a coffee table and proclaimed, with fearless self-confidence, that when the United States wanted to do something, it did it. The loss in Vietnam robbed the United States of its totally unrealistic, romantic sense of omnipotence. It left Americans feeling like other people who have suffered losses and indignities. It took some getting used to.

1

The raucous divisions of the 1960s between supporters and critics of the war, between hard hats and long-haired protesters, echoed through the years, affecting issues as diverse as immigration and abortion, gun control and the environment, and, of course, war and peace. While neither side had a monopoly on patriotism, both claimed it, poisoning the political atmosphere even further. One especially shameful example focused on a Senate race in Georgia in 2002 between Democratic senator Max Cleland, a Vietnam veteran who had left three limbs in the jungle swamps, and his Republican challenger, C. Saxby Chambliss, who did not serve in the military. It was an ugly race, during which Chambliss, in a TV advertisement, maliciously linked Cleland with Osama bin Laden and Saddam Hussein, in this way questioning the Democrat's loyalty and patriotism. Chambliss won the election.

The story of Vietnam, the war and its aftermath, runs like a bleeding wound through recent American history, affecting every president from Gerald Ford to Barack Obama and raising profound questions about their prerogatives and powers. How can a president avoid another Vietnam? Should a president commit troops to war only when "national interests" are directly involved? How are U.S. interests to be defined these days? Must a president have an "exit strategy" before committing troops? Should he, like George H. W. Bush at the time of the Persian Gulf War, use overwhelming military force, getting out as quickly as he got in? Or should he, like Ronald Reagan, shy away from using any military force, even after the killing of 241 U.S. Marines in Beirut? Does a president still need congressional backing, as Lyndon Johnson believed, or can he act on his own authority, considering, in this age of terrorism, the need for swift action?

These questions have no easy answers. When confronting such post-Vietnam challenges as terrorism and asymmetrical warfare, presidents have often found themselves haunted by the "ghosts" of Vietnam, as though, magically, in the entrails of a lost war, they may yet find a solution to their current problems, or discover a mistake they can avoid, or detect a way around the dysfunction and frustration they see and feel.

Presidents from Harry Truman in the mid-1940s to Nixon in the late 1960s bear a particular responsibility for the disaster in Vietnam. How could one president after another make so many unfortunate decisions? They did have other options. Nothing was written on tablets of stone. Yet, step by step, they committed the prestige and power of the United States to a colonial war in Indochina that soon morphed into a civil war, a colossal blunder that ended up wasting tens of thousands of American lives and millions of Vietnamese lives. These presidents reached their decisions in profound ignorance of Vietnam's history and culture. They lived in the cauldron of the cold war, and they worried about falling dominoes, seeing the loss of Vietnam as a step toward more catastrophic losses throughout the Pacific. And often in these years one heard a variation of the old politically charged question, once aimed at President Truman: "Who lost China?" Now, a Republican eyeing the White House might consider a campaign strategy rotating around the question, "Who lost Afghanistan?" The candidate's answer would almost certainly be Barack Obama.

Our story, to be clear, is not about the Vietnam War. That story has already been told by Stanley Karnow, Neil Sheehan, William Prochnau, John Prados, and many others. Our story is about the legacy of that war. Whatever the specific issue or provocation—whether it was the capture of the *Mayaguez* in 1975, the Soviet invasion of Afghanistan in 1979, the deaths of the 241 Marines in Beirut, Lebanon, in 1983, the Persian Gulf War, or the wars in Iraq and Afghanistan—Vietnam always seemed to have a seat in the Oval Office, playing a surprisingly critical role in many presidential decisions. The loss of Vietnam has profoundly changed how presidents decide questions of war and peace and how they interact with Congress, the public, and the world. In short, Vietnam has infiltrated the presidential DNA, even though presidents have struggled with this DNA in different ways.

Vietnam has also disrupted a familiar pattern in presidential politics of honoring and favoring those candidates who have served in the military. Since the founding of the Republic in 1776, military service during wartime has been a preamble to political reward. The commanding generals in three of America's major wars went on to become two-term presidents: George Washington after the Revolutionary War, Ulysses S. Grant after the Civil War, and Dwight D. Eisenhower after World War II. Andrew Jackson, the flamboyant hero of the War of 1812, rode his fame into the White House, as did Zachary Taylor, a general in the Mexican War. Theodore Roosevelt, commanding his Rough Riders, captured the public's imagination in the Spanish-American War and went on to win the White House. John Kennedy and Richard Nixon both launched their political careers in 1946 as World War II veterans, winning seats in the House of Representatives en route to their successful presidential campaigns.

Up until 1992, every successful presidential candidate since World War II had served his country in uniform during wartime. Then a baby boomer named Bill Clinton, who had danced through hoops to avoid service in

Vietnam, upset the traditional pattern by defeating a World War II hero, George H. W. Bush. In 1996 Clinton beat another World War II veteran, Robert Dole, badly wounded during the Italian campaign. In 2000 George W. Bush, a Texas governor who had joined the National Guard to sidestep Vietnam, outmaneuvered and beat Democrat Al Gore, an incumbent vice president who had served honorably as an army journalist in Vietnam. In 2004 Bush won again, defeating John Kerry, a Massachusetts senator who had fought in Vietnam and won medals for courage and valor. Kerry's Vietnam service, ironically, was a major factor in his defeat, as chapter 8 recounts. And in 2008 Obama, a young Democratic senator from Illinois, only thirteen years of age when the war ended, beat John McCain, a Republican senator from Arizona who had been shot down over North Vietnam and then spent five years in a Hanoi prison camp.

Clearly, any identification with Vietnam, whether as a military hero or an honorably discharged veteran, proved a political liability rather than an asset; avoiding military service in Vietnam was not a bar to election. The war drained American politics of the need for a commander-in-chief to be a veteran of military service.

Vietnam changed other patterns, too. The soldiers of the Vietnam War were primarily draftees, serving in the military as part of a broad system of compulsory national service. Nixon believed that the widespread antiwar demonstrations on college campuses were fueled by fears of the draft and the dangers of fighting in Vietnam. In 1969, the same year that he decided to start the withdrawal of American troops from Vietnam, he also decided to phase out the draft. Now the United States goes to war with an all-volunteer force, and there are few antiwar demonstrations on college campuses.

After Vietnam, the Pentagon surveyed the strategic landscape, and cringed. America's strategic arsenal had been depleted, its budget repeatedly cut or frozen in the country's focus on Southeast Asia. The army, navy, air force, and Marine Corps had all been diminished and demoralized. Left with feelings of shame and anger, many veterans found it hard to admit that they had been defeated; that in the jungles of Vietnam, the vaunted American military had somehow lost its fighting edge, its capacity to produce miracles on the battlefield.

It took more than a decade to rehabilitate the American military, and longer still to restore feelings of national pride. Part of this turnaround resulted from the development of a new kind of officer corps, highly educated, academic, determined to avoid leading troops into another Vietnam-style conflict. They spent time at universities and in think tanks, and they came up with new theories and doctrines of warfare. General David Petraeus, for example, obtained a Ph.D. from Princeton; his dissertation was on the lessons and mistakes of Vietnam.

The shadow of the American failure in Vietnam fell on every president from Gerald Ford to Obama, as each one, in his own way, grappled with foreign challenges of unprecedented complexity:

—Gerald Ford decided to use overwhelming force to liberate a merchant ship, the *Mayaguez*, seized by Cambodian pirates. Operating in the immediate aftermath of the Vietnam War, he worried that allies and adversaries would consider the United States a paper tiger.

—Jimmy Carter, appalled by the bloodletting of Vietnam, yearned for a bloodless presidency dedicated to peaceful endeavors. For a time, he succeeded: diplomacy produced a variety of agreements with Panama, China, the Soviet Union, Israel, and Egypt, all impressive accomplishments. But then came the seizure of the American embassy in Tehran and the Soviet invasion of Afghanistan. Prodded by his national security adviser, Zbigniew Brzezinski, Carter secretly armed an anti-Soviet force of fanatical mujahidin fighters to take on, slow down, and ultimately defeat the Soviet troops.

—Ronald Reagan was shocked by the terrorist murder of 241 U.S. Marines in Beirut. He knew who did it and where they were. Though he boasted of American power and position, he did not retaliate, even though American warships were then off the coast of Lebanon. After Vietnam, he did not want to put them through another difficult military adventure whose outcome was uncertain. Reagan also encouraged the creation of a new military doctrine, later called the Powell Doctrine, to determine when and under what circumstances the United States would or should enter a foreign conflict.

—George H. W. Bush, an adherent of the Powell Doctrine, sent a half-million-man army to the Middle East to evict Iraqi troops from Kuwait. He led a swift and successful operation and then withdrew the American troops. He refused to go as far as Baghdad and capture Saddam Hussein, because he was concerned that the United States could get too deeply involved in another foreign war.

—Bill Clinton, when faced with crises in Somalia, Haiti, and Kosovo, used diplomacy and the threat of force to gain an acceptable solution. He did not want to send ground troops anywhere. He feared another Vietnam, the war he hated and escaped with student deferments. His antiwar aides shared his strong aversion to the use of American military force unless absolutely necessary.

—George W. Bush, after 9/11, became a war president, believing that the world had to be put on notice that no one could assault the United States with impunity. He uprooted the Taliban regime in Afghanistan, and then invaded Iraq, where he got bogged down for a long time and where officials feared another Vietnam.

—Barack Obama, proclaiming that Afghanistan was not Vietnam, raised the number of American troops in Afghanistan to 100,000 in an effort to head off a Taliban takeover of the country. But he has been tormented by an enveloping fear that slowly but inexorably he was being drawn into another Vietnam. He made much of a July 2011 exit strategy, but then kicked the can down the road to December 2014, postponing the date for a substantial withdrawal of American troops. He seemed stuck in a war with no acceptable outcome.

In many of their decisions about war and peace, about foreign and political strategy, these seven presidents have been living with the gloomy legacy of a war lost decades ago. Words such as "Vietnam," "quagmire," or "syndrome" have become instant shorthand for the popular image of the United States getting trapped in another long, costly, and unwinnable war. No president can any longer reach critical decisions about committing troops to battle in faraway lands without weighing the consequences of the American defeat in Vietnam. That war still casts an unforgiving shadow over Oval Office deliberations. Unwanted, uninvited, but inescapable, Vietnam refuses to be forgotten.

1

Ford: Finally, the War Ends

My options were few.

—GERALD R. FORD, Remarks at a Symposium, Cantigny, Illinois, March 5, 1997

WHEN GERALD R. FORD picked up the fallen standard of American policy in Vietnam on August 9, 1974, after replacing the disgraced Richard M. Nixon, he felt "duty bound to honor my predecessor's commitment."[1] In fact, each American president since Harry Truman had felt "duty bound" to "honor" his "predecessor's commitment" to Vietnam. Facing the dangerous challenges of the cold war, they formed a unique partnership on the issue of Vietnam; they became a band of brothers, determined to protect one another's reputation, and that of the nation.

The Origins of the Commitment

On April 12, 1945, when Franklin D. Roosevelt died and Truman became president, Vietnam, a small country in Southeast Asia, lived on the far periphery of America's national interests. It was a French colony, and Truman was preoccupied with ending World War II. Only after Germany and then Japan surrendered did the new president come to appreciate the exploding challenges of the postwar world. None was more compelling than the global spread of communism. Stalin's Red Army occupied Eastern Europe, and the communist parties of France and Italy seemed on the edge of winning national elections. In Asia, Mao Tse-tung's army was sweeping toward victory in China, and Ho Chi Minh's guerrilla fighters were the emerging power in Indochina.

Truman launched an anticommunist counteroffensive that included the Truman Doctrine, which benefited Greece and Turkey; the Marshall Plan, a landmark aid program for Western Europe; the remarkable Berlin airlift, designed to break the Soviet blockade of Berlin; and the creation of the North

Atlantic Treaty Organization (NATO). In 1949 the Soviets tested their first nuclear bomb, breaking the American monopoly, and months later, Mao raised the red flag over Beijing. In this climate of building tension known as the cold war, Truman did not hesitate in June 1950 to involve American troops in the Korean War. It would have been politically unacceptable for Truman to stand by while another Asian country followed in China's path. Only five years after the end of World War II, the United States was again at war.

Because Truman needed France as a reliable ally against Stalinist expansion in Europe, he did not object to France's postwar reimposition of colonial rule in Indochina; and when France asked for American economic and military help, Truman quickly obliged, opening a $160 million line of credit, which expanded year after year. The United States also extended its diplomatic support, but in a manner so sloppy that Dean Acheson, Truman's secretary of state, once described it as a "muddled hodgepodge." The United States was "willing to help" the French, Acheson told Congress, but "not to substitute for them."[2]

And yet, within a few years, the United States did indeed "substitute" for the French. It happened quickly, at a time when the domino theory became the gospel of American policymakers. So it was no surprise that when Mao recognized Ho as leader of Vietnam in January 1950, Truman opted a month later to recognize the pliant French puppet, Bao Dai, as leader. This clash set the stage for a much deeper American involvement in Vietnam. Acheson revised his diplomatic vocabulary, tying the future of Vietnam to the security of the United States. "We are lost," he told British foreign secretary Anthony Eden, "if we lose Southeast Asia without a fight."[3] It was the start of a slippery slope.

After the Korean War, which concluded in 1953, Dwight Eisenhower wanted no part of another large-scale American military engagement on the Asian mainland, but he did send ten B-26 bombers and 200 air force personnel to help the French in their losing effort at Dien Bien Phu. In 1954, after the Geneva Conference split Vietnam into two parts, he recognized South Vietnam as a newly independent, noncommunist nation, a member of the "free world." In early 1955 he established the U.S. Military Aid and Advisory Group (MAAG) in Saigon, replacing France as the major foreign supporter of the South Vietnamese regime. Finally, in 1959, Ike infused the deepening American commitment to South Vietnam with powerful words, which later were used by other presidents to justify their expansion of the war: he said he had reached the "inescapable conclusion" that America's "national interests" were linked directly to the continued independence of a noncommunist South Vietnam.[4] Translation: America may have to go to war again to achieve this end.

John Kennedy sent "military advisers" to South Vietnam, increasing the number from 700 when he came to office to 16,000 by the time of his assassination, and Lyndon Johnson presided over a major escalation of the conflict, sending a half million U.S. troops. By the time Richard Nixon came to office in January 1969, the United States was already losing the war, facing deep dissent at home and probable defeat in the rice paddies of Vietnam. Nixon privately acknowledged, "There is no way to win this war. . . . But we can't say that, of course."[5] When Gerald Ford became president, following Nixon's resignation in August 1974, the Vietnam War was flickering to a sorrowful end. The commitment Truman had commenced died in disgrace. It was Ford's responsibility to bury Vietnam, but he and his successors found that Vietnam stubbornly refused to be buried.

A Ford, Not a Lincoln

Like many veterans who had served in World War II, Ford returned to find a different America. He had gone to war an "isolationist," believing that the United States should avoid "entangling alliances."[6] Grand Rapids, Michigan, was his world—"a strait-laced, highly conservative town" of "hard-working and deeply religious" Dutch immigrants.[7] Furniture was the principal industry, football the principal sport. But after the war, while there were still Dutchmen in Grand Rapids, everything else had changed: General Motors, auto parts, labor unions, and a comparatively large influx of southern blacks had moved into town. Ford, back from his naval duty in the Pacific as an officer on the USS *Enterprise*, a combat aircraft carrier, checked out the new Grand Rapids and realized that the war had changed him, too. He later acknowledged, "I had become an ardent internationalist." Prewar, his heroes were football players; now, his hero was a politician, the esteemed Senator Arthur Vandenberg, who stunned the GOP establishment by supporting the foreign policy of Democratic president Harry Truman. "The U.S.," Ford wrote, echoing Vandenberg's sentiment, "could no longer stick its head in the sand like an ostrich."[8]

In 1947 Ford stumbled upon a political opportunity that he could not resist. He had been working as a lawyer deeply engaged in community affairs. He loved people and politics. His Republican representative in Congress, Bartel J. (Barney) Jonkman, an old, "fervent isolationist" on the House Committee on Foreign Affairs, was bucking both Truman and Vandenberg in opposing the Marshall Plan. "No, no, no," he would rail from his privileged perch on Capitol Hill, not a penny for American aid to Europe. In Grand Rapids, a few Republicans, Ford among them, wondered whether Jonkman was too much of a political anachronism to represent their changing community. "Leave him be," Ford was advised. "He can't be defeated."[9] But in June 1948 Ford decided to challenge Jonkman in the GOP primary. To everyone's amazement, he beat him and then, in the election, overwhelmed the Democratic opponent, winning almost 61 percent of the vote.[10] Foreign policy was the issue, and Ford successfully attached himself to Vandenberg's internationalist philosophy. Grand Rapids had entered the world.

When Ford arrived on Capitol Hill in January 1949, he found himself in the company of, among many others, John F. Kennedy, Lyndon B. Johnson, and Richard M. Nixon, all three of whom were to precede him to the White House, where they made the unfortunate decisions that led the United States into the longest, most divisive foreign war in its history, a war that it ultimately lost. Ford proved to be an effective member of Congress, capable of listening, learning, and legislating and, when appropriate, cozying up to party leaders.

In the summer of 1953, as a member of the House Appropriations Committee's Defense Subcommittee, Ford visited Vietnam, then under the "nominal control" of the French, who seemed to have "no real plan for combating Communist insurgents led by Ho Chi Minh." Three words in his travel diary conveyed his impression of the French colonial regime: "speeches, pictures, ballyhoo." The French thought they would win the war. "They laid on a big briefing," outlining "their strategy to crush Ho and his forces." Four months later, Ford noted, the French were defeated at Dien Bien Phu. "Spit and polish, it turned out, was no match for the jungle fighting expertise of the Viet Minh."[11] Ford was clearly not impressed by the French, but he was by the communists. Shortly after the French collapse, the United States stumbled into Vietnam as principal backer of the anticommunist cause.

Many years later, Ford opened up to Bob Woodward and Christine Parthemore of the *Washington Post* that "there was a fundamental mistake made back after World War II, when the French had committed to support the Vietnamese." If France had not returned to Indochina, its old colonial empire, and if the United States, consistent with its anti-colonial tradition, had strongly objected to France's return, even threatening to cut its economic and military aid, then, Ford believed, the United States could have avoided getting trapped in the Vietnam quagmire. But France did return to Indochina, the United

States did not object, and ultimately, after Dien Bien Phu, the United States replaced France in a colonial war. "We were on the wrong side of the locals," Ford concluded. "We made the same mistake that the French did, except we got deeper and deeper in the war. We could have avoided the whole darn Vietnam War if somebody in the Department of Defense or State had said: 'Look here. Do we want to inherit the French mess?'"[12]

During the Eisenhower years, Ford acted like the Eagle Scout he had once been. He backed Ike when the United States threw its support behind the de facto creation of two Vietnams after the 1954 Geneva Conference; when it dumped Emperor Bao Dai and installed the autocratic Ngo Dinh Diem; when it began to slip military advisers into South Vietnam; and when Ike, in a major statement of policy, declared in 1959 that the survival of an independent, non-communist South Vietnam was in the "national interest" of the United States. During the 1950s, though he had his doubts, Ford never raised an objection to U.S. policy in Indochina, reflecting the broad indifference of congressional leaders to White House policymaking, especially when the White House was in Republican hands.

When John Kennedy became president in 1961, Ford supported his Vietnam policy too. When Kennedy proposed a foreign military aid bill containing a considerable sum of money for South Vietnam, many in the GOP rose in opposition. Ford, however, organized a moderate coalition of Vietnam supporters in both parties and saved the legislation. He also backed Kennedy's controversial decision to send more than 16,000 military advisers to South Vietnam.

Toward the end of his life, Ford entered a world of academic speculation that had intrigued and baffled scholars for many years: if Kennedy had lived and then had won a second term in 1964, would he have pulled American forces out of Vietnam? Ford never bought into that speculation. "If Kennedy regretted his decision to commit U.S. ground forces to Vietnam," he said, "he kept his regrets to himself. Nothing he did before he died suggests to me that he harbored such regrets—much less that he intended to withdraw the troops and, in effect, acknowledge his error in sending them there in the first place."[13]

On November 22, 1963, when Kennedy was assassinated and Johnson was sworn in as president, Ford "just couldn't believe it." In many respects, he admired Johnson. LBJ had been "extraordinarily effective" as Senate majority leader up until 1961, and as vice president "he had done well too."[14] But in Ford's judgment Johnson did not measure up to being a president. Even after his landslide victory in the 1964 election, Johnson acted in ways that troubled

Ford. LBJ loved his Great Society program. And yet he allowed himself to slip more deeply into the war in Vietnam. Ford wondered whether the war would disrupt the Great Society and whether the war could even be won. Ford saw him as "a President in anguish, haunted by the specter of [Kennedy] . . . governed by memories of the 1950s, when the debate over 'who lost China' helped to poison American politics" and "influenced . . . by the harsh memory of Munich, where appeasement only led to W[orld] W[ar] II[,] a conflict of unimaginable savagery."[15]

But when President Johnson called, Ford saluted. "Jerry," Johnson said, "I want to appoint a bipartisan blue-ribbon commission to investigate the assassination of President Kennedy. . . . I want to have two members from the House. Hale Boggs is going to be one, and I want you to be the other."[16] Ford agreed, and his participation in the commission raised his stature in the House, on television, and in the nation. In January 1965 he defeated the House minority leader, Charles Halleck, to take over the House's top GOP post. He saw the job as a major step toward becoming Speaker of the House, at the time his ultimate dream in national politics. Political public relations were part of his new duties; he was to put a pleasant Midwestern face on House Republicans. Everett Dirksen, a marvelously colorful character from Illinois with a deeply resonant voice, had the same job for Senate Republicans. Thus on television a new duo in American politics was born: the Ev and Jerry show. Once a week, the broadcast sparkled with their criticism of the Democrats and their defense of the Republicans. It was a political hit. On only one issue did the nation's two top Republicans ever disagree: Vietnam. Dirksen always supported Johnson's foreign policy, even as he plunged the country more deeply into a costly war; Ford, on the other hand, openly opposed Johnson's periodic bombing pauses, favoring a more effective use of the air force, meaning more bombing, not less. Ford also attacked Johnson's "shocking mismanagement" of the war, believing that the president could not have both guns and butter, and that one day he would have to raise taxes and pay the political price.[17] In March 1968 Johnson shocked everyone, including Ford, by announcing that he would not run for reelection. Vietnam had become too much of a burden.

In 1968 Richard Nixon campaigned as the candidate with what became known as a "secret plan" to end the war. He did not, in fact, have a secret plan but wanted to oversee a "strategic retreat" from Vietnam, a very difficult wartime maneuver; he sought to emulate none other than Charles de Gaulle, who managed to extricate France from the Algerian War with a degree of national honor. Perhaps, Nixon hoped, he could accomplish the same thing in Vietnam. Out with honor, he thought, assuming incorrectly that Vietnam was similar to Algeria, and Vietnamese similar to Algerians.

In his memoirs, Ford asked some relevant questions about Vietnam. Had U.S. civilian and military leaders really analyzed Vietnam's history and culture? Did they have a clear strategy? At the end of the day, did the American commitment in Vietnam make sense for the United States, globally in terms of its reputation and nationally in terms of societal tranquility and budgetary sacrifice? "The answer to these questions," Ford conceded, "is probably no." But he then asked another question: "Can we win this war?" He reflected that in the late 1960s, "I felt certain—given four basic assumptions—that we would prevail":

—If the United States used its military power "fully and appropriately."

—If the South Vietnamese could raise their military prowess to the level where they could defend themselves without American forces.

—If the South Vietnamese people would rally around their flag and support the war effort.

—If the United States, meaning Congress, would continue to fund the war effort, which was costing more and more each year.

Ford was unrealistic in raising these four "ifs," and he quickly seemed to realize his dilemma. He wrote with obvious candor:

> To varying degrees, none of these assumptions proved out. The war dragged on and on, and the damage it caused this country both domestically and internationally was truly staggering. Our greatest loss, of course, was the 58,000 American dead and the more than 100,000 who suffered serious injuries. Next came the loss of U.S. prestige around the world. The conflict created deep divisions among the American people and discredited our military. Lastly, LBJ's decision to provide both guns (the war cost us $150 billion) and butter without a tax increase had resulted in a terrible disruption of our economy. It would take America a long time to recover from these wounds.[18]

But during the Nixon years, even as his doubts deepened, Ford was always the loyal Republican and the patriotic American. When Nixon ordered American troops into Cambodia and then Laos and when he sent waves of B-52 strategic bombers over Hanoi and Haiphong, blitzing North Vietnam's capital and port over the Christmas holiday in 1972, Ford vigorously defended the president's controversial policy, never allowing a crack of daylight to shine between himself and Nixon. When Nixon transformed global diplomacy by visiting Beijing and then Moscow, temporarily isolating Hanoi in a new tri-angular vise, Ford was all over television praising the president's brilliance and creativity. And when in January 1973 Henry Kissinger finally concluded a face-saving compromise agreement with North Vietnam, ending America's role in the long and painful war, Ford was elated, as much for the country as for his own career; the Speaker's chair was now coming into focus.

But he could see that the agreement itself was tenuous, principally because, as he later wrote, "The North Vietnamese . . . never considered the Paris peace accords as the end of the conflict."[19] There were two other questions troubling Ford: would Congress continue to fund the war after all American troops were withdrawn and prisoners of war returned, and would the president, already burdened by the Watergate scandal, have enough political clout to resume military action against North Vietnam in the event of communist violations of the Paris accords?

As though the Paris accords had not signaled a negotiated end to the war, the North Vietnamese picked up where they had left off. They resumed their infiltration of troops and supplies into South Vietnam. Ford quickly recognized that because of Watergate, the president could not focus on Vietnam nor retaliate against the communists, meaning, for all practical purposes, that "North Vietnam could violate the accords with impunity."[20] The scandal had paralyzed the president; it had also encouraged Congress to pass legislation blocking any further American military action in Indochina. For Congress and the American people, the war was over; for Nixon, so, too, was his presidency, though it took several more months for the historic, president-toppling drama of Watergate to unfold. By the time it did, Vietnam was already over the horizon as a daily story. Only its legacy was left to haunt and bewitch the White House, as one president after another tried valiantly to bury both the Vietnam War and the cold war and meet the unexpected challenges of the age of terrorism.

On December 6, 1973, Ford—after Nixon had selected him to replace the scandal-tainted Spiro Agnew—took the oath of office as vice president, his left hand on a copy of the Jerusalem Bible his son had bought for the occasion. It was opened to Psalm 20: "May [God] answer you in time of trouble." His House colleagues gave him a standing ovation. "I am a Ford, not a Lincoln," the new vice president candidly told the chamber.[21]

By the following April, the Watergate scandal dominated the news on television and in newspapers. No other topic, no matter how urgent, could break into the national dialogue. During his weekly briefings for the vice president,

Kissinger told Ford that he was deeply worried that Watergate was jeopardizing the nation's foreign-policy agenda, making it much more difficult for him to challenge North Vietnamese violations of the Paris accords and defuse rising tensions in the Middle East.

The turmoil in Washington sparked speculation that Nixon might soon be impeached or forced to resign and that Ford, once considered a safe and convenient vice presidential selection, might soon become president of the United States. In his meetings with Nixon, Ford began to speak with more confidence and power. At one point he told Nixon that he could no longer support his "stonewalling" of congressional requests, and on another occasion he objected to Nixon's supposedly asking Nelson Rockefeller, "Can you see Gerald Ford sitting in this chair?" But Ford's mix of loyalty and hurt snapped on June 5, when he told a GOP fund-raiser in Columbus, Ohio, that Nixon was "innocent of any involvement in any cover-up" only to learn hours later that Nixon had been named an "unindicted co-conspirator" in the cover-up by a federal grand jury. Instinctively, Ford began to pull back from Nixon. "I was in an impossible situation," he later stated. "I couldn't abandon Nixon. . . . Nor could I get too close to him, because if I did I'd risk being sucked into the whirlpool myself."[22]

On August 8 Nixon asked Ford to come to the Oval Office. "I've made the decision to resign," Nixon announced solemnly. "It's in the best interest of the country." He added, "Jerry, I know you'll do a good job." Then, appearing more relaxed, the president provided Ford with a lengthy briefing on domestic and foreign affairs, stressing especially the need to strengthen NATO, conclude the strategic arms limitation agreement with the Soviet Union, and protect South Vietnam and Cambodia. Nixon emphasized Kissinger's key role: "Henry is a genius," he said, "but you don't have to accept everything he recommends. He can be invaluable, and he'll be very loyal, but you can't let him have a totally free hand." Interestingly, Nixon never mentioned Watergate in his briefing, did not rail against the media, and showed no vindictiveness toward anyone. He recommended Rockefeller to be Ford's vice president, but then added graciously, "It's your choice."[23] Years later, when Ford considered this historic moment, he reflected on the Nixon persona: "a brilliant mind . . . great sensitivity to the public's political mood . . . unique ability to analyze foreign policy . . . abhorred details . . . very shy . . . a loner . . . seemed to prefer dealing with paper work to dealing with people . . . a terribly proud man [who] detested weakness in other people . . . very bitter about members of Congress who wanted to cut and run from our obligations in South Vietnam . . .

detested those lawmakers who were trying to hamstring his efforts to settle the war from a position of strength." Finally, Ford noted, "his pride and personal contempt for weakness had overcome his ability to tell the difference between right and wrong."[24]

When Ford returned to his office after his climactic meeting with Nixon, his first call was to Kissinger. "Henry, I need you," Ford told the secretary of state. "The country needs you. I want you to stay. I'll do everything I can to work with you." Kissinger, skilled at massaging a presidential ego, responded, "There will be no problem. Sir, it is my job to get along with you and not yours to get along with me."[25]

On August 9, at noon, Nixon formally resigned, having told the nation the night before, "I have never been a quitter. . . . But, as President, I must put the interest of America first." He told his cabinet and White House staff, "Always remember . . . others may hate you, but those who hate you don't win, unless you hate them, and then you destroy yourself." Also at noon, Ford took the oath of office as president of the United States. "My fellow Americans," he said, in comforting tones, "our long national nightmare is over. Our Constitution works. Our great Republic is a government of laws and not of men." Ford offered "prayers" for "our former President . . . and his family." He closed by calling on the Almighty: "God helping me, I will not let you down."[26] And thus began the short, accidental presidency of Gerald R. Ford, which coincided with the final, humiliating collapse of the American undertaking in South Vietnam.

Only a Miracle Could Save South Vietnam

Even before Ford took the oath of office, Kissinger had already written an obituary on what the Vietnamese called "The American War." In his memoirs, the secretary wrote: "I knew that Cambodia was doomed and that only a miracle could save South Vietnam. North Vietnamese communications to us grew progressively more insolent. There was no longer even the pretense of observing the Paris Agreement. And our legislated impotence added humiliation to irrelevance."[27] Granted, Kissinger tended to strike a pose of innocent grandeur amid uncontrollable and malevolent forces, but putting aside his role—and Nixon's—in the development of this diplomatic debacle, he did paint an honest portrait of the end of an era of American ineptitude in Indochina. For Ford at this time, history imposed a more humble task: that of the mortician, whose job it was to bury a lost war. The scope of the failure in

Vietnam came into sharper relief as Watergate forced Nixon's resignation, Congress withheld funding for South Vietnam, and North Vietnam systematically proceeded with its reunification of the country under communist rule.

The landmarks of this historic defeat were everywhere, though Ford fought gallantly against the obvious and what some considered the inevitable. The Central Intelligence Agency (CIA) compiled another National Intelligence Estimate for the new president. "Communist military forces in South Vietnam," it started, "are more powerful than ever before. . . . The evidence points toward a marked increase in military action between now and mid-1975. . . . At a minimum the Communists will sharply increase the tempo of fighting by making greater use of their in-country forces and fire-power."[28] It did not yet predict an all-out offensive but considered one very likely if Hanoi sensed that the moment was right. And events in Washington and South Vietnam moved Hanoi persuasively in this direction.

Ford pardoned Nixon, igniting a new political storm, and the Democrats scored significant victories in the November 1974 midterm elections, strengthening antiwar sentiment on Capitol Hill. A deep sense of war weariness seemed to settle over the country, certainly over Washington, and the news from Saigon brought no reassurance. Although Ford sent a string of letters to Nguyen Van Thieu promising support, the South Vietnamese leader faced the reality of shrinking supplies of ammunition and increasing doses of American criticism in the media and in Congress. In October Ford signed a military appropriations bill providing $700 million for South Vietnam, and in December he signed a foreign assistance bill setting aside $617 million for all of Indochina. Ford had asked for an appropriation of $1 billion.[29] In fact, only about $200 million in aid actually reached Saigon. The handwriting was on the wall, clear enough for anyone in Saigon and Hanoi to read: no matter how forceful Kissinger's arguments, nor matter how plaintive Ford's appeals to national honor and patriotism, the United States was showing the world that it wanted "out" of this war.

And yet in Hanoi the Politburo was actually split on the question of whether the United States would again intervene in the war that the Paris Peace Accords clearly had not ended. Aging revolutionary Pham Van Dong told his colleagues that though the U.S. bombers might return, the ground troops, he was certain, would not, "even if we offered them candy." Another of the leaders, Le Duan, encouraged as much by the ineffectiveness of the Army of the Republic of Vietnam (ARVN) as by congressional caution, advocated an aggressive strategy for reunifying Vietnam under communist rule.

He wanted "to create conditions for a general uprising in 1976," timed for the next American presidential election campaign, and "if opportunities present themselves," he wanted to "seize the moment" and move even more expeditiously toward victory.[30]

In late 1974 Kissinger asked his Vietnam expert, Richard Smyser, to check the reliability of fresh intelligence showing a considerable increase in North Vietnamese troop infiltration into South Vietnam. Upon examining all the intelligence available to him, Smyser told Kissinger that, in his judgment, the North Vietnamese were indeed getting ready for a big move. "I told him that the North Vietnamese did not focus mainly on American elections but on what they judged to be the situation (and the chances for victory) in South Vietnam," Smyser recalled. "I said that they could very well attack in 1975 if they thought the military and political situation in the South was favorable. The build-up suggested that their attack would come in 1974–75, not a year later. It should not come as a surprise to us."[31]

In early January 1975 the North Vietnamese, ready for not just another offensive but perhaps the climactic offensive of the war, chose their first target with care, eager to test the ARVN's strength in the Central Highlands. Shifting from a strategy of guerrilla warfare to a more familiar, traditional kind of warfare, they sent 8,000 well-armed, regular army troops against an ARVN unit protecting Phuoc Binh, a provincial capital in a sparsely populated mountainous area bordering Cambodia. For more than a week, the North Vietnamese pounded the capital with artillery and rocket fire. When it was clear that the South Vietnamese were not going to be reinforced, the communists stormed into the capital, seized control, and raised their flag. This time, unlike in 1972 when they took another provincial capital, Quang Tri, but then were forced to abandon it, they were determined to hold on, thus sending a signal to all of South Vietnam that the communists were again on the move. Thieu was shocked by the complete collapse of his army garrison at Phuoc Binh, and he made a snap decision that he would later regret, ordering his forces into a broad retreat across the country. His order had a cataclysmic effect, exactly the opposite of what he wanted; it accelerated the disintegration of many ARVN units, raised questions about his military acumen, and deepened fears among many Vietnamese that the United States was abandoning them.

Ford, discouraged by events in South Vietnam, rushed to Congress with fresh requests for additional military aid. He asked for a $1.4 billion aid package for South Vietnam and Cambodia. "With adequate United States military assistance," he said, "they can hold their own. We cannot turn our backs on

these embattled countries."[32] He urged a high-ranking congressional delegation to visit Saigon. He put his case to powerful columnists. Ford seemed truly
to believe that, with another infusion of American aid, South Vietnam and
Cambodia could still be saved. He could not accept the congressional consensus that further support for South Vietnam, whether measured in pennies or
billions, was a waste of money.

On March 10 the North Vietnamese moved suddenly against Ban Me
Thuot, the squalid capital of Darlac Province. The operation was under the
command of General Van Tien Dung, at age fifty-eight the youngest member of the Politburo. Highly professional, patient, and calculating, he sent his
troops on a deceptive feint toward Pleiku, sucking the ARVN into a mistaken
reinforcement of the city. He then ordered the bulk of his three regular army
divisions to attack Ban Me Thuot, softening it up with artillery and rocket fire
before sending tanks and troops into the city and overwhelming the surprised,
bewildered ARVN force.

As one provincial capital after another fell to their advancing troops, the
North Vietnamese debated the big question: should they go for the gold prize
now, or should they continue their offensive, cautiously probing, pushing,
acquiring another provincial capital or two, until they reached that magic
moment in the campaign when the enemy collapsed and they rode triumphantly into Saigon? On March 24 the Politburo decided that the time was
ripe for victory. It sent a new set of instructions to General Dung: he was
to "liberate" South Vietnam. He was to move on Saigon before Thieu had a
chance to defend it. And he was given a tight timetable. He had until the last
week of April to start the offensive. "From then on," an aide declared, "we
were racing the clock."[33]

Thieu reacted to the unexpected loss of Ban Me Thuot by redeploying
ARVN to protect larger, more heavily populated coastal and southern regions
of the country and to prepare a counteroffensive against a suddenly more
aggressive enemy. He placed General Pham Van Phu in charge of the Central
Highlands. Phu was corrupt and totally without imagination. Thieu knew of
his reputation but still assigned him to the job. Even under the command of a
brighter, more effective officer, it might already have been too late. The redeployment quickly disintegrated into a sloppy, disorderly rout, and the counteroffensive never materialized. Phu, outclassed and outmaneuvered by Dung,
requisitioned a helicopter, gathered his family and cronies, and departed from
the spreading battle in the Central Highlands, leaving more than 200,000
ARVN troops and their families without a leader.

Into this growing vacuum flowed more and more North Vietnamese troops, tanks, trucks, and armaments. Pleiku fell, and soon thereafter Kontum. Surprised, Hanoi had not expected so sudden and stunning an enemy collapse. Usually cautious, the Politburo now moved in for the kill, ordering another wave of regular army troops to cut across the demilitarized zone (DMZ) and flood all of Quang Tri Province. Within days, they entered the capital city of Quang Tri and then advanced further south toward the old imperial capital of Hue. More than a million panicked refugees fled on the main, clogged highway toward Danang, South Vietnam's second largest city, already overflowing with other refugees and retreating troops. In a short time, communist forces reached the outskirts of Danang, firing rockets into the central square, terrifying citizens into finding any means of escape.

On March 26, as the situation in Danang worsened, the State Department announced that the United States would begin evacuating thousands of Vietnamese refugees and all U.S. personnel from the endangered city. Boeing 747 cargo planes would fly them to Saigon and then on from there. Confusion, chaos, and the usual bureaucratic snafus impeded a smooth evacuation.

On March 29 an impatient Edward Daley, president of World Airways, flew one of his own jumbo jets into Danang. The pockmarked runway was jammed with frantic citizens. Almost 300 Vietnamese boarded the plane in ten minutes, while several fell to their deaths as they tried to cling to the aircraft. The following day, Easter Sunday, five days after Hue had succumbed to the North Vietnamese, Danang fell to 35,000 advancing communist troops.

Ford, tired and testy, then left for a golfing vacation in Palm Springs, California, much to the unhappiness of his press secretary, Ron Nessen, who worried justifiably that Americans would see the president relaxing with his Hollywood friends in one news story and then in another see thousands of South Vietnamese women and children fleeing for their lives.[34]

It was on the flight to California that Nessen, a former NBC war correspondent who had survived five assignments in Vietnam and developed a love for the Vietnamese people, got a flash report that Danang had just fallen to the communists. Crestfallen, he brought the news to the president. Ford read the report, Nessen recalled, but said nothing.[35] Nessen, though, thinking of his Vietnamese friends, later broke down in tears.[36]

The traveling White House press corps, seeking Ford's reaction to the fall of Danang, caught up with him at one point during his vacation. The normally affable Ford would usually stop, exchange pleasantries, and answer a few questions. This time he tried walking past the reporters without answering their questions, like the imperial president he never wanted to be. At first he moved slowly and then, to everyone's surprise, much more quickly, until finally he was running, apparently as fast as he could. Ford finally reached the welcoming comfort of his bulletproof limousine, which no question could penetrate. It was an unforgettable sight.[37]

Before leaving for California, Ford had met in the Oval Office with Kissinger, General Brent Scowcroft, and General Frederick Weyand, the army chief of staff, to review the crisis. Even this late in the Saigon saga, they were still unable to get a handle on the damage, and they wondered whether the ARVN could mobilize a counteroffensive and whether Saigon itself was now in imminent jeopardy. As though he could still affect the outcome of the war, Ford decided to send General Weyand to South Vietnam and Cambodia on a fact-finding mission. Ford set a strict deadline of no more than a week. When the others had left the room, photographer David Kennerly, who had worked for *Time-Life* in South Vietnam for more than two years and had been in the room taking pictures, remarked to Ford, "Vietnam is falling to pieces." Kennerly wanted to see for himself, to accompany Weyand and provide another perspective. Ford nodded. "Do it," he said.[38]

April 1975 opened with a presidential plea that 2,000 South Vietnamese orphans be evacuated immediately and flown to the United States. The money, Ford assured his former colleagues, would come from a special $2 million foreign aid children's fund. A devastating footnote: during the orphan evacuation, one C-5A transport plane, carrying 243 orphans and 66 adults, crashed soon after takeoff, killing everyone on board.

Other questions crowded Ford's desk. What about the 6,000 Americans still in and around Saigon? Would they also be evacuated, and if so, when and how? Defense Secretary James Schlesinger, who was often odd man out in the Ford White House, urged that their evacuation begin promptly. He cited the obvious dangers. Ford and Kissinger opposed a quick evacuation, concerned that ARVN troops, disappointed by what they could interpret as a U.S. betrayal, might then turn their guns on the remaining Americans. This dispute between Schlesinger on the one side and Ford and Kissinger on the other persisted to the very end; Schlesinger tended to be much more realistic about the crisis than the president and his secretary of state.

On April 5 Weyand returned with a report that seemed wildly disconnected from the stormy political and military reality in Saigon. He told Ford what Ford wanted to hear: that with additional U.S. military aid, costing roughly $722 million, the Thieu regime in Saigon could be saved.

Kennerly, in his private briefing for the president, was unyieldingly pessimistic, providing the other perspective he had promised: "Cambodia is gone,"
he said, "and I don't care what the generals tell you; they're bullshitting you if
they say that Vietnam has got more than three or four weeks left. There's no
question about it. It's just not gonna last."[39]

Would Ford cling to the slim reed of hope provided by Weyand? Or would
he believe Kennerly? Neither in his memoir nor in previously secret cables
or communications did he reveal his true beliefs. He continued to read the
somber CIA and U.S. embassy reports from Saigon, with their clear, underlying message: "Get out, it's over." But by word and action he conveyed the
impression that the United States still could affect the outcome of the war.
On April 10 Ford went to Congress with a televised appeal for $722 million in
military aid and $250 million for economic and humanitarian assistance. "The
options before us are few," Ford said, "and the time is very short." Kissinger
had advised Ford to deliver a "go down with the flags flying" speech, blaming
Congress for the debacle in Indochina, but Ford had waved him off. Instead,
Ford tried to reach for the soul and conscience of the country and remind
Congress that, despite Watergate, the United States still had global responsibilities. "We cannot . . . abandon our friends while our adversaries support
and encourage theirs," he told his former colleagues. "Let us put an end to
self-inflicted wounds. Let us remember that our national unity is a most price-
less asset. Let us deny our adversaries the satisfaction of using Vietnam to pit
Americans against Americans. At this moment the United States must present
to the world a united front."[40]

Not once was Ford's appeal to Congress interrupted by applause. Even the
Republicans sat on their hands. Popular reaction also was unenthusiastic. Just
a thousand or so calls and telegrams reached the White House in support of
the president; two-and-a-half times that number opposed him.[41] If Ford had
delivered the speech on the day of his inauguration, he might have been able
to arouse more sympathy and support from the public and Congress. But no
longer. A former colleague from the House, Donald Riegle of Michigan, had
advised the president that "the American people and the elected Congress
had decided to close the book" on Vietnam. Another friend, Republican Bob
Michel of Illinois, thought Ford could and should make "a clean break with
Vietnam" and have no "sense of guilt over Vietnam and Cambodia during
his stewardship, because he is in an altogether new ball game since Nixon
and Watergate."[42]

A few days later, on April 14, the Senate Foreign Relations Committee requested a meeting with Ford. The request was highly unusual, but Ford agreed. They all gathered in the Cabinet Room. The atmosphere, Ford remembered, was "extremely tense." Kissinger and Schlesinger described the political and military positions, and the Senate reaction was swift and decidedly negative. "Get out, *fast*," the senators urged. Republican Jacob Javits of New York said, "I will give you large sums for evacuation . . . but not one nickel for military aid." Democrat Frank Church of Idaho discouraged a large-scale evacuation of all loyal Vietnamese, fearing that such an effort "could involve us in a very large war." Democrat Joe Biden of Delaware, years later to become vice president, echoed Church's fears. "I will vote for any amount for getting the Americans out," he told Ford. "I don't want it mixed with getting the Vietnamese out."

Ford thought the senators were "incredibly short-sighted." The United States "couldn't just cut and run." After an hour, the meeting ended with Ford politely telling the senators that while he respected their views, he disagreed with their opinions. "If we try to pull out right now," he warned, "it'll lead to panic and the chaos will jeopardize the lives of untold Americans."[43] What Ford knew at the time but did not tell the senators was that the communist Khmer Rouge were surrounding the Cambodian capital, Phnom Penh, and Ambassador John Gunther Dean and his staff were burning official documents, packing, and making other last-minute preparations before being helicoptered to safety. Cambodia was, as Kennerly had warned, days away from falling under communist control. It fell on April 17.

The problem now was South Vietnam. While the evacuation from Cambodia, which involved a comparatively small number of people, could proceed smoothly, the numbers in South Vietnam were considerably higher, posing huge logistical difficulties. In addition to the 6,000 Americans still in country, there were at least 100,000 Vietnamese who had worked for the United States and who wanted and deserved consideration. Counting their families, the number of potential evacuees could swell to nearly a million. How could they be extricated without triggering the "panic" that Ford feared? Could anyone be certain, he asked, that angry government troops would not open fire on the departing Americans? Besides, how was one to measure Vietnamese loyalty? The questions were almost biblical in complexity. Was the ambassador's driver more deserving of evacuation than the soldier who fought in a losing cause? Was Thieu's cabinet assured of evacuation while other Vietnamese had to take their chances? Up until the last moment, Ambassador Graham Martin acted as if he believed Saigon could be successfully defended. He opposed any form of evacuation, and he worked the phones from Saigon to Capitol Hill trying to encourage additional aid for the ARVN.

But Ford finally concluded that even if Saigon somehow could be saved, the evacuation of the remaining 6,000 Americans was prudent and probably necessary. On April 16 he formally ordered the evacuation of all "nonessential" Americans. The evacuation was to start immediately. Martin, a flinty, highly experienced diplomat who had lost a son in the war and who cared deeply about the Vietnamese people, picked the same day to send Kissinger a cable claiming that no American was in imminent danger. It often seemed in those final days that Martin in Saigon was pursuing one policy while Kissinger in Washington was pursuing another.

For example, Kissinger, using back channels to the Kremlin, tried to negotiate an understanding with North Vietnam allowing the United States to evacuate its citizens from South Vietnam in a safe and orderly way. Brezhnev, enjoying the spectacle of an American defeat, was Kissinger's middleman to Hanoi. The Soviet leader assured Kissinger that while North Vietnam did not seek to humiliate the United States and would not interfere with the evacuation of its citizens, the Hanoi government wanted all Americans out of South Vietnam quickly. They agreed on a final date of May 3. Kissinger did not tell Martin about his understanding with Moscow and Hanoi, and their relations tumbled into a deep freeze.

Martin, meanwhile, was working his own diplomatic game. He was frantically toying with the highly inflammable notion of ousting Thieu in a coup and replacing him with a general, such as the always-available Duong Van Minh, known popularly as "Big Minh," who might be acceptable to the communists in a new coalition government. Martin was not thinking clearly; the communists, already on the cusp of a long-delayed victory, no longer needed a coalition government to serve as a way station to power. Thomas Polgar, the CIA station chief in Saigon, collaborated with Martin in concocting this conspiracy, but his boss, Director William Colby, rejected the plan, arguing persuasively that the United States was complicit in the 1963 coup to oust Diem, which, he said, was a blunder of monumental proportion.

Kissinger by this time wanted only to see the war come to a quick end. At one meeting, using loose language to conceal his impatience, the secretary was heard to mumble, "Why don't these people die fast? . . . The worst thing that can happen would be for [South Vietnam] to linger on."[44]

On April 21, having learned of the Martin-Polgar conspiracy, mindful of the Diem coup and murder, and judging a communist victory to be only days away, Thieu packed his bags and four days later fled to Taiwan. He had sniffed an American betrayal as far back as the summer of 1969, when Nixon began to withdraw American forces from South Vietnam.

Thieu's flight ended Ford's illusionary quest for additional economic and military aid for South Vietnam. "Communist forces moved closer and closer to the capital," Ford later recalled. "I faced the fact that the end was near."[45] The depressing results of the battle at Xuan Loc, a junction town thirty-five miles northeast of Saigon, provided him with further proof. Forty thousand North Vietnamese regular army troops encountered unusually fierce resistance from the ARVN, whose soldiers fought well but ultimately lost the battle. The North Vietnamese sped south, heading for Saigon.

Ford publicly recognized the obvious in a speech at Tulane University on April 23. He no longer tried to justify the American involvement in Vietnam. Instead, he attempted simply to put the war in a historical context, in effect pronouncing the end of an American misadventure that took too many lives, accomplished little, and lasted for more than twenty-five years. "Today, Americans can regain the sense of pride that existed before Vietnam. But it cannot be achieved by refighting a war that is finished," he declared. "These events, tragic as they are, portend neither the end of the world nor of America's leadership in the world."[46] Ford was deliberately putting distance between his view of the war and the Nixon-Kissinger view. Nixon had always argued that the United States could only walk away "with honor," or else its international reputation and leadership would be irreparably harmed. Not so, Ford concluded; the country would survive its bloody and embarrassing defeat in Vietnam and once again flourish. Nixon had traditionally taken a more gloomy view of Vietnam, Ford a more optimistic one. Kissinger, who had not been given a chance to read the Ford speech, was furious and disappointed.

Now the president faced two immediate, practical problems: getting the remaining Americans out of harm's way in Saigon, and then managing the challenge and costs of housing, feeding, and transporting more than 100,000 Vietnamese who had labored on America's behalf over the years.

The final days were hectic and uncertain. On April 28 Scowcroft interrupted a meeting in the Cabinet Room, where Ford was talking with his chief economic and energy advisers, with bad news for the president. Communist forces, now on the outskirts of Saigon, had fired rockets and artillery shells at Tan Son Nhut Airport, making a mockery of Hanoi's promise to Kissinger that North Vietnam would not hinder a safe evacuation of American personnel from Saigon and forcing the U.S. Air Force to stop its evacuation flights. The communists hit and destroyed a C-130 transport plane and killed several marines. If they continued rocketing the airport, then Ford would have to initiate Option IV, the mass evacuation by helicopter of thousands of Americans and South Vietnamese. Ford waited a few hours, hoping the shelling would stop. Eventually it did stop, but before the evacuation could resume, hundreds and then thousands of desperate refugees rushed on to the runways and refused to leave. Planes could neither leave nor arrive. "The situation there was clearly out of control," Ford concluded.[47] Shortly before midnight, out of other options, he resorted to Option IV. Thus began the largest helicopter evacuation in history.

The Signal Was Crosby and Christmas

According to a prearranged plan, Bing Crosby's famous rendition of "I'm Dreaming of a White Christmas" was beamed all over Saigon, the signal to Americans and Vietnamese that the final evacuation was beginning. They were to drop everything and rush to certain predesignated places. Pandemonium quickly replaced the plan. As rumors spread of an impending rocket assault on Saigon, mobs of hysterical Vietnamese raced to the airport and the embassy. Thousands stampeded the embassy and a nearby building, many climbing the walls to reach the helicopters on the rooftops; when filled, the choppers would take off with dozens of other Vietnamese clinging to their runners. It was a scene of emotion, fear, desperation, and humiliation, clearly marking the end of an era. Television pictures captured the attention of the world, friend and foe alike: the most powerful nation on earth had been reduced to a helicopter escape after losing the first war in its history to a small country in Southeast Asia.

Martin, suffering from exhaustion and pneumonia, had refused to pack and ship his special collection of Asian curios out of the country. Up until the last minute, in a state of stubborn denial, he could not accept the fact that the war was ending with an American defeat and a communist victory. Finally, holding the embassy flag, he slowly boarded a helicopter, which brought him and his wife safely to a ship off shore. Several times on that fateful day, Kissinger had ordered Martin to leave the embassy, but he had waved off the secretary, saying he would take such an order only from the president.

Option IV took eighteen hours, an amazingly brief time for a humanitarian miracle by helicopter never before attempted or accomplished.[48] The rescuers used 70 helicopters and flew 630 sorties. When it was all over, the pilots could hardly believe they had rescued 1,373 Americans, 5,595 Vietnamese, and 85 third-country nationals.

At any point in the evacuation, North Vietnamese troops, then in command of Saigon, could have shot down the helicopters. Instead, under strict orders from Hanoi not to interfere with the American evacuation, they just watched this final withdrawal of American forces. "Let them go home," they seemed to be saying. One day, Hanoi suspected, Vietnam would need the United States as an economic partner or as an ally against China, a neighbor with a long record of expansionism. Many years later, communist officials took the lid off their strategic calculations at the time of the American pullout. The "American War," as they put it, was over, but their contest with China was never-ending.

At the White House, Kissinger and Nessen briefed reporters on the final evacuation, which they described as a complete success, with all of the Americans safely removed. Considering the importance of the news, it was a surprisingly short briefing, attended by few reporters. Many of the others were already writing their stories on the basis of television coverage. After Kissinger and Nessen left the podium, Scowcroft greeted them with the news that, in fact, there were still 129 marines in Saigon.[49] Not all of the Americans had been evacuated, and what they had just told the reporters was not true. Donald Rumsfeld, then the White House chief of staff, also joined in an impromptu summit. What they knew was that a helicopter was then on its way back to Saigon to get the marines, a job that would take no more than two hours. Neither Nessen nor Kissinger had intentionally lied. No big deal, they thought. But Rumsfeld interjected: "What if they don't get out . . . and they could end up getting killed?" Rumsfeld had been in Congress during the worst days of the war and felt the government had not been "totally straight" with the American people about the war. He remembered telling his White House colleagues, "I don't think we ought to have this war end on a lie."[50] Everyone agreed that Rumsfeld had a point. Nessen was sent back to the briefing room to tell the reporters about the 129 marines, soon to be the last Americans to leave Saigon. As the marines were helicoptered to safety, thousands of North Vietnamese troops raised a communist flag over the presidential palace. They had won.

Ford had one other task, a "special obligation," as he put it, before he could close this chapter in the Vietnam saga. He wanted to help those Vietnamese refugees who had left Vietnam but had nowhere to go. Thailand would not give them asylum. Neither, he learned, would Malaysia, Indonesia, or the Philippines. On April 30, a day filled with the dark headlines of defeat, Ford turned to Congress with an appeal for $507 million to care for the Vietnamese refugees. It took Congress less than a day to say no. It wanted no part of Vietnam. Senate Democratic whip Robert Byrd of West Virginia put it bluntly: "There is no political support for it in this country."

"Unbelievable!" Ford responded in despair. After World War II, the United States had opened its doors to more than a million displaced people. After the Hungarian uprising in 1956, the United States had welcomed 50,000 Hungarian refugees. After Castro stormed to power in 1959, more than a half million Cubans were admitted to the country. Ford assumed the role of moral leader in a personal crusade to help the Vietnamese, arguing that they deserved legal admission to the United States as well as American help in getting jobs and housing. They had sided with the United States in the struggle against communism in Indochina, and, as American allies, deserved American assistance.

Ford found a few supporters in Governors Reubin Askew of Florida, James Longley of Maine, and Dan Evans of Washington. George Meany, president of the American Federation of Labor and Congress of Industrial Organizations (AFL-CIO), said his union would help. So did the American Jewish Committee, which felt a special sympathy for homeless refugees. Ford himself traveled extensively through the country, selling his belief that the United States had to help these Vietnamese. "It was a matter of principle," he wrote later. "To ignore the refugees in their hour of need would be to repudiate the values we cherish as a nation of immigrants, and I was not about to let Congress do that." Slowly, under this steady presidential pressure, America began to open its doors. Refugee camps were established. Private citizens and organizations volunteered their time and resources, and more than 100,000 Vietnamese refugees came to the United States, ultimately enriching American society.[51]

Ford had won his personal battle, but the United States had lost the war. Now one president after another had to face the consequences of a lost war.

2

Ford and the Mini-Challenge of the *Mayaguez*

Vietnam was there as a great big flashing light, saying "Be careful of these entanglements."
—STROBE TALBOTT, Interview, December 4, 2007

THE FIGHTING STOPPED, but in many ways, the war continued. It was no longer the bloody conflict that had convulsed the nation. Now Vietnam seemed to morph into historical digressions about war, peace, and presidents; code words suggesting unwanted and unwinnable wars; and troubling strategic questions that barged into the Oval Office like unwelcome guests, whether a Democrat or a Republican sat behind the desk.

One of the best chroniclers of the American presidency, *Washington Post* reporter Bob Woodward, believes that the Vietnam War runs through the White House and the government like a "bare, 10,000-volt wire."[1] Not the war itself; that had ended on April 30, 1975, when the United States, wounded and humiliated, helicoptered its way out of South Vietnam. Now it was the haunting legacy of the war, particularly the way in which it influenced every president since Gerald Ford to remember the painful lessons of this lost war when considering the use of American military force. A president might stress the need for a clear mission statement, or an exit strategy, without quite realizing that he was responding to a mutation of the Vietnam experience. For example, Vietnam was at the table when both Ford and George H. W. Bush concluded that they needed to use quick, overwhelming military force while avoiding long and costly wars in Cambodia or Iraq.

On the morning of May 12, 1975, exactly twelve days after the collapse of the American misadventure in South Vietnam, the world came knocking at President Ford's door in the form of a crisis in Southeast Asia, and it wanted to know how the United States would respond. Had it lost its will to lead and, if necessary, to fight? The *Frankfurter Allgemeine Zeitung*, a respected

German newspaper, ran a front-page editorial with the eye-catching head-line, "America—A Helpless Giant," which reflected growing European doubt about America's willingness to defend its global interests. Ford, aware of this problem, felt that the United States "would not permit our setbacks to become a license for others to fish in troubled waters."[2] And yet on this beautiful Mon-day morning in springtime Washington, someone was indeed fishing in "trou-bled waters" off the coast of Cambodia, and Ford was suddenly faced with the first serious challenge of the post-Vietnam era.

National Security Adviser Brent Scowcroft interrupted the president's morning schedule with the disturbing news that an American merchant ship, the SS *Mayaguez,* had just been seized off the Cambodian coast in interna-tional waters. At the moment not much more was known. In addition to its crew of thirty-nine, the *Mayaguez* carried food, paints, chemicals, and sup-plies and was lazily making its way from Hong Kong to the port of Sattahip in southern Thailand. Radio Operator Wilbert Bock had managed to send a last-second distress call: "Have been fired on and boarded by Cambodian armed forces. Vessel being escorted to unknown Cambodian port." Captain Charles T. Miller probably did not know (though clearly, in retrospect, he should have known) that in the week before the seizure of the *Mayaguez,* the Cambodians had fired on or captured twenty-five other ships or fishing boats in roughly the same area without warning or explanation. The captured vessels were assumed to have been released.[3]

Later in the morning, Ford raised a number of rhetorical questions with his spokesman, Ron Nessen. "What would you do?" he asked. Nessen, surprised, did not answer. "Would you go in there and bomb the Cambodian boat and take a chance of the Americans being killed? Would you send helicopters in there? Would you mine every harbor in Cambodia?"[4]

At noon Ford convened a meeting of his National Security Council (NSC). Very quickly the discussion leaped the boundaries of a ship in distress to the broader ramifications of America's image in the post-Vietnam world. Would the United States be seen as a "paper tiger," weak and irresolute, humbled by its crushing loss in Vietnam, or would it meet this new challenge with strength and determination? The Khmer Rouge, who had seized control of Cambodia only weeks earlier, seemed cocky and defiant, pressing their claim to a string of nearby islands believed to be rich with oil reserves. Secretary of State Henry Kissinger felt instinctively that the United States had to respond swiftly and decisively to this unprovoked challenge. By meeting's end, the question was not whether, but how, where, and when, the United States would act.[5]

Ford instructed Defense Secretary James Schlesinger to assemble an impressive show of American strength in the Gulf of Thailand, including the aircraft carrier *Coral Sea,* other warships, and a 1,110-person amphibious brigade from the Third Marine Division based in Okinawa. It was more than enough power to mount a rescue and, Ford hoped, to project the image of a powerful, resolute America, still able, despite its recent defeat in Vietnam, to display, and if necessary use, its military power. He also ordered three navy P3 Orion antisubmarine reconnaissance planes at the U.S. Air Force Base at Utapao, Thailand, to take turns tracking the *Mayaguez.*[6]

Ford had his eye on a dramatic rescue. In the back of his mind was the unhappy memory of the USS *Pueblo*'s seizure by the North Koreans in 1968. For eleven months, eighty-two crewmen were held in the port of Wonsan, many beaten and forced to sign false confessions about links to the CIA. American diplomats had unsuccessfully sought an immediate release, basing their case on the fact that the ship was in international waters, while the North Koreans, dismissing American demands, argued that the *Pueblo* was a spy ship. Ford did not want the *Mayaguez* seizure to turn into another *Pueblo* stalemate, not so soon after the Vietnam defeat. A Pentagon official told a *Time* magazine reporter: "What if the Cambodians used the Mayaguez crew the way that the North Koreans used the Pueblo crew? I'd hate to think what would happen to the remaining American position in Asia. Yet, that was a possibility we had to face if the crew was not returned."[7]

The president, who during the Vietnam War was categorized as a hawk, also turned to diplomacy, but here his options were severely limited. He wanted Kissinger to convey an urgent warning to the Khmer Rouge: release the *Mayaguez* and its crew immediately, or else. Or else what? Bomb the *Mayaguez* and possibly kill its crewmen? Unacceptable. Invade Cambodia? Impossible, so soon after Vietnam. Protest to the United Nations? Yes, but with what result? There were times when words carried no weight, and this was one such time. Kissinger reminded the president that the United States had no diplomatic relations with the new Khmer Rouge government in Cambodia. What about the Chinese? Perhaps they would be willing to serve as middlemen; that was Kissinger's hope. A few hours later, he was to be disappointed but not totally surprised: the Chinese diplomat summoned to the State Department to receive and transfer the U.S. demand refused even to touch it.

By day's end, a split had developed between Kissinger and Schlesinger, nothing new in their contentious relationship. Kissinger, like Ford, wanted swift retaliation. The world was waiting to see whether another "little shit-ass country," as Nixon had once described Vietnam, could embarrass the United States, and do so with relative impunity. No, Kissinger argued, this must not be allowed to happen. Schlesinger took a less belligerent approach. He believed that after Vietnam it would be wiser for the United States to sheathe its military might for the time being and play the diplomatic card, no matter how unrewarding it might be at the beginning. Besides, he said, military action might not achieve the desired goal. No one knew exactly where the crew was being held. Were they still on the *Mayaguez,* or had they been transferred to another boat, or to a number of other boats, or even to a prison cell on the Cambodian mainland? Were the Khmer Rouge under orders to kill the crewmen as soon as the United States attempted to rescue them? If the United States took out the two gunboats flanking the *Mayaguez,* there would soon be other gunboats. If the United States bombed Cambodia, producing unavoidable civilian casualties, the Khmer Rouge would score propaganda points throughout the world.

Moreover, the facts that day were slippery. To begin with, where was the *Mayaguez?* All day long the president and his men had been receiving contradictory reports about the location of the ship: first, in the morning, that it was steaming toward Cambodia; then that it was anchored off Koh Tang Island, a highly fortified base about thirty-four miles from the Cambodian shore; later in the afternoon that it was again steaming toward Cambodia; and in the evening, at 10:30 p.m., that it had been spotted off the island of Poulo Wai, where it had originally been seized. One of the two gunships guarding the *Mayaguez* fired at a U.S. reconnaissance plane when it swooped in under low clouds for a look. But then at 1:30 Tuesday morning, Scowcroft woke Ford with the news that the *Mayaguez* was again on the move, heading toward the mainland, now less than an hour from the resort town of Kompong Som, also known as Sihanoukville. At 2:30 a.m. Scowcroft called again. The *Mayaguez* was now reported to be anchored one mile north of Koh Tang. But where was the crew?

A few hours later, Schlesinger telephoned the president. They spoke for more than an hour. Dawn was then breaking over day two of the *Mayaguez* crisis. In fashioning his evolving response, Ford kept returning to the U.S. experience in the *Pueblo* crisis. Determined to avoid a repeat performance, he stressed the need for quick action. He ordered his defense secretary to make absolutely certain that no Cambodian vessel be allowed to make the journey from Koh Tang to the Cambodian mainland.

At 10:22 a.m. Ford opened another NSC meeting. It was devoted entirely to the *Mayaguez* crisis. Kissinger reported that Thailand's prime minister,

Kukrit Pramoj, had informed the U.S. ambassador in Bangkok that he would not permit the United States to use its Thai bases for action against Cambodia. Ford nodded sympathetically but believed that deep down the Thais understood that the United States had no option but to use its Thai bases. As the crisis escalated, the base at Utapao became a central hub for offensive action against Cambodia. The Thais knew it, the Cambodians knew it, and the world knew it.

That morning's military intelligence raised the possibility that some or all of the crew had been moved to Koh Tang Island or to the Cambodian mainland, but there was no confirmation. A second U.S. reconnaissance plane, circling over the island for intelligence, was fired upon, hit, and badly damaged. Other U.S. planes—F-4 Phantom fighters, A-7 Corsair light-attack bombers, and F-111 fighter bombers—streaked out of Utapao Air Base, despite the prime minister's objections, and attacked eight Cambodian gunboats leaving Koh Tang for the mainland, first by firing across their bows and then, when they did not change course, directly at them, sinking three of them and damaging four others. Late that evening, an American pilot spotted another gunboat leaving Koh Tang Island, presumably for the mainland. In his A-7 Corsair, he went after the boat, but when he got close and prepared to shoot, he saw eight or nine men with "Caucasian faces" on board.[8] The pilot radioed for guidance. Within seconds, his query reached Admiral James L. Holloway III, the chief of naval operations, who was at an NSC meeting at the White House. Holloway turned to Ford for a decision. "You get a message to that pilot to shoot across the bow," the president replied, "but do not sink the boat."[9]

"Higher authority has directed that all necessary preparations be made for potential execution early on the 15th to seize the Mayaguez, occupy Koh Tang Island, conduct B-52 strikes against the port of Kompong Som and Ream Airfield, and sink all Cambodian small craft in target areas," read a top-secret memo sent from Washington to all the appropriate admirals and generals.[10]

Again, among the president's closest advisers, Schlesinger was odd man out, opposing the use of the B-52 as too heavy-handed, too aggressive, too reminiscent of U.S. operations in Vietnam. Kissinger, Scowcroft, and Nelson Rockefeller favored the use of the B-52. Ford cast the deciding vote: yes on the B-52. He wanted the Cambodians to know that "we meant business." He wanted not just the release of the ship and crew; he wanted the world to know that the United States was back.[11]

But then, unexpectedly, from the back of the room, photographer David Kennerly had his say: "Has anyone considered," he said, "that this might be the act of a local Cambodian commander who has just taken it into his own hands to halt any ship that comes by? Has anyone stopped to think that he might not have gotten his orders from Phnom Penh?" A silence fell over the room. "If that's what has happened," he continued, "you know, you can blow the whole place away and it's not gonna make any difference. Everyone here has been talking about Cambodia as if it were a traditional government. Like France. We have trouble with France, we just pick up the telephone and call. We know who to talk to. But I was in Cambodia just two weeks ago, and it's not that kind of government at all. We don't even know who the leadership is. Has anyone considered that?"[12] Ford was the sort of self-confident president who could tolerate an unorthodox burst of advice from a youthful photographer; surgical air strikes by navy jets off the carrier *Coral Sea* suddenly made infinitely more sense than a B-52 blitzkrieg of Cambodia.

Ford did what he had planned to do from the very beginning: he issued final orders to rescue the *Mayaguez* and its crew. At Utapao Air Base, American military forces under the command of Lieutenant General John J. Burns were ready for combat. The destroyer *Holt* headed toward Koh Tang Island, where the *Mayaguez* was last seen. A small force of marines huddled on deck. The *Holt* approached the *Mayaguez*, and to everyone's surprise, no shots were fired. The heavily armed marines quickly boarded the merchant ship and discovered that no one was there. Bowls of warm rice and tea were found in the galley, suggesting a hurried exit. The marines, anticipating a firefight, were somewhat disappointed, but, in the final analysis, pleased to be able to raise an American flag on the ship's fantail. No casualties. Mission accomplished, almost.

On Koh Tang itself, it was a different story. A retired air force lieutenant colonel, John F. Guilmartin Jr., wrote years later, "It looked like a walk, but virtually everything that could go wrong did." He added, "Seemingly self-evident lessons about the importance of accurate intelligence at the cutting edge and the dangers of high-level intervention in tactical decisions went unheeded."[13] Eight helicopters, carrying 175 marines, flew into withering fire from enemy positions along the beach. Five helicopters either crashed or were disabled, and just 110 marines were able to land on the island.[14] "The marines and helicopter crews never received the good intelligence available about the island's defenders," Guilmartin noted. "They went in expecting 18 to 40 lightly armed militia but instead found a reinforced battalion of elite Khmer Rouge naval infantry."[15] The marines managed to establish a beachhead, but they were pinned down by intense small arms fire from Cambodians hidden in a wooded area nearby. U.S. planes blasted Cambodian strongpoints, and soon the marines were able to take effective control of the island. But then, another surprise: just as there had been no crewmen aboard the *Mayaguez,* there were none on Koh Tang. Where were they?

Ford felt an obligation, under the War Powers Act, to consult with Congress about his military action in the Gulf of Thailand. Twenty-one congressional leaders of both parties were invited into the Cabinet Room at 6:40 p.m. on May 14. When the president entered, they rose to their feet and applauded. Using maps and aerial photographs, Ford explained the dimensions of the crisis. Up to this point, the members nodded their acceptance of the president's rescue plan; but when he described air strikes against military facilities on the Cambodian mainland, three prominent Senate Democrats—Mike Mansfield of Montana, Robert Byrd of West Virginia, and John McClellan of Arkansas—strongly objected.[16]

"Sure, it was a risk," Ford admitted later, "but one that I had to take."[17]

"I thought we were going to use minimum force," McClellan said. "Do we have to do it all at once? Can't we wait to see if the Cambodians attack before we attack the mainland?"

"It's too great a risk," replied Ford.

"I want to express my deep concern, apprehension and uneasiness at this near invasion of the Indochina mainland," interjected the usually mild-mannered Mansfield. "We have plenty of firepower there in the two destroyers. Frankly, I have grave doubts about this move."

Byrd wondered why Ford had waited to consult with Congress.

"I had a choice between doing too little and too much," Ford explained. "If I did too little and endangered the Marines, I would have been subjected to very legitimate criticism."

"Allow me to press this respectfully," Byrd continued. "Why weren't the leaders brought in when there was time for them to raise a word of caution?"

"We have a government of separations of powers," Ford replied. "In this case, as commander in chief, I had the responsibility and obligation to act. I would never forgive myself if the first wave of Marines was attacked by twenty-four hundred Cambodians." The debate continued for a few more minutes. Then, this formal consultation having been completed, Ford asked his former congressional colleagues to pray with him for "the very best."[18] Through much of the Vietnam War, one president after another wrestled with Congress about which branch of government, the executive or the legislative, had the ultimate authority to declare and prosecute a war. Vietnam left both sides exhausted, the question never really resolved.

At 7:07 p.m., while the president was still meeting with congressional leaders, a radio station in Phnom Penh began broadcasting a nineteen-minute "news bulletin" attacking the United States but ending with word that the *Mayaguez* would be released. No word on when, no word on the crew. The Phnom Penh broadcast was routinely taped and translated by the CIA, and a summary was dispatched to the White House at 8:06 p.m., quick work by any standard.[19] There then ensued a fascinating but odd and highly unusual chapter in White House relations with the media during a national security crisis.

When the president was informed of the Phnom Penh radio broadcast, he told Kissinger to inform the Cambodians that the United States heard the announcement and would suspend all military operations if the crew was also released. But, again, since the United States had no diplomatic relations with Cambodia and no effective means of communication, there was no quick way of conveying Ford's position to the Cambodians; in the meantime, the fighting and killing would continue.

Kissinger had an idea. He summoned Nessen to his office, but Nessen was busy. Kissinger, already impatient, went into a rage. He sent Scowcroft to Nessen's office, and Scowcroft, as Nessen recalled, "grabbed me by the arm and literally pulled me to Kissinger's office." Kissinger told Nessen: "We have got to use you to get a message through to Cambodia!" The message was Ford's response to the radio announcement. "They've got to read it on the AP!" Kissinger believed that an Associated Press story, distributed worldwide, would be the fastest, most credible way to get the president's message to the Cambodians.

Nessen gently informed Kissinger that the United States had not yet announced the rescue mission. So how could it first announce its possible ending? Kissinger agreed. "Yes, do that first, and then do the message to the Cambodians. But hurry!"

Nessen raced to a crowded briefing room. It was past 9 p.m. He announced the rescue mission and then started reading the president's message, apparently too quickly for many of the reporters. "Would you read it slowly, please?" the journalists asked. "Listen to what I have to say!" the spokesman cried. "There is some urgency about it." The room went quiet, as reporters realized that the spokesman, for a change, might have something of importance to convey. Nessen read Ford's message: "We have heard a radio broadcast that you are prepared to release the S.S. Mayaguez. We welcome this development, if true. . . . As soon as you issue a statement that you are prepared to release the crew members you hold, unconditionally and immediately, we will promptly cease military operations." Nessen reread a phrase or two and then explained the government's need for speed. "We believe the news channels may be the fastest way for this message to get through," he said. "Go file."[20]

Reporters hurried to their telephones, television correspondents to their cameras, and Nessen returned to Kissinger's office in time to see the networks break into their regular programming to report both the launching of the rescue mission and the president's response to the Phnom Penh announcement. Then everyone waited. Schlesinger was monitoring the crisis from his Pentagon office.

On Koh Tang Island, the fighting had ended. The *Mayaguez* was again in American custody. But the condition of the crew remained a mystery. A few hours later came word, unconfirmed, that a fishing boat was approaching the destroyer *Wilson*, and people could be seen on deck waving white shirts. Who were they? A few minutes later, Schlesinger called Ford with the answer. All thirty-nine crewmen were now safe on the *Wilson*. In fact, the Cambodians had released them a couple of hours earlier and sent them on a fishing boat headed in the general direction of the *Mayaguez*. Ford excitedly told his advisers: "They're all out! . . . They're safe! Thank God!"[21]

Donald Rumsfeld, possibly thinking of the April 30 scene in Saigon when a number of marines were left behind, double-checked with Schlesinger about whether all the crewmen had been released; Schlesinger replied that he had three sources: the crew was all out, all in good shape.

U.S. war planes were still in action against Cambodia. Scowcroft wondered: "Is there any reason for the Pentagon not to disengage?"

"No," Kissinger replied, "but tell them to bomb the mainland. Let's look ferocious! Otherwise they will attack us as the ship leaves."[22]

A third and final air strike was ordered against oil-storage facilities on the mainland, and the marines were instructed to withdraw from Koh Tang.

Ford, breaking the news to the American people on television, said that "at my direction," the United States "tonight" recovered the *Mayaguez*, "landed" on Koh Tang, and "conducted supporting strikes against nearby military installations. . . . The vessel has been recovered intact and the entire crew has been rescued." By implication, Ford was congratulating himself, hoping to generate praise for his leadership under fire, but he also congratulated "the units and the men who participated in these operations for their valor and for their sacrifice." With that behind him, Ford took a sleeping pill and went to bed.

The morning mail contained 14,000 letters, telegrams, and phone calls praising the president's management of the crisis, but there were also irritating questions and some biting criticism, including queries about whether Ford had overreacted or acted too quickly.[23] But at the time most members of Congress chose to support the president. A few expressed reservations.

Representative Melvin Price (D-Ill.) called the rescue operation "a great boost to the country." Senator Adlai Stevenson III (D-Ill.) said, "Let no one mistake the unity and the strength of an America under attack." Senator Barry Goldwater (R-Ariz.), who had been following the crisis closely, said that if Ford had not rescued the ship and its crew, "every little half-assed nation would be taking a shot at us." Senator Hugh Scott (R-Pa.) complimented Ford: "He is a strong President and a man whose resolution held up under stress." Senator Mansfield offered a mixed assessment. He praised Ford for making "a very difficult decision" and felt "it was the right one," but he thought Ford should have "consulted" Congress before taking action against Cambodia. Under the War Powers Act, as Mansfield saw it, a president was obliged to do so before deciding to take military action. Senator Frank Church (D-Idaho), one of the original sponsors of the act, disagreed: "I really don't know what more a President can do in a situation that requires fast action."[24] Representative Carroll Hubbard (D-Ky.) summarized the general mood on Capitol Hill: "It's good to win one for a change."[25]

Newspaper reaction was decidedly mixed. Under the headline, "Barbarous Piracy," *New York Times* columnist Anthony Lewis wrote: "Once again an American government shows that the only way it knows how to deal with frustration is by force. And the world is presumably meant to be impressed."[26] The *Atlanta Journal*, with Vietnam very much on its mind, editorialized: "There seems to be a feeling of joy that at last we have won one. And indeed we have." The Tokyo newspaper *Yomiuri Shimbun* asked: "Why did [the U.S.] have to use a cannon to shoot a chicken?" Beijing and Hanoi predictably denounced the rescue mission as "an act of piracy," but Moscow's propaganda outlets were unusually silent. A French diplomat complained: "The same result might have been obtained with less violent methods and without the loss of lives." But a German diplomat was more sympathetic: "People understand that Ford could not just sit and wait."[27]

Ford felt that "all of a sudden" the gloom that had descended over the nation after the Vietnam defeat seemed to lift. His poll numbers shot up 11 points, which could do wonders for any politician's mood. "I felt I had regained the initiative," the president wrote, "and I determined to do what I could with it." But Ford admitted that he was "disturbed . . . a lot" by two aspects of the rescue operation. Casualties, for one. Forty-one Americans had been killed during the operation, and another fifty were wounded. "That was a high toll, and I felt terrible about it." Second was "high-level bumbling at the Defense Department," an extraordinary admission by a president. Ford had ordered four strikes against Cambodia, but only three were executed. On one run, navy jets had dropped their bombs into the Gulf of Thailand. Ford never learned why, though he asked more than once. "I was anxious to find out who had contravened my authority," the president later wrote. "The explanations I received from the Pentagon were not satisfactory at all, and direct answers kept eluding me. Perhaps I should have pursued my inquiry, but since we had achieved our objective, I let the matter drop."[28] Not quite. The widespread assumption at the time was that Schlesinger had been less than forthcoming in explaining Pentagon actions to the president and that Ford was simply uncomfortable with him as secretary of defense and displeased with his overall performance during the crisis. If there was any doubt about the president's judgment of Schlesinger, the man and the secretary, they were removed on November 19, 1975, when he sent Rumsfeld to the Pentagon to replace Schlesinger.

In the end, when it came to the *Mayaguez* crisis, there was never a serious question about whether the United States would launch an impressive rescue operation. The question was whether the world could be persuaded that the nation was not a "pitiful, helpless giant," as Nixon had feared it would be seen, but rather a superpower still capable, despite the defeat in Vietnam, of standing up to communist adventurism.

Shortly after the crisis eased, Ford left for a NATO meeting in Europe. His overarching worry at the time was that NATO was facing a "psychological" problem caused by the U.S. defeat in Southeast Asia. "In the wake of Vietnam," he thought, "would the U.S. remain firm against Communist aggression elsewhere? Could old allies still depend on us?"[29] Senator Mansfield, reflecting a rising but not yet alarming new wave of isolationism, proposed a withdrawal of thousands of U.S. troops from Western Europe. Ford discovered at the NATO meeting that his European allies wanted to know whether the United States would honor its overseas commitments. Ford pointed to the *Mayaguez* crisis as proof that the United States could and would act to protect its global interests.

In this case, Vietnam obliged an American president not only to use military force but also to employ it effectively and overpoweringly. Other presidents, such as Jimmy Carter, Ronald Reagan, and Bill Clinton, when confronted with national security challenges, reacted to the Vietnam defeat by trying to avoid military confrontations. They did not want to get "involved." Still others, such as George H. W. Bush, reacted by sending 500,000 troops halfway around the world when 150,000 would have been considered more than sufficient to do the job. Vietnam evoked no single reaction, but it was always on the mind of the president facing a decision to send American troops into battle.

3

Carter, Brzezinski, and Russia's Vietnam

We now have the opportunity of giving to the USSR its Vietnam War.
—ZBIGNIEW BRZEZINSKI, Interview in *Le Nouvel Observateur,* January 1998

TO PARAPHRASE TOLSTOY rather severely, all presidents reacted to the American defeat in Vietnam in the same way, except that each reacted in his own way. Gerald Ford, for example, felt the need to send an impressive armada of American power to the Gulf of Thailand not only to recapture a merchant ship hijacked by Cambodian pirates but also to "hose them down," to unleash the marines, and to bomb Cambodia; "to make it clear we are not getting out of the Pacific," as one official recalled.[1] Ford wanted the world to understand that the United States was still the most powerful nation on earth, not a "paper tiger," even though it had been brought to its knees a few weeks earlier by a decidedly smaller and weaker adversary. Four years later, in 1979, Ford's successor, Jimmy Carter, facing a challenge of infinitely greater import, did comparatively little in response. Iranian revolutionaries had seized the American embassy in Tehran and held American diplomats as hostages: it was an act of aggression, of terrorism, indeed, an "act of war," according to almost any international code of diplomatic conduct. But although Carter was under heavy pressure to retaliate and rescue the hostages, for many months he held his fire. When finally he did act, it was with a display of power so pathetically small that it exploded in failure in the empty deserts of Persia, bringing only further embarrassment to the United States.

Over the years, the range of presidential reaction to the Vietnam defeat was to swing widely from the Ford model to the Carter one: from the strutting use of American military power (by Ford, George H. W. Bush, and George W. Bush) to its deliberate underuse (by Carter, Bill Clinton, and, surprisingly, Ronald Reagan). In Afghanistan, Barack Obama has so far straddled both models. Even presidents who convinced themselves that using military power was preferable to not using it were reluctant to get entangled in a foreign adventure, unless the national interest was directly involved. Thank you, Vietnam.

From Peanuts to Presidency

When Jimmy Carter launched his presidential campaign in 1976, he introduced himself to the American people as a peanut farmer from Georgia, modest and religious, close to the soil, unblemished by Watergate scandal or Vietnam debacle, a new star on the horizon of the Democratic Party, a moderate governor from the South who would never lie and would always carry his own suitcase. *Why Not the Best?* was the title of his campaign autobiography, and it was the question he asked of a nation exhausted by the loss of a war and the shame of a president. He was also asking the nation to turn a new page in American history, away from a reliance on military power toward an assertion of old-fashioned American values, and he was given the chance.

Carter emerged out of the political nowhere, an obscure one-term governor of Georgia. He was, like his father, a successful businessman in Plains, but his ambition soared beyond this small rural community. As a boy, Jimmy Carter was already dreaming of attending the Naval Academy in Annapolis, Maryland. After finishing secondary school, he attended two colleges, restlessly moving from Georgia Southwestern to Georgia Tech; and when Annapolis belatedly beckoned in 1943, he quickly abandoned Georgia and transferred to the Naval Academy, where his intelligence and diligence were soon obvious to all. During the summer of 1944, with World War II still raging, Carter the midshipman was assigned to temporary duty on the USS *New York,* a battleship patrolling up and down the East Coast and the Caribbean. One day the ship was hit, possibly by a torpedo fired from a German submarine. "It was the closest Jimmy Carter would ever come to hostile action," wrote journalist James Wooten. "The Navy awarded a combat ribbon to everyone on board, including all the midshipmen from Annapolis."[2]

With his ribbon, Carter returned to Annapolis, where he continued his studies, graduating fifty-ninth in the 1946 class of 820 ensigns. Now married to another native of Plains, Rosalynn, he was sent on a variety of assignments with the navy. While working with Hyman Rickover, then a captain and later a crusading admiral, Carter developed a passion for nuclear-powered submarines, for a time studying nuclear physics at Union College. But in 1953, as he was about to be assigned to one of these new submarines, Carter got the bad news that his father had died, and he felt a family obligation to return to Plains. He quit the navy and took over the family farms and business, a seed and farm-supply company.

The future president busied himself with community work in hospitals, schools, and especially his local Baptist church. Like many in his rural community, Carter saw religion as a powerful force in his life and later became "born again."

He won his first two runs for public office, serving in the state senate in the mid-1960s, a time when the rising civil rights movement challenged the prevailing racist sentiment in Georgia and other southern states, and when the Vietnam War called southern patriots to military service in the jungles of Southeast Asia. In 1966 Carter ran for governor and lost. One day, while still a candidate, he appeared before the Atlanta Press Club. Bruce Galphin, a columnist for the *Atlanta Constitution,* listened to the aspiring candidate and felt sorry for him. His "honesty" about the war, Galphin wrote, "is almost painful." According to Galphin, Carter "said Viet Nam wasn't an issue in the Georgia governor's race . . . but then went on to talk about it, to admit it was complex and finally to confess, 'I don't have any solutions.' He would have done better to stop after saying it wasn't an issue."[3]

Throughout his political career, including even his term in the White House, Carter always dealt with the raw reality of Vietnam as if it were somebody else's problem, a contagious disease best left to others to manage. He would assert that on the one hand the war had little relevance to his plans, whatever they were at the moment, and then on the other hand acknowledge that the war utterly baffled him and that if he were responsible for running the war, he could not do it effectively. Jody Powell, who was to become one of Carter's loyal aides, described his own views about the war as "extremely conflicted." He assumed Carter's views were close to his own.[4]

In 1970, with Powell at his side, Carter ran once more for governor, and this time won. He governed as a new southern politician, courageous enough to renounce the region's segregationist history, and at the same time appealing enough to reach unashamedly for national recognition as a candidate for vice president and even president of the United States.

During the run-up to the 1972 presidential campaign, one Democratic hopeful after another journeyed through Georgia, seeking Carter's endorsement. Carter regularly invited the visiting Democrat to join him for dinner and spend the night at the governor's mansion. He wanted to display southern hospitality, but, just as important, to take the measure of a string of potential rivals. One morning, feeling particularly pleased with himself, Carter turned to Powell and pronounced: "You know, I'm better than any of them. I'm going to run."[5]

At the 1972 Democratic National Convention in Miami, Carter moved aggressively to position himself as a vice presidential possibility. He sent feelers to the front-running presidential candidate, South Dakota's Senator George McGovern, a World War II hero who opposed the Vietnam War, to see whether he might be acceptable as a running mate, but got nowhere.

Not one to stand on political principle, Carter quickly adjusted his compass and swung to the hawkish right, delivering the nominating speech for Senator Henry "Scoop" Jackson of Washington, a well-known supporter of the Vietnam War, who stood little chance of winning the party's nomination. The convention was dominated by McGovern supporters. Still, when Jackson asked Carter to nominate him, Carter happily accepted, not because he thought Jackson would or could be nominated, but because he hungered for the national publicity.

There was enough of the southerner in Carter, the former naval officer, to feel closer to hawk than dove. Just as Powell felt a deep sympathy for the men and women in uniform, so Carter, too, felt a special compassion for the troops and perhaps for the war itself. His son Jack had enlisted in the navy in 1968 and served on a salvage ship in Vietnam, but he was eased out in 1970 under less-than-ideal circumstances: he was caught using drugs. Later, in an oral history interview, Jack stripped away the protocol and explained: "They were busting me out of the Navy in a fairly mellow manner, about the time Dad was getting elected governor of the state of Georgia."[6] Later still, in 2005, the former president went a step further in an interview with the British *Telegraph* newspaper: "He told me he smoked marijuana there [in Vietnam] with most of the other people in his company. When his superior officers asked if he did so, Jack told the truth."[7]

When Carter, Powell, and the other Georgians talked of their "conflicted" views about the war, they understood why they opposed McGovern so strenuously. Wooten, in his book, placed their opposition in a special historical context. They came from a "different tradition," he wrote, "in which military service was the expected if not the mandatory avocation of every young man. . . . If they had personal doubts about the propriety of the war—and it is extremely doubtful that they did—they kept them to themselves. Theirs was a creed that essentially agreed with Robert E. Lee's suggestion that 'the call of one's country is a high one, and the call of one's country to war is the highest.'"[8]

But because support for an unpopular war was perhaps as tricky a proposition for a rising politician as opposition, Carter was forever trying to strike an Olympian pose of selfless detachment. "Who can say who is responsible for Vietnam?" Carter asked during a talk to the League of Women Voters in 1972. "This is certainly not a partisan fault. Eisenhower, Kennedy, Johnson, Nixon have all struggled unsuccessfully, but in a dedicated way, to deal with a difficult problem, and they are still struggling, the leaders of our Nation, with this matter." Sounding very understanding, Carter added, "I think there is an overwhelming support in our Nation to end the [Vietnamese] war and to get our people back home. This almost unanimous commitment is one for which leading governmental leaders are searching to find a way."[9]

When Carter spoke, Nixon was already heading toward a landslide victory, fresh from headline-catching summits in Beijing and Moscow and endless negotiations with the North Vietnamese in Paris. But could 1976 be the year for a relative newcomer to make a run for the presidency and win? In September 1972 Carter convened his senior advisers and posed the question. "With the Vietnam War coming to a close," Hamilton Jordan, who was to become Carter's chief of staff at the White House, recalled answering, "domestic problems and issues were apt to be a more important consideration, the problem-solving ability of the American government was very much in question, and someone outside of Washington and outside the Senate, a governor who had proved that problems could be dealt with effectively by the state, could win."[10] And who was that governor? Carter, of course, they all agreed.

In 1974 Carter formally decided to run for president. No one in his family or his immediate entourage was surprised. It seemed that he had been running for president from the moment he became governor. That summer the Democrats met in Louisville, Kentucky, in part to check out their presidential hopefuls, including Carter. One day the Georgia governor called a news conference to outline his plans for the nation, and he reserved a large room, apparently believing that he already commanded national attention. But for whatever combination of reasons, only two reporters showed up: an Associated Press reporter and Andrew J. Glass of Cox newspapers. Unfazed, Carter detailed his plans and took a few questions, at one point in an answer using the phrase "when I am president," not "if I become president." He did not use the phrase in a boastful manner; he seemed simply to be projecting his own deep belief that, one day, he would be president.[11]

A few months later, on December 12, 1974, with the Vietnam War in its final phase and the North Vietnamese already moving in for the kill, Carter declared his candidacy for president of a very tired nation. Others were also thinking of declaring—Senators Birch Bayh of Indiana, Henry Jackson of Washington, and later Frank Church of Idaho; Representative Morris Udall of Arizona; and Governors George Wallace of Alabama and Jerry Brown of California—but all decided to wait for a better time. Carter saw no reason to wait. Before a single other Democrat would join him in the presidential race, Carter had already traveled 50,000 miles in thirty-seven states, giving more than 200 speeches and quickly becoming the darling of the media, which portrayed him as the candidate from beyond the Beltway, the new southern governor, the moderate the Democrats needed, a likely winner, just as Hamilton Jordan had predicted.[12] To the surprise of the political establishment, Carter captured the key early states of Iowa and New Hampshire, developed momentum, attracted bundles of cash, and by June wrapped up the nomination and selected Senator Walter Mondale of Minnesota, a Hubert Humphrey protégé, as his vice presidential running mate.

Mondale recalled years later that when he entered the Senate in 1965, he was not even sure where Vietnam was, but when he visited Vietnam and started asking questions, he learned that the official version of the war was often at odds with reality. Once, after a visit, he asked Secretary of Defense Robert McNamara: "Why is it that if you put black pajamas on Vietnamese, they are the best fighters, but if they put on South Vietnamese uniforms, they are the worst fighters?" McNamara paused for only a moment before pronouncing: "I'm late for a meeting." Mondale added, "I slowly started rethinking; and as I did, [I'd talk to] Humphrey and anybody who'd listen to me at the State Department, that we needed to change course. But they were stuck." Mondale said that his support for the war, however reluctantly offered, was "the biggest mistake of my political career."[13]

Carter, for his part, never deviated from his belief that Vietnam was "no longer very important." In fact, in early 1976 he posed a rhetorical question to a reporter. "You know what McGovern's biggest mistake was?" He answered his own question. "He never should have made the Vietnam War an issue."[14] Carter carefully sidestepped such issues as the cost of the war in lives and treasure and hewed more comfortably to those reflecting his personal and religious beliefs, including the legal and ethical question of what the United States should do about the draft dodgers and deserters who had refused to serve in Vietnam.

Many young Americans had fled to Canada. In 1974, shortly after Nixon's resignation, Ford proposed a compromise program for dealing with this problem. Draft dodgers would perform some sort of community service, and deserters would serve a tour in the military, as their way of avoiding penalties or punishment. A Presidential Clemency Board would be established to review records and reach judgments.[15] For Carter, the Ford proposal missed the point. He drew a philosophical distinction between a "pardon," which he supported, and "amnesty," which he opposed. At a rally in Reno, he explained the distinction. "To me, amnesty means that what you did was right and you are to be congratulated for it," he said. "Pardon means that what you did, whether it was right or wrong, is forgiven. So I'm going to declare a pardon and forget the Vietnamese war and let those young people come home."[16]

During the first televised debate between Ford and Carter, it was no surprise that the amnesty/pardon issue was raised. Ford explained his program, but lost in the exchange. "He [Carter] no doubt scored some points when I was asked how I could justify pardoning Nixon while refusing a blanket pardon for all draft dodgers and deserters," Ford later wrote. "I explained my reasoning and discussed the earned amnesty program. Carter jumped all over that, said he favored a full pardon for draft evaders and declared that 'what the people are concerned about is not the pardon or the amnesty of those who evaded the draft but whether or not our crime system is fair'" to those who are poor and lack influence.[17]

The Vietnam War also emerged during the campaign as an example of a "Doleful" malapropism. This time it was during the vice presidential debate in Houston on October 15, 1976, where Mondale debated Ford's running mate, Senator Robert Dole of Kansas. He of the sardonic wit snapped at one point that all the wars of the twentieth century were "Democrat wars." He had been asked about his criticism of Ford's pardon of Nixon. Embarrassed, not wishing to open any daylight between himself and Ford, he responded that Watergate was not much of a campaign issue, "any more than the Vietnam War would be, or World War One or World War Two or the Korean War— all Democrat wars, all in this century."[18] Dole, himself a disabled World War II veteran, was then subjected to sharp ridicule and criticism in political and journalistic circles, and was forced to recant.

The race tightened toward the end of the campaign, with Ford narrowing the gap significantly, but Carter clung to his lead and won. The country wanted a change from Vietnam and Watergate; they wanted the Democrats. Carter had campaigned as a "new" voice of traditional American values, deep faith, modesty, and hard work. At the time of his election, Carter struck many of the journalists who covered his campaign as an incredibly ambitious, intelligent, self-confident politician without a doubt in his mind about whether he could do the job of president of the United States. God, he believed, would always be at his side, helping and encouraging him to do the right thing. If he approached his new Oval Office responsibilities with a trace of the modesty he urged on others, it was not apparent. If he was troubled by the prospect of another Vietnam challenge, that one day he would have to make the awesome decision, reserved specifically for presidents, to send, or not to send, American troops to fight in yet another foreign war, this, too, was not apparent. He intended to turn a page in American history, and for a time he did. He was determined to raise the banner of human rights and bury the burden of Vietnam and the anguish of Watergate; in the process, he rejected war as a preferred instrument of American foreign policy and flashed a smile of friendship and integrity to the world. And he prayed, literally prayed, that the world would smile back.

No longer would America be noted for dirty wars, such as the one just finished in Vietnam; he hoped that now, in his administration, America would shed its militarist past and resume its rightful role as the custodian of human rights. As he said in his 1981 farewell address, "America did not invent human rights. . . . Human rights invented America." Nevertheless, a question loomed in the background of Carter's evocation of human rights: what would he do when "human rights" conflicted with "national interest," as it inevitably would? Which would come first? Furthermore, if he deplored the use of military force, would he ever use it, and when?

To Move beyond the Vietnam War

On his first full day in office, January 21, 1977, President Carter sent Proclamation 4483 to the Office of the Federal Register, delivering on his campaign promise to "pardon" the draft dodgers and deserters of the Vietnam War, not all of them, but many of them. It was the first step in his plan to bury the Vietnam obsession and expunge it from the national psyche.

The proclamation granted "a full, complete and unconditional pardon to: (1) all persons who may have committed any offense between August 4, 1964 and March 28, 1973 in violation of the Military Selective Service Act . . . restoring to them full political, civil and other rights."[19] It was not a blanket pardon, for it listed two clear exceptions. Those who used "force or violence" in their antiwar activities and those who deserted their "duties and responsibilities" would still be subject to punishment under the law. During the height of the Vietnam War, in the late 1960s and early 1970s, more than 100,000

Americans avoided military service by fleeing to foreign countries, most of them to Canada.[20]

Carter's pardon kicked off a hot debate between those who wanted everyone pardoned, including the deserters, as Carter himself had strongly recommended during the campaign, and those who demanded strict punishment of all draft dodgers and deserters. "It was a very difficult political issue," Carter told interviewer Brian Williams in 2006. "But it was the right thing to do, and I was just following up, basically, on the heroic action that President Gerald Ford had taken in trying to heal our nation, and to give us a chance to move beyond the Vietnam War, and obsession with Vietnam, into another era of life."[21] By 2006 Carter could forget that thirty years earlier, he had not praised Ford for "heroic action" but instead had been sharply critical of his position. Former presidents have a way of bonding that includes exaggerated praise and convenient amnesia.

Carter's second step was strictly confidential. Within days of assuming office, he asked his impressive team of national security advisers, led by Secretary of State Cyrus Vance, Secretary of Defense Harold Brown, and National Security Adviser Zbigniew Brzezinski, to explore the possibility, daring in its timing and symbolism, of establishing some form of diplomatic contact with Vietnam, the nation that had just inflicted a stinging defeat on the United States. This step reflected his desire to turn his back on the Vietnam War and also represented a very practical way of opening a channel for regular communication with Hanoi about, among other things, American prisoners of war, a particularly emotional issue in the United States. Carter wanted to send a presidential commission to Hanoi. Vance, who succeeded Kissinger, was charged with "working" the problem. Through intermediaries, the new secretary of state got word to Hanoi that the United States was serious about negotiating the POW issue, and other issues, if appropriate.

For weeks Vance heard nothing from Hanoi. The North Vietnamese probably suspected that Carter, a new and problematic personality on the international stage, was playing games. On February 19, 1977, Brzezinski informed Carter that "there has been no answer to your proposal for a delegation to visit Hanoi," and that "the story is now leaking out after being held together by a large number of Americans and foreign governments."[22] A week later Brzezinski speculated that if a presidential commission actually did go to Hanoi, it would "quite likely return with a somewhat unsatisfactory Vietnamese accounting for the MIA's."[23] In which case, Brzezinski cautioned, Carter would have to figure out how to handle the League of Families, which was convinced that Hanoi held hundreds of American POWs. Carter's push for an early breakthrough in U.S.-Vietnamese relations was aborted. Hanoi seemed uninterested, China was beckoning, and China, in Carter's view, was a much more important prize.

Even this early in his administration, Carter showed signs of tilting back and forth between Vance's "idealistic, lawyerly approach" to foreign problems and Brzezinski's more "hard-edged, Soviet-leery approach."[24] Depending on the issue, Carter would try to balance the advice of both advisers, always convinced that at the end of the day he would make the decision and they would follow his lead. Leslie H. Gelb, an accomplished foreign policy analyst who worked in Carter's State Department, wrote that Carter rejected the Nixon-Kissinger emphasis upon East-West relations, based on U.S.-Soviet competition, and favored instead focusing on north-south relations and the "developing world," and, whenever possible, playing "America's strongest power card: its values and its role as preeminent champion of human rights."[25]

After Carter turned his back on Vietnam, he seemed also to turn his back on the cold war, rejecting its MAD (mutually assured destruction) underpinning and projecting an image of peace and joy more appropriate to a Sunday morning sermon. He thought he could end the cold war by simply putting it into his "out" box. In one of his early speeches, he used a phrase that was to come back and haunt him: he lashed out at America's "inordinate fear of communism," even as signs accumulated in many parts of the developing world of a more aggressive Soviet expansionism; and when in late 1979 the Soviet Union invaded Afghanistan, Carter was shocked and disappointed.

When most officials were still trying to find the rest room, Brzezinski was already sending Carter a "Weekly National Security Report," a "top secret," "highly concise" account of "(1) Opinions, (2) Facts, (3) Alerts, (4) Concerns and (5) Reactions" for his "weekend reading." "Perhaps after a few weeks," Brzezinski suggested in his opening paragraph, "you can let me know whether this is helpful or whether it is merely a redundant reading item." It was "helpful," indeed, both to Carter and Brzezinski. On page one of the first report, Carter wrote in his neat script: "I like it, J." From then on, week after week, for four years, except on those occasions when Brzezinski was traveling, Carter would receive a four- to six-page, "Top Secret" and occasionally "Eyes Only" weekly summary of Brzezinski's private thinking about world affairs, which the president appeared to appreciate.[26] In this way, the former professor from Columbia University beat out the lawyer from Wall Street to become the president's principal source of information and opinion about matters of national security. Later, Brzezinski would say that he and Carter needed only to exchange glances to know what the other was thinking.

It was an odd marriage of convenience between the Bible Belt president who believed he existed to do great and noble things in the world and the Polish-born scholar who worried deeply about Soviet plots and plans. Carter might have been looking North-South, but the Soviets were still operating East-West; and in weekly report after report, Brzezinski tried to focus the president's attention on the new Soviet challenges—from adventurism in Africa to stubbornness in the unfolding negotiation on strategic weapons—by highlighting the importance of U.S.-Soviet relations.

In private talks with Carter, Brzezinski would describe the Soviet Union as a "giant with arms of steel and a totally rotten stomach." Strong, yes, but with deep, internal weaknesses, which could and should be exploited. While Carter viewed human rights as an American blessing, a gift from God to be bestowed on the world, Brzezinski saw "human rights" as an "offensive tool" in a widening global confrontation with the Soviet Union. It underscored the immorality of Soviet policy. Vietnam, the professor believed, was not only the "first war that we really lost"; it was also a defeat of historic importance. It encouraged the Soviet leaders to believe that Hanoi's victory was unmistakable proof that they were winning the global struggle between East and West, between the communist and the capitalist systems. Brzezinski, a student of Soviet politics, was certain that the Kremlin leaders would now try to take advantage of America's vulnerability.[27] And he was right.

The president, though, was marching to a different drummer, at least in the early years of his administration. Tom DeFrank, who covered the Carter White House for *Newsweek*, labeled the president's view of the Soviet Union "naive in the extreme." Making matters worse, Carter mixed naïveté with hubris and misjudgment. Though he considered the Soviet system "fundamentally corrupt," he also believed he could strike historic agreements with Brezhnev, such as an updated strategic arms limitation agreement. His emphasis, early on, was on summitry. "If Leonid Brezhnev and I were in a room together, I could make him understand the flaws in his system," he mused. Brzezinski, who believed summitry, not carefully prepared, could be dangerous, once derisively commented, according to DeFrank: "Yes, and in what language would God be negotiating?"[28]

Alexei Arbatov, a respected Russian political scientist at the Carnegie Moscow Center, shared Brzezinski's instinctive caution about summitry, stressing that the aging Soviet leaders, most in their seventies and a few already in their eighties, lived in their own ideological bubble, totally incapable of seeing or understanding the complexity of the real world. They saw the American defeat in Vietnam not as an early case study of asymmetrical warfare, in which tenacious nationalist guerrillas could outmaneuver an exhausted superpower, but rather, as Brzezinski suspected, as vindication of their faith in the ultimate triumph of communism over capitalism. Arbatov—whose father, Georgy Arbatov, was a well-known specialist on American domestic and foreign policy, often serving at summits as a spokesman for the Kremlin—believed that Brezhnev and his octogenarian colleagues reached what was for them a logical conclusion: with America licking its wounds, withdrawing, and retreating, and with a new president hailing human rights, never an issue to be taken too seriously by the Kremlin, the Soviet Union could accelerate "its own expansion in the third world" and go on the offensive.[29]

Soviet leaders felt vindicated by the U.S. defeat and decided to take advantage of the power gap left by the Americans, explained Vladimir Lukin, a former Russian ambassador to the United States. The risks were minimal, the Soviets thought, and the gains could be huge. At the time, no one in the Kremlin seemed to remember Stalin's warning in the early 1930s about becoming "dizzy with success." Afghanistan, which would prove to be the Soviet Union's own Vietnam, was still a few years away. The U.S. defeat became a trap, Lukin lamented. Bad as it was for the United States, it came to be worse for the Soviet Union. Ironically, the American defeat in Vietnam encouraged a procession of Kremlin leaders to make decisions that led ultimately to the collapse of the communist system and the end of the cold war. Yet few could imagine such historic consequences flowing from the North Vietnamese victory in Vietnam, certainly not Carter and certainly not Brezhnev.[30]

Drop Kick Me, Jesus, through the Goal Posts of Life

Holding aloft his banner of "human rights," which attracted both praise and concern, Carter plunged into world affairs with the excitement of a kid in a candy store. No problem was beyond his reach. He wanted to end American control of the Panama Canal, he wanted to negotiate a new Strategic Arms Limitation Agreement with the Soviet Union, he wanted to normalize relations with China, he wanted to do the impossible in the Middle East by persuading Israel and Egypt to establish diplomatic relations, exchange embassies, and ambassadors and sign a peace treaty. Remarkably, the president achieved a number of his foreign policy goals, and in rather quick order. He was energetic, determined, and pragmatic, an Oval Office bulldog who refused to take no for an answer. He wanted to be in charge of everything, including the schedule of the White House tennis court. When he learned that there was not enough time in the day to absorb the large number of memos that found their way to his desk, he took a speed-reading course. When the slowness of the bureaucracy frustrated him, he installed speakers in his office so he could listen to soothing Mozart or, since his tastes were eclectic, country music, one favorite being "Drop Kick Me, Jesus, through the Goal Posts of Life."[31]

Central to Carter's calculations was changing America from Sparta to Athens, from losing causes such as Vietnam to winning ones such as human rights. He sincerely believed that America had to return to its roots as a glowing symbol of peace and progress; he would be its messenger.

EXAMPLE ONE: THE PANAMA CANAL TREATY

Before the Panama Canal opened for business in 1914, on the eve of the First World War, a transport ship had to travel more than 14,000 miles from New York to San Francisco via Cape Horn, on South America's southern tip. It was always a long, uncertain, rocky, and expensive journey. Taking advantage of the Panama Canal, the same ship, carrying cargo from the East Coast to the West Coast, would travel only 6,000 miles, a much shorter and less expensive journey. One of the most difficult engineering projects in history, the forty-eight-mile-long Panama Canal was an instant success. From year to year, the number of vessels and the tonnage of cargo increased. By 2008 roughly 15,000 vessels passed through the canal every year, carrying roughly 310 million tons of cargo.

For much of its history, the Panama Canal was the property of the United States, though it traversed the territory of a theoretically sovereign country. In 1903 an adventurous Theodore Roosevelt forced Panama to sign a set of treaties granting the United States a ninety-nine-year lease for control of a canal, which the United States was only then starting to build, and a strip of land on both sides of the canal, which the U.S. Army would guard. Before nationalism ignited passions in Panama and other parts of Latin America, Roosevelt's treaties were profitable and manageable. Once nationalism took root, however, the Panama Canal became, for many, a handy symbol of "Yankee imperialism." Over the years, a rising tide of anti-American sentiment led to riots and demonstrations, and 1964 was a particularly bloody year.

In Washington, Congress began to hear calls for change. Could the United States retain control over transit through the canal while yielding sovereignty in all other ways to the government of Panama? Would the United States have to give up all control? Newspaper editorials pressed for action, for some sort of compromise. In quieter times, the Johnson administration might have considered a number of propositions, but Vietnam absorbed everyone's attention; Panama would have to wait. The Nixon administration, equally absorbed with Vietnam, was even less inclined to negotiate with Panama. Only after the Paris Peace Accords were signed in January 1973 did negotiations between the United States and Panama get started, but they did not progress.

For Carter, Panama was low-hanging fruit, and he quickly reached for it, brushing aside conservative opposition to any change. He depended on the resourceful Sol Linowitz, the nimble diplomat who once ran Xerox, to pursue an agreement. Linowitz shuttled between Washington and Panama City, swiftly whittling down the differences, until he came up with an agreement acceptable to both sides: Panama would acquire full control over the Panama Canal on December 31, 1999, and the United States would be assured of the neutrality of the canal, meaning that it would always be open to American shipping. Carter and General Omar Trujillo signed the agreement on September 7, 1977. The United States regained a measure of Latin American respect, while retaining access to the canal. Carter had turned a page in Latin America, and Vietnam seemed to be slipping from memory.

EXAMPLE TWO: MIDDLE EAST PEACEMAKING

If you fancied yourself a prince of peace, what better place to strut your stuff than the Middle East? Peace was possible, Carter decided, not with the old Kissingerian style of "shuttle diplomacy" but rather with a new style of presidential leadership and engagement aimed ultimately at a comprehensive settlement between the Israelis and the Arabs. Low-lying fruit this was not to be.

As the 1973 Yom Kippur War was ending, Kissinger inaugurated his famed shuttle, traveling between Israel and one Arab country after another trying to negotiate "interim agreements," or step-by-step arrangements, that might lead to peace at some time in the distant future. He operated under the assumption that the Arab world was not ready for peace with Israel and might never be, and that Israel would settle for nothing less than guaranteed security based on peace treaties with its Arab neighbors. When Israeli forces encircled the Egyptian army near the Suez Canal, days away from destroying it, Kissinger saw a diplomatic opening: if he could persuade Israel to spare the army and thereby salvage a degree of Egyptian honor, would the Egyptian leader be willing to strike an interim land-for-peace deal with Israel? With any other Arab leader at the time, the answer would probably have been no, but, with Anwar Sadat, the answer was yes.

A few years later, this modest understanding opened the door to a groundbreaking Sadat visit to Jerusalem, and then to a peace treaty and diplomatic relations between Israel and Egypt. None of this would have happened without a bold and courageous leader of Egypt, a shrewd prime minister of Israel, and the personal involvement of an American president. Carter injected his full power and prestige into the Camp David negotiation, and, after thirteen grueling days and nights, he finally reached a peace agreement between Egypt and Israel, a rare example of personal courage and determination producing a historic breakthrough.

To succeed, Carter needed Anwar Sadat and Menachem Begin, two of history's least likely collaborators. Each was deeply suspicious of the other, but in the end they shared a Nobel Peace Prize, an outcome surely not on Begin's mind when he came to power on June 21, 1977, or on Sadat's when he succeeded the Egyptian firebrand, Gamal Abdel Nasser, on October 15, 1970.

At first American officials referred to Sadat as a "clown." They misjudged him badly. By the end of the 1973 war, he had become the indispensable Egyptian: brave, smart, the one Arab leader who could set an example for the others.

"Welcome! Welcome!" Whether Sadat was welcoming a visiting secretary of state or an American television reporter arriving for an interview, his deep baritone would echo through the ornate reception room in the Tahra Palace or in the enchanting garden of the spacious presidential villa outside of Cairo, fragrant with jasmine shrubs and shaded by ancient banyan trees. Usually he was in uniform, but he acted so graciously informal that one might have imagined him on a tennis court in a Washington suburb. No matter how tricky the negotiation, he smiled whenever he saw the lens of an American camera, and he had a wickedly attractive smile, even when he had nothing of consequence to say to a journalist. He was one of the few foreign leaders to understand the power of the media, and he treated the small entourage of reporters who accompanied Kissinger as potential allies, shaking their hands, joking with them, using them not only as foils in a diplomatic duel but also as sources of information about the secretary's strategy. If Hollywood had to cast an Egyptian leader for this role at this time, it could not have selected anyone better. And to complete the picture, Sadat was uncommonly sophisticated, cunning, and bold.

Sadat had tried war as an instrument of policy; now he decided to try personal diplomacy, and it shattered the mold. No more shuttles, no more Geneva conferences, no more balancing Moscow off against Washington. Sadat, with panache, decided to visit Jerusalem; it was televised, dramatic proof of his desire for peace with the Jewish state.

On November 19, 1977, after careful negotiations with the Israelis and well-orchestrated interviews with American TV anchors, Sadat arrived at Ben Gurion International Airport, where he was greeted by past and present Israeli leaders and an army of journalists with cameras. Sadat's eyes were moist when he kissed Golda Meir, prime minister during the 1973 war. Israelis watching on television cried.

Sadat made all the proper stops, from the Yad Vashem memorial to the Al-Aqsa Mosque. When he addressed the Israeli parliament, or Knesset, he spoke of peace and an end to war, and he received a standing ovation.

At the White House, Carter, like tens of millions of other Americans, watched the Sadat visit on television and then issued a statement saying that "the hopes and prayers of all Americans" were with both Sadat and Begin. He added the obvious: "The arrival of President Sadat in Israel is an historic occasion." If Sadat could blaze new trails by visiting Begin in Israel, Carter concluded, then he himself could blaze newer ones by inviting them both to Camp David, the presidential retreat in suburban Maryland, for an unprecedented trilateral summit. Carter studied the lives of the two leaders. Sadat, he sensed, was ready to make history, but was Begin?

Throughout his life, the Israeli leader took pride in his uncompromising Zionism and his dedication to Israeli democracy. Born and educated in Poland, where he studied law, he moved to Palestine and led the militant Irgun resistance to British rule and then, after independence in 1948, the right-wing Likud Party. He once said that in the early 1950s he disagreed so strongly with Prime Minister David Ben-Gurion's decision to accept "blood money" from Konrad Adenauer's Germany that he was tempted to rally his supporters, stage a coup, seize power, and then return the money; but he could not move against the established order. He cherished democracy.

In his office, Begin always wore a dark suit and tie, so uncharacteristic of the casual style of Israeli leaders. "One day I knew that I would be Prime Minister," he said with the certainty of a Carter, "but I wanted to be Prime Minister of a democracy. I wanted the power that comes from an election." He paused. "So I waited."[32] He waited through eight successive Likud defeats to the Labor Party, which had governed Israel for the first thirty years of its existence. And then, in 1977, Likud won for the first time, and Begin became prime minister. On September 5, 1978, he and Sadat arrived at Camp David.

The negotiation was exceedingly tough, which was expected, and confidential, which was not expected. Carter had begged the two belligerents to avoid a war of words. The Israelis were master leakers, but, miraculously, not on this occasion. Reporters had access only to the official White House briefing. On September 6 Carter, Sadat, and Begin met together for the first time. On September 7 they again met together. On September 8 Carter met separately with each leader. On September 10 Carter invited Sadat and Begin to tour the Civil War battlefield at Gettysburg. For the next week, it was not clear whether success was possible. But Carter, undaunted, pursued his dream, day after day, night after night, and on September 17 he was able to announce a breakthrough in negotiations for peace in the Middle East.[33]

On September 18 a proud president went to Capitol Hill and addressed a special joint session of Congress. Carter was accompanied by Sadat and Begin. The president, enjoying the moment, proclaimed that the Camp David agreements had turned an "impossible dream" into a realistic expectation of peace. *New York Times* reporter Hedrick Smith wrote that Carter had clearly emerged as the victor politically, and columnist Tom Wicker went even further, saying the agreement not only raised Carter's popularity level, but it also lessened concerns about his competency in handling the country's many challenges.[34] Carter's optimism was ultimately rewarded. Six months later, on March 26, 1979, Egypt and Israel signed a historic peace treaty, the first ever between Israel and an Arab state.

Example Three: SALT II, the Treaty Reached but Never Ratified

From the very beginning, Carter wanted to update the SALT I agreement, which Nixon and Brezhnev had signed in 1972. It recognized "strategic parity" between the United States and the Soviet Union. Up to that time, the United States had enjoyed a clear advantage. But after the Cuban missile crisis, which Soviet leaders saw as a major defeat, they began to invest heavily in missiles, warheads, tanks, and in time a "blue water" navy, all of which had the effect by the beginning of the 1970s of righting the strategic balance between the two superpowers. Hence SALT I. As the Soviet Union strove for parity, the United States slipped into the morass of Vietnam, spending its money there and not on strategic weapons.

It was during this time that an ideological argument erupted in the Kremlin, encouraged in part by the emerging realization among top Soviet leaders that the Americans might not be able to win in Vietnam. No one believed they could lose, but they were clearly being stretched to the limit by the North

Vietnamese. The argument centered on whether the Soviet Union should readjust its global strategy. One ideological faction, pressing the goals of "proletarian internationalism," argued that ideally there should be little cooperation between capitalism and communism; that Moscow should push its advantage wherever and whenever possible, short of triggering another direct confrontation between the two superpowers. The opposing faction, supporting "peaceful coexistence," believed that the competition between the two nations should continue and that it would lead inevitably to a communist triumph, but that there was no need in a dangerous nuclear-armed world to be deliberately provocative.

"Some of the most serious Soviet internal debates," said Sergei Rogov, director of the Moscow Institute on the USA and Canada, "were between the people who said 'peaceful coexistence' and 'proletarian internationalism' [and] those who said 'proletarian internationalism' not 'peaceful coexistence.'"[35] In the buildup to Hanoi's ultimate victory in 1975, the proletarian internationalists appeared to be gaining the upper hand, even though the Soviet government officially supported the Paris Peace Accords. Once Hanoi decided to crush the Saigon regime, the Soviets rushed massive quantities of military and economic aid to North Vietnam to ensure its success and win its allegiance in the ongoing Sino-Soviet struggle.

When the Soviets, like so many others around the world, observed the humiliating American pullout from Saigon on April 30, 1975, they began to imagine the unimaginable. Burdened throughout their history with a deep sense of insecurity, they had trouble absorbing one new development on the world scene: the mighty United States, in their minds the leader of the capitalist world, was in stunning retreat. Some in the Kremlin wondered whether the strategic balance was shifting once again; whether the Soviet Union might now be stronger than the United States. Rogov, a young communist at the time, articulated a thought many of his more idealistic colleagues could only dream about: "the global victory of communism," he recalled, might no longer be "something which we should fight for eternally but something that could happen in our lifetime." Reduced to the dry calculations of arms-control negotiations, this meant that the Soviet Union would no longer be satisfied with "nuclear parity," the basis of SALT I. Now, in Rogov's words, "we felt we no longer had to be second to America; we felt we could become Number One."[36]

Of all of Carter's advisers, it was probably only Brzezinski who could have put his finger on the Soviet pulse at that time, and he worried about a wave of "renewed aggressiveness" resulting from the American defeat. In many parts of the developing world, he saw signs of Soviet expansionism. In Africa, for example, the Soviet Union used tens of thousands of Cuban proxies along with "Soviet advisers" to extend communist influence in Angola, Mozambique, Somalia, and Ethiopia. In the South China Sea, where the Soviets had never had a foothold, they were now occupying the Vietnamese port of Cam Ranh Bay, which featured the large naval base the Americans had built and then abandoned. This major extension of Soviet power and influence sent ripples of anxiety through the Forbidden City in Beijing. By supporting a leftist coup in Afghanistan, they were bringing this once remote kingdom into the fierce East-West competition. Suddenly a different kind of question was being asked by Carter's advisers: could Brezhnev be angling to extend Soviet power toward the Persian Gulf and thus be in a position to control oil shipments? Even closer to home, Castro's Cuba was beginning to push a more aggressive policy in Central and South America.

Brzezinski wondered about the "legacies of Vietnam and Watergate," and on May 5, 1978, he wrote Carter: "My concern for the future is not that the Soviet Union will emerge as the dominant world power, imposing a 'Pax Sovietica.' I fear something else: that the destructive nature of Soviet efforts will increasingly make it impossible for us to give order and stability to global change and thus prevent the appearance of a more cooperative and just international system. We will become more isolated and fearful and inward looking," and the world might then conclude that "the Soviet Union is on the ascendancy and the U.S. on the decline."[37]

Brezhnev had always been a supporter of "peaceful coexistence." Could he be losing his grip on power? As far back as 1971 he had trumpeted the "irreversibility" of détente. But within a few years, as Brzezinski noted, Brezhnev saw his "two main Western interlocutors—Nixon and Brandt—fall from office," and then, during the 1976 presidential campaign, he saw Ford moving so far to the right that another strategic arms limitation agreement seemed to be "slipping from their grasp." Brezhnev seemed "dismay[ed]" and "bitter."[38] Carter's policy of human rights irritated Brezhnev, and Brzezinski's own reputation as a Polish-born, anticommunist critic bugged him. A British journalist, Edward Crankshaw, who had covered Soviet affairs for decades, noted the fragility of Brezhnev's political position: "The Soviet leadership is in deep disarray," he wrote. "Brezhnev is 72 and has been intermittently ill." And so, Crankshaw continued, "We are now being treated to a show of frightfulness by a lot of frightened men to show how strong they are."[39] Mondale, much more realistic about the Soviet leadership than Carter, thought "the USSR was going to collapse, and they were doing desperate things to seem powerful."[40]

Still, arms negotiations between the two sides resumed, and on March 11, 1977, in another of his weekly reports, Brzezinski assured Carter that American negotiators were working "intensively" on a new U.S. position.[41] Carter wanted progress, but he did not have to make an immediate decision, and the talks lumbered along.

By June Brzezinski was reporting a slowdown in the negotiations. The United States wanted an agreement, but, Brzezinski kept asking himself, had Brezhnev lost his passion for arms control? One problem, he soon learned, was that Carter was a puzzle to Brezhnev. Sometimes, in discussing U.S.-Soviet relations, Carter would sound like Vance, detached and sympathetic, extending a hand of friendship; but on other occasions he would sound like Brzezinski, suspicious and belligerent, extending a clenched fist. The Soviets thought Carter was a confused and probably weak president, a one-termer. Brezhnev, to make matters worse, had a disconcerting way of personalizing national relationships. During the Nixon administration, for instance, he thought he understood U.S. policy, because he thought he understood Nixon. Or during the Ford administration, because he had met Ford and liked him, he thought he understood him. Carter was a new and baffling personality, and even Brezhnev's experienced Washington ambassador, Anatoly Dobrynin, did not yet have a fix on Carter.

Finally, on June 18, 1979, after many long, excruciating negotiations, Brezhnev and Carter met in the glittering Redoutensaal in Vienna's Hofburg Palace to sign the SALT II agreement, aimed at setting qualitative and quantitative limits on the strategic nuclear arsenals of the two superpowers. SALT II conformed to Carter's self-image as a pilgrim of peace. It was another milestone in his journey to put America on a post-Vietnam trajectory of no more wars.

While both leaders enjoyed the pomp and ceremony of superpower summitry, each had more serious reasons for coming to Vienna. The United States wanted to contain the worrisome expansion of Soviet nuclear weaponry, and Carter thought he might be able to persuade Brezhnev to stop his dangerous escapades in Africa, the Middle East, and Asia. He again exaggerated his powers of persuasion. The Kremlin's aging leadership was rattled by the recent normalization of relations between the United States and China, which Brezhnev saw as a direct threat to his country, and he wanted assurances from Carter that the United States would never sell weapons to China.

At the signing ceremony, the Soviet leader, in a typically Russian gesture of joy, hugged and kissed Carter, leaving the peanut farmer from Plains looking momentarily discombobulated. For a president already under critical scrutiny at home, the summit kiss was not the image he intended to project. Brzezinski, meanwhile, stressed verification and newly imposed limitations on Soviet missile expansion.

Carter flew directly to Washington and reported to Congress on the SALT II signing, the second time in two years he was able to boast about a historic accomplishment: first the Camp David agreement and now a strategic arms limitation agreement. Carter was, for a brief time, enjoying his diplomatic coups.

EXAMPLE FOUR: CHINA, ALONG TWO TRACKS

Carter was always fascinated by China. When he was a boy, he read glowing reports of Christian missionaries spreading the gospel among a grateful people. He also read family letters from "Uncle Tom" Gordy, a U.S. Navy sailor, who described port calls in China: squalid cities filled with poor, hungry, desperate people for whom religion was an unaffordable luxury. In 1949 as a young naval officer, Carter visited China on a U.S. warship, making his own port calls in Tsingtao and Hong Kong, then a British colony. His curiosity was aroused, but it was not until February 1977, a month after he became president, that he could begin to satisfy not just his curiosity but also his desire to "normalize" relations between the American and Chinese people. He was now in a position to build on the Nixon-Kissinger breakthrough in 1972, the opening of liaison offices in Washington and Beijing in 1973 and the Ford visit to China in 1975. Now it was his turn, and he moved with characteristic self-confidence.

He invited Huang Chen, China's liaison chief based in Washington, to the White House, where they had a long talk, longer than the one he had with Soviet ambassador Dobrynin, which raised more than a few diplomatic eyebrows. After a general review of the Sino-American relationship, Carter stressed his interest in a rapid improvement in diplomatic relations. Since ambassadors usually have no authority to go beyond diplomatic platitudes, he did not expect anything more than a pro forma response; but the Chinese diplomat surprised him. Huang Chen spoke openly about the Soviet threat. Whenever he mentioned the Soviet Union, as Carter later wrote, he turned "antagonistic" and "distrustful." Still, throughout the meeting, Huang Chen exuded an extraordinary sense of imperial grandeur. After all, he represented the "Middle Kingdom."[42]

One day a China scholar who later became one of Bill Clinton's experts on the National Security Council visited Huang Chen's liaison office in Washington. After a long talk there, he left feeling amazed at the disappointment the Chinese were expressing about Carter's pursuit of SALT II and better relations with the Soviet Union. "Jesus," he said, "these guys are really strung out about the Russians!" Apparently the Chinese had no inhibitions at that time about discussing their growing concerns about Soviet policy. The scholar continued: "I remember very vividly, in '76, '77, how they were sounding alarms to us, that we were not fully appreciating how dangerous the Russians were, and that we needed to increase our vigilance against the Russians. They were very concerned that we were underestimating the threat from the Soviet Union."

Brzezinski, who maintained a working dialogue with Huang Chen and other Chinese diplomats, struck the same note in an April 22, 1977, report to Carter: "The main Chinese concern remains the global strategic posture of the U.S.," he wrote. "The Chinese repeatedly condemned the 'appeasement' posture of the U.S. in SALT and even more so in Africa. Disappointingly, they drew no distinctions between Carter and Ford Administration policies toward the USSR."[43]

Also in 1977 Carter took another step toward normalization. He appointed Leonard Woodcock, the respected leader of the United Auto Workers, to be the next chief of the American liaison office in Beijing. By the time Woodcock got to China that July, Carter had already drafted a normalization agreement with China, refining its contents in a series of top-secret meetings with Vance and Brzezinski. He was ready for Woodcock to make a formal presentation to the Chinese and was certain that they would respond positively.

In the spring of 1978, largely as a result of Brzezinski's prodding, the quest for normalization accelerated. Using his clout as national security adviser, Brzezinski kept urging Carter to see China as another "offensive tool" against the Soviet Union. In one weekly report after another, he underscored continued Soviet adventurism in Africa, Latin America, and Asia and stressed the need for a more assertive American foreign policy, gently but repeatedly raising questions about the president's approach. Brzezinski wanted Carter to "exploit" Soviet "weaknesses," the "inner contradictions" in the Soviet system. "It would create pressure on them, they would realize they can't win, the competition itself would put strains on them and turn the tables against them."[44]

But Carter resisted Brzezinski's urgings, perhaps because he was uncomfortable with his aide's aggressive style. The president felt more comfortable with Vance's dignified, by-the-book diplomacy. While Brzezinski was eager to leapfrog obstacles, such as Taiwan, and embrace overarching strategic breakthroughs, such as enlisting China in his fight against the Soviet Union, Vance and the president decided to proceed step by step, negotiating trade deals, then cultural exchanges, and, as relations eased, the issue of Taiwan, and finally, down the road, normalization. All of this would take time, and Brzezinski thought the United States did not have much of it.

In April 1978 Brzezinski finally got Carter's permission to visit Beijing. In his weekly reports, he had been hammering away at Vance's approach to China, at first indirectly but then with uninhibited bluntness, referring to the State Department or Vance himself, or Richard Holbrooke, the assistant secretary of state for East Asian affairs, whom he openly distrusted and disliked, as "obstacles" to a sound China policy. On April 21 he told Carter that Vance's efforts to withdraw American troops from Korea (actually a presidential initiative) were "unsettling" and "precipitate"; that his negotiating the normalization of relations with Vietnam made "little sense"; that "our naval presence" in the Pacific was "inadequate" to meet the "growing Soviet" threat; that "U.S. weakness vis-à-vis Moscow justifiably [caused] China to view us as a less attractive partner"; and, cutting to the heart of his argument, that "we have failed to use the China card against the Soviets."[45]

On May 17, 1978, as Brzezinski was preparing to leave for China, Carter sent him a personal letter of instruction, which, from its style and tone, one could imagine was drafted by Brzezinski himself. It ran five pages, and though it straddled the administration's twin approaches to normalization, it tilted decidedly toward the Brzezinski approach. Proof was on the first page: "The United States and China . . . have parallel, long-term strategic concerns," the president wrote. "The most important of these is our common opposition to global or regional hegemony by any single power."

"Hegemony," in the language of the time, meant Soviet domination. Should the United States and China normalize their diplomatic relationship—which was then a matter of when, not whether—the two would act as though they were in an unofficial alliance against the Soviet Union. Carter stressed in an almost pro forma way that of course he wanted peace with the Soviet Union, but he also urged Brzezinski "to establish a shared perspective" with China about "the Soviet military challenge" and to "develop political collaboration."

Aware of China's concerns about his negotiations with the Soviet Union on strategic nuclear weapons, Carter sought to explain, through Brzezinski, that SALT II was "not a product of weakness but the consequence of prudence." Then he laid out his vision of "the Soviet threat": "My concern," he wrote, "is that the combination of increasing Soviet military power and political shortsightedness, fed by big-power ambitions, might tempt the Soviet Union both to exploit local turbulence (especially in the Third World) and to intimidate our friends in order to seek political advantage and eventually even political preponderance. This is why I do take seriously Soviet action in Africa and this is why I am concerned about the Soviet military buildup in Central Europe. I also see some Soviet designs pointing towards the Indian Ocean . . . and perhaps to the encirclement of China through Vietnam (and perhaps some day through Taiwan)." In case his point was missed, which was unlikely, Carter then repeated that his policy was designed "to shape an international system not subject to hegemony by a single power."[46]

On his way to Beijing in late May, Brzezinski stopped in Tokyo, where he had a chance to practice his activist diplomacy. The Japanese and the Chinese were at that time negotiating a joint declaration of principles. One contentious issue was the use of that same word, "hegemonism." The Chinese wanted the word to be inserted in the declaration; the Japanese thought it too provocative. Prime Minister Takeo Fukuda sought Brzezinski's counsel. "Use it," the American adviser said. "We have no objections to that." The word was used in the declaration, much to Moscow's displeasure and Brzezinski's delight.

In China, Brzezinski broke protocol. He did not negotiate with a senior Chinese adviser on national security, someone who was his equivalent on the protocol ladder; instead, he negotiated directly with China's supreme leader, Deng Xiaoping, and they got along famously. Vance, on his trip to China in August 1977, had gotten "hung up" on the contentious issue of Taiwan and did not make progress with normalization; Brzezinski sidestepped the issue, telling Deng that "history will take care of that one." The United States had no fundamental interest in Taiwan, he added, and the Carter administration supported the Shanghai communiqué. It was clear that Deng was ready to make progress; he embraced Brzezinski's vague formula about Taiwan, which had been the principal stumbling block up to that time. When it was obvious that Deng and Brzezinski were singing from the same sheet of music, they moved on to "Soviet hegemony." "The real issue," Brzezinski said, preaching to the choir, was that "you're threatened by hegemonism," and the United States was also worried about it; so "all of a sudden there is something in common here that's big, that's really big, and that led from one thing to another."[47] Discussing his China visit many years later, Brzezinski looked like the cat that swallowed the canary, content not only with the result but also with his role in negotiating it.

Carter considered the Brzezinski trip "very successful." Deng had emerged as an active and sympathetic interlocutor, and normalization seemed only months away. In his diary, Carter wrote that Brzezinski "was overwhelmed with the Chinese. I told him he had been seduced." By November the negotiation was rumbling toward a successful conclusion. In December Brzezinski met with Chai Zemin, the new chief of the Chinese liaison office in Washington and handed him a letter of invitation from Carter to Deng for the Chinese leader to visit the capital soon after the normalization of relations, which, Carter had proposed, should be on January 1, 1979. Deng accepted Carter's invitation and agreed to the January 1 date. "We will adopt the draft of the United States," he told Woodcock, "and I accept the President's invitation to visit your country."

The formal announcement was made simultaneously in Washington and Beijing on December 15.[48] Carter was worried about a Taiwan backlash and an explosion of conservative opposition. He got neither, much to his relief, suggesting that the American public at least considered normalization to be a logical extension of the earlier Nixon breakthrough.

In late January 1979 Carter greeted Deng at the White House. Carter was impressed by the Chinese leader; one might say "overwhelmed." That night, in his diary, Carter used eight favorable adjectives to describe Deng: "small, tough, intelligent, frank, courageous, personable, self-assured, friendly," adding, "it's a pleasure to negotiate with him." Their focus was twofold: Sino-American relations and Soviet hegemony. Deng at one point told Carter, as Carter wrote in his diary, that "the Soviets will launch war eventually," and it was important to "coordinate our activities to constrain the Soviets."[49] Carter and Deng seemed to agree on everything.

To this day, in his office at the corner of 18th and K streets in Washington, D.C., Brzezinski proudly points to a photograph showing Deng having dinner at Brzezinski's home—Deng sitting on one side of the table, he on the other. It was his crowning accomplishment, bringing the United States and China together against the Soviet Union: an accomplishment that was soon to be tested.

. . . And Then It All Came Tumbling Down

If Jimmy Carter's term could have ended in early 1979, he would have been rated a successful president in the arena of foreign affairs. He had entered the White House with an idealistic vision: no longer would the United States be seen as the nuclear-armed giant that had stumbled into a colonial war in Vietnam and, unbelievably, managed to be defeated by peasant warriors; now, behind the banner of human rights and individual liberty, the United States would again become peacemaker to the world, leaving Vietnam in the dustbin of history. Carter's record in this respect was impressive. He had started with a grand gesture toward Latin America: the Panama Canal Treaty. Then he swung his attention to the troubled Middle East, where the idea of a peace treaty between Israel and Egypt was unimaginable; yet at Camp David he negotiated just such a treaty. A SALT II agreement with the Soviet Union and normalization of relations with China were both on Washington's agenda, but they were not inevitable byproducts of presidential attention. Carter exploited both opportunities and produced two substantial diplomatic victories.

Yet, for several reasons, Carter was seen as incompetent, and this deeply disturbed him. One reason, wrote Brzezinski on September 13, 1979, was "the excessively critical and even prejudiced views of the Washington press corps." But media criticism, critical and occasionally even prejudiced, has been endemic to Washington politics; it explained little. What was crucial for Brzezinski was how the world saw the U.S.-Soviet relationship. Here he returned to one of his favored critiques: that "the Soviet side" was seen "increasingly" as "the assertive party" and "the U.S. side" as the "more acquiescent." "The country craves, and our national security needs, both a more assertive tone and a more assertive substance to our foreign policy."[50] He offered options to the president, such as "ostracizing" Cuba, condemning Soviet adventurism in Africa, and "doing more" for national defense. In his view, to do less would "stamp this administration as weak." In retrospect, it seems quite extraordinary that a national security adviser could be so persistently critical of a president and get away with it. Vance had his own view: after Vietnam, he argued that the United States should be less confrontational, not only because an accommodating policy made more sense but also because the United States needed time to recoup after a long, debilitating involvement in Southeast Asia.

But even if Carter had acted on all of Brzezinski's recommendations, he still might not have been able to raise his stature at home and abroad. Every successful politician needs luck. Carter had plenty of it in 1976, when he ran for president. Three years later, he had very little of it; 1979 was, for him, an especially cruel year. It started with an Islamic revolution in Iran and ended with the Soviet invasion of Afghanistan. Carter seemed blindsided by both.

The Shah Leaves, the Ayatollah Arrives

On January 16, 1979, the shah of Iran fled to Egypt, a sick and dispirited man. He had once been the reliable anchor of Washington's Mideast strategy. In Carter's 1977 New Year's Eve toast, Iran was described as "an island of stability" in a troubled region. Ever since 1953, when the CIA manufactured a coup against Mohammed Mossadegh, a mercurial prime minister who was thinking about nationalizing the oil industry, and the young shah was installed, Iran had been a close and trusted American ally in the cold war, an anti-Soviet oil well that spouted the American line and bought American arms. From his imperial throne, the shah looked down on a complex society, proud of its Persian legacy, profiting from its economic expansion and a manageable degree of political diversity, and yet torn inside by a simmering civil war between modernization and Islamic doctrine. In 1963 the war burst into the open, as religious leaders demanded more of the Koran and less of the West.

The shah chose to crack down. Using the pervasive powers of SAVAK, the National Intelligence and Security Organization, he smashed this religious rebellion, but not the smoldering resentment of the Islamic hierarchy, which quietly nurtured a new generation of nationalistic, religious zealots. Sitting on top of this cauldron was an angry ayatollah named Ruhollah Musavi Khomeini, who was at first imprisoned by SAVAK and a year later exiled. He was determined to return, he said, when Iran showed signs of becoming a new caliphate.

For a time, SAVAK, narrow-mindedly egged on by the CIA, contained the Islamic discontent, arresting, brutalizing, or killing thousands of religious dissenters. But when Carter came to power, hailing his new policy of human rights, the shah's continuing crackdown led inevitably to tension in the U.S.-Iranian relationship. Carter's instinct was to criticize the shah; human rights were being systematically violated in Iran. But faced with the cold calculus of the cold war, he needed a shah-led Iran, and he lived with the illusion that he could have both the shah and human rights. On this issue, as on so many others, Brzezinski and Vance disagreed. Brzezinski argued that a stable, pro-Western Iran was more important to the United States than a feel-good trumpeting of human rights, while Vance adhered to Carter's call for human rights and democracy as the better path for ensuring a pro-Western Iran.

As late as November 7, 1978, two months before the shah's forced departure, the United States considered the situation in Iran to be "reasonably stable." In a revealing backgrounder, Brzezinski told reporters at the time that "we feel quite confident that the shah will be able to surmount" his current problems. "He has the means, the will and the latent support."[51] Brzezinski was wrong. In fact, the shah had dwindling support, even among his closest advisers, and he was suffering from terminal cancer. Despite a secret agreement between SAVAK and the CIA to exchange intelligence, little was being exchanged. "Our intelligence," Brzezinski acknowledged, "could be a hell of a lot better. We are superb on facts, very poor on political intelligence. And this is not only the CIA but the State Department, too. Very few cables are worth reading. *The New York Times* does a much better job. We really don't have good systematic reporting which gives us a good feel for what's going on in the world."[52] He knew that in August 1978 the CIA had produced a report saying that Iran was "not in a revolutionary or even a pre-revolutionary situation."[53] It was unclear why Brzezinski was expressing so much confidence in the shah's survivability when he had so little confidence in U.S. intelligence.

Sixteen days after the shah's departure, on February 1, 1979, Ayatollah Khomeini returned to Tehran more bitter than ever. His son had been killed by SAVAK. Referring to the Iranian leadership, he told a rapturous throng of Iranians who had swarmed to the airport, "I will strike with my fists at the mouths of this government."[54] Prime Minister Shahpour Bakhtiar desperately tried to maintain his government's control over the country, but he was helplessly engulfed in the passions of an Islamic revolution. Khomeini appointed a sympathetic lawyer, Mehdi Bazargan, as prime minister. What had once been an "island of stability" suddenly became a base of religious instability, and, according to the White House, a threat to the entire region. The United States was facing the disruptive power of Islamic fundamentalism, and the Carter administration was baffled by this challenge, consistently underestimating both its staying power and its appeal to the wider Muslim world.

Carter tried to cope, watching the revolution unfold, knowing that it was hurting U.S. interests and yet feeling that he was unable to do anything about it. Again, as in the final days of the Vietnam War, the United States looked like a paper tiger.

On February 11, as rebel fighters loyal to Khomeini overwhelmed government troops, Iran flipped from a failing monarchy to a triumphant theocracy. On April 1 Iran took the next step, renaming itself the "Islamic Republic of Iran," with the ayatollah serving as its supreme leader.

As Khomeini rose in global prominence, the shah became a wandering refugee, traveling from one country to another, unable to find either proper medical care or a permanent home. His cancer had spread. In late October two of his American friends, Henry Kissinger and David Rockefeller, pleaded with Carter to allow the shah to come to New York for treatment. Carter, who had been very reluctant, agreed, and his problems multiplied. The shah and his entourage arrived in New York, where they stayed for a brief time, clearly unwanted, before leaving for Panama and then Egypt, where he died in July

1980. Carter had considered the possibility that accepting the shah could lead to the Iranians' taking Americans as hostages, but, under pressure from the Republican establishment, he let the shah in.

On November 4 several hundred student radicals, all of them followers of "the imam's line" and furious at Carter's decision, stormed the U.S. embassy in Tehran, seized sixty-six Americans, and demanded that the shah be returned to Iran immediately for trial and execution. It was not clear at the time whether they were vamping or operating on the ayatollah's orders; whether they intended to hold the Americans for a week, a month, or a year; or whether they were shopping for a swap of the shah for their hostages. What followed was a hostage crisis that lasted 444 days. Not until January 20, 1981, when Ronald Reagan was sworn into office, were the hostages finally released. The crisis, which was an all-consuming story in the United States, ruined Carter's chances of reelection. And as in 1975, during the final days of the Vietnam War, it demonstrated America's inability to cope with asymmetrical warfare, this time in the form of a challenge from student radicals. In fact, from a military point of view, the United States could have crushed the Iranian revolution if the Americans had acted decisively, but Carter was hoping for a bloodless solution.

Such hopes collapsed when the ayatollah publicly threw his support behind the students. Once the ayatollah set the tone, everyone followed his lead. Overnight, the students became symbols of national pride. Hundreds and then thousands of Iranians set up nocturnal vigils around the embassy, echoing the student demand for the shah's return. The students themselves seemed to take a perverted pleasure in their new power, blindfolding the Americans and forcing them to walk, head down and humiliated, in front of the world's cameras. When a few Iranian politicians summoned the courage to warn the ayatollah about possible American retaliation, Khomeini was dismissive. It was not clear whether the ayatollah was acting with due deliberation or recklessly riding the crest of a popular revolution, whether he was aware that, according to international law, the embassy seizure could be interpreted as an act of war, or whether he was oblivious to such matters and was simply playing a game of domestic politics, Iranian-style, using the embassy seizure to obliterate his political foes.

One day David Aaron, Brzezinski's deputy on the National Security Council, raised this possibility with Carter. "It seems to me," Aaron said, "that the radicals are using this to eliminate everybody we talk to, and they are really doing this to discredit the so-called moderate politicians."[55]

Perhaps, but neither Carter, Aaron, nor any of the other senior advisers knew. They were all guessing, trying to avoid a calamity. It was so outrageous an action that Carter assumed that the Khomeini government would soon bring the students to their senses and the crisis would pass, certainly by Christmas. When Aaron challenged the president's assumption—"You know, Mr. President, despite everything, this thing could go past Christmas"—Carter chose to ignore him. Carter was depending on Vance and his deputy, Warren Christopher, to find an acceptable diplomatic way out of this crisis; and, if they failed, he was hoping his chief of staff, Hamilton Jordan, who was piling up frequent flyer points traveling from one part of the globe to another for hush-hush negotiations with Iranian officials said to be "close to the ayatollah," would somehow pull a miracle out of the hostage hat, but he, too, failed. Aaron told Carter that the Arabs had a saying about Iranians: "They will take you to the water, and you will come back thirsty." And he added, "We came back thirsty every single time," a reference to all the diplomatic efforts, some tempting, most disappointing, none successful, that were being tried.[56]

As the weeks and months passed, Carter found himself trapped in a crisis that seemed only to get worse. When the student rebels released some of the hostages, women and African Americans, for a moment Carter thought maybe they would then release all of them. But again he misread the signal. The students were actually playing to the galleries, and the ayatollah's rhetoric grew harsher still. On several occasions the president did consider a rescue mission, but he was very reluctant to give the green light, and at that time serious preparations never got off the ground. Carter had always hoped that after so many thousands of lives had been wasted in Vietnam, he could lead America to a new age of peace where all problems would be resolved by negotiation and goodwill. He wanted his administration to pass into history as the only one without a presidential order to kill. The Joint Chiefs of Staff, definitely not gung-ho about dropping marines into Tehran, proposed a number of military options, but each time Carter was unwilling to pull the trigger. The Oval Office became his bunker. He rarely traveled. His advisers began to worry about his reelection prospects, but he waved off all talk of politics. Carter was fixed on only one thing: getting the hostages out of Tehran safe and sound. At first, the American people supported his approach, and his poll numbers shot up. But as time passed and the hostages were still hostages, his poll numbers began to drop.

Complicating Carter's hostage problem was a perfect storm in the American economy. Serious unemployment combined with double-digit inflation created turmoil and uncertainty all over the country. And when another Arab oil embargo forced Americans to wait hours in gasoline lines, tempers flared, and Carter was blamed. The combination of a deteriorating economy and the hostage crisis effectively killed his reelection prospects even before the 1980 presidential campaign got off the ground.

Rosalynn Carter, who often substituted for the president on political trips, tried to persuade her husband to "do something." "Like what?" he would ask. "Couldn't you mine the harbors?" she replied. But Carter would respond that such an action could lead to the Iranians' taking "the hostages out one at a time . . . before a firing squad, [and] then what?" He counseled patience.[57]

Mondale visited with his former colleagues on Capitol Hill. They were sympathetic, but they, too, wanted action, Mondale recalled. "They all said, 'Carter has to do something. He is losing us.' Then, I went to Carter, and he said, 'I know what they are saying, but I won't have that on my conscience.'"[58]

For a time during the winter of 1979–80, Carter placed so high a premium on saving the life of every single hostage that he seemed to be losing sight of other presidential responsibilities, one of which was the ability, when necessary, to order American military power into action. His predilection for pacifism seemed to stifle his decisionmaking powers during the hostage crisis. Another president might have acted against the student radicals soon after the embassy seizure, recognizing that while several of the hostages might have been killed in the rescue operation, the others would probably have been liberated, and the United States would have shown a degree of toughness and resolve consistent with its superpower status.

One day Kissinger visited Mondale, and they discussed a possible rescue mission. Inevitably a question of biblical simplicity arose: is the national interest, as Kissinger defined it, worth the life of a single hostage, or five hostages, or twenty? Mondale argued Carter's case. Was there a rescue mission so perfect in concept and performance that it would ensure the safety of all the hostages? No, said Kissinger, and there never would be. "One of the things that worried us," the vice president responded, "was that we will give the radicals over there a chance to get rough with our hostages. We have been through this a lot, and there is no guarantee it couldn't happen." Kissinger replied that the hostages were professional diplomats. "When you go into the Foreign Service," the former secretary of state observed, "you agree to take risks for your country, and this is that kind of situation." No rescue mission was perfect, but a mission was needed.[59]

Carter and Mondale both understood that with each passing day the American people were converting the hostages into secular saints. Yellow ribbons were wrapped around trees and posters all over the country. Bumper stickers were passing reminders of the unsolved crisis. Hostage families were constant guests on morning and evening television programs. Lobbying groups were changing the crisis into a cause. Sunday sermons were filled with sympathy but also advice for the president. ABC's *Nightline* became a must-stop fill-in before bedtime and its host, Ted Koppel, a credible interpreter of the unfolding drama.

On April 11, 1980, Carter told his aides that he was "seriously considering an attempt to rescue the hostages," something that had been an option for months.[60] He could not, after a while, resist the building pressure for action, even though he knew that action carried risk with no assurance of success. He felt trapped by circumstance but compelled to act.

The top-secret mission, code-named Operation Eagle Claw, called for eight helicopters to fly from an aircraft carrier in the Persian Gulf and meet up with six C-130 transport planes and 132 Delta Force commandos and Army Rangers on a deserted airstrip in eastern Iran, Desert One, in official terminology. After refueling, the helicopters, loaded down with heavily armed commandos and Rangers, would fly to an empty canyon in a Tehran suburb, where, camouflaged, they would spend the day. That was Desert Two. In the dead of night, a procession of trucks would arrive and ferry the commandos and Rangers to the occupied embassy. And, just like that, swiftly, silently, the hostages would be sprung, hustled into the waiting trucks, which would then take them to another deserted air base on the outskirts of Tehran, and quickly flown to freedom—all before a single Iranian got out of bed and noticed what had happened. Except—blame it on a sandstorm, faulty mechanics, the need for strict radio silence, or just plain lousy luck—the mission had to be aborted, which proved to be a humiliating embarrassment to Carter.

Carter met with Colonel Charlie Beckwith, who was selected to command the mission. Beckwith asked: "Mr. President, did your family ever live in the Florida panhandle?" "Oh, yes," Carter replied, "that's where my family came from, and later they moved on to Georgia." "Well, that's where I'm from too," Beckwith said. "Our families probably picked cotton together." Carter shook his hand. "Charlie, I want you to know that no matter what happens, if anything goes wrong, any problem arises, I will take all the responsibility." And, as Aaron recalled, "He sure did."[61]

Beckwith, the swashbuckling warrior who created the Delta Force, was buoyantly optimistic about the mission. Though it was complicated and dangerous, and to some even fanciful and crazy in its complexity, he was positive that all the parts would fit. Vance and Christopher were decidedly pessimistic, regarding Carter's "go" decision to be a repudiation of all their negotiating efforts. Vance, deeply disappointed, informed Carter that he intended to resign, whether the mission was successful or not. Brzezinski nodded his approval but wondered what would happen if it failed. Jordan, at wit's end after so many fruitless efforts at a negotiated solution, agreed with the decision.

Carter added a final condition: if, during the rescue, Beckwith's team was to run into a hostile crowd in Tehran or elsewhere, they were to use nonlethal crowd control agents. This was madness, for Beckwith would then have no authority, even in self-defense, to open lethal fire on Iranians. A Delta captain said, "The only difference between this and the Alamo is that Davy Crockett didn't have to fight his way in." Beckwith's deputy, Major Bucky Burruss, objected, but had been told, "No, the president insists."[62] Carter wanted a bloodless mission, although it was difficult to see how he could have imagined that 132 commandos and Rangers could arrive in Iran in eight helicopters and six C-130 transport planes and rescue fifty-three Americans locked up in an embassy occupied by student radicals, without firing a single shot. Beckwith and Burruss decided, presidential order notwithstanding, that they would do what they felt they had to do to accomplish the mission, even if that meant shooting Iranians.

Everyone understood that all the parts would have to fit for the mission to succeed. Beckwith built in very few redundancies. He needed six helicopters for the rescue, but added two more, just to be sure. He wanted only his trusted Delta Force to do the job, but General David Jones, chairman of the Joint Chiefs of Staff, added a small Ranger team. Two of the six C-130s would carry fuel balloons for all refueling operations, and the other four C-130s would carry the commandos, the Rangers, and all of their necessary operational gear to Desert One.

The problems started early in the mission. For the sake of security and surprise, strict radio silence was the order of the day. As the C-130s approached the first landing strip on April 24, 1980, they ran into a haboob, a typically Persian sandstorm that erupted out of the desert like a giant skyscraper of sand, miles wide and high, effectively blocking pilot visibility. The planes were forced to slow their descent, but one by one they managed to land safely. Out of nowhere, unplanned, came a bus with a few dozen passengers riding across the airstrip on a journey from one small town to another. Beckwith's men stopped the bus and apprehended the passengers, who seemed harmless enough. The helicopters, though, ran into much worse trouble. Because of radio silence, they were not warned about the obstructing haboob. The result was that one helicopter after another stumbled into the massive sandstorm. The pilots could not see where they were going or keep track of one another, and dust got into their engines, slowing them down considerably. Only five helicopters were usable.

Beckwith had to decide whether he could proceed with only five helicopters. Much to everyone's disappointment, he opted to abort the mission, informing Washington of his decision. Carter was devastated, but perhaps in a small corner of his heart he was also relieved: no one was hurt, and maybe no one would learn about the failed mission. Unfortunately, as everyone prepared to leave the airstrip and the dust was swirling around the planes and helicopters, making visibility and movement extremely difficult, the rotating blades of one departing helicopter smashed into one of the two C-130s carrying a fuel balloon. It was an accident, obviously. Most of the crew managed to get off the plane and the helicopter, but the collision touched off a series of small fires that quickly raced through the C-130 until they reached and ignited the fuel balloon. Suddenly, a thunderous universe of flame turned night into day and set off the reserve explosives, from small arms fire to rockets and missiles, hitting everything on Desert One and tracing crisscrossing paths across the sky, destroying the C-130 and seven of the eight helicopters. Most important, it killed eight crewmen.

The news reached the White House at 6 p.m. Carter's closest advisers had gathered to monitor the rescue attempt. The phone rang, and Carter answered. His jaw dropped as he listened to General Jones report on the debacle in the Persian desert. Carter asked only one question: "Are there any dead?" He got the answer he had spent his entire presidency trying to avoid. The president slowly dropped the receiver back into its cradle. His face pale, Carter told his team what had happened. Jordan ran into the bathroom and vomited. The others stood silently. Finally Vance, leaving the administration in any case, approached Carter and said, "Mr. President, I'm very, very sorry."[63]

Drawing the Soviets into the Afghan Trap

Seven weeks after the student rebels seized the American embassy in Tehran, Soviet troops invaded Afghanistan. Brzezinski, Mondale, and the others, to different degrees, shared Carter's shock and surprise, and they supported his decisions to boycott the upcoming Moscow Olympics and withhold wheat deliveries. But Brzezinski also saw the invasion as a dream come true: a precious opportunity to suck the Soviet Union into its own Vietnam War, with consequences, he believed, that could rock the Soviet empire. What the Americans had suffered in Vietnam, Brzezinski now envisaged for the Soviet troops in Afghanistan: a long, costly, ugly guerrilla war that would have the twin effects in time of not only blunting the Soviet offensive in the developing world but also weakening both the Red Army and the Soviet Communist Party, and perhaps the Soviet Union itself. It was a bold vision requiring an even bolder strategy. It would involve a new "strategic relationship" with China; a secret, U.S.-backed military alliance against Soviet aggression in Afghanistan; an infusion of money and weapons to the mujahidin fighters; and the sparking of an Islamic fundamentalist crusade against the Soviet invaders, which had the unintended effect years later of returning to haunt the Americans.

In a 1998 interview with the French publication *Le Nouvel Observateur*, Brzezinski was asked whether he regretted having sent arms to the mujahidin. "Regret what?" Brzezinski snapped.

> The secret operation was an excellent idea. It had the effect of drawing the Russians into the Afghan trap, and you want me to regret it? The day that the Soviets officially crossed the border, I wrote to President Carter, "We now have the opportunity of giving to the USSR its Vietnam War." Indeed, for almost 10 years, Moscow had to carry on a war unsupportable by the government, a conflict that brought about the demoralization and finally the breakup of the Soviet empire.

The follow-up question: "And neither do you regret having supported the Islamic fundamentalism, having given arms and advice to future terrorists?"

Brzezinski: "What is more important to the history of the world? The Taliban or the collapse of the Soviet empire? Some stirred-up Moslems or the liberation of Central Europe and the end of the cold war?"

Reporter: "Some stirred-up Moslems? But it has been said and repeated [that] Islamic fundamentalism represents a world menace today."

Brzezinski: "Nonsense! It is said that the West had a global policy in regard to Islam. That is stupid. There isn't a global Islam. Look at Islam in a rational manner and without demagoguery or emotion. It is the leading religion of the world with 1.5 billion followers. But what is there in common among Saudi Arabian fundamentalism, moderate Morocco, Pakistan militarism, Egyptian pro-Western or Central Asian secularism? Nothing more than what unites the Christian countries."[64]

Obviously Brzezinski considered the undermining of the Soviet state to be far more important than the hatching of Islamic fundamentalism. He knew about the dangers of Soviet totalitarianism; he did not yet know about the dangers of Islamic fundamentalism.

The possibility of a Soviet invasion of Afghanistan had hovered over administration deliberations all year. On March 28, 1979, Arnold Horelick, the top CIA expert on the Soviet Union, sent a memo to his boss, Director Stansfield Turner, alerting him to the likelihood of Soviet intervention in Afghanistan in support of the leftist regime of President Nur Mohammed Taraki, which was tottering under relentless rebel assault.[65] The Brezhnev Doctrine held that once a country went socialist or communist, it was to remain socialist or communist forever; and if Taraki needed assistance, political or military, he was to get it. But, Horelick noted, if the Soviets intervened with military assistance to prop up the Taraki regime, then "Pakistan, Iran and perhaps even China" would send "barely disguised covert military assistance to the insurgents." Escalation on both sides was built into the Afghan quandary, one teasing the other into further action. Horelick's conclusion? "The Soviets may well be prepared to intervene on behalf of the ruling group."[66]

On April 24 Horelick sent another alert, advising that the Soviet Union was becoming increasingly involved in Afghanistan, sending more advisers, more military materiel. And, as if to set up a pretext for further intervention, Soviet propagandists began to accuse the United States and China of fomenting the rebel revolt against Taraki, arguing that the Soviet Union had no option but to help him. Still to be decided was how much help, in what form, and when.[67]

At the same time, the United States was weighing its own options. None seemed more consequential than a strategy deliberately intended to pull the "Soviets into a Vietnamese quagmire," as Pentagon official Walter Slocombe said. At a key meeting, David Aaron asked two mind-concentrating questions. First, did the United States have an interest in "maintaining and assisting the insurgency," and if so, what was it? Second, if the United States did assist the insurgency, might it not be running "too great" a risk of provoking the Soviet Union into a rash counteraction that could tip the whole region into a wider war?[68] In a succession of top-level meetings, Vance argued that the risk was clearly too great, while Brzezinski argued that it was a risk worth taking. Not for the first time, the Vance-Brzezinski split dominated American deliberations. For Vance, nothing was more important than managing the nuclear dangers inherent in the U.S.-Soviet relationship, which was becoming increasingly fragile. For Brzezinski, it was taming and, if possible, defeating the Soviet regime, which was, in his view, recklessly pushing its luck and fomenting trouble all over the world. Carter was caught in the middle, but with each month, as reports reached him of further Soviet encroachments into Afghanistan and the presence of a Soviet combat brigade in Cuba, known to be there for many years but largely ignored by a succession of American officials, he seemed to tilt more toward Brzezinski's view than Vance's. And if the Soviets were to be stopped in Afghanistan, the Chinese would have to be brought into the game. They were the key. No one could have been happier than Brzezinski, who from day one had wanted to play the "China card."

The turning point in U.S. policy came not after the Soviet invasion but six months earlier, when on July 3, 1979, Carter had signed a presidential "finding" authorizing covert assistance to the mujahidin insurgents.[69] It was code-named Operation Cyclone. The finding, though modest in its early form (a half-million dollars was allocated), opened the door to direct American support of the anti-Soviet insurgency in Afghanistan. It was to be nonlethal in character but deadly in intent; the tools of propaganda, from radio to pamphlets, began to be slipped across the Pakistan border into mujahidin hands, as well as economic assistance and hard cash. When word of Carter's decision reached Pakistan and Saudi Arabia, they pressed Carter to go further and send arms and military supplies to the insurgents, who were doing surprisingly well against an initial Soviet force of 80,000 troops equipped with all the modern weapons of war. Brzezinski, who had written repeatedly about "an arc of crisis" in South Asia, now envisaged "an arc of Islam" that could be mobilized to fight godless communism.

For Brzezinski and other "China tilters," as they were called, the stage was being set for a Vietnam-style war. In late August, as a direct consequence of Carter's July 3 "finding," the United States decided to play its "China card." Mondale flew to Beijing on August 24, and before he left on September 3, he had transformed the U.S.-China relationship into what was known as a "strategic partnership," no longer just the traditional diplomatic exchanges of one country with another, but now two countries tied by mutual interest into an anti-Soviet crusade focused initially on Afghanistan but soon to be much broader in scope.

"I visited with Deng Xiaoping," Mondale later recalled. "I brought information . . . about Soviet locations across the border. I brought listening devices. We agreed to the sale of satellite and other equipment that they hadn't had before, and I told them we were going to [modify] export control rules [for] them. We changed their status . . . to a friendly nation."

"We did a lot to better our relationship with China," he continued, "and all these led to a discussion of a military relationship for the first time in the history of these two countries."[70] At the time, Mondale knew that the Chinese (and the Egyptians) were providing weapons to the mujahidin rebels, including an early Chinese version of the Stinger missile, a shoulder-held, antiaircraft missile the rebels used against Soviet helicopters with unexpected success. By the time Defense Secretary Harold Brown visited China in January 1980, the "military relationship" was already in springtime bloom.

Also included in the Mondale package was a remarkable plan for the United States to build and operate a top-secret, highly sophisticated listening post in Sinkiang Province bordering on Soviet Central Asia. It was designed to check on Soviet missile launches, among other things. The intelligence was to be shared by both countries. That a closed totalitarian society such as China's would allow the United States to run an anti-Soviet intelligence operation on its territory was an extraordinary indication not only of China's willingness to cooperate with a former enemy but also of its chronic fear of a Soviet attack. Brzezinski had calculated that Deng Xiaoping was ready for a protective American embrace, and he was right. For both sides, this was a "huge confidence-building measure," to quote a senior American official. "It had Deng's fingerprints all over it," he said. "They protected the site, we basically ran it, and we both benefited from it."

After the Mondale visit, things moved swiftly. In Kabul, Taraki was murdered in factional communist violence, and Hafizullah Amin, seen even by the Kremlin as an even more extremist Marxist, seized power. The rebels took advantage of the chaos, extending their reach into areas of Afghanistan formerly denied them. Interestingly, Amin frightened the Soviet leaders. He was on the one hand too rigid an ideologue and on the other hand too unpredictable; there were rumors he might even be exploring a deal with the Americans, which the old men in the Kremlin were sufficiently self-deluded into believing. They faced a range of unfamiliar and bewildering options. Most important, perhaps, the U.S. defeat in Vietnam was leading them into "miscalculations [and] misinterpretations," according to Sergei Rogov.[71] They thought they could now extend their power anywhere and everywhere, and the United States could not stop them. If Afghanistan needed Soviet assistance, Afghanistan would get it, no matter the risks.

Alexei Arbatov, whose work and contacts brought him into close contact with the Kremlin, recalled that the old men "believed they were doing a noble thing saving Afghanistan from chaos . . . and from an American occupation."

There was no American occupation, and none was likely, but they feared one could flow from a rebel victory. They were told by Red Army generals that if the Americans moved into Afghanistan, the Soviet Union would have to dispatch an "additional 80 divisions" to protect the Soviet-Afghan border, and that would lead to a total reorganization of the Soviet military. Brezhnev believed that the Soviet Union would then be truly encircled by NATO to the west, China to the east, and America in Afghanistan. "Nobody put under doubt that stupid assessment," Arbatov said of the eighty divisions, adding that it was "completely groundless, but that was taken at face value. . . . The Minister of Defense got this from the Main Operational Director—that 80 divisions would be needed, and we had to prevent it."[72]

In Washington the "China tilters," led by Brzezinski, were clearly winning the internal debate. CIA director Turner warned of an imminent Soviet invasion of Afghanistan. The question now was how urgently, broadly, and publicly the United States would support the mujahidin insurgents. In October Carter began to send millions of CIA dollars to Pakistan for the purchase of Soviet-style military equipment for the insurgents, equipment manufactured in Egypt and China. Turner also sent communication equipment to the insurgents, essential for coordinating their hit-and-run guerrilla war against the Soviets. When the Soviets finally upped the ante and invaded Afghanistan on Christmas Day, 1979, U.S. support for the anti-Soviet insurgents expanded exponentially. It had started modestly; but once the Soviet forces moved into Afghanistan, funding for the support rose from $20 million to $30 million a year in 1980 to $630 million a year by 1987. Just as the Soviets had exploited the Cubans in their proxy wars in Africa, now the Americans were exploiting the Afghan insurgents in their proxy war against the Soviet Union. It could be argued that the Soviets were in fact responding to U.S. provocations, stupidly drawn into a Vietnam-style war, but their motivation was obviously more complicated.

But how far would they go? On January 16, 1980, Turner sent an "eyes only" memo to Carter warning that although the Soviets, in his view, were not implementing "a highly articulated grand design for the rapid establishment of hegemonic control over all of southwest Asia," they might have the more limited objective of establishing a "pro-Soviet Iran." As a result of the invasion of Afghanistan, Soviet forces were now on the eastern and northern borders of Iran, opening the possibility of sneaking Soviet arms and supplies to the Baluchi, Azeri, and Kurdish separatist movements, with the aim of toppling Iran's Islamic regime and bringing it into the Soviet empire.[73] Brzezinski agreed with

Turner. "At the time," he recalled, "Iran was falling apart, with Baluchistan potentially the next area for play." If the United States could frustrate Soviet ambitions in Afghanistan, then the Americans could stop a Soviet power play in Iran. "I was basically trying to organize an international coalition, trying to make it difficult for the Soviets to take over Afghanistan."[74]

When Carter delivered his State of the Union address on January 23, 1980, it was clear that he shared Brzezinski's concerns. Indeed, he carried his concerns to the point of articulating a new Carter Doctrine for the Persian Gulf that was similar to the 1947 Truman Doctrine, the start of the American policy of "containment." "An attempt by any outside force to gain control of the Persian Gulf region," he said, "will be regarded as an assault on the vital interests of the United States of America, and such an assault will be repelled by any means necessary, including military force."[75] He quickly established the Rapid Deployment Force for the protection of the oil supply lines through the Persian Gulf. He asked the Senate to postpone ratification of the SALT agreement; it never was ratified, although it was honored. He canceled economic and cultural exchanges between the United States and the Soviet Union. He announced that the United States and its allies would send munitions, food, and other supplies to Pakistan, everyone understanding that Pakistan was simply a relay stop into Afghanistan. The president who tried so gallantly to sheathe America's sword after the Vietnam War was again waving it before the world after the Soviet invasion of Afghanistan. He saw the invasion as a watershed in global politics and in his own thinking about global politics. He called it a "blatant violation" and "a grave threat to peace." The invasion, Carter said, "has made a more dramatic change in my own opinion of what the Soviets' ultimate goals are than anything they've done in the previous time I've been in office."[76]

To the Soviet leaders, including the usually cool Ambassador Dobrynin, the administration's outrage was, as Dobrynin later wrote, "feverish" and "agitated." Brezhnev, who had got on so well with Carter in Vienna, "cursed" him "heartily." Andrei Gromyko said, as Dobrynin recalled, that Carter was "acting like an elephant in a china shop." "For all my experience of anti-Soviet campaigns in the United States," Dobrynin noted in his memoir, "I had never encountered anything like the intensity and scale of this one."[77] It was the "opening of a new Cold War." It was also a time of triumph for Brzezinski. Finally, he had the president's full attention, and support.

In early February Brzezinski went on a well-publicized week-long trip to Pakistan and Saudi Arabia, two countries crucial to American policy. When a week earlier the foreign ministers of thirty-five Muslim countries condemned the Soviet invasion of Afghanistan, it was music to his ears. He was on a roll. He told Pakistani president Mohammed Zia-ul-Haq that the freshly articulated Carter Doctrine committed the United States to his country's defense in the event of a Soviet attack. As proof of his seriousness, he left a fifteen-man military team in the area to look into the country's defenses and arms requirements. One day, in an optimistic mood, he visited Pakistan's border with Afghanistan. He asked a Pakistani soldier toting a Chinese-made rifle to shoot it, and the recoil left the soldier on the ground as bullets flew from the rifle. No one was hurt. "Any casualties?" joked Brzezinski.

At a stop at a refugee camp straddling the border, Brzezinski told a crowd of Afghan refugees, "You should know that the entire world is outraged," adding, "God is on your side."[78] In Saudi Arabia, home of the Wahhabist strain of puritanical Islam then being exported to the Afghan rebel fighters, Brzezinski extracted a commitment from the royal family that the Saudis would match every dollar the United States spent on the anti-Soviet insurgency.[79]

For the rest of the year, Brzezinski was on Turner's back, demanding that the CIA deepen the American commitment to the Afghan insurgents. And it did, even going so far as to open a secret program to train militants in the United States and the United Kingdom. What the United States learned very quickly was that the Soviet forces were not very adept at fighting "wars of national liberation." Like the Americans in Vietnam, they had been trained to engage the enemy on a battlefield, as they had fought the Nazis in World War II. They were used to tanks and planes. They were unfamiliar with the unforgiving terrain and with guerrilla war, and Brzezinski wanted them to bleed, and then to bleed some more. Aaron recalled that the "Russian military was not what people thought it was." First of all, only 20 percent of the Soviet troops were actually engaged in fighting the mujahidin; the others guarded camps, garrisons, airports, and cities. And second, Aaron said, the Soviet helicopter "had a ceiling that made it difficult for them to [fly] over certain mountains" in pursuit of rebel bands, which could often attack and then escape with relative impunity. "The Russians never adapted to the kind of war they were fighting," Aaron said.[80]

It was clear from Brzezinski's weekly reports to the president that he felt the Carter administration never got credit for a set of policies that (1) established a strategic partnership with China; (2) built up an insurgent army of Islamic fundamentalists who took on the vaunted Red Army, inflicted massive casualties, and forced a humiliating Soviet withdrawal; and (3) in this way set in motion the ultimate collapse of the communist state. And that listing did not mention the Camp David Agreement or the Panama Canal Treaty. "What do we do for an encore?" Brzezinski asked in jest, as he surveyed the political landscape in advance of the 1980 presidential election campaign.[81]

Despite its triumphs, the Carter administration resembled a Greek tragedy. The flaws were apparent from the beginning, and Carter, bright and diligent as he was, was the wrong knight in shining armor. He tried desperately to create a warless world. It was a hopeless task. He wanted more than anything to bury Vietnam, to banish it from the national consciousness, but found himself joined at the hip to a national security adviser who had concocted a strategy designed to suck the Soviet Union into its own Vietnam. He was a deeply religious man, who trumpeted the cause of human rights; and yet as he grappled with the Soviet invaders in Afghanistan and the ayatollahs in Iran, he put forth the Carter Doctrine, returning America to the image of a global Sparta he wanted so much to change, and sparking an Islamic fundamentalism that brought such severe pain to the country he loved. He organized a totally unrealistic rescue mission; he wanted it to be bloodless, but it failed miserably. The ayatollahs waited until the first minute of his successor's presidency to release the hostages. They wanted him to suffer, and he did. Also, through much of his administration, the economy was in crisis, with inflation and interest rates in double digits, gas lines irritating the public, and a second oil embargo torpedoing any chance of recovery. Politically, Carter beat back the political challenge of a popular Kennedy from Massachusetts but then lost to a Hollywood actor. If, on his trip back to Plains, Georgia, where it all began, he entertained the thought that life was not fair, he could be forgiven.

4

Reagan, Grenada, Lebanon, and the Marines

No More Vietnams.
—RONALD REAGAN, May 30, 1980

REPUBLICAN MYTHOLOGY HAS it that Ronald Reagan "won" the cold war: that when he took the oath of office on January 20, 1981, the United States was in free fall, the victim of Jimmy Carter's mismanagement; and that during Reagan's eight years in the White House, the United States not only regained its footing but also emerged as leader of the Western world while its archenemy, the Soviet Union, was swiftly losing its superpower status. True, but misleading.

Reagan was certainly in office during this historic rearrangement of global power, and his policies played an important role in ending the cold war. But were it not for the skillful diplomacy of his successor, George H. W. Bush, and the political realism of his principal adversary, Mikhail Gorbachev, the peaceful dismantling of the Soviet Union, the tearing down of the Berlin Wall, and the reunification of Germany might not have happened—at least, not when they did. And were it not for the political and economic changes then sweeping through the Soviet Union, the cold war might have limped along, Reagan or no Reagan, for another decade or two.

The changes were profound. They included the death of Brezhnev in 1981 and the quick succession and passing of Yuri Andropov and Konstantin Chernenko, two old, ailing Politburo members; the emergence of Mikhail Gorbachev in 1985 as a young, dynamic leader; his new policies of "glasnost" and "perestroika," which transformed Soviet life from a rickety dictatorship into a reform-oriented but still communist autocracy; and the devastating Soviet military defeat in Afghanistan, where thousands of young soldiers were killed and many more thousands wounded, where military discipline had deteriorated and drug use proliferated—all in an asymmetrical war frightfully reminiscent of the American disaster in Vietnam. Carter's national security adviser Zbigniew Brzezinski had hoped that the Soviet Union could be drawn into its own Vietnam "trap" in Afghanistan, and though no longer in a position of power, he watched with the deepest satisfaction as the Red Army, time and again, not only failed to suppress the mujahidin insurgency but also suffered grievous losses. Gorbachev, on taking office, spoke of Afghanistan as a "bleeding wound," a war that, no matter the political consequences, had to be ended. And quickly in the mid-1980s he moved to end it and focus on the pitiful state of his suddenly shaky empire.

During the Brezhnev-Andropov-Chernenko transition, which coincided with his first term in office, Reagan denounced the Soviet Union as the "focus of evil in the modern world," and TASS, the Soviet news agency, responded by denouncing his "bellicose, lunatic anticommunism." U.S.-Soviet relations were, at best, on hold. But during his second term, which coincided with the rise of Gorbachev, Reagan engaged in a series of headline-catching summits, which had the effect of improving bilateral relations to the point where, during their Reykjavik summit in 1986, both leaders could actually discuss the elimination of all of their nuclear weapons. Reagan had clearly come a long way, from his old, instinctive anticommunism to his new "trust, but verify" formula for superpower coexistence.

This presidential journey from old to new was not that of a woolly-headed actor looking for another leading role. Reagan had always believed that the United States must negotiate from a position of strength. When he took office, it was the prevailing view of U.S. intelligence, faulty in the extreme but rarely challenged by the president's senior advisers, that, since the American defeat in Vietnam, the Soviet Union was in the ascendancy in global affairs and the United States in decline. Reagan, who agreed, felt that until the United States recaptured its earlier dominance in strategic weaponry and economic power, there was no point in engaging the Soviet Union in another round of strategic arms talks or another trade agreement. In fact, the Soviet Union then stood on the cusp of historic collapse, but U.S. intelligence, not for the first time, missed the signals. Just as it had failed to see the rise of Islamic fundamentalism in Iran, it failed to appreciate the internal rot and corruption in the Soviet state and the political disintegration of the Kremlin hierarchy. Because he assumed that U.S. intelligence was right, Reagan was wrong in his reading of Soviet capabilities. He was absorbed with two problems closer to home, both significantly worsened by the American defeat in Vietnam in 1975: one was a deeply troubled economy, the other was a military machine that was, to quote Robert

McFarlane, who was to become one of Reagan's national security advisers, "in a terrible condition."[1]

"No More Vietnams, No More Betrayal of Friends"

So said presidential candidate Ronald Reagan on May 30, 1980, an elaboration of his slogan "No more Vietnams," which resonated through many of his stump speeches.[2] Like Jimmy Carter, Reagan tried throughout his political campaigns to distance himself from the Vietnam War; it was not, after all, his war. But his core beliefs surfaced in a succession of speeches and interviews. As he put it in 1976: "Let us tell those who fought in [Vietnam] that we will never again ask young men to fight and possibly die in a war our government is afraid to win."[3] In this way, Reagan boxed the political compass: he was against the war; but if he had to fight in Vietnam, he would fight to win. Nothing less would do. Winning was the American way, and Reagan, as both actor and politician, had a feel for the American way.

It could be said of this man from Tampico, Illinois, that, given his political success, one could imagine his DNA stretching all the way back to George Washington. But there was little in his background to suggest that he would become a two-term governor of California and a two-term president of the United States, one of the most popular chief executives in American history and a trailblazer in American conservatism.

Reagan was born in 1911 into a Democratic family. His father was a traveling salesman and his mother worked as a seamstress to make ends meet. He and his brother, Neil, attended Eureka College, where Reagan enjoyed acting and began to dream of a career in Hollywood. He was for a brief time a sportscaster. In 1937 he managed to get to California, where he took a screen test. His smile and aw-shucks sincerity were appealing enough to win a Warner Bros. contract, and he starred in a number of movies, most notably *Knute Rockne, All-American,* and *Kings Row.* Most of his other movies were ranked "B" and were easily forgettable. During World War II, Reagan's military service was centered on the Los Angeles area, where he made training films for the armed forces.

After the war, he dipped into politics and learned, rather quickly, that he was good at it. During the controversial McCarthy period, when the senator from Wisconsin accused many in Hollywood of being soft on Soviet communism, Reagan served as president of the Screen Actors Guild, a position that obliged him, however reluctantly, to defend his suspect colleagues.

Reagan gradually swung his political allegiance to the Republicans, voting for Eisenhower in 1952 and 1956 and Nixon in 1960. When he finally switched parties in 1962, he was already thinking of switching careers. His reputation as a new voice of California conservatism attracted national attention; in 1964, when asked to speak in support of candidate Barry Goldwater, he delivered a televised speech of such eloquence that GOP bigwigs immediately began to think of Reagan as governor of California and maybe even president of the United States.

In 1966 the budding politician ran for governor against a popular Democratic incumbent, Edmund "Pat" Brown. Reagan won. His Hollywood fame and velvety voice helped launch his new career. In 1967 CBS News paired Reagan with Robert Kennedy, at the time a senator from New York, to appear on *Town Meeting of the World*. The network billing could not have been better for the ratings: both were rising stars presumed to have presidential ambitions. The program focused on the Vietnam War, the most hotly debated issue of the day. Democrats were delighted, Republicans were anxious; it was assumed that Kennedy would clobber Reagan, who was, after all, "just an actor." The actor, though, was carefully coached and won easily. The next morning, political reporters all over the country slapped their heads, realizing that they had better take another look at this actor-turned-politician.

As governor, Reagan rarely mentioned the Vietnam War, but the war was everywhere as radical student protests rolled over California's college campuses, mixing civil rights with the antiwar movement to form a volatile political cocktail. Reagan was offended by the student violence. In 1969 he ordered the California Highway Patrol, the Oakland Tactical Squad, and then the National Guard to suppress protests at Berkeley. "I'm convinced we win when we defy the little monsters," he said.[4] Reagan was playing to the conservative galleries, and he was being heard.

In 1972 Reagan discouraged speculation about a presidential run. Nixon had all the advantages of incumbency, and Reagan had time. "It has been my privilege as a governor to receive in-depth briefings on the war and the international situation," he wrote to the Young Americans for Freedom. "As a result, I'm in full support of the president's Vietnamization policy."[5]

When Ford replaced Nixon in 1974, Reagan saw an opening. After Ford pardoned Nixon, Reagan mounted a spirited primary challenge in 1976. He came close but lost. During the campaign, he sharpened his Vietnam rhetoric, slipping "No more Vietnams" into his campaign speeches. He was striking the image of a reasonable but deeply concerned conservative. Not far away was

1980, and, by all accounts, 1980 was to be his year. Though he would have preferred to ignore the sad legacy of Vietnam, he could not; it nipped at his heels.

Had Vietnam cut into presidential powers? Yes, Reagan responded. "I believe the greatest blow to the power of the presidency has resulted from Vietnam. The world today has a belief that a president of the United States cannot respond to a crisis or emergency as presidents have in the past—some 125 times. There is a danger in this."[6]

"No more Vietnams"—what exactly did he mean? "What I meant by that," he explained to reporter Elizabeth Drew, "was never again must this country ever ask young men to fight and die in a war we're afraid to let them win."

"Are you saying that you wouldn't have gone in or that we should have gone in and fought it in a way to win?" Drew questioned.

"I was one who never believed we should have gone in. . . . I've always believed in the MacArthur dictum that you don't get involved in a land war in Asia. But the troops were sent in; once we sent them in, then you have made a commitment to the men you're asking to fight that you are going to give them every resource to win this thing and get them home as soon as possible."[7]

In his memoir, Reagan went further: "I think, as MacArthur did, that if we as a nation send our soldiers abroad to get shot at, we have a moral responsibility to do *everything* we can to win the war we put them in. I'll never forget one prophetic remark by MacArthur: 'If we don't win this war in Korea, we'll have to fight another war—this time in a place called Vietnam.' Until then, I had never heard of Vietnam. I only knew about a place called French Indochina. How right he was."[8]

On August 18, 1980, Reagan brought his campaign to Chicago, where he addressed the Veterans of Foreign Wars (VFW). After again stressing, as he had in 1976, that American troops ought never to be sent "to fight and possibly die in a war that our government is afraid to win," Reagan added a sentence that depressed his poll numbers but inflated his sense of righteous indignation. "We dishonor the memory of 50,000 young Americans who died in that cause," he said, "when we give way to feelings of guilt as if we were doing something shameful, and we have been shabby in our treatment of those who returned." Then the added sentence: "It is time that we recognized that ours, in truth, was a noble cause."[9] Noble cause? Vietnam, a war the United States lost, a war that cost more than 58,000 American lives, a war that damaged American interests?

Reagan's pollster, Richard Wirthlin, watched his boss's poll numbers tank. For his part, Reagan cherished the audacity of the sentence, not just because he (not his speechwriters) wrote it, but because he thought it was true. In their analysis of the 1980 campaign, reporters Jack W. Germond and Jules Witcover wrote:

> Some primordial political instinct told him that was also something the members of the VFW would like to hear. For any actor, applause lines are basic sustenance. What Reagan did not foresee, however, was that those few words would be viewed as an attempt to open up national wounds that had scarcely healed. And what he did not recognize, because the insertion of the phrase slipped by his staff, was that making this point would divert the press from the main point of his speech—that Jimmy Carter was following policies of "weakness, inconsistency, vacillation and bluff" on national defense issues.[10]

A few days later, pool reporters cornered Reagan on a flight to California. Was he sorry he added the sentence? He replied that he was not. And had the focus on Reagan's comments drowned out his attack on Carter? At times like this, Reagan would often shrug and smile. "That's because you fellas every once in a while are more interested in finding something sensational than in printing the facts."[11]

Reagan was not simply engaging in campaign rhetoric when he wrote that Vietnam had sapped the strength of the American presidency—"the greatest blow," he had called it. In so many ways, when he became president, he learned the limits that the war had imposed on his new office.

Rebuilding America's "Military-Industrial Complex"

Many years later, Richard Perle, who served in Reagan's Pentagon under Defense Secretary Caspar Weinberger, remembered the sorry shape of the U.S. military after the Vietnam War. Morale problems were widespread, weapons so poorly maintained as to be unusable. Since the first Nixon administration, most of the Pentagon's budget had gone into financing the losing war in Southeast Asia; little had gone into strategic modernization.[12] The upshot was that Reagan, Weinberger, Perle, and other senior officials believed that as a direct result of the Vietnam War, the United States was falling behind the Soviet Union in a shifting global balance of power. Urgent action was now Reagan's top priority. The new president, for whom the very idea of America's losing its strategic edge to a communist adversary was unimaginable, ordered a dramatic expansion and revamping of the Pentagon budget—spending limits be damned!

Reagan's "powerful" message, as he put it, was that "we weren't going to stand by anymore while [the Soviet Union] armed and financed terrorists and subverted democratic governments. Our policy was to be one based on strength and realism. I wanted peace through strength, not peace through a piece of paper."[13] But was a policy based on "strength and realism" possible in a time of American retrenchment, when a "sense of withdrawal" permeated the ruling establishment? He listed possible explanations: "the Vietnam War, the energy crisis, and the inflation and other economic problems of the Carter years—or the frustrations endured by the Carter administration over the failure of its policies in Iran. Whatever the reasons, I believed it was senseless, ill-founded, and dangerous for America to withdraw from its role as superpower and leader of the Free World."[14]

Reagan's first defense budget, for 1982, ran to $185 billion, almost a $30 billion increase over Carter's last budget. His second military budget jumped to $210 billion, his third to $227 billion, and his fourth to $253 billion. In his first four years in office, Reagan's annual military budgets totaled about $875 billion, roughly 60 percent more than Carter's four defense budgets, which added up to $512 billion.[15]

Overseeing Reagan's military budgets was Frank Carlucci, his deputy secretary of defense. A former Foreign Service officer who had served Nixon as director of the Office of Economic Opportunity and Carter as deputy director of the CIA, Carlucci focused on spending the expanding military budgets on modernizing old weapons and building new ones. When he arrived at the Pentagon, he was shocked to find the military in "terrible" shape. "Mission capability," he soon learned, was "way down." It was "a hollow army with an air force that couldn't fly."[16] Instead of procuring weapons on an annual basis, which delayed and complicated the development and production of new weapon systems, he instituted, for the first time in Pentagon history, a multi-year procurement program and listed thirty-two specific "initiatives" regarded as crucial to restoring the nation's military prowess.

Most on Reagan's new defense team seemed to share Carlucci's judgment about the sorry state of the military. James Webb—an assistant secretary of defense who later served as secretary of the navy and later still as a U.S. senator—recalled that the "American military in the early years of the volunteer army was in really bad shape, and the big part of that was the people coming in. . . . The disciplinary problems, the drug problems, the racial problems, the education problems—they were all there."[17] Another senior official spoke about "indiscipline in the army, a very serious set of problems, with drugs and alcohol." To emphasize his point, he added that some officers refused to enter a barracks at night "unless armed."

Colonel Lawrence Wilkerson, who worked for Colin Powell at the State Department, described the situation as "absolutely horrible." In the late 1970s he commanded a mechanized rifle company at Fort Benning, Georgia, and he found himself engaged much more in "unsuitability hearings" than in training spit-and-polish soldiers for combat. "We were recruiting from a six-state area— Alabama, South Carolina, Georgia, North Carolina, Tennessee, and so forth. . . . We were recruiting anything we could find." One of his responsibilities was to conduct a weekly honor review on York Field, the biggest parade field at Fort Benning. "I had a 280-man rifle company, and I was . . . [hard] pressed every week to find 42 soldiers I could put on that field, who would stand there and look good and be disciplined and perform in front of Chinese, Spanish, French and other visiting leaders. . . . One time . . . I dipped into the bag as deeply as I could, put 42 men on the field, and every one of them was an African-American." Apparently that was a problem for the commanding general. Wrong image, he thought. He told Wilkerson "never to do that again." Wilkerson responded: "General, then get me some soldiers, because those were the only 42 soldiers I could put on the field." He was keenly disappointed in the quality of his recruits, not because they were raw but because they were below his standards: not suitable for military service, in his judgment. Through these time-consuming but necessary "unsuitability hearings," Wilkerson "put people out of the army at a pace that was just blistering." He demanded minimum quality for a professional army, and in those days he had serious trouble reaching his goal.[18]

"The army was broken," concluded Milton Bearden, a veteran CIA officer. "We were going through a nervous breakdown."[19]

McFarlane, who "often" discussed military strategy with Reagan during the 1980 presidential campaign, served twice in Vietnam. "At the end of the war, the military was in terrible condition," McFarlane remembered.

> The UA [unauthorized absence] rate was very high, drug use very severe. We had difficulty in both recruitment and retention. We were having a hard time getting enough volunteers, establishing this volunteer army. Those we got were not high school graduates, or there weren't enough of them. The quality of the force in terms of education, ability to be trained and perform effectively, taking into account drug availability, was simply very low. Readiness was very low. . . . The fleet became decrepit, airplanes couldn't fly. . . . Readiness was very bad, and drug busts were very high.[20]

Carter actually increased his annual defense budgets, and his defense secretary, Harold Brown, tried valiantly to hold off the further deterioration of the American military. But the "operations and maintenance" of military supplies and equipment continued to drop to perilous levels. According to McFarlane and others, it took about ten years to restore the American military to acceptable levels of performance.

The Politicization of Intelligence

Reagan found that Vietnam had also affected the quality of American intelligence; it politicized what had been an apolitical activity. Bearden provided an early illustration. He was a "young first-tour case officer" dispatched to a divided Germany in 1967. Thrilled by his assignment, he plunged into the intelligence business. Somehow, in East Germany, the CIA managed to pick up "the sons of some very big guys" in the North Vietnamese leadership. The "sons" were touring communist-controlled Eastern Europe. Bearden's job was to debrief them. "I started very faithfully recording all [they said]," he recalled, "and sending all the intelligence reports to Washington. Then the questions started coming—to ask them about the effects of the bomb[ing]." Following orders, Bearden asked the "sons" about the bombing. "Yes, they would say, it's a nuisance, it would disturb their day, but that's it." Bearden's superiors in Washington were not satisfied. They wanted to know whether the bombing had brought the North Vietnamese "to their knees," whether it had begun to "affect the national morale." Bearden suddenly felt the floor tremble. "I am sitting there as a young case officer," he recalled. "I am saying to my manager, you know what they're doing, don't you? They are trying to tell you to send in the intelligence report so that they can give it to Lyndon Johnson and tell him that, in fact, the bombing policy is good and these guys are on their knees." The manager turned to Bearden. "You're not going to do that, are you?" he asked. "I said, no, I can't do that." And he didn't.

Bearden then stepped back and painted a broader picture. "Whenever the intelligence begins to come out against something important to the White House, then it gets politicized," whether it concerned Vietnam or the Soviet Union.[21]

Morton Abramowitz, a career Foreign Service officer, who was, in the aftermath of Vietnam, an assistant secretary of defense and who later ran the State Department's Office of Intelligence and Research, agreed with Bearden. In Abramowitz's view, Vietnam was responsible for the "politicization of intelligence." It led to "lying" and "deception" to cover mistakes and misjudgments.

"Our intelligence system, is, I believe, broken for many reasons. . . . [It] doesn't know who it works for any more . . . Congress, the public."[22] Through the Reagan years, quality intelligence was always in short supply.

The Murder of 241 Marines in Beirut

For a number of reasons, not least of which was the often haunting legacy of the Vietnam War, Reagan never did go after the terrorists who, on October 23, 1983, killed 241 U.S. Marines in their Beirut barracks, even though he knew who they were and where they were. Therein lies a most intriguing tale of presidential mismanagement and bureaucratic infighting.

The early years of the Reagan administration were a fat and glorious time for what Eisenhower once dubbed "the military-industrial complex." Billions were being poured into the procurement of new weapons systems and the modernization of older ones, and no one seemed to worry about cost. The military spending also benefited the ailing economy. Visiting European dignitaries, like de Tocquevilles of old, admired America's entrepreneurial spirit, its ability to bounce back from adversity. One French official, seeing an "economic recovery," told Reagan that it "bodes well for Europe."[23] Reagan's sunny rhetoric also had a positive effect on both Wall Street and Main Street.

Toward the end of 1983, as the Reagan team planned the president's reelection campaign, his tone toward the Soviet Union changed from one of suspicion and hostility to one of promise and hope for a better tomorrow. That such an adjustment fit perfectly into his campaign strategy for 1984 was officially advertised as pure coincidence; unofficially it was good, old-fashioned politics. The American people were tired of war, inflation, and Arab oil embargoes. Reagan, a good judge of the public mood, looked out at the cities, farms, and prairies of what he had called "the last best hope of man on Earth," and smiled with confidence. He told the American people that it was again "morning in America," which he described as "a shining city on a hill." They listened to his rhetorical music, even as the demands of a turbulent world pierced the bubble of Reagan's optimism and reintroduced a familiar question about presidential power in the post-Vietnam world: whether presidential power had really been cut back; and whether a president could commit troops to battle without congressional approval and public support, and, if so, for how long a time.

October 22–23, 1983, was a weekend like no other in the Reagan presidency. It was to have been a relaxing one, the president testing his golf swing for the first time in years in Augusta, Georgia, but it proved to be a challenging one. A crisis in the Caribbean and a tragedy in Lebanon dramatically upended his agenda.

On Saturday morning he was awakened just after 4 a.m.[24] with the not totally unexpected news that the Organization of Eastern Caribbean States (OECS) had officially asked the United States to invade Grenada, an island neighbor ninety miles north of Venezuela. Radical Marxists had seized power on the island, and the OECS was worried that Grenada would soon become another Cuba. The White House was equally alarmed. McFarlane, the newly appointed national security adviser, had wondered whether the OECS was considering military action against Grenada and whether it needed American assistance. Small island nations such as St. Kitts and Barbados, on their own, could not have unseated the new Marxist regime, supported by Cuba, but the OECS, with military assistance from the United States, could do the job. Hence the unusual 4 a.m. request.

Reagan, in robe and pajamas, greeted McFarlane and Secretary of State George Shultz in the Eisenhower Cottage, where he was staying. They reviewed the exchanges between the OECS and the United States that led to the official request for assistance. Though McFarlane informed Reagan that "our intelligence on Grenada was very poor," he strongly recommended that the president agree to the OECS request.[25] Political turmoil convulsed the island, and there were reports of widespread violence. Hundreds of American medical students were clearly in danger. Reagan did not have to be reminded that if the situation continued to deteriorate, they could become hostages of anti-American fanatics, a newer version of the Iran hostage crisis, and he wanted no part of that.

"The United States is seen as responsible for providing leadership in defense of Western interests wherever they may be threatened," McFarlane, who had served Reagan in other posts before becoming national security adviser, lectured the president in this middle-of-the-night seminar. "For us to be asked to help and to refuse would have a very damaging effect on the credibility of the United States and your own commitment to the defense of freedom and democracy." Reagan "never hesitated. 'You're dead right,' he said. 'There's no way we can say no to this request.'"[26] By phone, Reagan then instructed Vice President George H. W. Bush, in Washington, to take charge of preparations for an American invasion of Grenada. He was to tell the OECS that "we recognize the problem" and "we'll be glad to respond."[27] Reagan then asked McFarlane, out of curiosity, how long it would take for the Pentagon to prepare an invasion. Forty-eight hours, he was told. "Do it," he said. At which point, Reagan, satisfied, "went back to sleep."[28]

For Reagan, this was not a difficult decision, though perhaps it should have been. After all, he had just ordered an American invasion of a sovereign country that, up to that point, had taken no hostile action against the United States. But Reagan was a founding father of the dominoes-are-falling club. He sincerely believed that if Grenada fell to the Marxists, other Caribbean islands would fall on his shift. Unacceptable, he concluded. He was also obsessed with the possibility of a hostage crisis in Grenada, similar to the one that had so seriously damaged his predecessor's tenure in office. Also unacceptable. And then there was Vietnam. For Reagan, the war was a quiet migraine, an unsettling memory he could not shake. It beat with metronomic regularity through his politics. In deliberations with aides or with members of Congress, Reagan kept referring to the "post-Vietnam syndrome," which he defined as "resistance of many in Congress to the use of military force abroad for any reason." He "understood," he wrote, what "Vietnam had meant for the country." But he tried to turn the page. "I believed that the United States couldn't remain spooked forever by this experience to the point where it refused to stand up and defend its legitimate national security interests."[29] He flashed the green light for an American invasion of Grenada, in part to end the "post-Vietnam syndrome," to show Congress, America, and the world that under his leadership, the United States would again stand tall in defense of its interests. But to discourage congressional concerns about "another Vietnam" brewing in the Caribbean, he ordered absolute secrecy. He did not even inform Prime Minister Margaret Thatcher, a favorite of his, though Grenada was technically a member of the British Commonwealth. He assumed that the invasion, once ordered, would be swift and successful, and everyone, including Thatcher, would be happy.

The next morning, Reagan was awakened even earlier. At around 2:30 a.m.[30] McFarlane called with the horrific news that dozens, perhaps hundreds, of sleeping marines in Beirut had been killed when a truck, loaded with dynamite, exploded in their barracks. Once again, his advisers, stunned by the news, convened in the Eisenhower Cottage. Reagan looked older, his complexion gray with fatigue and anger. Shultz and McFarlane had been marines, and they were especially shaken. "I felt as though I had been stabbed in the heart," McFarlane later wrote.[31] Shultz described the killings as "the worst experience I ever had in public service."[32]

In words and pictures, the scene in Beirut was being conveyed to Augusta, and it only got worse and worse. "I haven't seen carnage like that since Vietnam," said Marine Major Robert Jordan, a spokesman in Beirut.[33] The truck was a Mercedes, stuffed with TNT. In the quiet of a summer dawn, it had snaked its way through and around steel fences and sandbag barricades as it approached the four-story barracks in an exposed corner of the Beirut International Airport, which also served as the marine administrative headquarters. The Mercedes headed for the main entrance, picking up speed as it zigzagged around obstacles. A marine sentry, late in detecting the danger, fired five shots at the truck, hoping to kill the driver. Another marine, in desperation, threw himself in front of the truck, obviously to no avail. Neither could stop the truck, which smashed into the building and exploded, creating a crater thirty feet deep and forty feet wide. All four stories collapsed in the explosion.[34]

Less than two minutes later, another truck, also loaded with explosives, drove into a building in the southern Beirut suburb of Jnah, two miles from the marine barracks, where a French force of 110 paratroopers was housed. The explosion leveled all eight stories, causing dozens of casualties.[35]

The attacks, terrorist in nature, were obviously coordinated, using the same techniques, the same trucks, and the same type of explosive. The message was also the same: get out of Lebanon.

The president decided to return to Washington immediately. Twenty-four hours earlier, he had agreed to invade Grenada, a small island in America's backyard, an easily manageable target. Now, in Beirut, he faced a far more serious challenge in a Middle Eastern capital torn apart by sectarian violence and religious rivalry. When a year earlier Reagan had dispatched 1,500 marines to Lebanon as part of a multinational peacekeeping force, he did not expect nirvana, but he did hope to bring a measure of stability to a country wracked by civil war. It was a mission of modest dimension, but it ended with the slaughter of 241 marines, and it confronted Reagan with the no-win choice of either getting more deeply involved in the Lebanese civil war or abandoning the mission entirely and withdrawing. The situation also deepened a bitter split between two of the president's closest advisers: Shultz at State, who argued that the marines were a stabilizing presence in Beirut and should not be withdrawn; and Weinberger at the Pentagon, who belittled the marine presence as "small" and "without any kind of mission, without any kind of knowledge of when the matter ends, without any specific goal to be achieved," and said they should be withdrawn.[36]

Reagan's first decision of consequence, hardly surprising considering the U.S. flight from Vietnam in 1975, was that the United States would not leave Beirut, a decision that satisfied the Shultz wing of policymaking. The marines would fulfill their mission. But, four months later, the marines were pulled

out of Beirut, a decision that satisfied Weinberger and the Joint Chiefs of
Staff. Between the murder of the 241 marines on October 23, 1983, and the
withdrawal of the remaining marines on February 26, 1984, a revealing story
emerged about a president who, despite all his tough talk about America's
restored pride, did essentially nothing to avenge the killing of the American
marines. He did nothing for a number of reasons: the running dispute between
Shultz and Weinberger; the reluctance of many of his civilian advisers and the
Joint Chiefs to bomb Arab communities, the advantages and disadvantages
of a foreign war during a presidential campaign; and always, like haunting
background music, "Vietnam," translated in this case as Reagan's feeling that
the American people, "spooked" already, could not tolerate another Vietnam.
And yet Reagan had just ordered the invasion of a Caribbean island, in part to
show the world that the United States had overcome Vietnam.

Question: why withdrawal in one case and invasion in the other? William
Perry, defense secretary in President Clinton's first term in office, offered one
explanation. In recent decades, there was "no reluctance," he said, to fight
"another army."[37] The Pentagon, then, saw a traditional enemy in Grenada: an
army, an air force, small, targetable, and easily destroyed. Even if the enemy
had been formidable and armed with modern weapons, so long as it fought
a traditional war, the Pentagon felt a high degree of confidence in its capaci-
ties to engage the enemy and destroy it. In Lebanon, it saw a different kind of
enemy. And, as Perry said in a broader context, the Pentagon would instinctively recoil from getting "involved in a guerrilla war where the people are
shooting at you and planting bombs in the roads."[38]

Suddenly, to Weinberger, Carlucci, and others in the Pentagon, Lebanon
looked too much like Vietnam, and they wanted no part of it. Their reaction
to Lebanon in the 1980s echoed the message of British writer T. E. Lawrence's
experiences in Iraq in the early 1920s, related in his *Seven Pillars of Wisdom*:
To make "war upon rebellion is messy and slow, like eating soup with a knife."

The Lessons of Lebanon

How and why did Reagan get involved in a Lebanese civil war in the first place?
It was not by planning, surely.

In fact, the White House did its best to whistle past the Middle East grave-
yard, focusing instead on rebuilding the American economy and the military.
In December 1981, when a young National Security Council (NSC) staffer,
Douglas Feith, returned from the Middle East with the disquieting news that, in

his judgment, Israel's Prime Minister Menachem Begin and Defense Minister Ariel Sharon were planning to wipe out the Palestine Liberation Organization (PLO) with a lightning strike into Lebanon, where the PLO was based, he was ignored. The Israelis, in April 1982, had withdrawn from the Sinai, and they had assured the U.S. Middle East envoy, Philip Habib, that they would not attack the PLO in Lebanon unless they were attacked first. No one really sniffed a crisis. Moreover, neither the president nor his famed troika of White House advisers (Chief of Staff James Baker III, Deputy Chief of Staff Michael Deaver, and Counselor Edwin Meese III) were blessed with much knowledge, or curiosity, about the Middle East. They asked few questions about the buildup of tension between the PLO and Israel. When the PLO opened a fresh round of cross-border attacks into Israel in the spring of 1982 and the Israelis swiftly retaliated, the Reagan White House still seemed oblivious to the rising danger. What the Americans did not yet appreciate was that the Middle East was always ready with a basketful of surprises, many of a disruptive type.

On June 3 Palestinian terrorists attempted to kill Shlomo Argov, Israel's ambassador to the United Kingdom, violating an odd code of conduct up to that time that neither side would assassinate leading figures on the other side. If the Israelis were looking for an acceptable pretext to launch an all-out offensive against the PLO, the attempt on Argov's life provided it. On June 5 Israeli war planes softened up PLO positions in southern Lebanon, and on June 6 Israeli ground troops moved into Lebanon. At first, Israel explained that it intended to go no further north than the Litani River in southern Lebanon, ridding the region of PLO fighters in the process. But in fact the Israelis went much further. Within days, they blasted their way into the southern suburbs of Beirut, and the White House was surprised as well as furious. Israel had not leveled with its most important ally. According to McFarlane, "The Israeli government repeatedly lied to Washington about its intentions."[39] Once in Beirut, the Israelis went about the business of systematically destroying the PLO establishment. Sharon was in charge of the Israeli offensive, and he used the full power of the Israeli military to accomplish his mission. After four weeks of intense fighting, Israel dominated southern Lebanon. It controlled access to Lebanon's capital and fanned out into the Bekaa Valley. In direct combat, the Israelis destroyed most of Syria's surface-to-air missile batteries and, in a series of surrealistic dogfights in the blue skies over Lebanon, shot down eighty-two Syrian jet fighters, losing only one of its planes, a jaw-dropping exhibition of Western superiority over Soviet-made aircraft. Syria had suffered a stinging military defeat, and so had the PLO.

The Americans were of two minds about the Israeli victory. They could not help but be impressed by the skill and courage of the Israeli Defense Forces, but they also knew they needed quickly to arrange a cease-fire acceptable to the PLO and its Arab backers. In the Middle East, the United States always had to balance the ticket. Within weeks, the United States worked out a cease-fire in Lebanon, and Reagan proposed a new framework for peace between Israel and its Arab neighbors, including the Palestinians. But Begin had other plans. He was determined, one way or another, to destroy the PLO.

On August 10 the Israelis opened a massive fourteen-hour air bombardment of West Beirut, which had become the unofficial capital of the PLO, a military stronghold protecting thousands of PLO fighters, their families, and tons of supplies. The television reports were devastating: Israeli fighter planes zooming out of the skies, swooping down over West Beirut, dropping bombs on tenements; billows of black smoke, fire everywhere, women carrying babies, children scurrying about in the flaming chaos, bodies scattered about, bloodied in the bomb blasts. Israel, which had once prided itself on being a lonely David against the Arab Goliath, now looked like Goliath against the Palestinian David. In the Middle East, war was perception as much as reality. In defeat, the Palestinians were picking up sympathy; in victory, the Israelis were losing friends. No one watching these TV reports from Beirut could fail to appreciate the horror of the Lebanon war, a conflict between Israel and the PLO that happened to be taking place in Lebanon.

In the early morning hours of August 11, during his national security briefing, Reagan looked grim. He had seen the TV reports, and he was appalled. One of his closest advisers, Michael Deaver, known to be anti-Begin, had urged the president to express his strong disapproval of the Israeli bombing of West Beirut to the Israeli leader. Surprising everyone at the briefing, Reagan placed a call directly to Begin and, without his usually comforting note cards, laced into the Israeli prime minister and warned him, as McFarlane recalled, "in terms as severe as I had ever heard him use," that if the Israeli air attacks did not stop immediately, the United States would have to "reassess its relationship with Israel." Reagan concluded, "Our entire relationship is at stake!" End of conversation.[40]

Begin for the next few days held his fire, while Habib desperately tried to negotiate an arrangement satisfactory to both the PLO and Israel. Though drastically weakened, the PLO still commanded about 14,000 troops; Israel had not destroyed it. Habib proposed a compromise: that the PLO be allowed to withdraw from Lebanon. Dispersed to the four winds of Arabia, it would no longer be an immediate, existential threat to Israel, but it would be allowed, even in defeat, to retain a degree of dignity.

Israeli leaders were split. Most of them were reluctantly prepared to go along with the compromise, but a few, including Sharon, were ready to continue the fight. Finally, on August 16, PLO chief Yassir Arafat agreed to the Habib compromise, but with one crucial condition: that the PLO withdrawal from Lebanon be protected by a multinational force. Arafat was worried about an Israeli betrayal. Begin, fearing an open rupture in relations with the United States, something no Israeli prime minister could easily survive, also yielded to Habib's entreaties.

With the PLO and Israel in rare agreement, Habib arranged for 800 U.S. Marines, 400 French paratroopers, and 800 Italian troops to be rushed to Lebanon. Their mandate was loosely phrased and poorly understood. They were to guard against any possible Israeli attack during the PLO withdrawal. Then they were to remain in Lebanon for up to thirty days, until the Lebanese Armed Forces replaced them and assumed responsibility for protecting Palestinian refugees. The arrangement left unanswered the questions of which refugees—those still in West Beirut or those in the Palestinian camps—were at issue, and what would happen if the Lebanese Armed Forces did not replace the multinational force in thirty days. Precision, as well as goodwill, was in short supply. On August 21, with heavily armed multinational troops providing security, the 14,000 PLO fighters withdrew from Lebanon.

In Washington, while the State Department was hastily arranging the multinational force, Defense Secretary Weinberger pulled every string to frustrate the operation. The defense secretary voiced his opposition to the idea of positioning American troops in any Arab country, even for as short a time as envisaged in Lebanon. He denounced the Israeli offensive in Lebanon, and he warned that Arab oil shipments to the United States could be jeopardized. Weinberger thought he had a sympathetic ally in Reagan. The president also was decidedly unhappy about the Israeli offensive, and he offered only lukewarm support for the idea of a multinational force moving into a volatile Lebanese crisis. But he was persuaded by Shultz and McFarlane that the Habib compromise was the best the United States could extract from the PLO or Israel at this time. Besides, it was to be temporary. Weinberger, in obvious disagreement with his boss and his colleagues, took matters into his own hands, as he was to do a number of times in this crisis. According to McFarlane, whose respect for the defense secretary would not have filled a thimble, Weinberger, "without consultation or notification," issued a "fateful—and treacherous—order" to the effect that as soon as the PLO fighters withdrew from Lebanon, the marines were also to leave. They were to go "back aboard ship," which they quickly did. The French and the Italians quickly followed. The Beirut newspapers noted the marine arrival and departure: "Last In, First Out."[41]

Events then exploded in rapid-fire fashion. On September 14 Bashir Gemayel, a charismatic Phalangist leader, who had just been elected president of Lebanon, was murdered by terrorists supported by Syria. He had been Israel's great Christian hope, the only Lebanese leader believed to be capable of reconciling differences among the many warring factions and establishing a peaceful modus vivendi with Israel. He was succeeded by his older brother, Amin, known to be a loose-living playboy with none of the vision, discipline, and courage needed to lead Lebanon in those tumultuous times. Reagan, in his diary, wrote, "We . . . fear the worst."[42]

On September 16, in West Beirut, the Palestinian refugee camps of Sabra and Shatila were attacked by Phalange militia, while Israeli troops watched from the sidelines. The Israelis could have stopped the rampaging militia, but they did not. The result was a massacre heartless even by Middle Eastern standards. More than 600 men, women, and children were slaughtered, apparently as tribal retribution for the killing of Bashir Gemayel.

"Why? How?" asked Reagan, a "look of uncomprehending despair" on his face. "What could move people to do something like this?"[43] McFarlane had briefed the president about other massacres in the history of this part of the world, but this was on Reagan's shift, and he seemed to blame the Israelis. He did not blame his old friend Weinberger, whose arbitrary decision to pull the marines out of Beirut opened the door. Had the marines not been withdrawn, had they remained in position to protect Palestinian dependents, which was part of the original deal between Habib and Arafat, the massacre would not have happened. Weinberger was, according to McFarlane, "criminally irresponsible" for denying marine protection to "these hapless innocents."[44] Weinberger defended his decisions as being consistent both with the national interest of the United States and the president's own views.

All the president's men, except Weinberger and Joint Chiefs of Staff chairman General John W. Vessey Jr., voted to send the marines back into Beirut in a newly reconstituted "multinational force."[45] Guilt was a large part of their motivation. Reagan unveiled this step on September 20. The marines, he announced, would return with the mission of supporting the Lebanese government "to resume full sovereignty over its capital."[46]

Over the next six months, as the civil war spread through Lebanon, the marines gradually found themselves in the unenviable position of supporting one of the major factions in the war; namely, the troops loyal to Gemayel and his cohorts. This alliance evolved naturally: Gemayel represented the "government," and the marines were there to help the "government" with training and military supplies. Marine commandant P. X. Kelley naively played into Gemayel's game of seduction, saying on CBS's *Face the Nation* that he would follow the Lebanese army commander "into battle anywhere." Gemayel's national security adviser, Wadia Haddad, claimed: "I have the United States in my pocket," and a few other advisers warned their foes, "Toe the line. We are not alone."[47] If at the beginning of their "presence" the marines were seen by the Lebanese people as friends, after a while they began to be seen as "stooges" of the Gemayel regime, as participants, however unwitting, in their civil war. After a while, it was not unusual to see young Lebanese throwing rocks and obscenities at the marines during their street patrols.

On March 16, 1983, someone threw not a rock but a grenade at the marines during a patrol, injuring five of them.[48] On the same day, when a Lebanese dignitary assured Reagan that the president was "much loved" in Lebanon and that other American presidents "advanced so far and then retreated," Reagan responded like a proud peacock. "I told him I didn't have any reverse gear."[49]

On April 18 a suicide bomber drove a Chevrolet pickup truck into the front door of the U.S. embassy in Beirut, setting off a massive explosion that destroyed the face of the building and killed more than sixty people inside, including seventeen Americans. "First word," Reagan noted that night in his diary, "is that Iranian Shiites did it—d . . n them."[50]

On May 17, almost one month after the embassy attack, the United States midwifed a peace agreement between Israel and Gemayel's government, an agreement so decidedly in Israel's favor that it was almost doomed to fail. It spoke unrealistically of security, trade, and diplomatic relations. Gemayel's foreign minister, Shafik al-Wazzan, expressed concern that it would only antagonize Gemayel's opponents and heighten tensions in the country. During the summer, when it became clear that the agreement could not be implemented, Lebanon edged toward collapse.

On September 4 Israel abruptly pulled its forces out of the Shouf Mountains near Beirut and withdrew to southern Lebanon. Various factions sought to gain advantage: the Druse, allied with Lebanese Muslims, Syria, and the newly formed, Iranian-sponsored Hezbollah; all in opposition to Gemayel's

Maronite Christian party; questionable loyalists in his own army; and finally the Phalangists.

On September 7 the U.S. embassy reported that the Lebanese army, consisting at the time of three infantry brigades, was running out of ammunition, and morale was flagging.

On September 10 the Druse alliance, backed by Iranian Revolutionary Guards, began to attack one of the three brigades guarding the small mountain village of Suq al-Gharb overlooking both the presidential palace and the U.S. ambassador's residence in Beirut. The battle continued through the night. Shrapnel fell into the ambassador's swimming pool and a mortar in his courtyard.[51]

The following day, September 11, McFarlane—in Beirut as Reagan's personal Mideast representative—learned that seven Lebanese soldiers had been killed and forty-three others wounded. He read the casualty report with alarm. He expected another attack later in the day, and he had little to no confidence that the Lebanese army brigade could survive it. McFarlane sent a "flash cable" to Washington: "There is a serious threat of a decisive military defeat which could involve the fall of the Government of Lebanon within twenty-four hours," he wrote. "Last night's battle was waged within five kilometers of the Presidential Palace. . . . This is an action message. A second attack . . . is expected this evening. Ammunition and morale are low and raise the serious possibility that the enemy . . . will break through and penetrate the Beirut perimeter." His cable ended with a dramatic flourish. "In short, tonight we could be in enemy lines."[52]

On September 19 four American battleships—the guided-missile cruisers *Virginia, John Rodgers,* and *Bowen* and the destroyer *Radford*—opened fire against Druse, Syrian, and Palestinian forces. American five-inch shells, 360 of them, rained down on the anti-Gemayel troops, who were slowly forced to withdraw from the town, which now lay in shambles.[53]

Unmistakably, the United States had now entered the civil war as a combatant, and on that day it won the battle; the "enemy" withdrew. McFarlane noted, in defense of his position, that Iranian advisers and trainers, speaking in Farsi, and Syrian troops, speaking Arabic, had also participated in the battle.[54]

On September 25 mortars fell once more on the American ambassador's residence. The timing was odd, because the next day Syrian President Hafez al-Assad accepted American terms for a cease-fire in Lebanon.[55]

On September 28 Congress, worried about Lebanon becoming another Vietnam, was engaged in hot debate about whether to pull the marines out of Beirut or give Reagan more time, as he had requested. At issue was a law passed during the Vietnam War defining a president's "war powers." After seven hours, the House of Representatives voted 270-161 to give Reagan another eighteen months. John McCain, then a freshman member of Congress from Arizona, joined twenty-six other Republicans in denying Reagan the extra time. He thought Lebanon looked too much like Vietnam. "The fundamental question is, What is the United States' interest in Lebanon? It is said we are there to keep the peace. I ask, what peace? It is said we are there to aid the government. I ask, what government? It is said we are there to stabilize the region. I ask, how can the U.S. presence stabilize the region?" The key was Syria, and McCain did not think Syria was impressed by the show of American naval power. "Are we prepared to use this power?" McCain asked. "I do not think so," he said, "nor do I believe the Syrians think so."[56]

On October 17 McFarlane got his reward for the Lebanon cease-fire: he was appointed Reagan's national security adviser. If he thought for a moment that he had "solved" the Lebanese crisis, he was soon proven to be wrong. Proof arrived on the weekend of October 22–23, when the United States was confronted with the twin crises of Grenada and the marine massacre in Beirut.

Grenada was comparatively easy. Indeed, the U.S. invasion of Grenada, which Reagan applauded as a complete success, served as a convenient cover for his failure to respond adequately to the terrorist murder of 241 marines. Years later, in his memoir, Reagan described Beirut as "the source of my greatest regret and my greatest sorrow as president."[57] "Regret" and "sorrow" were hardly the appropriate words to describe his refusal to act against the terrorists and to rein in his freelancing secretary of defense and end the costly squabbling over foreign policy in his cabinet.

Reagan was president. He had the authority to end the infighting, set policy, and advance American interests in the Middle East. Before him was a clear choice; Shultz arguing for engagement, Weinberger for disengagement. Engagement would likely have involved the use of military force; disengagement offered the comfort of a casualty-free retreat. In the post-Vietnam era, for this president, at this time, disengagement made more sense. He still talked a good game, but when it was time for a decision, he punted. "In the weeks immediately after the bombing," he later wrote, "I believed the last thing we should do was turn tail and leave."[58] And yet, fearful of another Vietnam, he waited a few months and then pulled the remaining marines out of Beirut. According to McFarlane many years later, his decision opened the door to the terrorism that has plagued the region and the world ever since. "I am convinced we could have stopped it then, just as it was starting, but Reagan chose not to."[59]

In the final analysis, decisionmaking in the Reagan White House all came down to a certain head gesture, a gentle smile, an ambiguous phrase or two. Rarely did Reagan fully engage in a detailed discussion of foreign policy options. Loyal and devoted advisers, such as Shultz and Weinberger, would retreat from an Oval Office discussion of options with clashing impressions, allowing each to pursue a policy he thought the president had just approved, but, on the other hand, might not have approved. Because everyone seemed so intent on letting "Reagan be Reagan," no one shouted, "Stop!" The resulting uncertainty and sloppiness led to policy confusion, misdirection, and embarrassment, not only among the advisers but also among nations, and it damaged America's interests and reputation.

Robert Timberg, author of the acclaimed *The Nightingale's Song,* described two Reagans in explaining the president's reluctance to express a firm decision: the public Reagan, who "looked like a president and acted like one," and the private one, "passive, incurious, often befuddled."[60]

So long as the president did not explicitly say no, he ruled no option out; and this very vagueness could then be interpreted by such adversaries as Shultz and Weinberger as a sort of yes for the option each wished to pursue. In the Beirut crisis, Weinberger took infinitely more advantage of the Reagan style than Shultz, and it led to an open rupture between the president's two top advisers. McFarlane, the national security adviser, sided with Shultz, and Vessey, the chair of the Joint Chiefs of Staff, went with Weinberger. The president understood that there were two warring factions in his official family. It was not that he enjoyed the debate, which other presidents might have relished; it was just that he seemed to rise above the squabbling or he seemed indifferent to it, and in the end did nothing to stop it.

On the day of the marine massacre in Beirut, Reagan convened his senior advisers for an urgent White House meeting. He had always promised "swift and effective retribution" against terrorism, and there was every reason to believe that, this time, he would respond with a mailed fist. "The first thing I want to do is to find out who did it and go after them with everything we've got," he said.[61] He was angry, and his message, in this instance, was clear. In a written directive, he ordered the CIA quickly to identify the culprits, and the Pentagon, just as quickly, to produce plans for retaliating against them. Given the magnitude of the tragedy and the president's deep personal grief at the murder of 241 marines, one would have imagined that the administration would have clicked its heels, saluted, and retaliated with unmistakable force; one would have been pitifully wrong. The State Department and the NSC went in one direction, the CIA in another, and the Pentagon did not move at all, stuck in Weinberger's unbudgeable belief that it would be counterproductive to U.S. interests in the Middle East to strike at the Arabs.

The CIA soon traced the bombing of the marines to a splinter Shia commando force known as the Husaini Suicide Forces. It was led by Abu Haidar Musawi, a radical Shia who had split off from the mainline Amal in 1982 to form the more extremist Islamic Amal, which soon morphed into Hezbollah.[62] Enter the Iranian Revolutionary Guards, who had been closely cooperating with the Syrians in the Bekaa Valley. They embraced, supported, and armed the Islamic Amal. The Iranian Revolutionary Guards and the Islamic Amal were in the Al Shams Hotel and the Sheik Abdullah Barracks in the historic town of Baalbek.

There was other intelligence that incriminated the Iranians and the Syrians. On September 27, four weeks before the marine massacre, the National Security Agency (NSA) reported on a message, highly classified, containing instructions from Iranian ambassador Ali Akbar Mohtashemi in Damascus for Musawi in Baalbek to concentrate his terrorist offensive against the multinational force and, in particular, to "take a 'spectacular' action against the U.S. Marines."[63] Not known was whether the NSA shared this intelligence with other parts of the U.S. government. Because U.S. intelligence was generally "stovepiped," meaning routinely kept within each agency, rarely shared, the NSA did not open its books on the Mohtashemi memo to Musawi until after the marine bombing. Admiral James A. Lyons Jr., who was then deputy chief of naval operations, learned about the memo only on October 25, two days after the Beirut tragedy. He should have been briefed earlier.[64]

The CIA also had learned that Majid Kamal, a senior Iranian intelligence agent responsible for coordinating the terrorist activities of pro-Iranian cells in Lebanon, was in Beirut on the day of the bombing, and seven intercepted Iranian messages pressed for attacks on U.S. and French interests, including the marines.[65]

CIA director William Casey raised the obvious question at a meeting: should the United States now launch a retaliatory strike against Islamic Amal and its allies in Baalbek? His answer was yes. The president, after all, had asked who had conducted the attack and where they were. Casey's analysts had screened NSA intercepts and studied "overhead" or satellite imaging. Shultz, satisfied, quickly backed Casey. So did McFarlane. The president expressed no opinion;

he listened to his advisers. Weinberger, who had consistently opposed an American presence in the multinational force, argued with renewed passion against any U.S. attack in Lebanon. "If you don't know what you're shooting at," Weinberger said, according to McFarlane, "you're going to hit a lot of innocents. The impact of that on our relations [with the Arab world] would be very severe." Weinberger played a valuable card: he knew that Reagan always worried about "collateral damage." The president turned to Casey. "Well, Bill, I want you to focus on this. I can't allow killing Americans with impunity," he said, but he also did not want to kill innocent Arab civilians indiscriminately.[66] Casey, though he had full confidence in his intelligence, promised another, even more rigorous, review of all relevant intelligence within a few days.

The meeting about the barracks bombing ended on this inconclusive note, and Reagan and his team shifted their focus to final plans for an invasion of Grenada; advance teams had already landed on the island. When the October 25 invasion took place, it naturally grabbed the headlines, and for a brief time the tragedy in Beirut seemed to fall into second place in the national consciousness. Reagan felt a temporary sense of relief, the success in Grenada assuaging the grief over Beirut. He wrote in his diary on October 27, "Success seems to shine on us & I thank the Lord for it. He has really held us in the hollow of his hand. . . . Everything is going well in Grenada. We're mopping up." On October 30 he wrote, "The press is trying to give this the Vietnam treatment but I don't think the people will buy it."[67]

Shultz was thrilled by the Grenada invasion. "It was the first time we used military force," he recalled. "After Vietnam, it was a shot heard round the world. We were back in the game. We were saying to the people in Angola, everywhere where Soviet advisers and Cuban proxies were, that we were on their side. We will help you."[68] But Grenada was not a "shot heard round the world." It was not heard in Beirut or Baalbek or Damascus, where the Grenada invasion had little resonance. Far more compelling was the American inaction. Days passed, and the United States did not lift a finger in retaliation. In the Middle East, retaliation was as natural as the sun rising in the morning and setting at night; no retaliation was what was unnatural, suggesting weakness or cowardice.

On November 7, on the eve of a presidential visit to Japan and South Korea, Reagan paused long enough to hear an updated Casey report on the Beirut bombing. "We believe," Reagan noted that evening, "we have a fix on a headquarters of the radical Iranian Shiites who blew up our Marines. We can take out the target with an air strike & no risk to civilians. We'll meet 7 A.M. tomorrow as to whether we order the strike now or while I'm away." The only issue, it seemed, was timing; the decision had been made. But on November 8, before leaving, Reagan backed off. "Short meeting re a possible air strike in Beirut against those who murdered our Marines," he wrote. "Decided we don't have enough intelligence info as yet."[69] One day he had the intelligence; the next day he did not have it?

Somebody got to him, and that somebody was Weinberger, supported by the Joint Chiefs, who wanted no part of an American presence in Beirut and certainly no part of an American attack against Arab targets in Lebanon. The defense secretary, whose friendship with Reagan was deep and long-lasting, returned to an argument now familiar to the president, and one that he often made on television. Beirut, Weinberger believed, was "this most dangerous of all situations. . . . We shouldn't be there, and we should get out. . . . It was always argued by those of us in our government who wanted to keep them there, that this would be 'cutting and running,' and 'Marines never retreated,' and various other nonsensical slogans that had no meaning in this kind of situation."[70] Everyone understood that the "marines" in this debate were Shultz and McFarlane, who had both served in the Marine Corps.

Chairman Vessey recalled that "the [Joint Chiefs] would have been overjoyed to hit the enemy, but we simply did not have the evidence." The marine bombing, he said, was easily "the saddest day of my life." Time and again, though, Vessey leaned on two key points: he did not think U.S. intelligence was reliable in this instance, or adequate, and he did not think U.S. interests would be served by an attack on the Islamic Amal. Displaying an acute sensitivity to Arab concerns, the army general said, "The Arabists [at the Pentagon] told us that there were historical sites at Baalbek, and if we hit them and destroyed them, we would be doing more harm to American interests in the region [in the long term]. We also had to worry about collateral damage." For him, the key issue was intelligence: whether the United States had the evidence to proceed with a strike. "Basically," Vessey concluded, "we didn't have the intelligence. McFarlane may say we did, but we didn't."[71]

For Shultz, the ex-marine, "cutting and running" was not a "nonsensical slogan"; it was a real problem. He once told a television audience, "If people see you, in the face of opposition, see you cut and run, that's not some slogan. That is something that hurts you badly."[72] He was deeply concerned that vacillation or inaction in this case would create the image of the United States, as he once put it, as "the Hamlet of nations, worrying endlessly over whether and how to respond."[73]

"Direct" and "Unambiguous," and Yet Vague Enough

On November 14 Reagan returned from his trip to Asia. After a seventeen-hour flight, he was tired, of course, but he still had a decision to make about the Beirut bombing. Would he, at long last, order an air strike against the Islamic Amal in Baalbek? Shultz, McFarlane, and Casey were in the "yes" camp; they thought it was extremely important for the United States to send a signal to the Arab terrorists that they had gone too far. Weinberger and Vessey were in the "no" camp; they were convinced that an air strike would be counterproductive. Reagan convened another NSC session. "We have some additional intelligence," he wrote in his diary on November 14, "but still not enough to order a strike."[74]

McFarlane, however, repeatedly insisted on a dramatically different account. "The President," he wrote, "gave his approval for a retaliatory strike to be conducted on November 16. It was a direct, unambiguous decision."[75] Indeed, "all of us were quite moved by photographic evidence of a mockup training site that was analogous in virtually every respect to the site actually hit, and this mockup site in the Bekaa valley involving a road, a turnoff, a building structure, gave us very high confidence that that was, that that had been, the rehearsal area for the conduct of the attack."[76] McFarlane added, "This time Casey really nailed it. He was quite firm in telling the president, 'This is why I know who did it, and this is the nature of the target, and this is my confidence that we can hit it without significant collateral damage.'"[77]

McFarlane described White House plans for a joint American-French air attack on the terrorist site. "The president approved it," he recalled. "[He approved] an air raid, and we coordinated with the French, who'd also been hit, and they agreed to attack with us. . . . The president said, 'Let's do it' . . . and that was that." But that was not that. The events of November 16 were a surprise to McFarlane; early that morning, he learned that Weinberger had aborted the attack.

> "Wait a minute. This cannot be!" I called Cap [Weinberger], and I said, "I don't understand," and he said, "I just don't think it's the right thing to do. There's too great a risk of a backlash in the Arab states if we start killing Arabs." I said, "Cap, you said that . . . and you said it well, and the president heard you and he decided, and you've violated a direct order

from the president." He said, "Well, I'd be glad to be accountable and talk to the president about it." And I said, "Well, I think you better come over and do that."[78]

If Weinberger did, there was no record of it. McFarlane, for his part, did meet later that morning with Reagan, who seemed worried. "His body language demonstrated that he was very, very troubled," McFarlane recalled, "and yet I don't say angry, which bothered me at the time. He leaned forward in his chair and said, 'I just don't understand it, Bud; what happened?' And I said, 'You heard the ideas . . . you knew Cap had reservations, but you made a decision, and Cap decided later not to do it, and you cannot let this stand, Mr. President. . . . You just can't let this stand.'"[79]

"Gosh, that's really disappointing," Reagan responded. "That's terrible. We should have blown the daylights out of them. I just don't understand."[80] Years later, McFarlane recalled that Reagan could not "confront a close personal friend," Weinberger. "Reagan had this way of pursing his lips when an issue involving a personal friend came up," McFarlane remembered.[81]

Shultz's recollections conformed to McFarlane's. "The 241 Marines were killed," he said, "and the president gave the order [but Weinberger] didn't want to do it." Shultz, in trying to explain the defense secretary's insubordination, spoke of the president's concern about eight hostages, one of whom was an American associated with the American University in Beirut, who were being held by the terrorists at a training camp in the Bekaa Valley. "The training camp, we knew about it," Shultz went on, "that was the logical place for them to hold the hostages. The president was very concerned about this issue of hostages, and he did not want to [run into the trap] Carter was in [with the hostages in Tehran]. Cap found some wiggle room there, and used it." He added, "[We had] a great disagreement."[82] There have been other examples in recent history of cabinet squabbles, most notably the differences that arose between Colin Powell and Donald Rumsfeld over the war in Iraq; but none that reached the level of bitterness and anger exhibited by Shultz and Weinberger in the early 1980s.

On November 16 Reagan noted in his diary, "The Israelis burned Naba Chit known to be a camp of the Iranian Shiites believed responsible for the car bomb attacks. That was one of the targets we were looking at but didn't feel we had enough information yet."

On November 17 Reagan continued on this theme: "Surprise call from France—they were going ahead without us & bombing our other target in

Lebanon. They took it out completely."[83] Every now and then Reagan seemed to live in his own world, confirming what was comfortable and familiar, evading what might be a problem or an embarrassment. He did not raise objections to the Israeli or French actions and never changed his position that he did not have enough intelligence to proceed with an American strike. It is not clear why he would have been surprised that the French proceeded without the United States; French paratroopers had been killed, and the country's national pride had been offended. Often in Mideast diplomacy, the United States has allowed the Israelis to carry its dirty water, knowing that the Israelis would undertake unpopular and controversial actions that the United States supported but was unwilling for different reasons to execute or acknowledge. This might have been one of those.

"Evacuate All the Marines"

A casual reader of *The Reagan Diaries*, a book of unintended revelations about the Reagan presidency, might have missed what national security adviser McFarlane later labeled "one of the worst defeats" of the Reagan years in the White House.[84] On January 23, 1984, Reagan noted, "We're going to study a possible move of the Marines to the ships offshore but an Army force on shore to train the Lebanese army in anti-terrorist tactics."[85] On February 15 Reagan sent Congress an eight-page memo outlining his plans to relocate the marines.[86] McFarlane later described Reagan's withdrawal of the marines as "a powerful signal of paralysis within our government."[87]

Years later, in his memoirs, Reagan acknowledged that the situation in Lebanon had worsened considerably by early 1984. "The Lebanese army was either unwilling or unable to end the civil war into which we had been dragged reluctantly," he wrote. And "the war was likely to go on for an extended period of time." The president's decision: "I gave an order to evacuate all the Marines to ships anchored off Lebanon" before being "moved on to other assignments."[88]

Morton Abramowitz remembered that "we didn't know what we were doing in Lebanon. . . . We didn't understand the situation. . . . We got out because we weren't confident about what was going on [there] any more. . . . Normally, [if someone had killed 241 marines], we'd go in and beat the [hell] out of them. [But] Reagan was very realistic. He said, 'This is a morass. We don't know what we're doing. Let's not get involved.'" Abramowitz reached back to Vietnam for further elaboration. "Vietnam made us very careful," he said. "For a generation . . . many of us were scared about getting involved, about casualties."[89]

"We had to pull out," Reagan explained in his memoir. "By then, there was no question about it: Our policy wasn't working. We couldn't stay there and run the risk of another suicide attack on the marines. No one wanted to commit our troops to a full-scale war in the Middle East. But we couldn't remain in Lebanon and be in the war on a halfway basis, leaving our men vulnerable to terrorists with one hand tied behind their backs."[90]

It is a sad commentary on American politics that a president had to wait years before telling the truth to the American people about an embarrassing change in policy. His diary was a record of the moment, which conformed not only to his flexible sense of truth and reality but also to the political needs of the time; his memoir afforded him a degree of candor and historical perspective but also an opportunity for self-justification, which he seized again and again. Reagan could seek sympathy and understanding by writing in his memoir, "Perhaps we didn't appreciate fully. . . . Perhaps the idea of a suicide car bomber. . . . Perhaps we should have anticipated,"[91] perhaps this and perhaps that, but the marine tragedy in Beirut was the direct result of terrorist rage and narrow-minded American policy, ignorance and arrogance, all on Reagan's watch. *New York Times* reporter Thomas L. Friedman, who covered the marine tragedy, wrote that the United States "learned in Beirut, maybe even more than in Vietnam, [that] the world has undergone a democratization of the means of destruction."[92] He was referring to asymmetrical warfare: pitting terrorists against states, targeting civilians as well as soldiers, exploiting roadside bombings and modern media technology in an all-out fight against super-sophisticated armies.

The Reagan-Weinberger-Powell Doctrine

Reagan understood that since Vietnam, and especially since Lebanon, the rules of warfare had changed, and that it was imperative for the United States to adopt a new set of principles for applying its military power in foreign conflicts. He left the drafting and elaboration to Weinberger, but he had four principles in mind, all rooted in the American experience in Vietnam:

1. Never commit U.S. power unless the cause is "vital to our national interest."

2. Nothing "halfway or tentative."

3. Unless there is "reasonable assurance" of popular and congressional support, don't "commit our troops to combat." He added, with specific reference to the Vietnam experience, "We all felt that the Vietnam War had turned into such a tragedy because military action had been undertaken without sufficient assurances that the American people were behind it."

4. Combat must always be a "last resort" option, "when no other choice is available."[93]

Reagan hoped that future presidents would follow these four principles. They were, for him, the lessons of the Vietnam War. It could be argued that by ordering the marines out of Beirut in February 1984, he was following the logic of his four principles. He was, by this order, avoiding a fight without a clear end, without popular and congressional support, and without a sharply defined mandate and endgame. But it is difficult to understand, then, why he committed the troops to Beirut in the first place, why he allowed his senior aides and commanders to place the marines in a civil war, why he left them in such an exposed and dangerous position, and why he did not retaliate against the killers. If there ever were a Beirut symphony commemorating the marine tragedy, the notes would be Reagan, Shultz, Weinberger, McFarlane, Gemayel, and the terrorists, but the melody would be Vietnam.

A Soviet Version of Vietnam

Reagan was the last American president to spend his full time in office dealing with the cold war. During his second term, which he won overwhelmingly, he met on an almost annual basis with Soviet leader Mikhail Gorbachev, and their relationship warmed to the point where they discussed the elimination of all nuclear weapons, a goal so wildly unrealistic that their senior aides never seriously considered it. They attempted to balance the promise of their new relationship with the residual habits of the cold war: they wanted to contain and possibly reduce their nuclear arsenals, but neither could resist tweaking the other whenever the occasion arose. Reagan indulged in this practice more than Gorbachev, who had little time for old tricks. Upon taking office in 1985, Gorbachev was absorbed with the daunting task, as he saw it, of preserving the communist system, which was in a state of rapid disintegration. Almost immediately, he spoke about withdrawing Soviet troops from what was clearly a failing, reckless adventure in Afghanistan. Reagan, rather than ease Gorbachev's path, seemed determined to rub salt in an open and humiliating wound. He and his hard-line CIA chief, Bill Casey, decided that it was in America's national interest to win in Afghanistan. Reagan never defined what constituted a win, but he wanted more than a Soviet version of Vietnam.

In July 1986 Casey invited the tough CIA agent Milton Bearden to become station chief in Islamabad, Pakistan, with full responsibility for the American aid program to the mujahidin, the Islamic radicals battling Soviet troops in neighboring Afghanistan.[94] Bearden, just home from a rough assignment in the Sudan, thought Afghanistan sounded like a cushy job. He was wrong. "Casey and Reagan decided . . . Let's break the rules. Let's ramp up the money and let's . . . try to win," Bearden said.[95] Bearden elaborated on Casey's surprising order to up the ante:

> "I want you to go out to Afghanistan, I want you to go next month," Casey said, "and I will give you whatever you need to win." Yeah. He said, "I want you [to go] there and win." As opposed to, "let's go there and bleed these guys," make a . . .Vietnam. "I want you to go there and win. Whatever you need, you can have." So he gave me the Stinger missiles and a billion dollars.[96]

Gorbachev had already indicated that he was going to leave Afghanistan. The United States could have opened the door to this anticipated Soviet pullout and waved goodbye, but it took a more belligerent approach, consistent with the maxim: when your enemy is down, kick him.

Shortly after Bearden arrived in Islamabad, the floodgates on aid to the mujahidin were opened. The aid came from a strange and informal coalition, led by the United States, that included Pakistan, Saudi Arabia, China, Iran, and others, each with a running grievance against the Soviet Union. By the time the last Soviet soldier left Afghanistan on February 15, 1989, having left more than 13,000 dead comrades behind, the United States had already contributed more than $10 billion worth of arms and munitions to the mujahidin cause, which soon spawned Osama bin Laden's deadly band of terrorists known as al Qaeda. Throughout this effort, Bearden worked closely with Alistair Crooke, a British intelligence agent. The more the Soviet Union bled, the happier they were. "The important thing to know," Bearden stressed, "was how many people in the Warsaw Pact and in China who were willing to sell us Warsaw-Pact ordnance to shoot Russians with." He smiled. "This is such a wonderful world we live in."[97]

One day, according to reporter Steve Coll, a special envoy from the State Department arrived in Islamabad, checked the aid program for the mujahidin, toured the battlefields of Afghanistan, and then wrote a highly controversial, top-secret cable to Washington questioning the underlying concept of American support of Islamist radicals. He believed that the strengthening of Islamist radicals was a huge, historic blunder, one that would come back and bite the United States.[98] Bearden, in almost violent disagreement, argued that the aid program was in fact a success. Finally, Bearden won.

Brzezinski had wanted to suck the Soviet Union into its own Vietnam War. He wanted it to suffer, amid rising casualties and fading glory, in full view of the rest of the world, just as the United States had in Vietnam. Reagan and Casey, having succeeded in accomplishing these goals, wanted to use Soviet losses in Afghanistan as a weapon not only against the Soviet state but also against the ideology of communism itself. According to Russian analyst Alexei Arbatov, "The Soviet Union was doomed to collapse, but Afghanistan was like a trigger."[99] There were other reasons, too, but the Soviet defeat in Afghanistan paralleled the American defeat in Vietnam and contributed mightily to the ultimate collapse of the Soviet state.

Years later, in an official history of the Soviet involvement in Afghanistan, General Alexander Lyakhovsky, a veteran of the war, went to great lengths to disconnect the Vietnam parallel from his nation's experience in Afghanistan:

> It is not only unfair but even absurd to draw such parallels. There cannot be any comparison here, because these two missions are diametrically opposite. . . . Starting with the fact that nobody invited the Americans in Vietnam, whereas the Soviet troops were sent to Afghanistan after numerous requests from the legitimate Afghan government. . . . We came in not with the goal to occupy and split the country, as it happened as a result of American actions, not with the goal of capturing foreign territory, but with the goal of providing internationalist assistance in defense of sovereignty and territorial integrity of Afghanistan. We never pursued any selfish goals or set any conditions.[100]

Shakespeare might have said that the general, perhaps, protesteth too much.

5

Bush I: Burying Vietnam

That war cleaves us still.
—GEORGE H. W. BUSH, Inaugural Address, January 20, 1989

Vietnam has made us paranoid, it has terrorized us, it has blinded us to our own interests.
—DAN QUAYLE, Speech on the Senate Floor, August 4, 1983

We cannot put the United States through another Vietnam.
—COLIN POWELL, *My American Journey*, 1995

THE PRESIDENTIAL CAMPAIGN of 1988 added a fresh face to American politics—that of a baby boomer named James Danforth Quayle, aged forty-one. Quayle was tapped for the vice presidency on the GOP ticket by presidential candidate George H. W. Bush, thus becoming the first of his heralded generation to enter the top tier of American governance. The Bush-Quayle ticket won handsomely, and the boomer from Huntington, Indiana—boyish-looking, blue-eyed, conservative—suddenly found himself one heartbeat away from the presidency. He seemed utterly unprepared for this challenge, evoking questions of whether he had been prepared for a different challenge earlier in his life. During the Vietnam War, Quayle had sidestepped military service in Vietnam by enlisting in the Indiana National Guard. At the time, he never dreamed that one day he would be chosen to be vice president.

An Associated Press political reporter, Jonathan Wolman, made the obvious connection between Vietnam and the campaign. "The Bush campaign wanted a baby boomer, they got one, and he carries the baggage of his generation," Wolman wrote. "This is not World War II we're talking about, this is the Vietnam War and millions of kids were trying to avoid it. In Quayle's case, he is wrestling with the image of a rich kid who chose law school over Vietnam and traded on his family influence to make his dreams come true."[1]

In the most unintended of ways, Quayle came to personify the political and cultural crosscurrents of that large baby-boomer generation born in the post–World War II years of 1946–64. Each of its milestones was celebrated and analyzed: turning forty, turning fifty, turning sixty, retiring. *Time* magazine named this generation its 1966 Man of the Year.

Those born at the beginning of the baby boom, such as Quayle, Bill Clinton, Al Gore, and George W. Bush, were shaped by a tumultuous decade—the 1960s—marked by the growing U.S. involvement in Vietnam, as well as the civil rights movement, greater efforts for women's equality, and an increasingly youth-oriented culture. The Vietnam War served as a backdrop to their high school and college years, and their decision about Vietnam—whether to enlist, be drafted, join the National Guard or Reserves, be exempted for medical reasons, flee to Canada—was a crucial one.

For young men considering a political career, the decision had even bigger implications. For many years, military service was seen as an honorable, even necessary, feature of an aspiring politician's résumé. All the presidents who held the office in the years following World War II had served, most of them during wartime: Harry Truman, a National Guardsman, who fought gallantly in Europe during World War I; Dwight Eisenhower, a commanding general and supreme allied commander in Europe during World War II; John Kennedy, a naval officer in the Pacific, commended for heroism during World War II; Lyndon Johnson, another naval officer who served in the Pacific; Richard Nixon, still another naval officer with Pacific service; Gerald Ford, naval officer, action in the Pacific; Jimmy Carter, an Annapolis graduate and naval officer; Ronald Reagan, an army officer who made World War II training films; and Bush I, who joined the navy at age eighteen, immediately after graduation from prep school, and became its youngest aviator, renowned for participating in fifty-eight combat missions and winning the Distinguished Flying Cross. As it turned out, Bush, who failed in his bid for a second term in 1992, would be the last of the World War II–veteran presidents. The last nominee of that generation was Bob Dole, the unsuccessful Republican standard-bearer in 1996, who had been severely wounded while serving in the army during the war. But by that point, military service was less important as a selling point.

World War II was seen as a "good war." Those who fought in it were honored as what Tom Brokaw has termed the "greatest generation." Indeed, after major wars the American people elected generals, not politicians, to be their president: George Washington after the Revolutionary War, Ulysses S. Grant after the Civil War, Ike after World War II. But Vietnam shattered the link between military service and political acceptability—it seemed to have spoiled the well, going on for too long and costing too much in lives and treasure. Military service for many of the baby boomers apparently lost its allure in the jungles of Southeast Asia. Quayle and later Bush II chose a middle course: they joined the National Guard but never shot a bullet in anger. Clinton never even joined the National Guard, protesting against the war while a graduate student at Oxford. Gore served in Vietnam as a military journalist, in part to spare his father any political embarrassment during his Senate reelection race in Tennessee.

Ironically, in the post-Vietnam period, a candidate who clearly ducked combat in Vietnam could beat a candidate who had served honorably in Vietnam or in earlier wars; pre-Vietnam, one would have imagined just the opposite. In 1992 Clinton beat Bush I; in 1996 Clinton beat Dole, a World War II hero; in 2000 Bush II beat Gore and then in 2004 beat John Kerry, a Vietnam War hero; and in 2008 Barack Obama, who was too young to have served in Vietnam, beat John McCain, an Annapolis graduate, a pilot, and a prisoner of war in Vietnam for five-and-a-half years.

When Bush chose Quayle to be his running mate, hoping to put a youthful spin on his ticket, he unintentionally opened up a hornet's nest of bad memories and old controversies. The questions for Quayle—why he chose the National Guard, whether he needed family influence to get in—were cut of faded cloth that magically regained a degree of luster during the 1988 campaign.

At his first news conference, shortly after his selection, memorable for one answer more than any other, Quayle acknowledged that he would not have enlisted in the National Guard if he had known in 1969 that he would one day be selected as a vice presidential candidate. "I did not know in 1969 that I would be in this room today,"[2] he said in a throwaway line that generated a storm of negative comment among reporters and absolute anguish among his political handlers. One of Bush's advisers, Charlie Black, prompted to reflect on the 1988 campaign, recalled the Republican Convention: "The National Guard thing dominated our convention for two-and-a-half days," he recalled. "[Quayle] had apparently avoided service in Vietnam using special favors and influence, [and] he never overcame [that]. . . . I think it was too much stream-of-consciousness. He shouldn't have put [it] that way, but what he was getting at was, 'if I . . . knew I was going to get a chance to run for president or vice-president, I would have gone ahead and served full time in the army.' I think that's what he was trying to say."[3]

According to reporter Jules Witcover, apparently "all he had on his mind was getting married, going to law school and raising a family." At one point in the news conference, Witcover looked over at Quayle's handlers. They were, he wrote, "aghast at what their presidential nominee had wrought."[4]

From Quayle to Powell

At the same time, the country witnessed a fresh take on military strategy. It belonged to Colin Powell, at the time national security adviser to President Reagan. "There is . . . no fixed set of rules for the use of military force," he once wrote. "To set one up is dangerous." He meant that there was more than one way to use military force in a war, more than one way, as he put it, to get out of a burning apartment building. The elevator might be the most convenient means of escape, but not necessarily the best. "No, you run to the stairs, an outside fire escape or a window," he said, listing his options.[5]

Yet as he reviewed American military capabilities, he felt the need to advance a new "set of rules" to govern the use of military force in the event of a crisis, rules that arose out of both the dismal experience of the Vietnam War and the marine tragedy in Beirut. They came to be called the Powell Doctrine.

Powell always rejected authorship, believing, in fairness, that it was not he but Caspar Weinberger, Reagan's secretary of defense, who had originated the new doctrine. Powell joked that it was neither he nor Weinberger but Sun Tzu, author of the old Chinese classic study of war, called *The Art of War*, who first came up with the basic principles of "objective" and "mass" in determining any approach to fighting a war.[6] Or perhaps it was the nineteenth-century German theorist Carl von Clausewitz, who impressed Powell by stating that "no one starts a war . . . without first being clear in his mind what he intends to achieve by that war and how he intends to achieve it."[7]

Weinberger took parts of Sun Tzu and most of von Clausewitz and came up with his own post-Vietnam doctrine of war. His test was the marine deployment to Lebanon in the early 1980s. He had opposed it strenuously, and it ended in tragedy. In a speech at the National Press Club on November 28, 1984, with Powell, his military aide, in attendance, Weinberger publicly raised the question that had privately tormented the Reagan administration for a long time: when should the United States use its military force? "Under what circumstances, and by what means," the secretary asked pointedly, "does a great democracy such as ours reach the painful decision that the use of military force is necessary to protect our interests or to carry out our national policy?"[8] The question had been subjected to serious debate in the Reagan administration.

In his memoir, Reagan wrote with disarming simplicity that his successors must carefully review all options before committing American troops to battle, and they must have certain "principles" in mind. The "cause," he stressed, must be "vital" to American interests. It must command the support of Congress and the American people. And if force was to be employed, it must be employed only as a "last resort" and only for the purpose of "winning."[9] At first blush, Reagan's recommendations had an appealing obviousness. On closer examination, they produced only more questions. How would he define "winning" in a guerrilla war, for example? Would it be by the destruction of the Islamist radicals based in Baalbek, which, from a military point of view, was easy to accomplish; or by the destruction of their sponsors in Iran, which posed a much more complex set of problems? If he ever addressed these questions, he stopped short of providing the answers, which he normally left to others.

But Reagan had obviously been impressed by Weinberger's argument. His ideas flowed directly from his defense secretary's doctrine, which was designed specifically to limit the use of American military power. Weinberger wanted it to be used with exceptional care and with a clear end in sight. He feared nothing more than escalation by stealth, approaching a problem on cat's paws. He worried constantly that an American president, not wanting to get into a fight and yet feeling the heat to show the flag and flex a muscle, might decide to take one small step into the fray, as much to satisfy a congressional critic as to respond to a legitimate national interest, and then take another step and another. Eventually, the United States, by virtue of its growing footprint, would become involved and ultimately committed to the fight. Weinberger's doctrine contained six cautionary markers, which he hoped would alert any president to do his best to avoid another gradual Vietnam-like escalation from involvement to commitment:

1. The vital national interests of the United States or its close allies had to be at risk.

2. The war had to be fought wholeheartedly, with the "clear intention of winning."

3. If force is to be used, it should be in pursuit of "clearly defined political and military objectives."

4. Constantly reassess whether the use of force is necessary and appropriate.

5. There must be "reasonable assurance" of congressional and public support.

6. Use force only as a "last resort."[10]

Presumably, according to this doctrine, if a president faced a crisis, he would review these six markers and be governed by them. If he was satisfied that vital national interests were at risk, that he had the support of Congress and the public, and that he would be using force only as a last resort, then he would commit his troops to battle, and he would do so wholeheartedly and with the intent to win—except, according to marker 5, he would constantly reassess whether his decision was right or wrong. Almost by definition, a reassessment would undercut a wholehearted commitment. If during one such reassessment the president was to decide that military force was not really necessary or appropriate, what would he then do? Would he stop the war, readjust his strategy, or pull out? A change of this magnitude would bring into question the original commitment to winning. And, if during another such reassessment, the president discovered to his dismay that he was losing the support of Congress, would he still pursue the war and ignore Congress? Or would he change his strategy to accommodate Congress?

Weinberger's deputy, Frank Carlucci, and his military aide, Colin Powell, differed from Weinberger on one major point. "I disagreed with Cap on the idea of public support," Carlucci said. "I think it's the job of the president to mobilize public support and to lead. You don't want to wait on something hopeless . . . to wait for public support to mobilize before protecting the national interest."[11]

For his part, Powell said, "We may not have public support at first, but we needed to go on." In Panama, for example, "we went [in], got engaged and disengaged so quickly that public support didn't become an issue."[12] Powell did not dismiss the importance of public support, but he felt it could not be allowed to impede a military operation deemed to be crucial to the national interest.

Weinberger was a shrewd and stubborn official. He understood that the stars might never be in perfect alignment. He was not trying to create the ideal military strategy. He was trying to avoid another Vietnam, which stood like an 800-pound gorilla in all his calculations. "We cannot fight a battle with the Congress at home," he said in his Press Club speech, "while asking our troops to win a war overseas or, as in the case of Vietnam, in effect asking our troops not to win, but just to be there."[13]

Powell, always attuned to the political arguments of the day, added his own sophisticated spin to the Reagan recommendations and to the Weinberger markers. He linked military strategy to politics, and he framed the issue in a series of questions:

Is the political objective we seek to achieve important, clearly defined and understood? Have all other nonviolent policy means failed? Will military force achieve the objective? At what cost? Have the gains and risks been analyzed? How might the situation that we seek to alter, once it is altered by force, develop further and what might be the consequences?[14]

In his memoir, Powell stressed that "when we go to war, we should have a purpose that our people understand and support; we should mobilize the country's resources to fulfill that mission and then go in to win." He, like Weinberger, always thought of the Vietnam War as the strategic model to be avoided at all costs. "In Vietnam," he continued, "we had entered into a halfhearted half-war, with much of the nation opposed or indifferent, while a small fraction carried the burden."[15] Colonel Lawrence Wilkerson, one of Powell's aides in 1989, thought he understood the Powell Doctrine. "For a democratic republic as ours," he explained, "it is better to act massively and decisively, and produce lots of carnage perhaps, but have the short time necessary to achieve victory—be a lot better than [be there] a long time and be defeated. If you are going to use force . . . use it quickly, massively and get out."[16] For this reason, more than any other, Powell, like Weinberger, opposed the marine deployment to Lebanon. It took too much time, it did not have a clear objective, and it was losing public support.

Enter George H. W. Bush

When the national debate over the Vietnam War was at its height during the late 1960s and early 1970s, it was angry, volatile, and deeply divisive. It split the country into warring camps and buried the old adage about foreign policy differences dying at the water's edge, except among those politicians who lived by pre-Vietnam standards. Such a one was George H. W. Bush, son of Prescott Bush, a Wall Street banker who became a GOP senator from Connecticut, and grandson of Samuel Prescott Bush, a successful industrialist and entrepreneur from Ohio. The Bushes were wealthy, patrician, and patriotic. On Vietnam, as on other foreign policy matters, they supported the president, whether Republican or Democrat.

As a young man, George H. W. Bush moved his family to Texas in search of oil and big bucks. Though he often wore boots and tried speaking with a Texas twang, he never lost his New England roots or outlook, contributing, many thought, to his 1964 loss in a run for the Senate. More important, though, was Lyndon Johnson's landslide; it was not a good year for Republicans.

Bush could have hunkered down into bitter partisan warfare but instead played an active role in a Great Society project in his local county, knowing well that the Great Society was an LBJ signature program. "If that placed him on Lyndon Johnson's side," wrote a Bush biographer, "so did the war in Vietnam." Bush supported Johnson's war policy. "He had no doubt that the president was right on target. His own war experience . . . shaped his understanding of what it was all about."[17]

In 1966 Bush lowered his political sights, ran for a House seat, and won. Once in Washington, he dropped "any pretense to being a Texas conservative," aligning himself with "moderate, civic Republicans."[18]

As antiwar protesters around the country chanted, "Hey, hey, LBJ, how many kids did you kill today?" Bush decided to visit the battlefield in December 1967, taking advantage of the New Year's break in the legislative calendar. He wrote to a friend, who had expressed his opposition to the war on moral grounds:

"I think you are wrong on the immorality aspect of it all," Bush said. "I just don't buy that this is an immoral war on our part. If you want to argue that all war is immoral—fine; but this selectivity and this blind willingness to emphasize the weakness of the South Viet Nam government while totally overlooking the terror of the VC and the past slaughters by Ho and the boys I can't buy."

Bush also refused to criticize Johnson in a personal way. He remained, even in opposition, a proper New England gentleman: "Look, I don't go [for] LBJ, I vote against him all the time, but I'm not going to take that mean step which strips the man of any feeling and assigns to him unthinkable motives."[19] In 1970, when Richard Nixon, a Republican president, was pursuing his "triangular diplomacy" to back out of the war, Bush struck a continuing note of compassion for Johnson. "One of my real regrets about the Johnson presidency," he wrote, "was the personal abuse that was heaped on the President—the name calling. The direct allegations, usually chanted in epithet, that he wanted war or encouraged killing. How gross! How unfair. It is ironic that the steadfastness of Pres[ident] Johnson at certain critical times laid a groundwork for the Nixon plan which is winding down the war."[20]

With two terms in the House under his belt, Bush ran once again for the Senate in 1970. He was defeated by Democrat Lloyd Bentsen, who, interestingly, ended up as the vice presidential nominee on the 1988 Democratic ticket led by Massachusetts governor Michael Dukakis. But in 1988 it was Bush who won and Bentsen who lost.

After his unsuccessful run in 1970, Bush held a variety of high-level posts. He was U.S. ambassador to the United Nations and to China, chairman of the Republican National Committee, and director of the CIA. And, of course, for eight years, he was Reagan's vice president—all preparatory to his campaign for the presidency in 1988, which, while successful, was marked by especially nasty advertising. One of his gurus, Roger Ailes, responsible for many of the TV ads, said after the election, "If you didn't like '88, you're going to hate '92."[21] Ailes imagined another dirty campaign.

Bush's opponent in 1988 was Governor Dukakis, the son of Greek immigrants, frugal, hard-working, liberal, and well educated. He had served in a peacetime army from 1955 to 1957, and four times he was elected to the Massachusetts state legislature, where he was renowned for his intelligence and industriousness. In 1974 he ran for governor and won. In 1978 he lost but bounced back to win two more gubernatorial terms in 1982 and 1986. Dukakis, unlike Bush, did not support the Vietnam War, but he rarely spoke up in opposition to it.

During the campaign, Bush staffers, inspired by Ailes and Lee Atwater, saw many advantages in challenging Dukakis's patriotism, tying him to an African American murderer and labeling him a "liberal" and therefore unfit to be president. Bush was a gentleman while governing but a tiger during his campaign for the number-one job. He sanctioned the Ailes/Atwater approach to negative campaigning.

The Democrats, who, for a time, led in the race, emerged from their July convention in reasonably good shape, but their fortunes turned after the Republican convention a month later. A *Newsweek* magazine poll showed Bush beating Dukakis by 51 to 42, and the gap grew in the next few weeks. Surprising to many, the National Guard controversy surrounding Quayle did not end up hurting the Republican ticket. In fact, 74 percent of the American people said their opinion of Quayle had not been affected by his guard service.[22]

Quayle, ambitious, wealthy, deeply conservative, had been waiting for some time "for lightning to strike," as he put it in his autobiography. "There were plenty of strengths I could bring to a ticket headed by George Bush," he wrote with no trace of modesty.[23] When Bush called him with news of the vice presidential selection on August 16, Quayle could not contain his enthusiasm. Lightning had struck. He reacted, wrote Herbert Parmet, "like a school kid at a prep rally, almost jumping with glee."[24] When he actually met Bush later in the day, he seemed "unable to restrain himself, physically grabbing his benefactor."[25] "Nearly punching Bush in the stomach, Quayle cried, 'Let's go get 'em!'"[26] Usually cool, experienced political reporters watched the scene in astonishment. Quayle had been seen as a "lightweight," a "mediocrity." Why would Bush make such a selection?

In one of the top floors of the Marriott Hotel overlooking the convention center, Charlie Black, Senator John McCain, and Representative Henry Hyde were briefing reporters about the GOP platform. They had not yet been told about the Quayle selection. Reporter John Harwood burst into the room. "I'm sorry to interrupt, but everybody needs to know that Bush . . . is going to announce Quayle." Who? Quayle? You kidding? Most of the reporters did not wait for answers. They scampered from the room, the remaining few now peppering the briefers with questions about Quayle, not about the platform. Black thought Bush would have chosen Dole, someone with experience, someone who had been "around the track" once before.[27]

On August 17 Quayle attended a high-level meeting in Bush's hotel suite. "I remember Baker asking me, 'You served in the National Guard?' and my telling him yes. But the subject was just left hanging in the air," Quayle wrote. Apparently not one of Bush's key advisers anticipated the turmoil then stirring in newsrooms around the country. "There was no follow-up, no anticipation of questions that might arise from it . . . . my service in the Indiana National Guard was honorable. No strings were pulled on my behalf to get in."[28]

In fact, reporters soon learned that strings were pulled, and influence was exerted. What they found was that Wendell C. Phillippi, once a managing editor of one of the Quayle newspapers and a retired National Guard officer, had spoken with Quayle about guard service. Quayle apparently wanted to know whether it was likely that the Indiana National Guard was going to be called up for duty in Vietnam. Phillippi then spoke with a well-placed friend, Major General Alfred F. Ahner of the National Guard, asking that Quayle be accepted.[29] In this way, Vietnam was back in the headlines, thanks to the young senator just selected to be the vice presidential candidate.

But outside of Indiana and the Senate cloakroom, Quayle was a relative unknown. He was a young conservative politician from Huntington, Indiana, the son of James Quayle, publisher of the *Huntington Herald-Press*, and grandson of Eugene Pulliam, owner of a number of newspapers, including the *Indianapolis Star* and the *Arizona Republic*, who had enjoyed a meteoric career in politics despite a reputation for only modest accomplishment.

Like his father and grandfather, Quayle attended DePauw University in Greencastle, Indiana. As a freshman in 1965, he found DePauw to be a "sleepy place, where the handful of student radicals were never taken seriously." In

1968 he voted for Nixon, "partly because I thought he would end the Vietnam War sooner and more honorably than anyone else."[30] According to reporter Witcover, Quayle, like many Hoosiers, "wore his patriotism on his sleeve."[31]

He could have acted in conformity with his patriotism. There were many opportunities. He could have volunteered for the army, navy, or air force, he could have fought in Vietnam; but instead he joined the National Guard, like thousands of others who wanted a respectable way out of the fighting. In 1968, when Quayle entered his senior year of college, an especially brutal year in the war, the waiting list for service in the National Guard was exceptionally long. Pull was necessary to get on the list, and lots of pull to get to the top of the list, which was where Quayle found himself at the time of his college graduation. Quayle's service in the guard was undistinguished. Three months before his honorable discharge in 1975, he took a routine evaluation test and scored far below average. His score was 56, the average was 75.[32]

Quayle wanted to go to law school, more to acquire a pedigree for politics than to study or practice law. He applied to Indiana University, but because of his less-than-stellar college grades, he was not accepted at the main campus but did get into the night school in Indianapolis. It was during this nocturnal cruise through law school that he met his wife, Marilyn, a fellow student; they were married in 1972. After graduation in 1974, he set up a firm with his wife called Quayle and Quayle.

In 1976, at age twenty-nine, Quayle was recruited by the Indiana GOP establishment to run for a House seat then occupied by an eight-term Democratic incumbent named Ed Roush. Quayle ran as an outsider, someone unblemished by politics, and he won going away. Two years later, he was reelected. In 1980 he saw another opportunity. Referring to himself as a "Vietnam-era veteran," Quayle ran against Democratic senator Birch Bayh. Genuine Vietnam veterans objected to Quayle's self-designation, and he dropped the term.[33] It didn't matter. He upset the three-term incumbent anyway, obviously benefiting from Ronald Reagan's sweeping victory that year.

Four years after setting foot in the House, Quayle was already in the Senate, where he attracted attention by spouting a particularly hard line on national defense, on Vietnam, on fighting the spread of communism, and on critics of the president's policies in Central America. The critics were complaining that Reagan was "leading us down the same bloody, unwinnable, tragic road that we experienced in Southeast Asia nearly 20 years ago," Quayle said in 1983. "The real legacy of Vietnam," he argued on the Senate floor, was that "it has so paralyzed our thinking that rational debate is virtually impossible. Vietnam

has made us paranoid, it has terrorized us, it has blinded us to our own interests." He added, "We are afraid, half-hearted, unable to act in our self-interest
and the interests of our friends. Mostly because of Vietnam, we have all but
lost the ability to use the principal tools of policy formation—economic, political, diplomatic and military tools—with finesse and judiciousness as well as
with determination and purpose."[34]

Obviously, Quayle—who won a second Senate term in 1986—spoke with
passion about Vietnam's debilitating impact on the country, but he never
seemed to dig deeply into the real reasons. Reporters Bob Woodward and
David S. Broder, in a biography of Quayle, explained how Vietnam affected
his judgment and his policy: "Neither then [during the Vietnam War] nor
now does he seem to have reflected seriously about the dilemma that Vietnam posed for the nation and for millions of individual citizens—or the way
it shattered the previous generation's foreign policy consensus," they wrote.
"Asked what he thought Vietnam did to the country, Quayle said, 'It certainly
did weaken us [because] around the world we became perceived as impotent.' The lesson he drew from the period, he said, was: 'State your missions
clearly. State your objectives clearly. Make sure you can achieve them, and
then achieve them. I mean, it is not much more difficult than that.'"[35]

Quayle, during the buildup to the Persian Gulf War in January 1991, had
clearly been listening to Powell and just as clearly had absorbed his doctrine.
Or had he?

A week after unveiling Quayle as his vice presidential selection, George
Bush recognized that he had made a big mistake. Like Reagan, Bush was a
disciplined diarist, and, on August 21, 1988, he confided with embarrassment,
"It was my decision, and I blew it, but I'm not about to say that I blew it."[36] If
he was really looking for a bright, young, discreet, and loyal confidant, another
George H. W. Bush, with whom he could share ideas and insights about a
nation and a world in rapid change, he chose the wrong man. Quayle was
loyal, he bubbled with enthusiasm, he exuded a blind faith in traditional conservative values; but he was not especially bright, nor was he experienced in the
ways of the world. If he had been vice president during the height of the cold
war, useful as a ready spokesman for anticommunism, he might have been of
more use to Bush; but he was vice president when the cold war was crumbling
and a new Middle East war was brewing, and he had little to contribute to the
president's consideration of problems, except an instinctive antagonism for
all things Soviet and a pugnacious approach to most other problems. Bush
deserved better, but, as he himself said, "I blew it."

As vice president, Quayle was properly honored, but his responsibilities were kept limited. "Where could he do the least harm?" seemed to be the question. He was put in charge of the Council on Competitiveness, he was made the first chairman of the National Space Council, he attended the requisite number of funerals, he kept tabs on congressional doings, and he stood near the president at those public events requiring his presence, according to the rigid rules of White House protocol. But his capacity for mindless, embarrassing inarticulateness made headlines anyway.

A New World Order

It was then hardly surprising that Quayle was not the first person Bush consulted when a political revolution began to sweep through Eastern Europe in the late 1980s. Bush had Brent Scowcroft as national security adviser, James Baker as secretary of state, Dick Cheney as secretary of defense, Colin Powell as chairman of the Joint Chiefs of Staff, and Robert Gates as deputy director of central intelligence with whom to consult, and he had two other assets: first, invaluable experience in foreign affairs, and, second, a personal telephone directory filled with the names and numbers of foreign officials he had met and stayed in touch with over many years. In his hand, the telephone became a powerful instrument of diplomacy.

One number, often dialed, was Gorbachev's in the Kremlin. The relatively new Soviet leader faced historic challenges at home and abroad, and Bush wanted to be sympathetic, but only up to a point. The Red Army was in virtual rebellion toward the end of the Afghan War. The economy was near collapse. Allegiance to the Soviet Communist Party was almost nonexistent. The communist system was tottering. Desperately, Gorbachev launched two domestic programs designed, he hoped, to reform the state and restore communism to its former glory. One was called *perestroika*, his way of modernizing the creaking economy, and the other, *glasnost*, was intended to introduce a measure of personal freedom by loosening up rules on censorship and travel. What happened, though, was not the reform of the Soviet system, as Gorbachev had hoped, but rather the disintegration of the Soviet system. Communism as a governing philosophy was dying. The most heavily armed region in the world was suddenly without clear governmental authority.

Bush did not have to be told that he was coping with potential catastrophe. Questions arose about who would control the nuclear weapons, whether Gorbachev could survive, and whether a military coup was in the works. And an even larger strategic question hovered over all of the other questions: was this really the end of the cold war? And if it was, what would replace it? Would there be a new world order?

Gates, looking back at this time, wrote, "When you are confronting challenges that you know will alter the course of history, it can become downright scary. From 1989 to 1991, we shot the rapids of history, and without a life jacket."[37]

Several of Bush's closest advisers, including Quayle, Cheney, and Gates, were still very suspicious of Gorbachev and his new policies. The Soviet Union was a superpower, they noted, with roughly 12,000 nuclear warheads pointing at the United States and 390,000 troops in East Germany. According to Bill Kristol, who was Quayle's chief of staff before becoming a TV pundit and magazine editor, Quayle was "very concerned about an excessive drawdown in defense spending." He was not offering his own formula for success; but he did sit in on many of the meetings and, when asked, expressed his "very hawkish" views. Kristol admitted, "We weren't centrally involved."[38] Clearly, Quayle was not a key player.

Bush, Baker, Cheney, Powell, and Scowcroft were the key players, and in one meeting after another, they wanted to take advantage of Gorbachev's emergence as a Soviet leader willing to shake up the old system. Gates was an unofficial notetaker. He wrote that Bush and Scowcroft "consistently pushed for bolder initiatives," especially in nuclear arms negotiations, while Cheney and Powell, representing the always more cautious military chiefs, as well as Baker, already deep in negotiations with the Soviets, resisted these initiatives. It was logical, considering the importance of German reunification—a key issue at the time—and U.S.-Soviet arms control, that sharp differences arose within the Bush administration, principally between Cheney and Bush.

"If 'prudent' was supposedly one of his favorite words in public," Gates wrote of Bush's approach, "his vocabulary of choice in private, as he looked to Europe and the USSR, was 'boldness' and 'opportunity.'"[39] Cheney flashed a cautionary signal, especially on cutting U.S. troop levels in Europe. The defense chief argued that the Europeans did not want the United States to pull tens of thousands of American troops out of Europe. Bush, a bit testily, vented his impatience with Cheney's grip on the past. He had been talking regularly with Gorbachev, and he sensed a golden opportunity for positive change in the superpower relationship. He thought that if he yielded on one point, Gorbachev would yield on another. It was worth the risk. Bush turned to his defense secretary. "So, we are sitting with 270,000 troops? Offering no reaction to Soviet actions? The world is changing, and we're going to change with it," he said, his annoyance with Cheney hard to hide. "Why do we always need the same number of troops and bombs? Let's test the Soviets. Ask them to do something that they would never do. Otherwise, we'll have passed up an opportunity, we'll have to make unilateral cuts, and we'll get nothing for it. Let's not have slight, begrudging change, but respond boldly. We have an enormous opportunity to do something dramatically different. . . . I don't want to miss an opportunity."[40]

While Bush spoke with Gorbachev, Baker was visiting frequently with Eduard Shevardnadze, the Soviet foreign minister, who shared Gorbachev's vision of a less dangerous tomorrow. This remarkable quartet delicately walked back from the brink of cold war confrontation and inaugurated a new period of U.S.-Soviet relations based on mutual accommodation. Were it not for Bush's diplomatic skill and Gorbachev's wise willingness to adapt to real-ity, many of the changes would not have happened. What they accomplished was truly historic:

—The relatively peaceful disintegration of the Soviet state

—The formation of a new Russia

—The independence (more or less) of most of the former Soviet republics, with little or no violence

—The peaceful reunification of Germany and its absorption in NATO

—The end of the Warsaw Pact and the subsequent independence of its member states

No one could have imagined that these changes would take place, and so quickly, but they did. The cold war was cascading to a historic conclusion.

In its place, Bush dreamed of building a "new world order" filled with promise and hope, rooted in a cooperative partnership between the United States and Russia. He wanted a world order that was as much post-Vietnam as it was post–cold war.

Bush's dream was first tested in the Persian Gulf. In the summer of 1990, Saddam Hussein, the tyrannical, totally unpredictable president of Iraq, described by Gorbachev as "an adventurer . . . a person who did not have a sense of reality," ordered thousands of troops—eventually numbering more than 300,000—toward the border with Kuwait.[41] Was he positioning himself to invade a fellow Arab state? Unlikely, most Arab leaders believed. Still, Hosni Mubarak of Egypt rushed to Baghdad for reassurance. Saddam Hussein, he believed, could only be bluffing. Having finished his costly eight-year war with Iran the year before, Saddam was restlessly picking fights with neighboring

Kuwait, arguing about oil prices with the Organization of Petroleum Export-
ing Countries (OPEC), and seeking mischievous ways of extending his influence throughout the Persian Gulf. But irritating as Hussein could be, he was
not mad, not so irrationally impulsive as to invade another Arab country, or
so Mubarak chose to believe.

During the Iran-Iraq War, the United States had sided with Hussein's Iraq.
The Iranian hostage crisis was still a humiliating memory in America, and for
the hard-nosed realists in the White House, Iraq represented an attractive gasoline station, potentially a good place for American investment. On Reagan's
behalf, Donald Rumsfeld, then a roving ambassador to the Middle East, had
traveled to Baghdad for "friendly" talks with Hussein; so had a procession of
congressional delegations, all returning to Washington with essentially positive reports about Iraq and Hussein. Bush, too, once in the Oval Office, had
expressed a wish for improved relations with Iraq, even though he recognized
that Hussein was an untrustworthy character. When Powell and General Norman Schwarzkopf, commander of the Persian Gulf region, began to knock on
Bush's door with disturbing intelligence about Iraqi troop buildups near the
Kuwaiti border in mid-July, the president at first brushed aside these warnings. Scowcroft shared the president's head-in-the-sand attitude, nonchalantly
opining to Bush that Hussein was engaging in nothing more than "a policy
of bluster" toward Kuwait.[42] Hussein had often threatened to absorb Kuwait
into Iraq; now, perhaps, the officials thought, he was upping the ante, moving
beyond threats to sending troops to the Kuwaiti border in an effort to increase
pressure on the ruling family to hand over an oil field, or an island, or a port.

On July 26 Hussein unexpectedly summoned U.S. ambassador April
Glaspie to his office. Hussein repeated that he had no intention of invading Kuwait, and Glaspie repeated the standard American refrain. "We have
no opinion on the Arab/Arab conflicts, like your border disagreement with
Kuwait," she said.[43] Though she had no intention of signaling American indifference, far from it, Hussein might well have read it as a yellow light from the
United States to pursue his objectives in Kuwait. For the next few days, he
ordered more troops to the border. Tanks were on the move. Logistics units
were sprouting up. Powell called Schwarzkopf. "Norm, are you looking at
what I'm looking at?" he asked. "Yes," replied Schwarzkopf.[44] Both generals understood immediately that Hussein was putting Iraq in a position to
invade Kuwait and perhaps Saudi Arabia, while using Glaspie, military feints,
and disinformation to confuse his enemies. By the time Hussein sent his formidable army into Kuwait on August 2, opening an Arab/Arab war sure to

affect oil prices and deliveries to the industrialized world, it was "too late," Powell realized, to head off "a major, major crisis with profound implications."[45] The United States had profoundly underestimated the danger posed by the Iraqi leader.

On August 2, after learning of the invasion, Bush convened his senior advisers for a meeting that Schwarzkopf described as "disorganized" and Powell saw as "quite a garble."[46] There was, Scowcroft felt, "no sense of outrage," no sense that the world had just turned a corner, "just a resigned approach to a fait accompli."[47] The questions—how would the invasion affect oil deliveries, world financial markets, Arab sensibilities, the shaky balance between Israel and its neighbors—were predictable and lacked urgency. If any decision was reached at the meeting, it was the obvious one: that the United States should go to the United Nations and condemn Hussein, which happened that day in the form of the first of twelve resolutions. None was to have any effect on Hussein.

After the meeting, the president paused before cameras and microphones. A reporter asked whether he was thinking about sending troops to the Middle East. Not wishing to go down that road, at least not then, Bush answered, "I'm not contemplating any such action, and I again would not discuss it if I were," a response that prompted speculation that he was looking toward diplomacy, not military action, as his way of handling the Kuwaiti crisis.[48] The president then flew to Aspen for a speech on the restructuring of the U.S. military and a meeting with British prime minister Margaret Thatcher, who reportedly prodded Bush not to "go wobbly." Actually, Bush was neither wobbly nor decisive. The invasion was not yet a day old, and his sense of Hussein's ultimate intentions not yet clear. Was the Iraqi leader reaching for all of Kuwait in order to settle for half or a third of it? Or was he gambling on much more, such as control of the Saudi oil fields and a chokehold on the industrial West?

Cutting through the policy fuzz, Scowcroft told the next National Security Council (NSC) meeting on August 3 that the Iraqi invasion of Kuwait had brought the United States to a fork in the road: the United States could recognize that the invasion affected the country's "vital national interests," demanding a clear, firm, and direct American response, or the U.S. government could see it as just another Middle East problem that could be managed through diplomacy and UN intervention. Scowcroft came down on the side of swift and resolute American action. Deputy Secretary of State Larry Eagleburger pounded the table. "Absolutely right," he said. Then, from around the table, came the crucial diplomatic and military questions for the United States to consider in this very early phase of the crisis, posed less for their rhetorical flourish than for their practical effect on policy and action.

One important question was whether Hussein would stop at the Kuwait border, or whether he would continue into Saudi Arabia and the oil fields.[49] Saudi Arabia was the key, protecting its oil fields an absolute necessity. Bush invited his national security team to join him at Camp David the following day to discuss military options.

But first Cheney and Scowcroft called the Saudi ambassador, Prince Bandar, for urgent consultations. They wanted Saudi permission to fly a large number of American troops into Saudi Arabia. Cheney shared American intelligence on Iraqi troop movements and stressed that the United States was "ready to help you defend yourself from Saddam." Bandar was doubtful. "Like Jimmy Carter did?" he asked.

The Saudi ambassador was referring to a recent embarrassing episode in U.S.-Saudi relations. When Ayatollah Khomeini overthrew the shah of Iran in 1979, Saudi Arabia asked for quick U.S. military assistance. Carter sent ten F-15 jet fighters but then announced they were unarmed. The Saudis felt publicly humiliated.

Cheney, aware of this contretemps, played his big card. He proposed that the United States send 100,000 troops to Saudi Arabia "for starters."

"I see," Bandar said. "You are serious."

Cheney suggested that Bandar check immediately with the king, who, still uncertain about the United States, hedged his bets. He wanted to hear first from a Saudi delegation scheduled to visit Washington.[50]

Bandar also met with Scowcroft at the White House. Scowcroft stressed U.S. seriousness about Cheney's troop proposal. Bandar said that the king felt that the United States was not a reliable ally. "Frankly," Bandar explained, "we're afraid, you say you'll help, and then the going'll get tough, and you'll pull out and we'll be left." Bandar repeated his Jimmy Carter story, putting it in the broader context of America's defeat in Vietnam. Scowcroft replied, "That will not happen. We're serious, we're deadly serious, and we . . . want to know if you are."[51]

For Colin Powell, this was the moment of reckoning. The United States seemed on the edge of war in the Middle East, and his mind shot back to Vietnam. "If you are going to put us into something," he believed, "then you owe the armed forces, you owe the American people, you owe just your desire to succeed, a clear statement of what political objective you're trying to achieve and then you put the force to that objective, and you know when you've accomplished it, you take the initiative out of the hands of your enemy." State your political objective, apply the necessary force, win, have an exit strategy, and then get out. But at the meetings of August 2 and 3, when Powell, as chair of the Joint Chiefs of Staff, raised the question of a clear political objective, he was chastised. Indeed, he was told by Cheney, "Look, you just do military options. Don't be the Secretary of State, or the Secretary of Defense or the National Security Adviser . . . you just do military options."[52]

Powell, though, remembered Vietnam, where he had served, and he remembered Beirut, where Weinberger had opposed American intervention. "It [was] a horrible war . . . and we stick our troops in the middle of it without thinking through what it is they're trying to accomplish," Powell recalled.

> An "interpositional force" was the very lovely term that was invented for it. But suddenly, someone started killing those Marines and then the Marines fired back and then political officials said, "Let's shoot battleship shells at them." This wasn't military judgment, this was a political judgment, and guess what, we made people very, very mad. . . . These Marines at the airport, [they] were essentially relatively defenseless with no particular mission, and I carry that to its logical conclusion: it resulted in the death of 240 Marines. . . . And so this is also weighing on my mind.[53]

Powell was, as he later described himself, "the ghost of Vietnam"[54] in the garb, and with the stars, of an army general. And he was the father of a "doctrine." One day, he said, "when R. Jeffrey Smith from the *Washington Post* came to me to ask about a 'Powell Doctrine,' I didn't know what he was talking about. It wasn't in any Army manual. So Jeffrey wrote this article about the Powell Doctrine. I once wrote an op-ed piece [saying] that I am not a wimp, I just want to know what we are going for." He continued: "If we are going to send our kids into harm's way, let's know why. . . . My doctrine comes from classical military theory . . . going back to Sun Tzu."[55]

This time, unlike in Vietnam, Powell wanted to be sure that if the United States was going to war, it would have a clear political objective, it would apply overwhelming military power, it would win, and it would leave. "It was my responsibility," he stressed, "not only to provide for military options [as Cheney had demanded] but to help them [the president and the secretary of defense] shape clear political objectives for the military to help achieve. Now I'm not usurping their authority and I'm not, in my judgment anyway, going beyond my own authority. I think I'm doing my job as the principal military adviser to the President of the United States. There had been cases in our past, particularly in the Vietnam period, when senior leaders, military leaders, did not force civilians to make those kind of clear choices, and if it caused me to be the skunk at the picnic," so be it, he seemed to be saying.[56] He was determined to ask, time and again, what was the political objective? What did we really want to achieve?

When Bush's advisers reconvened at Camp David on August 4, his political advisers sat on one side of the table, his military advisers on the other, and the meeting very quickly got down to the defense of Saudi Arabia. Kuwait was already in Hussein's hands, a puppet regime installed, and a reign of terror begun. As Powell recalled:

> There were several crosscurrents going on in the meeting. One crosscurrent was "Can we get the Saudis to accept the forces that we want to send?" Keeping in mind that this general, who sometimes is accused of not having military options, sat with Prince Bandar at three o'clock the Friday—the 2nd—in Dick Cheney's office, and laid out to Prince Bandar a deployment of US forces that would initially go up to one hundred thousand and my dear friend Prince Bandar said, "Whew, you guys aren't kidding." Now this is thirty-six hours after the invasion, so the suggestion that we didn't have military options, we weren't providing military options, I think falls a little flat when we presented to Bandar our military option involving one hundred thousand US troops going to the Kingdom, immediately, and this was less than thirty-six hours after the invasion.[57]

Bush made no decision at the August 4 meeting. He had first to learn whether Saudi Arabia would accept American troops and then whether Gorbachev would agree to sponsor a joint Soviet-American statement condemning Iraq and demanding its immediate withdrawal from Kuwait.

After the meeting, Cheney, Schwarzkopf, and other senior Pentagon officials flew to Riyadh to request the king's permission. By adding Cheney, his secretary of defense, to the delegation, Bush hoped to convey his seriousness. Shortly after their arrival, Schwarzkopf, using charts, graphs, and slides, laid out American strategy for the king. Earlier, on the plane, he had told Cheney that, in his judgment, the king would not make a decision right away. Cheney followed Schwarzkopf with his own presentation. He made three points: first, that the United States was prepared to defend the kingdom; second, that the United States would stay as long as necessary; and third, that when it was time to leave, the United States would take all of its forces out. There would be no residual American force left in Saudi Arabia. The king also examined U.S. photos of the massing of Iraqi tanks on the Saudi border, some seeming to cross the border. He engaged in a short, heated discussion with his senior advisers and then turned back to the Americans and said, "OK." Schwarzkopf "almost fell out of my chair" in amazement.

Cheney, double-checking, asked, "So, you agree?"

The king replied, "Yes, I agree."

The following morning, the Saudi defense minister asked, "When do you expect the first planes to arrive?"

The U.S. response was, "Within 12 hours, they'll be here."

"Within 12 hours?"

"Yeah, they're . . . on their way, as we speak."

Deliberately unspoken during this crucial exchange was Schwarzkopf's fear that if, at that time, Saddam Hussein were to cut across the Saudi border and occupy not only the oil fields but also Bahrain, Qatar, and the United Arab Emirates, he could do so without any meaningful military opposition. The Saudi army could not stop the Iraqi army, and even at top speed the United States needed three full months to build up its forces to defend Saudi Arabia.[58] In other words, Hussein had three months to strike with relative impunity, but he missed his chance.

Saudi agreement now in Bush's bank, the next urgent problem was the Soviet Union, a superpower in sharp decline yet critically important to Bush's plans for a post–cold war "new world order." The Soviet Union, for a long time, had been Hussein's patron saint and supporter, not only in UN diplomacy but also in weapons procurement and supply. Iraq had been Moscow's anchor in the Middle East. Therefore it would not have been surprising if Saddam Hussein still counted on a measure of Soviet sympathy and support, notwithstanding Gorbachev's negotiations with Bush about a new era in Soviet-American relations. In fact, only a year or two before, he might well have expected full Soviet support. On August 3, though, less than forty-eight hours after his invasion of Kuwait, he must have been stunned by an announcement from Moscow that the Soviet Union and the United States had agreed on an unprecedented joint declaration condemning his aggression and demanding an immediate Iraqi withdrawal from Kuwait. If Saddam Hussein needed proof that the world was changing, that, as Shevardnadze said, "this aggression [was] inconsistent with the principles of new political thinking and, in fact, with the civilized relations between nations," he got it in spades.[59]

The joint declaration was the concluding piece of an extraordinary visit to the former Soviet Union by Secretary Baker. He had left Washington on July 25 with no expectation of major developments in the world. Certainly, at that time, no one in the Bush administration was expecting a war in the Middle East. Trouble? Yes. Another buildup in Iraq? Yes. But not an invasion of another Arab country. Baker had his mind on problems in Asia and on another opportunity to deepen his friendship with the Soviet foreign minister during a rendezvous in Irkutsk, a city of half a million on the shores of Lake Baikal in Siberia. Months before, Baker had invited Shevardnadze to the American West, hoping that he would appreciate its relaxed and rugged beauty. In return, Shevardnadze had invited Baker to Siberia. When Baker arrived in Irkutsk in the predawn hours of August 1, he was greeted by the disturbing news from Iraq. Leaders in the Middle East had assured him that Saddam Hussein was a troublesome lout, but one "maneuvering for diplomatic advantage, not preparing for war."[60] Yet the latest American intelligence showed several infantry divisions leaving their bases in southern Iraq and heading for the Kuwaiti border.

After a full day of fishing and cruising on Lake Baikal, interspersed with conversations about the "new world order," Baker checked with the State Department. The Iraqi situation appeared to be worsening: more troops, more tanks, more war planes, all crowding the Kuwaiti border, some spilling across the line. Baker was told that the president was considering a call to Hussein to urge restraint. But by early morning, August 2, Iraqi forces had smashed into Kuwait.

When Baker met an hour later with Shevardnadze, he asked for Soviet assistance in restraining Hussein, not knowing at the moment what the foreign minister would say or do. He also asked Shevardnadze about reports that the Soviet Union was on the edge of another major arms sale to Iraq. Shevardnadze, obviously in the dark, shrugged off the very idea that Hussein would launch a cross-border attack into Kuwait. That would be crazy, totally irrational, he said. "Don't worry," he assured the secretary, foolishly. "Nothing's going to happen."[61]

As Baker and Shevardnadze were preparing for a news conference, Baker received more detailed intelligence: Iraq had indeed crossed the border. "I don't know if it's a partial grab," he said. "I don't know if they're going for the entire country, or if they plan to go beyond Kuwait." Baker's host was stunned. "This is just totally irrational," he exclaimed. "I know he's a thug, but I never thought he was irrational. It would be more like him to go in and then withdraw."[62] Baker, clearly seeking to take advantage of Shevardnadze's fury, urged him to stop arming Iraq and instead join the United States in condemning Iraq. Shevardnadze knew he could not on his own make a decision of such consequence. He told Baker that he would have to talk with Gorbachev, which meant, as a practical matter, that Shevardnadze would fly to Moscow and Baker would leave Irkutsk for a brief scheduled stop in Mongolia before returning to Washington. A stop in Moscow was not on Baker's itinerary.

However, hopping a ride to Moscow on Shevardnadze's plane were two of Baker's closest aides, Dennis Ross and Robert Zoellick. They went directly to the U.S. embassy, where Peter Hauslohner, an assistant to Ross, was eager to enlist their support for his idea of a joint U.S.-Soviet declaration condemning the Iraqi invasion. Zoellick pointed out that Baker needed to be in Moscow. Zoellick and Ross decided to stay in Moscow, discuss the possibility of a joint statement with their Soviet counterparts, and judge the prospects of success. If their talks held the promise of success, they would urge Baker to change his travel plans and fly directly to Moscow. They met with Shevardnadze's assistants, who indicated in a very positive way that the foreign minister would be willing to meet Baker at a Moscow airport to discuss a joint statement. However, they did not promise that he would agree to one.

At the White House, Bush did what he did best: he worked the phones, talking with a variety of world leaders, including Mubarak and King Hussein of Jordan. When he learned that Shevardnadze was willing to discuss a joint statement, he thought it made good sense for Baker to rearrange his schedule and fly to Moscow. A joint U.S. Soviet statement would be of considerable importance: it would confirm a new relationship between the superpowers and encourage the Arabs to stand as one in opposition to Saddam Hussein. Baker realized that his stop in Moscow was problematic. If he left without a joint statement, it would send the wrong signal to Iraq and other troublemakers. But he also realized that if he did not make the effort, there would be no joint statement.

While Baker was flying to Moscow, Ross met with Sergei Tarasenko at the Foreign Ministry. Tarasenko was one of Shevardnadze's principal deputies. Ross thought they would both check on the latest Soviet intelligence from Iraq, but Tarasenko had nothing better to offer than CNN, an American cable news network. Apparently the Soviets knew nothing more than the Americans, and both superpowers were embarrassingly dependent for late information upon CNN. Ross pressed Tarasenko to allow him to work on a draft for a joint statement so that when Baker arrived, Ross would be able to hand it to him. "It's time to demonstrate that we can be partners," Ross said with a sense of urgency. "We've talked about an evolution from competitors to cooperation. Now we have to talk about partnership. If we've really entered a new era, nothing is going to demonstrate it more than our being together, and nothing is going to demonstrate more clearly that we haven't entered a new era if we can't be together."[63] Tarasenko agreed and called Shevardnadze, who said, understandably, that he would have to talk to Gorbachev.

Ross left for Spaso House, the U.S. ambassador's residence, and drafted a tough, 135-word joint statement. It described the invasion as "brutal and illegal."[64] It called for an immediate arms embargo and added in blunt terms: "Governments that engage in blatant aggression must know that the international community cannot and will not acquiesce in nor facilitate that aggression." A few hours later, when Tarasenko appeared at Spaso House with a counterdraft, it was clear there was trouble. He proposed softer language and dropped the call for an arms embargo. Ross exploded: "Sergei, this is not a counterdraft. This is a counterrevolution! It's absolutely unacceptable. This becomes an argument not to do a statement at all. If this is all you can do, I'm going to call Baker and recommend that he not come."

"Relax," Tarasenko suggested. "Write it the way you want it, and we'll keep working."[65] Ross's brinksmanship seemed to be working. He resurrected the original draft. Tarasenko urged that one sentence be eliminated, about the United Nations being prepared to "consider further actions." Ross accepted the change. Tarasenko returned to the foreign ministry, apparently for further talks with Arabists concerned about the Soviet position in the Middle East. Four hours passed with no word from Tarasenko. Ross again lost heart. Finally, Tarasenko called and said the Arabists had agreed to the draft—except, he added sheepishly, the call for an arms embargo had to be dropped. Ross objected strenuously. Without the arms embargo, Ross cried, "there's no meat to the statement, no action."[66]

When Baker arrived in Moscow, Shevardnadze was already there, waiting in a holding room in the terminal building. His presence indicated that the Soviets were ready for a deal. Ross and Zoellick intercepted the secretary before he even got off his plane. They briefed him about the "arms embargo" hang-up, Ross expressing his disappointment. Baker struck a note of both resignation and determination. "Well, we're here," he said. "It doesn't do any good to worry. We have got to go through with it."[67]

The Baker-Shevardnadze talks lasted ninety minutes, the two ministers seated side by side in a corner of the room. Shevardnadze said that Gorbachev

had sent a letter to Saddam Hussein demanding an immediate Iraqi withdrawal from Kuwait but had received no reply. From a Soviet perspective, Shevardnadze continued, a joint statement made sense, except for two concerns:
one, the presence of 8,000 Soviet citizens in Iraq and another 900 in Kuwait,
and, two, the disturbing impact such a statement might have on other Soviet
client states in the Middle East. But, he added, Moscow was determined to
proceed. The Iraqi invasion of Kuwait "is just simply not civilized behavior,
and we can't remain aloof from this, even if they have been our friends."[68]
Baker responded that he had come to Moscow to demonstrate that "we can
and will act as partners in facing new challenges to international security." The
United States had 4,000 of its citizens living in Iraq and Kuwait, but "we [can]
not be deterred. . . . [W]ith a dictator like Saddam, the appetite comes with the
eating; we should not embolden him by backing off from an appropriate statement."[69] It had to have teeth. It had to have an arms embargo. Shevardnadze
was not yet ready to fold. "Well, what of the French?" he asked.[70] Would they
agree to an arms embargo? Baker said he would talk to them. He expressed
confidence that they would, ultimately.

It was a tricky moment. Shevardnadze was on the edge of agreement, but
he was still holding back, hoping perhaps that at the last minute Baker would
drop his insistence on the need for an arms embargo. Then Shevardnadze
proclaimed, "*Harosho,*" or "OK." "I can see it's important to you . . . I believe
this is an impressive statement." The call for an arms embargo remained in the
statement. Later Baker learned that Shevardnadze had acted on his own; he
did not have Gorbachev's approval to include the arms embargo clause in the
joint statement. "Eduard was a courageous man," Baker wrote in his memoir.
"He just did it on his own because he thought it right."[71]

Shevardnadze had one other concern, which he shared with Baker. Did the
United States intend to strike Baghdad? No, Baker assured him with less than
honorable candor. But he added: "If they do anything to our citizens, all bets
are off."[72]

As this momentous Moscow negotiation drew to a close, Baker recalled how
far the two superpowers had come in recent years. "This whole crisis would
have been put in the context of an East-West competition and confrontation,"
he said. "Then this would have been far more dangerous. That's a measure of
what we've accomplished." Shevardnadze nodded in agreement. "It's important to make this thing work," he added matter-of-factly. The two ministers
then held a news conference announcing a joint condemnation of "this blatant transgression of basic norms of civilized conduct."[73] Scowcroft praised the

Moscow agreement. "It dramatically put the two superpowers on the same side of a major crisis for the first time since the Cold War began," he said.[74]

Ten years earlier, the two superpowers had been locked in a fierce cold war competition. Now Baker, with Bush's blessing, was recognizing and dealing with a new Soviet morality and reality. On the plane ride back to Washington, Hauslohner complimented Baker. "Mr. Secretary," he said, triumphantly, "this is a dramatic day. It's the end of the Cold War."[75] There was some understandable hype in the diplomat's compliment. There were other dramatic days before the Soviet Union, in December 1991, formally dissolved and a new Russian Federation was proclaimed. Then, truly, the cold war ended.

Going to War in the Persian Gulf

Now, with both the Saudi agreement and the joint statement in hand, Bush and his team spent the autumn months of 1990 organizing the anti-Iraq international coalition, based at the time on a UN-supported program of sanctions. Along the way, Bush got private advice from the Egyptians and the Saudis that a single targeted air strike at Iraq might oblige Saddam Hussein to change his plans and pull out of Kuwait. Powell, supported by the Joint Chiefs, forcefully urged the president not to get sucked into half-measures. "We should not jump into a war that we were not prepared to prosecute to its conclusion," Powell said, mindful of the Vietnam experience.[76] He kept insisting on a clear, careful mission statement, and he promised that the U.S. military, knowing what it was being asked to accomplish, would do the job. Bush listened to Powell, nodding occasionally, but offered few insights into his thinking.

In late September, Powell joined Cheney, Scowcroft, and White House chief of staff John Sununu in the Oval Office. The president wanted to discuss the efficacy of the sanctions program. Would it do the job? How long would it take? Powell provided the military backdrop. He told Bush and the others how many troops, planes, tanks, and warships had already arrived in or near Saudi Arabia and how many were on the way. He laid out plans for defending Saudi Arabia and sketched out his ideas for evicting Iraqi forces from Kuwait, should the president make that determination. Implied throughout his presentation, not for the first time, was his plea for a clear mission and a clear endgame strategy. The president picked up his message. "It's good to consider all options," the president said, "but I just don't think we're going to have time for sanctions to work." Bush was thinking not only about the fragility of the coalition but also about the patience of the American people. He did not specify how much more time he was prepared to wait. "You don't know how long it takes sanctions to work," Powell echoed. One of his persistent worries about a sanctions-based strategy of waiting was that "you're not seizing the initiative from your enemy."[77]

Powell acknowledged that he was often described as a "reluctant warrior," a general who deep down hated war. "I'm guilty," he conceded. "If you can solve a crisis of this nature without a war, you certainly should try to do that. . . . But what I discovered as the months went by was that it wasn't going to work without a war." And to that end, he said he was "doing everything I could to put in place, with Schwarzkopf, a powerful, powerful force that would win decisively if that's what the president wished for."[78]

One crucial meeting came on October 30, 1990, when the president assembled his senior advisers in the Situation Room at the White House to hear Powell's latest assessment. The general had just returned from another of his frequent visits to Saudi Arabia. Scowcroft began. "Mr. President," he said, "we are at a Y in the road. Down one branch we can continue sanctions, which was the policy, and we can just be prepared to defend Saudi Arabia. Down the other branch we start to get the necessary political authority to go on the attack." Among Cheney, Baker, and Scowcroft, the conversation quickly revolved around the advisability of getting a UN resolution demanding an Iraqi pullout by a certain date. Bush, thinking first things first, wanted to talk about military planning. "Colin," he insisted, "let's hear from you."[79]

Powell had two large maps. He unrolled the first. "This is General Schwarzkopf's plan to defend Saudi Arabia," he began, "the mission he has been assigned." Powell never departed from his "mission" script. "My political masters," as he put it playfully, were responsible for giving the military a clear mission with an order to win. "Here's how [Schwarzkopf] would accept an Iraqi invasion in the empty desert . . . here's how he would cut it off, here's how we would do that."

Then Powell unrolled the second map. "Mr. President," he continued, "if you direct us to attack in order to eject the Iraqi army out of Kuwait, this is how we're going to do it." The room seemed suddenly quiet. Everyone leaned forward. In graphic detail, Powell spoke about "secondary attacks," the "air campaign," "the deep hook around the left side of the Iraqi forces," and then he told the president that "it would take a much larger force."[80]

"How much more?" asked Scowcroft.

"Nearly double," Powell replied. "About another 200,000 troops."[81] That the chair of the Joint Chiefs of Staff was proposing an American force of what would come to a half million for a war in the deserts of the Middle East was unprecedented and to a degree startling, and everyone in the room realized they were suddenly in a new game.

Powell also wanted "five or six carrier task forces," an exceptional show of naval power.[82] Bush had made up his mind that if war was on the near horizon, and it was, whatever Powell wanted, Powell got. "I did not want to repeat the problems of the Vietnam War," Bush later wrote, "where the political leadership meddled with military operations. I would avoid micromanaging the military."[83]

At the meeting, as Powell recalled, Bush asked, "Colin, you and Norm are really sure that air power alone can't do it?"

"Mr. President," Powell responded, "I wish to God that I could assure you that air power alone could do it, but you can't take that chance. We've gotta take the initiative out of the enemy's hands if we're going to go to war. We've got to make sure . . . there'll be no guessing."[84]

Powell, throughout this decisionmaking process, was always mindful of the painful lessons of the Vietnam War. As he later explained when asked to describe the policy of overwhelming force,

> If this is important enough to go to war for, we're going to do it in a way that there's no question what the outcome will be and we're going to do it by putting the force necessary to take the initiative away from your enemy and impose your will upon him. If you're not serious enough to do that, then you ought to think twice about going to war. It's the equivalent of being the biggest bully on the block. "I've got my knife, I've got my gun, I've got my stickball bat: are you sure you want to challenge me?"[85]

Bush pondered a range of opinions from his advisers. They all added up to one conclusion: sanctions would not work, not in an acceptable time frame, and the United States would have to go to war. Bush raised his head and pronounced, "Do it." For Powell, that was a "firm decision, no question about it."[86] The United States was going to war in roughly three months.

On November 8, several days after the midterm elections, Bush announced his decision to almost double the size of the American expeditionary force to the Middle East, adding more than 150,000 new troops to those already there and bringing the total to around 380,000.[87] It struck many as proof that Bush had made up his mind to fight, not to negotiate his way out of the crisis. Congress erupted in angry opposition. No one had been told, not even the

Republican leadership, all of whom were now publicly embarrassed by the dramatic escalation of the buildup. Many Democrats wondered why the president was not seeking his own Tonkin Gulf resolution, why he was not consulting with Congress. Hadn't he learned anything from the Vietnam disaster? Democratic senator Daniel Patrick Moynihan of New York struck a nerve when he suggested to Bush that the Kuwaitis, especially their leaders "who have taken over [the] Sheraton Hotel in Taif and they're sitting there in their white robes and drinking coffee and urging us on to war," were hardly worthy of American defense. "He never thought what Iraq had done to Kuwait was worth fighting for," Bush said in bitter disappointment.[88]

Baker, who was traveling around the world to come up with support for a UN resolution demanding an Iraqi withdrawal from Kuwait, was as furious as any congressional Democrat with the president's announcement: more so, in fact. He was about to confer in Moscow with Gorbachev and Shevardnadze about the advantages of a UN resolution when it now seemed perfectly clear that the United States was heading to war; the UN resolution would be seen as nothing more than a diplomatic fig leaf. In a snit, Baker telephoned Bush and strongly suggested that he embrace the congressional leadership on both sides of the aisle and explain his Iraq policy, which suddenly seemed to be going off the rails.[89]

In his diary on November 10, Bush acknowledged that "our system of consultation" needed work, and Congress had to be notified: "We've got to prepare the Congress for any action that I might have to take and the more phone calls we make under the heading of consultation, the better it is."[90] Consultation, though, was still not the same as concurrence. In 1964 Lyndon Johnson not only consulted with Congress but requested passage of the Tonkin Gulf resolution, which he used as congressional authority to go to war in Vietnam. Johnson had criticized both Eisenhower and Kennedy for beginning the military buildup in Vietnam without congressional authorization. Bush was making the same mistake. Scowcroft later wrote that a "lingering fear" still existed in Congress of a "drawn-out foreign military entanglement—remnants of the 'Vietnam syndrome.'"[91] And to address it, the Bush administration belatedly realized that it needed congressional authorization: a resolution backed by both houses of Congress.

Bush also realized that he needed a UN resolution, and that was his secretary of state's job, which Baker assumed and performed with skill and a dogged determination, traveling from one capital to another on what seemed a non-stop cavalcade, consulting, cajoling, pleading, bargaining, pushing, dealing, and, when necessary, striking a compromise in language without abandoning the ultimate purpose of a UN resolution.

On November 29, as his month-long chairmanship of the UN Security Council was rushing to a close, Baker, knowing he finally had corralled the necessary votes for a resolution, gaveled the meeting to order, the 2,963rd in its history and, in his judgment, "arguably the most important." He opened the meeting in dramatic fashion, reading a long quotation about "systematic" and "barbarous" aggression against innocent people, including the use of "terrible poison and harmful gases." One thought immediately about Kuwait, but Baker was actually quoting Haile Selassie, leader of Ethiopia, who had appeared before the League of Nations in 1936 to appeal for international assistance against foreign aggression. The league failed to act, and war followed. Now, Baker continued, "We must not let the United Nations go the way of the League of Nations." Baker posed the challenge: "If Iraq does not reverse its course peacefully, then other necessary measures—including the use of force—should be authorized." A deadline was imposed. If Saddam Hussein did not withdraw from Kuwait "unconditionally" by midnight, January 15, 1991, member states, operating under a UN mandate, would then have the right to "use all necessary means . . . to restore international peace and security in the area." The final vote was 12 (including the United States and the Soviet Union) in favor, 2 opposed (Cuba and Yemen), and 1 (China) abstaining.[92]

Even though the United Nations produced a diplomatic victory for the United States, it was not yet clear that Congress would back the war option. Vietnam loomed large in the "raging" debate. Memories of the long, lost, wasteful war dominated arguments advanced, ironically, by both the "isolationistic right" and the "Kingman Brewster left," as Bush noted on November 28.[93] Bush did not think he was asking for too much. He wanted Congress to support the UN resolution. He thought he was being reasonable. But memories of Vietnam frightened Congress and many Americans into believing that the United States would be drawn into another unwinnable war. Gorbachev shared these concerns. He told the president, "In my heart, as yours I am sure, the preference is to solve this without blood. It can all turn out very, very badly, worse than Vietnam."[94] Why worse? Because Iraq was in the middle of an oil field and Vietnam was in a corner of Southeast Asia.

Bush, in a series of meetings with congressional leaders, explained his strategy and his vision. He sincerely believed that if Iraq could seize Kuwait with impunity, then all of his hopes for a new world order would come crashing down, and a kind of global chaos would envelop the world.

As a way of winning support on Capitol Hill and in the Kremlin, of showing a willingness to "go the extra mile for peace," Bush considered a variety of high-level talks between American and Iraqi officials. One idea was for the Iraqi foreign minister, Tariq Aziz, to visit Washington and talk to the president. Another idea was for Bush to send a personal emissary to Baghdad, such as Baker, to meet with Hussein. And, finally, as a last resort, for Bush and Hussein to meet, but this idea was quickly squashed. Too complicated to set up—in any case, too late in the crisis for a summit.

Finally, on November 30, the day after the UN vote, Bush publicly proposed that Tariq Aziz come to Washington in the week of December 10 to meet with him, and that Baker go to Baghdad between December 15 and January 15, the day of the UN deadline, and meet with Hussein. The announcement was greeted with scorn and disappointment abroad—again, there had been no advance consultation—but relief and satisfaction at home. At least, the president was trying to avoid war.

In early December, Hussein played two cards. He said that he liked the idea of high-level talks, though the dates would have to be changed; and he released thousands of Soviet and American citizens who had been held in Baghdad against their will. Hussein was obviously playing to the galleries, but so, too, was Bush. Both leaders proposed different dates, but there was no agreement on any. Weeks passed. Iraq strengthened its position in Kuwait, and the United States continued its massive buildup in Saudi Arabia and the Persian Gulf.

In a year-end letter to his children, dated December 31, 1990, Bush wrote that there were "a scant 16 days" before the UN deadline expired. Maybe Hussein would still pull out of Kuwait, but Bush had his doubts. He asked rhetorically, "How many lives are you [Bush] willing to sacrifice?" None, "none at all," he answered. "The question of loss of life still lingers and plagues the heart." Bush focused on historical analogy. "If appeasement had given way to force" before World War II, he wondered, how many Jews would have been "spared the gas chambers"? How many Polish patriots would have been saved? He again made the case for international action against aggression—in his mind, there was really no choice. "So, dear kids, batten down the hatches." He then related what Democratic senator Daniel Inouye of Hawaii had told him: "Mr. President, do what you have to do. If it is quick and successful, everyone can take the credit. If it is drawn out, then be prepared for some in Congress to file impeachment papers against you." Bush agreed with Inouye. "He's 100% correct," Bush wrote, adding, "I shall do what must be done."[95]

On January 3, 1991, Bush proposed a Geneva meeting between Baker and Tariq Aziz on January 7, 8, or 9. The next day, Hussein accepted the proposal and suggested January 9. Done.

Word came from Arab capitals that Hussein did not believe the United States would, in the final analysis, use military force to evict Iraq from Kuwait. It was said that Hussein was interested in how the United States had lost in Vietnam. "Iraq's leader thought Vietnam had so traumatized the American psyche that we would never fight again," Baker later wrote.[96]

On January 9 Baker and Aziz met in Geneva. Baker handed Aziz a letter from Bush to Hussein. Its main point was to state yet again that Iraq had to withdraw from Kuwait without conditions. "There can be no reward for aggression," Bush wrote. "Nor will there be any negotiation." He hoped that war could still be avoided, but he warned: "What is at stake here is not the future of Kuwait—it will be free, its government will be restored—but rather the future of Iraq."[97] Aziz read the letter but did not take it with him. He left it on the desk. Baker felt the need to add his own warning. "There will be no stalemate . . . no U.N. ceasefire or breathing space for negotiation," he began. "If conflict begins, it will be massive. This will not be another Vietnam. Should war begin, God forbid, it will be fought to a swift, decisive conclusion." Colin Powell was not in the room, but his doctrine permeated the grim atmosphere. "If the conflict involves your use of chemical or biological weapons against our forces," Baker said, echoing Powell, "the American people will demand vengeance. We have the means to exact it. . . . [T]his is not a threat, it is a promise. If there is any use of weapons like that, our objective won't just be the liberation of Kuwait, but the elimination of the current Iraqi regime."[98] Baker closed with an appeal to Aziz, and through him Hussein, not "to misinterpret the different voices" in Washington as proof that the United States was divided by weakness and dispute. The United States, if necessary, would fight as one.

Aziz attacked the Bush administration and defended the Iraqi invasion of Kuwait as a defensive act against a war-hungry coalition consisting of the United States, Israel, and the Kuwaiti leaders. He warned that if the United States attacked Iraq, "you will be the enemy in many Arab countries." After the meeting, Baker returned to his hotel suite and called Bush. "There is no give," he reported. "They didn't give an inch. They're not prepared to change their position. They offered not one new thing, no single idea, and I told them that."[99]

Baker then reported to the press. His first word told the whole story. "Regrettably, ladies and gentlemen," he began, "in over six hours, I heard nothing that suggested to me any Iraqi flexibility whatsoever." A reporter asked for a description of the mood. "Somber," Baker replied.[100]

For the next three days, starting on January 10, Congress plunged into a final debate on a resolution to support the UN deadline of January 15. Edward Kennedy of Massachusetts strongly opposed any resolution. "There is still time to save the President from himself," he said. George Mitchell of Maine raised the question on many minds. "Why should it be an American war, made up largely of American troops, American casualties and American deaths?" he asked. Arlen Specter of Pennsylvania favored a resolution for fear that, without one, "the credibility of the United States will be diminished" and "the presidency as an institution" will be "incapacitated." On January 12, with only three days to go, the House voted 250-183 and the Senate voted 52-47 in support of a congressional resolution giving the president the authority to go to war. "I felt the heavy weight that I might be faced with impeachment lifted from my shoulders as I heard the results," Bush said. Then he added, "In truth, even had Congress not passed the resolution, I would have acted and ordered our troops into combat."[101]

His order came on January 17, shortly after the UN deadline expired. The United States went from Operation Desert Shield to Operation Desert Storm. U.S. warplanes bombed Baghdad. The air war first, then the ground war. Schwarzkopf had planned for 1,000 sorties a day, and that's roughly what he delivered. The air war was a complete success. Powell, getting reports from the front, could not help thinking about Vietnam. "When we came home from Vietnam," he recalled, "we had lost faith. You didn't wear . . . a uniform."[102] Now American warriors again seemed proud, determined. Powell wanted the American people to feel the same way. At a briefing on January 23, 1990, he said, referring to the Iraqi army, "First we're going to cut it off, and then we're going to kill it."

On February 24 the ground war began, and on February 27 coalition forces, mostly American, blasted their way into Kuwait City. Powell recalled that he and Schwarzkopf believed "we were close to accomplishing the assigned objectives given to us by our political leaders."[103] The Iraqi army had been ejected from Kuwait. The legitimate government had been restored. All hostages had been freed. A degree of strategic stability had been returned to the region. Powell asked for another day. Bush wondered, "Well . . . why not end it now?" One reason was that the Iraqi army was being decimated by American planes and tanks as it retreated northward into Iraq. Bloodied bodies, charred tanks and trucks were everywhere. Television coverage focused on the so-called

Highway of Death rather than on the obvious American victory. "We're pick-ing up some unfortunate baggage right now, some public baggage," Bush said. "I'd like you to consider that."[104]

An intense argument followed among Bush's senior advisers. Should the United States stop the war? Should it go on to Baghdad and get rid of Hussein? Bush had no appetite for a prolonged struggle, involving the possibility of street-by-street fighting in Baghdad. "It didn't enter my mind that we ought to do more," Bush later recalled. "When people came to me and said, 'It's over, we won,' that was fine."[105] The United States, he felt, had completed its Kuwait mission, and it was time to end the war.

Powell later explained: "We realized at the time . . . that it wasn't going to be VE Day or VJ Day. It wasn't going to be a total capitulation, units would get out, Saddam would survive, but the President felt he had accomplished his objectives and, if that's the case, why not stop the killing."[106] One hundred and forty-seven Americans had been killed in battle, not the thousands that earlier had been forecast.

The president announced to the nation and the world that Kuwait had been liberated. Mission accomplished. As Powell had promised, the war was swift and decisive, and it had a clear, recognizable end.

The troops returned to parades, a far cry from their return after Vietnam. Powell attended both the Washington and New York parades. "I was just thinking, as I sat in the stands watching Norm and the guys walk by and as I rode in the New York parade," he said years later, "this is incredible. We have come a far piece from the early 1970s when we came home to a state of being ignored. 'You guys just go off and leave us alone, forget about the draft. . . . We're going to cut you short on resources and we're not going to think about you very much.'" Powell was imagining the political leaders of the day dismissing the returning soldiers of Vietnam. He had been hurt, he and all of his buddies. But in Desert Storm the United States had a "professional, first-rate, well-led, military organization led by very solid political leaders," and he felt good.[107]

Had the "ghost of Vietnam" finally been laid to rest? President Bush seemed to think so. As Operation Desert Storm was ending, he said, memorably, "By God, we've kicked the Vietnam syndrome once and for all,"[108] adding the fol-lowing day, "The specter of Vietnam has been buried forever in the desert sands of the Arabian peninsula."[109] General Powell seemed to think so, too: "Vietnam was a chapter that I closed long ago," he said. "From 1973 roughly, to the time of Desert Storm, we rebuilt the army, we got rid of our syndrome, we internalized the way we're supposed to fight wars. We fought war that way in Panama when we went in and took down the Noriega regime, and we fought it again in Desert Shield and Storm. And those policies that we put in place, that strategy of how to fight wars, remains intact to this day. Those policies still remain the national policies. For some it might be the end of the journey from Vietnam, but my journey from Vietnam ended in the mid-seventies when I tried to be a part of the process of rebuilding the American Army. We suffer less from a quote syndrome than people like to think we do."[110]

Bush spoke like a president who won a war, and Powell like a dedicated soldier who led a successful international coalition against Iraq, when both spoke so confidently about shedding Vietnam from national deliberations about war and peace. Unfortunately, both were wrong, for the ghost of Vietnam rose again and again to haunt official consideration of American intervention in such conflicts as Somalia, Haiti, Bosnia, Kosovo, Iraq, and Afghanistan.

6

Clinton:
The First Baby-Boomer President

He would . . . have gladly enlisted in World War II.
—HILLARY RODHAM CLINTON, *Living History*, 2003

So began my personal bout with guilt.
—BILL CLINTON, *My Life*, 2004

ON NOVEMBER 16, 2000, Bill Clinton, the first baby-boomer president, arrived in Hanoi, now the capital of a united Vietnam eager for better relations with its former enemy. He had some unfinished business in this faraway land. The fifty-four-year-old Clinton, nearing the end of his two terms in office, was accompanied by executives from fifty of the biggest American corporations, including Coca-Cola and General Electric.

As a young man, Clinton had demonstrated against the war and, pulling every string, connived to avoid the draft and therefore service in Vietnam. As president, he wanted to forget the past and focus on the future, on reconciliation. But the past would not cooperate; it tugged at his conscience. So many Americans had died in the war he avoided, more than 58,000. Some were his friends. Vietnamese casualties were in the millions. In his memoir, Clinton would, in rare moments of self-disclosure, use the word "guilt" to describe his feelings about skipping the war. He spoke of himself as "the child of a World War II veteran," who "respected the military," and yet he found every way to duck military service in Vietnam. "So began my personal bout with guilt, one that was fought by many thousands of us who loved our country but hated the war."[1]

Clinton wanted, clearly, to lose himself in the "many thousands" who opposed the war, as though somehow, by avoiding service in the war, he was not guilty of anything all that unusual. There was one difference, though: he was the only one who opposed the war and then went on to become president of the United States.

Clinton spent three days in Vietnam, always on the brink of saying "I'm sorry" but not actually apologizing for the dead and wounded, the bombing, or the poisonous Agent Orange. His schedule included a number of tourist stops. One day, as he later told author Taylor Branch, an old friend, he "rang the scholars' gong in Hanoi's Temple of Literature, nearly a thousand years old," and he drew "enormous crowds everywhere."[2] On November 18 he drove to Tien Chau, a small, dirt-poor village where, thirty-three years before, an American F-105D Thunderchief had crashed, presumably killing its pilot, Lieutenant Colonel Lawrence Evert, one of almost 1,500 Americans listed as missing in action in the Vietnam War at the time of Clinton's visit. Investigators had recently uncovered bits of wiring and plastic and smaller bits of human remains. Clinton, wearing mud-covered work shoes, approached the worksite on a bamboo walkway.[3] It was an emotional moment for a president who knew that, had he turned a different corner earlier in his life, he might have had to fight and even face death in defense of his country, just as Evert had fought and died. A *Washington Post* reporter, Rajiv Chandrasekaran, wrote that Clinton's "eyes [were] welling with tears."[4]

"Look, neither side is ever going to fully get past it," said U.S. ambassador to Vietnam Pete Peterson, who had been a prisoner of war in Hanoi for six years. "Reminders of the war are everywhere. You drive by them every day."[5] "The trip to the MIA site," Clinton later wrote, "was an experience none of us would ever forget."[6]

By all accounts, Clinton's visit was a success. His antiwar credentials helped. "Mr. President," he was told by Pham Van Khai, the prime minister, "I can't tell you how much it means to me knowing that you opposed the war against our country." Clinton answered, "Yes, I did oppose the war," adding, "I thought it was wrong. But, at the same time, Mr. Prime Minister, I want you to know that the people who led us in that war had been fighting Communism a long time . . . I believe it was an honest mistake."[7]

Accompanied by his wife, Hillary Rodham Clinton, who had just been elected a Democratic senator from New York, Clinton represented not just star power; he represented a country of fast-moving technology that entranced the thousands of young Vietnamese who lined the streets and waved at his passing motorcade. When he reached the presidential palace, a large, mustard-colored building once the home of the French governor-general, the Vietnamese played a version of "The Star Spangled Banner" as President Tran Duc Luong welcomed the Clintons and the opportunity for better relations with the United States. "I've been struck by the friendliness of the people," Clinton said. "It is a very good omen for our relationship." Tran made a point of con-gratulating Mrs. Clinton on her victory. "We are all very happy," he smiled.[8] It was a comment and a scene unimaginable not too many years earlier.

Neither Bill nor Hillary Clinton had supported the Vietnam War, consid-ering it "misconceived and unwinnable," as she later wrote in her memoir. "I knew that Bill respected military service," she continued, seeking to put his avoidance of military service in Vietnam in a favorable light,

> that he would have served if he had been called and that he would also have gladly enlisted in World War II, a war whose purpose was crystal clear. But Vietnam tested the intellect and conscience of many in my generation, because it seemed contrary to America's national interests and values, not in furtherance of them. As the first modern President to have come of age during Vietnam, Bill carried with him into the White House the unresolved feelings of our country about that war. And he believed it was time to reconcile our differences as Americans and begin a new chapter of cooperation with our former enemy.[9]

A reporter asked Clinton as he headed to Asia whether he thought Vietnam was owed an apology for the war. "No, I don't," he replied.[10] On trips to Africa and Latin America, Clinton had apologized for earlier American actions. But in a country like Vietnam, still communist in governance, victor in America's first lost war, an apology was more than Clinton was prepared to offer. He had finally come to Vietnam, not as a soldier but as a president, and he had paid his respects. He had expiated his own sins.

Vietnam, the Searing Experience

In his eight years in office, Clinton rarely spoke in public or private about the "Vietnam syndrome," even though the ghost of the war was as much a par-ticipant in his deliberations about Somalia, Haiti, Bosnia, and Kosovo as was his secretary of state, his secretary of defense, or his national security adviser. Madeleine Albright, Clinton's UN ambassador during his first term and sec-retary of state during his second, spoke of Vietnam as "a searing experience for that generation of decision makers." A professor as well as a diplomat, Albright stated that "we all have our historic context." She explained, "Mine was Munich and World War II."[11]

For others, it was Vietnam. Anthony Lake, Clinton's national security adviser in his first term, powerfully influenced by his own experiences in

Vietnam as a young Foreign Service officer, recalled that Vietnam was rarely, if ever, mentioned in policy deliberations. "It's just . . . not done, because then you'd sound defeatist," he said. "But like sex in Victorian times," he added, "the fact that nobody talked about it didn't mean that it wasn't on everybody's mind . . . in some way; and even not in their minds but in their subconscious."[12]

Strobe Talbott, who roomed with Clinton at Oxford, knew him well, and served as his deputy secretary of state, remembered that "Vietnam was one of the defining experiences of his political life." Talbott said, "The lesson [of Vietnam] was always there. This nightmare of Vietnam . . . was not that far in the past that he'd forgotten it. . . . It was out there, and it stood as a reminder that you have to be very careful about such things as having a clear notion of purpose, being fully prepared for what the consequences will be, if you actually go in . . . and having an exit strategy."[13]

One lesson that policymakers had learned in the wake of Vietnam was that Congress had to be courted; it could not again be ignored. William Cohen, a Republican senator from Maine, who served as Clinton's secretary of defense in his second term, described a pattern of consultation with Congress about the crises in Bosnia and Kosovo. "We briefed the Congress almost every two and a half weeks. Fifteen or twenty people, they'd come down to the White House and we'd go through the charts each time. They'd say, 'OK, what's the strategy? What's the cost? What is the chance for success? And what's the exit strategy?"[14]

Samuel "Sandy" Berger, who knew Clinton well and served as his national security adviser in his second term, said that Vietnam—the "quagmire vision," as he put it—was "very much in all of our minds." Getting specific, Berger stressed that "every time the President deployed force, it was a very difficult decision for him. I think this is probably a legacy of Vietnam. I mean I think he had an acute sense that he was sending young American men and women to die."[15]

From Hope to Washington, D.C.

Bill Clinton had come a long way from Hope, Arkansas, where he was born on August 19, 1946, one year after the end of World War II, a "good" war. His mother was Virginia Cassidy Blythe, his father William Jefferson Blythe, who had died in a car crash three months before his son's birth. The future president later took the last name of his stepfather, Roger Clinton.

As a young boy growing up in Hope and later in Hot Springs, Arkansas, Clinton was a stellar student and a proficient saxophone player. His family was of modest means, aware of the value of a dollar, but he was never a deprived child. In the summer of 1963, excited about the politics and promise of John F. Kennedy's Camelot, he became a delegate to Boys Nation in Washington, D.C., where, during an event, he actually shook hands with President Kennedy, one of his early heroes. The photo of the two was later used repeatedly in his political ads, proof in this age of imagery that Clinton, even as a boy, was associating with Democrats of prominence, that he was a young man on the move.

Clinton had grades impressive enough to open doors at Harvard or Yale, but he was drawn to Washington, where he enrolled in Georgetown University's School of Foreign Service in September 1964. He actively pursued his passion for politics, holding positions in student government and, beginning in 1966, working in the office of his home-state senator, J. William Fulbright. As Fulbright delved more deeply into Vietnam politics, Clinton followed his lead, drawn inevitably into the rhetorical turmoil of an increasingly unpopular war. "When I went to work for the Foreign Relations Committee," Clinton wrote in his memoir, "I didn't know enough about Vietnam to have a strong opinion, but I was so supportive of President Johnson that I gave him the benefit of the doubt."[16] Within a brief time, though, influenced by Fulbright's deepening opposition to the war and his own awareness of the draft looming on his postcollege horizon, Clinton turned antiwar and so remained for decades to come, even when his opposition to the Vietnam War complicated his run for the presidency.

Wrestling with the Draft

For Clinton, the draft was a major problem. Hundreds of thousands of young American men had been drafted into military service, many ending up in Vietnam. In February 1968, when Clinton, a senior at Georgetown, was happily imagining postgraduate life at Oxford as a Rhodes scholar, Lyndon Johnson ended most postgraduate deferments, casting a cloud of uncertainty over Clinton's immediate future. Making matters worse, on March 20, 1968, Clinton was classified 1-A, fit to be drafted. "For the young men in the class of 1968, the draft now became an obsession," noted David Maraniss, one of Clinton's ablest biographers.[17] In theory, Clinton agreed with Johnson: graduate students should not be deferred just because they were graduate students, but still he was torn.[18] One day, in Fulbright's office, he saw a list of those who had been killed in action. One happened to be a high school friend. Clinton remembered the numbing impact that had upon him. "Seeing his name on the list, along with others I was sure had more to give and get in life, triggered the first pangs of guilt I felt about being a student and only touching the deaths in Vietnam from a distance," Clinton wrote.[19] For a time, he even considered dropping out of school and enlisting; but this thought had a very short shelf life.

His 1-A status haunted him throughout his summertime break in 1968, as he wondered whether he would be drafted. By this time, his stepfather, Roger Clinton, had died, but his uncle, Raymond Clinton, a mover and shaker with ties to the local Garland County Draft Board, bought time for Clinton— enough time, apparently, for his nephew to go off to Oxford without having received his draft notice.[20]

"I was told that I wouldn't be in the October call, and that I might get to stay beyond one term, depending on how many people my local draft board had to supply," Clinton wrote. "I wanted to go to Oxford badly, even if I got to stay only a couple of months."[21] He stayed, as it turned out, for two years.

Clinton thrived during his first year at Oxford, opting for a degree in politics; his classmates included Strobe Talbott and Robert Reich, both of whom ended up working in his administration, Talbott at the State Department, Reich as a secretary of labor. Among his friends, the draft was a constant topic of conversation. One of his closest friends, Frank Aller, upon receiving his draft notice, said he would refuse induction and stay in England. Aller "was particularly forceful with me," Clinton recalled, "telling me that, unlike him, I had the desire and ability to make a difference in politics, and it would be wrong to throw my opportunities away by resisting the draft. His generosity only made me feel more guilty, as the angst-ridden pages of my diary show."[22]

That winter, Clinton returned home for his mother's wedding to her third husband, Jeff Dwire; but once back in England, he reported to a nearby U.S. military base for a pre-induction physical exam. The doctor found him to be "one of the healthiest specimens in the western world," he noted in his diary, "suitable for display at medical schools, exhibitions, zoos, carnivals and base training camps."[23] Obviously a bit of gallows humor, suggesting perhaps that he thought his induction was not far off.

Yet months passed, and as one semester at Oxford led to another, Vietnam always shadowed him. In the spring of 1969, Clinton learned that one of his childhood friends, Bert Jeffries, had been killed in Vietnam, and on April 30 he received a draft notice, delayed in the mail, to report for duty on April 21.

Clinton called his draft board and was told that he could finish his semester at Oxford and then report for induction.[24]

During his 1992 presidential campaign, interestingly, Clinton failed to mention that he had received a draft notice, later explaining, as Maraniss put it, that it had "slipped his mind," an eyebrow-raising explanation since he had immediately telephoned his mother and stepfather to tell them about the draft notice and to ask what could be done.[25]

His first year at Oxford behind him and his draft notice in hand, Clinton returned to Arkansas. Some returning students would have succumbed to the inevitable and, after a visit to their draft boards, accepted their likely induction into the armed forces. But Clinton, in "a terrible emotional struggle,"[26] according to Fulbright staffer Lee Williams, checked out a range of alternative options. One such option was the ROTC program at the University of Arkansas Law School. If accepted into the program, Clinton knew that his pending induction into the armed forces would be canceled. He had discussed this possibility with Williams and Cliff Jackson, a Republican and fellow Arkansan who had also studied at Oxford. Years later, Jackson would evolve into a Clinton-hater; but back then he was a Clinton friend. He and Williams arranged meetings for Clinton with Colonel Eugene J. Holmes and Lieutenant Colonel Clinton Jones, the number one and two men at the ROTC program, who agreed to enroll him. Almost immediately, Clinton was reclassified from 1-A to 1-D, meaning he had outwitted the draft, at least for a time.

"I had mixed feelings," Clinton later wrote. "I knew I had a chance to avoid Vietnam, but somebody will be getting on that bus in ten days and it may be that I should be getting on it, too."[27] In his memoir, he described his torment, his many sleepless nights in a white reclining chair in his family's den. "I searched my heart," he wrote, "trying to determine whether my aversion to going [to Vietnam] was rooted in conviction or cowardice. Given the way it played out, I'm not sure I ever answered the question for myself."[28]

This self-serving self-portrait of a young, guilt-ridden Arkansan was intended to evoke sympathy among his friends. Once, he wrote a letter to Garland County Draft Board Chairman William Armstrong, dated September 12, 1969, asking to be returned to his original 1-A draft status, which would again have made him eligible for quick induction. But he never mailed the letter.[29]

Oxford beckoned, and Clinton returned to England. But he had changed. In his first year of graduate work, he was a committed student, engaging in late-at-night seminars and meeting frequently with his tutors. In his second year, he seemed more interested in the antiwar movement than in his studies.

He helped organize a major antiwar demonstration in London on October 15, 1969, the same day a series of protest rallies were scheduled to be held all over the United States. A month later, on November 15, he joined another antiwar rally in London. Later he journeyed behind the Iron Curtain, providing fodder for future critics. He went to Moscow for five days. There, by chance, he joined forces with a group seeking Soviet help on American prisoners of war and those missing in action in Vietnam.[30]

In the meantime, Clinton had changed his mind yet again about his draft status. While he never mailed the letter to William Armstrong, he did decide to put himself back in the draft, thereby severing his arrangement with the University of Arkansas Law School's ROTC program as well as his 1-D status. As Maraniss writes, "It is a difficult episode to sort out, muddled by Clinton's various accounts, which tend to be incomplete or contradictory, and by a scarcity of documentary evidence."[31] It remains unclear whether Clinton made his decision knowing that President Richard Nixon was making an important change in draft policy.

On October 1 Nixon opted to allow graduate students to finish their entire academic year instead of simply their current semester. That meant that Clinton could have it both ways: he could finish his second year at Oxford and, after reinstatement as a 1-A candidate for military service, which happened on October 30, he could look as if he was in no way evading the draft. "I was reconciled to the fact," he wrote, "that I'd probably be called up at the end of the Oxford year."[32]

On December 1, 1969, the draft policy changed once again. The Nixon administration instituted a draft lottery system, based on birthdays, and good fortune smiled on Clinton, whose birthday, August 19, put him at 311 in a possible field of 366. He still thought "I had a fair chance of being drafted,"[33] and on December 3 he wrote a long and remarkable letter to Colonel Holmes that was to play a major role in the 1992 campaign. He opened the letter by thanking the colonel for being "kind and decent" and for "saving me from the draft." The draft system was, in his view, "illegitimate," but he made an exception for World War II, when "the life of the people collectively was at stake." "I have written and spoken and marched against the war," he wrote, "a war I opposed and despised." So why did he ask to be reinstated in the draft? "To maintain my political viability within the system" was his candid response. He imagined, accurately as it turned out, that he had a promising career in American politics, and he did not want to undermine his prospects. He did not want to go to Vietnam, and he did not want to be a "resister," a draft dodger, so he gamed the system, first embracing the ROTC, though he had no interest in it, and then welcoming his 1-A draft status, when he suspected, given Nixon's changes, that he would never be drafted.[34]

Colin Powell, who survived two tours of duty in Vietnam and rose to be chairman of the Joint Chiefs of Staff and later secretary of state, offered a sympathetic context for Clinton's shifting tactics. "I had worked in the Reagan-Bush era with many hard-nosed men," he wrote, "guys ready to get tough with Soviets, Iranians, Iraqis, Nicaraguans, or Panamanians—all of whom were the right age, but most of whom had managed to avoid serving during the Vietnam War. Bill Clinton, in my judgment, had not behaved much differently from these men. The whole system of deferments and angles for escaping the fighting may have been technically legal. But it was class-ridden, undemocratic, and unjust."[35]

Politics, Yale, and Hillary

Clinton, having safely slipped past military service in Vietnam, now wanted to slip past the constraints of Arkansas, psychological as well as geographic. Instead of enrolling in the University of Arkansas Law School, he applied to Yale Law School, and was quickly accepted. Eventually he would teach at the University of Arkansas Law School, but at this point in his life he felt the need for the intellectual stimulation of New Haven and the political ferment of East Coast politics. He had loved Oxford ("two of the most extraordinary years of my life"),[36] though he never did get his degree, and he anticipated that he would love Yale. Clinton enrolled in September 1970 and was graduated in June 1973, five months after the United States and North Vietnam signed the Paris Peace Accords. The dark cloud of the Vietnam draft finally dissipated and soon disappeared. By the time he got his law degree, he knew he would never have to serve in the military and in Vietnam.

At Yale, Clinton focused on three subjects: law, politics, and Hillary. Shortly after his arrival, Clinton met a brilliant and bespectacled Wellesley graduate named Hillary Rodham, and they were clearly smitten with each other. She was already in her second year of law school. Their marriage in 1975 became one of the most famous, most analyzed in American history. Clinton enjoyed his legal studies, but he enjoyed politics even more. He helped Joe Duffey, a liberal antiwar Democrat seeking a Senate seat from Connecticut. Duffey lost. In 1972 he moved to Texas, where he became Senator George McGovern's state coordinator. Again, his antiwar candidate lost. Clinton returned to Yale for his final year.

In 1973, after his graduation, Clinton accepted a teaching job at the University of Arkansas Law School in Fayetteville. It was there that he launched his own political career. He mounted a long-shot challenge in 1974 to the Republican member of Congress representing the Third District, conservative John Paul Hammerschmidt, a respected World War II veteran. Clinton won the Democratic nomination at age twenty-eight. He reached out to Colonel Holmes and asked him, if possible, to return the letter he had sent him about the draft and the war. If released to the public, Clinton knew it would again focus attention on Vietnam, and Hammerschmidt would use it to hammer him on his opposition to the war. Holmes quietly obliged the candidate, but his aide, Lieutenant Colonel Jones, held on to a copy of the letter, which became controversial during the 1992 campaign. But in this campaign it was not a factor. Clinton lost by four percentage points, 52 percent to 48 percent.

In 1976 Clinton ran for state attorney general, a race he won and considered a stepping-stone to the governorship of Arkansas. Two years later, at age thirty-two, Clinton ran for governor, and won again. Smooth-talking, intelligent, moderate, Clinton became an instant media favorite, like Jimmy Carter a Democrat who could win in the deeply conservative South. He lost his bid for a second term in 1980, but won the governorship back in 1982 and continued winning in Arkansas until, in 1992, he won the presidency.

On to the White House

As governor for more than a decade, Clinton worked his way up the ladder of national politics, always seeking to strike a pose of moderation on controversial issues, neither too liberal nor too conservative, certainly not one of those old-style, free-spending Democrats. He helped create the centrist Democratic Leadership Council, and he served effectively as chairman of the Democratic Governors Association and the National Governors Association. In 1987 his presidential ambitions began to burst through the seams of his governor's garb; he was young, he was bright, he represented a "new" Democratic Party, he was a southerner. Why couldn't he be president? The question dominated the dinnertime conversation in Little Rock. His reputation, fair or unfair, as a draft-dodger and a womanizer punctured the balloon of this embryonic campaign, but there was enough of a flurry of speculation about his candidacy to produce a political prize. Democratic presidential nominee Michael Dukakis, the governor of Massachusetts, selected Clinton to deliver the keynote address at the Democratic National Convention. But it was, as speeches go, a calamity: rambling, boring, endless. "I had some good lines," Clinton recalled, "but, alas, the biggest applause I got was near the painful end, when I said, 'In closing. . . . ' It was thirty-two minutes of total disaster."[37] Dukakis lost; George H. W. Bush won, partly on the promise that he would never raise taxes.

The four years of the Bush presidency had a number of high points ("victories" in Panama and the Persian Gulf) and a low point (he did raise taxes), and in 1991, as another presidential campaign beckoned, Clinton rolled the dice. He thought Bush could be defeated. In August Clinton formed a presidential exploratory committee, and on October 3 he officially announced that he was a candidate for president of the United States.

Reporter and author David Halberstam reflected on Bush's poll numbers, which, after the Persian Gulf War, had "shot through the roof." He quoted from a conversation between Clinton and adviser Frank Greer:

> "Have you ever heard of the American people throwing out a president who conducted a successful war?" [Clinton] asked Greer. No, Greer answered, he had not, but this was a very different, much more volatile age. Because of the force of modern media, the old rules no longer applied. Political tides changed more quickly and less predictably, Greer suggested. "But I didn't even serve in the army and I was against the Vietnam War," Clinton said. "I didn't serve either and I was against it, too," replied Greer, who had helped run one of the anti-war moratoriums. Then Greer added, "And most of the country didn't serve either."[38]

Clinton's emergence as a baby-boomer presidential candidate in 1992 became the defining moment in the transition from the World War II generation to the Vietnam generation in presidential politics. Up until the Clinton run, Franklin D. Roosevelt (1933–45) had been the last candidate to win the presidency and not serve in the military. Subsequent presidents had served, several with distinction and heroism. Was Vietnam so wrenching and divisive an experience for the American people that it made military service for a presidential candidate irrelevant, or did it make it an even more essential ingredient in a presidential résumé? The Clinton candidacy seemed to prove that it was no longer essential, but the issue still resonated.

The field of Democratic candidates was jammed. It included, in addition to Clinton, Senators Bob Kerrey of Nebraska and Tom Harkin of Iowa, Governor

Doug Wilder of Virginia, former Massachusetts senator Paul Tsongas, and former California governor Jerry Brown. Reporter Dan Balz of the *Washington Post*, himself a baby boomer, spotted the contrasting differences between two of the candidates: Kerrey, a Medal of Honor winner for his Navy Seal service in Vietnam, who had lost part of his right leg in combat, and Clinton, who had cleverly avoided the draft and service in Vietnam. Both were, in their way, representatives of the new Vietnam generation.

"They are like bookends from the Vietnam generation," Balz wrote. "They have become clashing symbols in a party that has never fully resolved the ambiguities and divisions of that time. . . . [T]he public will have to wrestle with a new set of questions in judging its leaders. . . . For 20 years, Vietnam has shaped and divided the Democratic Party. After the Persian Gulf War, President Bush said the victory had helped to eliminate the Vietnam syndrome. Kerry and Clinton show that not all the questions have been wiped away." Certainly not with Clinton, who ultimately won his party's nomination, despite nagging questions about his draft status and his womanizing.[39]

In December 1991 George Stephanopoulos, then serving as a Clinton strategist, raised the draft issue. "We need some tighter answers," he warned. "It's going to come back." Stephanopoulos was expecting trouble on this issue. Both Bill and Hillary Clinton angrily disagreed. "Bill's not going to apologize for being against the Vietnam War," Hillary insisted. Clinton then spouted a "red-faced tirade against the war." Still, at Stephanopoulos's insistence, Clinton hired a research organization to investigate all aspects of his draft record so his campaign would be ready to answer any questions sure to arise during the campaign, "but it was already too late."[40] Reporter Elizabeth Kolbert of the *New York Times* wrote:

With the debate over Governor Clinton's draft status, the Presidential campaign seems to have run into a booby trap that was set 25 years ago. As the generation that came of age in the 1960's began to run for high political office, it was probably inevitable that someone would stumble into the snare. . . . With Governor Clinton, the question is whether he misled his local draft board to avoid conscription before 1969. . . . An official of his local draft board has said that he did mislead them; Mr. Clinton insists that he did not.[41]

In early 1992 Harkin took the Iowa caucuses, which was no surprise, but Clinton was leading in the New Hampshire primary, set for February 18, which was a surprise. Tsongas was supposed to be New England's favorite son. But on

January 19 a *Boston Globe* poll showed Clinton with 29 percent, Tsongas with 17 percent, and Kerrey with 16 percent.[42] Suddenly, Clinton was the front-runner in a key primary—that is, until late January, when the press turned its attention to Gennifer Flowers, an Arkansan, who told the country that she had had a twelve-year affair with Clinton. It was a bombshell, proof, if any were needed, that the rumors about Clinton's womanizing were now more than rumors. The campaign went into damage control, and to an extent succeeded, in part because both Bill and Hillary appeared on CBS's *60 Minutes* to acknowledge past problems in their marriage but also to profess their love for each other.

The Flowers issue seemed to be abating when a new crisis popped up, this one concerning the draft. A February 6 article in the *Wall Street Journal* by reporter Jeffrey H. Birnbaum detailed Clinton's draft history and his controversial relationship with the University of Arkansas Law School's ROTC program. Birnbaum wrote that Clinton's decision to enter the ROTC program took him out of the draft pool "during September and October of 1969, the critical two months when he expected to be called into service." The article quoted Colonel Holmes, who previously had posed no obstacle to Clinton's political ambitions, as saying, "Bill Clinton was able to manipulate things so that he didn't have to go in."[43]

The upshot, according to Stanley Greenberg, the campaign's pollster, was that Clinton's poll numbers were suddenly in "meltdown" mode. He had dropped to third place. "The draft did all the damage Gennifer didn't do," Stephanopoulos wrote.[44]

It was not just Clinton's presidential ambitions that hung in the balance; it was his entire political career. In the center of the storm was the letter Clinton had written to Colonel Holmes in early December 1969, which thanked Holmes for saving him from the draft. On February 10 ABC's Mark Halperin approached Stephanopoulos with a copy of the letter. When Stephanopoulos read the line about "saving me from the draft," his eyes popped. "That's it," he thought. "We're done."[45] James Carville, though, had a different take on the letter. Turning to Clinton, he cried, "This letter is your best friend, Governor."[46] And so it proved to be. The letter split Clinton's campaign into two camps. Younger aides considered its publication a death knell; older aides considered it a savior. Hillary Clinton exclaimed, "Bill, this is you! This is exactly what you were going through. This sounds like you, I can hear you saying this. This is terrific. This is just what it was like. Now they'll understand!"[47]

As Hillary went, so went the campaign, which ran the full text of the controversial letter in the regionally powerful *Manchester Union Leader* and, for good measure, bought two thirty-minute television call-in broadcasts for Clinton to answer any and all questions about the letter, the draft, and Gennifer. In addition, Clinton appeared on ABC's *Nightline*. Host Ted Koppel took the unusual step for an anchor of reading the entire letter, describing it as "quite a remarkable letter, actually, eloquent and revealing" and then prodding Clinton on whether there was anything to be "read into" the fact that Clinton got a high lottery number on December 1, sent his Yale Law School application off on December 2, and wrote his letter to Holmes on December 3. "I just don't remember," Clinton answered, "and there's nothing to read into it." Later in the interview, Clinton vowed to "give this election back to the people, to lift the cloud off this election," implying that sinister forces were at work attempting to steal the election from the "people." And who were these sinister forces? The media, of course. "All I've been asked about by the press are a woman I didn't sleep with and a draft I didn't dodge," sniffed Clinton. It was a good quote, even if not exactly accurate.[48]

Reporters Jack Germond and Jules Witcover described a "do-or-die push" by the Clinton campaign.[49] Everyone was in battle gear. Stephanopoulos wrote:

> Even if I had known for certain then that Clinton's closing statement wasn't really true, I would have had a hard time admitting it to myself. . . . [N]early anything we did, I believed, was justified by what was being done to us. Tabloid reporters were prowling the streets of Little Rock, offering cash for stories about Clinton. Almost all the rumors swirling around our increasingly gothic campaign—that Clinton sanctioned drug running from Arkansas's Mena Airport, that Clinton was a cocaine fiend, that Hillary was a secret lesbian—were both malicious and untrue.[50]

Late on February 18, after the polls in New Hampshire had closed but before the TV pundits could put their spin on the results, Clinton proclaimed himself "the comeback kid." He had come in second, winning 26 percent of the vote to Paul Tsongas's 35 percent, but he made second sound like first. The pundits admired "the comeback kid," who roared out of New Hampshire with full sails behind him to win the nomination and eventually the election. Bush had said at the GOP convention that "while I bit the bullet, he bit his nails,"[51] but Clinton still won with a plurality of 43 percent of the final vote; Bush got 37.4 percent and third-party candidate Ross Perot a surprising 19.

Richard Nixon expressed his shock and disapproval. "I still can't believe that Clinton won. I mean, I can believe it, but I don't want to believe it," he said. "I read in *Time* or some other place that Clinton told someone 'softly,' 'If I win, it will close the book on Vietnam.'" Nixon seemed to believe Clinton. "His victory . . . is proving that it was all right to be against the goddamned war. Everything we stood for . . . is going straight down the tubes."[52] Nixon should not have been so gloomy; actually, Vietnam survived Clinton's victory. It lived on in different ways.

"How did Americans come to choose their first baby-boom President, the third youngest in history, only the second governor of a small state, carrying more baggage than an ocean liner?" Clinton asked. He answered his own question by saying that the economy proved to be the number-one issue for the public, the deficit and health care were in second and third place, and character issues were "trailing."[53]

The Vietnam "Quagmire"—"It Was Very Much in All of Our Minds"

In early December 1992, President Bush's national security adviser, Brent Scowcroft, telephoned Samuel "Sandy" Berger in President-elect Clinton's transition office with a courteous if belated heads-up on an important decision. "Sandy," he said, "I want to let you know that President Bush tomorrow will deploy 20,000 troops to open up the food lines in Somalia." Berger was astonished. But before he could raise a question, Scowcroft assured him, "Don't worry . . . they'll be out before inauguration day."[54] Berger immediately reported the news to Clinton, who had his mind on the problems of transition, chief among them the troubled economy, which had been the focus of his campaign. Somalia was at least a world or two away. The president-elect gave his pro forma approval. He, of little military knowledge or experience, felt he had no option. The mission was obviously humanitarian: newspaper headlines spoke of tens, possibly hundreds, of thousands of Somalis dying of starvation; and though the mission was vague, it was to be relatively brief. Scowcroft was an honorable man, and he had given his word: "out," he had promised, before inauguration day. Besides, at the time Somalia seemed like a manageable distraction, carrying little if any political risk. It even paid a subtle diplomatic dividend: it demonstrated American sympathy for the Muslims of Somalia, even though the United States was at that time reluctant about helping the Muslims of Bosnia and Kosovo.

On reflection, Clinton may have felt that Bush's motivation might not have been entirely altruistic; after his bitter electoral defeat, he might have wanted to leave the White House in a manufactured blaze of glory, both guns spitting fire as he backed out of the saloon. It would be presented to the public, of course, as another example of Bush's capacity for statesmanship, leadership, and the sort of courage he displayed during the Persian Gulf War.

As Clinton prepared to assume the powers of the presidency, he understood that one of his top problems was going to be his shaky relationship with the military. He had publicly opposed the Vietnam War, he had avoided military service, and he had supported the presence of gays in the military, a position flatly at odds with the Pentagon's. Moreover, as a Democrat, likely to benefit from a post–cold war "peace dividend," Clinton was quickly portrayed by conservative Republicans as a president almost certain to be squishy soft on national defense, cutting into the Pentagon's budget and slashing funds for the Central Intelligence Agency. "I think Democratic presidents have more to prove that they are strong on defense as Republicans," observed William Cohen.[55] "President Clinton didn't want to [have to prove anything], but . . . the Republicans didn't trust him." Nor did they seem to trust national security to any Democrat, most especially Jimmy Carter, who, they claimed, had drastically weakened America's defense and damaged its reputation during the Iran hostage crisis. Now, by throwing his public support behind Bush's decision to send American troops to Somalia, Clinton hoped to strengthen his image as a new, moderate Democrat willing, when necessary, to use American power in defense of the national interest; and maybe in this way softening GOP suspicions of his national security credentials.

From the beginning, whether their charges were based on sound information or total fabrication, the Republicans found in Clinton a perfect target for a political pummeling, claiming that he and most of his advisers had been traumatized by Vietnam into a deep reluctance to use American military power in defense of the national interest. Years later, in a December 2007 interview, Berger had a ready, handwritten list on his desk of nine different times when Clinton used or threatened to use military force: when, to quote Berger, "we actually used force," as though that, in itself, was a noteworthy accomplishment. With a note of genuine pride, he read down the list:

1. Somalia, where "we managed that use of force for the first ten months of the Clinton administration."

2. Haiti, where "we fully anticipated knocking down the door."

3. Iraq, where "we destroyed the Ministry of Intelligence . . . in retaliation for the assassination attempt against President Bush."

4. Iraq again, where the United States launched "four days of saturation bombing on all of the targets of mass destruction that we knew about."

5. Bosnia, where "we deployed . . . in a peacekeeping mode, not a war-fighting mode."

6. Kosovo, "our most sustained use of force," an "air war, seventy-eight days of an air war."

7. Taiwan, a threatened use of force, where, after China "shot missiles towards Taiwan, we moved two air carrier groups near the Taiwan Strait as a dissuasive use of force."

8. Another threatened use of force, this time in Iraq, when "we deployed on the borders of Iraq."

9. Finally, Afghanistan, where the United States attacked the town of Khost in 1998, believing Osama bin Laden was there. "We missed him by two hours."

Berger insisted that, on the one hand, by the time Clinton came to office, the "Vietnam syndrome, defined as reluctance to use force, I think, had passed"; yet, on the other hand, "we were not impervious to the consequences of Vietnam, which was a defining event in our lives."[56] Berger then described a Clinton code of military conduct that closely paralleled Reagan's code, as formulated first by Weinberger and then by Powell. In the aftermath of the Vietnam War, as one administration followed another, each faced essentially the same set of questions about the use of American military power, and, with differences designed for the politics of the time, each tended to approach the use of military power with considerable caution, especially when the issue at hand was the commitment of ground combat troops—"boots on the ground," as it was often put. The specter of Vietnam would then rear its head and frighten presidents into either brandishing their swords or, with embarrassment, slipping them back into their sheaths and withdrawing from the front. George H. W. Bush was an exception, putting hundreds of thousands of boots on the ground in the Persian Gulf War.

"When we used force, we did it with caution and care," Berger stressed, "a function of having lived through Vietnam." When the United States struck the Ministry of Intelligence in Baghdad, "we did it at night" to avoid civilian casualties. Clinton was always extremely cautious about deploying combat forces to fight in another country. Even air power was authorized only after he had exhausted every other option. Like Powell, chair of the Joint Chiefs of Staff when Clinton took power, the president wanted a clear strategy, both to go in and to get out, and he wanted to be assured, in advance, that the United States would succeed. The fear of a Vietnam-like "quagmire" was, in Berger's words, "very much in all of our minds."[57]

Somalia, Where Insurgencies Were Hatched

When Clinton moved into the White House, U.S. troops were still in Somalia, Bush's hopes for a quick pullout dashed in the chaos of this ungovernable, desperately poor, and starving country in the Horn of Africa. In the best of times, Somalia was never a Swiss watch. The noblest of intentions often wilted and died in this basket case of everyday problems and unpredictable crises, one worse than another. What Bush had had in mind was simple enough. U.S. troops, working under a broad UN-sanctioned humanitarian mandate, named Operation Restore Hope, would break the stranglehold of the local warlords over food shipments and distribution and then quickly withdraw to UN bases near the capital city of Mogadishu or offshore to waiting ships. Presumably the people would then be fed. Famine averted. Mission accomplished.

But if the decision had been Clinton's, he would never have sent 28,000 troops to Somalia, the number eventually sent. Somalia was not high on his list of priorities. "He felt that a military adventure of some kind," said Leon Fuerth, national security adviser to Vice President Gore, "carried the risk of destroying his capacity to carry through the programs he had in mind to address the economy."[58] Clinton's natural inclination was to get out of Somalia, but in dignified fashion, by gradually cutting back on the number of U.S. troops and empowering the United Nations to complete the mission. "It was one of my jobs," said UN ambassador Albright, "to try to get the UN to take it over as quickly as possible." She recognized this was not an easy task. "We were asking the UN . . . to do a bigger job, in terms of disarming various people, [but to do it] with a smaller force."[59]

Richard Cohen, a columnist for the *Washington Post*, spotted the similarities between Vietnam and Somalia in a December 1992 column, before Clinton had taken office, but Cohen felt the United States was "throw[ing] off the shackles of Vietnam." And it was about time, he thought. "For too long, the very mention of that experience was enough to freeze policy-makers in their tracks and, more important, give the Pentagon the willies. It seemed every member of the Joint Chiefs of Staff took a blood oath to insist of their civilian bosses that never again would the military be asked to fight a war it cannot win."[60] In the *New York Times* the following day, Raymond Bonner was more definitive. "Somalia is not another Vietnam: America is not likely to get bogged down in a military quagmire."[61] Both writers, it seemed, were responding to a rising popular concern about Somalia becoming another Vietnam.

By the spring of 1993, U.S. troop levels in Somalia were cut from a peak of 28,000 to 4,500.[62] The Clinton administration had supported a plan broadening UN authority in Somalia to provide security and to embark on a number of nation-building projects, such as setting up regional councils and preparing for national elections, all under the protective blue helmets of the UN force. The stage was thus set for a "constant, day-to-day" tug-of-war between Ambassador Albright and UN secretary-general Boutros Boutros-Ghali over U.S. support for the expanded UN mission. "All of a sudden," as Albright recalled, "we were having the U.N. do all kind of things that it hadn't done since the Congo" in the early 1960s.[63]

Though Albright provided rhetorical encouragement to the UN mission, the United States, by its actions, was moving in the opposite direction and out of Somalia. Its policy was riddled with internal contradiction, and Boutros-Ghali was exasperated. "All my experience tells me not to trust the U.S.," he said one day. "You are unpredictable and change your minds too often."[64] Even when the House of Representatives in May passed a resolution of support for the UN mission, favoring the use of U.S. troops in this evolving nation-building effort, Boutros-Ghali was still unimpressed.

A month later one of the competing warlords, the ruthless and formidable Mohamed Farrah Aidid, who had welcomed U.S. troops to Somalia in December, suddenly switched his allegiance and his tactics. In an act of open defiance, on June 5 a small band of his ragtag army ambushed a UN peacekeeping force inspecting a suspected weapons cache and killed more than twenty Pakistani soldiers. The United Nations denounced the action and plastered Mogadishu with placards promising a $25,000 reward for information leading to Aidid's arrest. UN forces, including U.S. troops, attacked Aidid's headquarters and hangouts, hoping to capture the guerrilla leader. Fierce fighting ensued, many soldiers were killed, including Americans, but Aidid escaped. Clearly what had been a humanitarian mission was now being transformed into an asymmetrical guerrilla war between Aidid's followers and a UN peacekeeping army.

Black Hawk Down—And Things Changed

During the summer of 1993, American troops began to develop what has been described as ugly feelings toward the Somalis. Ambassador Robert Oakley was "appalled by the hatred of the Americans for the Somalis—the view that the only good Somali is a dead Somali . . . . [I]t reminded him of Vietnam, where our troops, in their need to survive in such a difficult war, had become even more bitter and [spoke] of the Vietnamese in the cruelest terms imaginable."[65] Though in Washington the administration was looking for a political solution, in Mogadishu American commanders were coming up with plans to go after Aidid once again.

On October 3 an elite American force, determined to do what the United Nations had so far failed to do, left their base and advanced on the Olympic Hotel in downtown Mogadishu, which usually served as Aidid's headquarters. Their aim was to capture or kill Aidid and his top lieutenants. The force consisted of 19 aircraft, 12 vehicles, and 160 Delta Force and Ranger troops, more than enough to accomplish their mission. They thought they had good intelligence; but they were new to guerrilla warfare in an urban environment, and they had badly miscalculated enemy strength, tactics, and resilience. They suffered a terrible defeat.

Aidid's militiamen, heavily armed with AK-47s and rocket-propelled grenades, operating on rooftops, and hiding in alleyways, obviously tipped off to the coming American assault, spotted the paratroopers slithering down ropes from the approaching helicopters. A ferocious firefight quickly erupted, and two UH-60 Black Hawk helicopters were shot down, crumbling to the streets with their blades still turning. Three other helicopters were badly damaged. The crew of one of the downed Black Hawks managed to escape from the burning wreckage and set up a tiny base of resistance, but the crew of the other Black Hawk was less fortunate. They were trapped, completely cut off. Through the night, they battled Aidid's militiamen.

Eighteen Americans died, dozens more were wounded; and when Aidid's men then dragged an American soldier through the crowded, cheering streets of Mogadishu, in full view of TV cameras and the international press corps, an exclamation point to their victory over the mighty American war machine, something snapped in the American people. A humanitarian effort, no matter how imperfect, was one thing; a deadly fight between American forces and Aidid's guerrillas was another, and it was totally unacceptable. From Congress came a clear message: either wipe out Aidid, or get out of Somalia. Though the formal announcement did not come for another month or so, the president decided on that fateful weekend to "get out of Somalia." Clinton "got stung" by Black Hawk Down, said Secretary Cohen, and he would never forget the experience.[66] "It was a huge disaster," said William Perry, deputy secretary of defense at the time, "a big story."[67]

Clinton had heard about Black Hawk Down while on a trip to California. He was surprised and furious. "How could this happen?" he wanted to know.[68]

Clinton had a finely tuned instinct for domestic politics; but in foreign affairs he was still learning. And there was a disturbing prelude to the Black Hawk fiasco. A week earlier the top U.S. commander in Somalia, Major General Thomas Montgomery, had fired off an urgent request to Les Aspin, through Powell, for additional reinforcements, including tanks, armored vehicles, and gunships. Aspin, in his most controversial decision as secretary of defense, turned down the request. It was a decision he was later to regret. His critics raised the obvious question of whether, with those reinforcements, the Black Hawk tragedy could have been averted.

By the time Clinton returned to Washington, Congress was demanding answers from him and Aspin. Members were overwhelmed by tens of thousands of calls and cables from irate voters demanding not only an explanation but an immediate withdrawal from Somalia. An NBC News poll on October 6, 1993, found that more than 50 percent of the American people feared that the American involvement in Somalia would become another Vietnam.

Clinton, privately, had already decided to get out of Somalia, but he had to wrap his gut decision in a dignified announcement. After several meetings, Clinton and his senior advisers concluded that an immediate withdrawal would undercut America's military posture all over the world, but eventually they agreed on a political, not a military, solution to their mini-war with Aidid—they would effectively let him off the hook—and on a quick but temporary buildup of American forces preparatory to a complete withdrawal by March 31, 1994. Clinton had carefully considered the advice of Democratic senators Sam Nunn and David Pryor that he should be mindful of the lessons of Vietnam: that if he was going to send more troops to Somalia, "he should ask for them all at once." Reporter Elizabeth Drew wrote that "Vietnam was a ghost Clinton couldn't shake. He was aware that his credentials as Commander in Chief were in question. . . . He knew that the men in uniform . . . looked down on him."[69] But the lesson Clinton took from Vietnam was to camouflage his decision to abandon Somalia with a buildup of forces in or near Somalia: a temporary buildup, as it turned out. He sent 1,700 more troops, 104 tanks and Bradley fighting vehicles, 4 Cobra attack helicopters, an additional 3,600 marines waiting offshore, and a naval battle group led by an aircraft carrier, the USS *Abraham Lincoln,* heavy with F-18 fighters.[70]

By these actions, Clinton eased some but clearly not all congressional concerns about Somalia, which bubbled to a climax during an Aspin appearance on Capitol Hill. The defense secretary performed abysmally. Rather than describing the full dimensions of the policy with the crisp authority expected during a national crisis, the usually rumpled Aspin, a former member of Congress from Wisconsin, chose to ask his former colleagues what they thought should be done. The atmosphere in the committee room turned white hot with anger and disappointment.

Within a few days, Perry recalled, "some of the key congressmen, including some of Les's friends, went to the president and said, 'He's gotta go.' . . . [They seemed] distressed by the fact that the secretary of defense didn't seem to be on top of it. . . . Within a few weeks, the president called in Les and told him [he had to go]. He didn't want to do that, but he was pressured by some key people in Congress." By the time Perry, in early 1994, replaced Aspin, the decision on total withdrawal from Somalia had been made. "There was no discussion of it," he recalled. "The government decided that that's what we were going to do, and nobody around argued with me about it." Perry agreed with the decision, which should have made implementation easier, but it proved to be tough going. "We didn't have a mission," he explained. "The warlords were gaining control, and the talk about 'the Vietnam syndrome' followed Congress and the country [everywhere]. . . . We didn't have [an exit strategy] from Somalia. Our exit strategy was pretty much a retreat, a retreat under fire. . . . That's the way we had to do it."[71]

"There was no exit strategy in Somalia," Berger lamented. "Our exit strategy was tragic. Our exit strategy was a disaster. . . . Quagmire . . . came back to haunt us in Somalia."[72] Warren Christopher admitted that "we probably allowed the [Somali] mission to get out of hand," adding, "there was 'mission creep' that we didn't want."[73] Albright, always the professor, pondered the situation in the wake of Black Hawk Down: "At home, at night, I questioned every aspect of what we had done. I had been a part of the decisions that had led to this. What had we done wrong? It was a nightmare."[74] Powell, for his part, considered the Somali operation "quicksand," and when he left the government, he urged the president to get out "soon" from Somalia.[75]

Richard Holbrooke, who had served in Vietnam with the State Department in the early 1960s, examined the Vietnam syndrome and the Somalia disaster and emerged with a syndrome of his own. He called it "Vietmalia," meaning, as Halberstam wrote, a situation where "a great power gets involved in some foreign country where American security is not involved. Because support for the policy is so fragile, and because even the policy makers have considerable doubts about what they are doing, the loss of just a few lives, and the televising of a few funerals, can spell the end of the policy."[76]

For Clinton, Somalia was his Bay of Pigs, his first test on the world stage, and it left him shaken, more reluctant than ever to put "boots on the ground," more concerned than ever about Holbrooke's concept of Vietmalia, which ended up inhibiting the United States from playing a proper role in other trouble spots. Clinton "derived the lesson [from Vietnam] that you have to be very goddamn careful about getting the United States embroiled in a foreign war," recalled Talbott. "And remember that his first experience with the use of force [in Somalia] was totally catastrophic."[77]

Morton Abramowitz, a former ambassador, linked the Somali experience to the bloodbath in another African country, Rwanda, where hundreds of thousands of people were slaughtered in a tribal war between Hutus and Tutsis. The United States should have done something, but "after Black Hawk Down," Abramowitz said, "they got so . . . scared" that Congress would balk at everything else, so they decided not to respond in Rwanda.[78]

Perry looked back on the Somali experience with sadness. Though Clinton, after leaving office, regretted not having done anything about Rwanda, Perry said that at the time "he had no thought at all [about doing anything]. I can tell you he didn't even consider it." Perry felt "Congress would have been outraged." He believed that a "modest show of force, even without sending a single soldier," might have slowed down the massacre. He persuaded a very reluctant Clinton to send an engineering battalion and a water purification machine to Rwanda. "Even then Congress was very unhappy,"[79] so deep was the fear that the United States would be sucked into another Vietnam-like situation.

No matter how energetically the Clinton White House tried to spin its message, the fact remained that the U.S. withdrawal from Somalia had a sharply depressing effect on America's global position. Intelligence officials with a responsibility for U.S. policy in the Middle East were picking up "chatter" suggesting that terrorists were less apprehensive about the use of American power following the pullout from Beirut. Richard A. Clarke, who later served as Clinton's national coordinator for counterterrorism, concluded that the terrorists saw Somalia as a clear-cut American defeat. "Once again, they told one another, the United States had been humiliated by a Third World Country. Just like Vietnam. Just like Lebanon. Just like the Soviets in Afghanistan."[80] Clarke remembered that when the United States withdrew from Lebanon, observers "throughout the Middle East" saw how "easily the superpower could be driven off, how the U.S. was still 'shell-shocked' from its defeat in Vietnam."[81]

The 1996 Presidential Campaign—
Again "the Slippery Draft Dodger" Wins

Clinton loved politics. When he met with his senior strategists to discuss his reelection campaign, he was the happy warrior. The polls showed that he could defeat any Republican challenger, including Kansas senator Bob Dole, a decorated World War II hero, and House majority leader Newt Gingrich, author of the successful Contract with America, and that Ross Perot, the third-party maverick who had done so well in 1992, was now losing his political appeal. Moreover, Clinton was at the time the beneficiary of two important triumphs, one domestic and one foreign, and he intended to milk both during his reelection campaign.

On the domestic side, the president squared off against a headstrong Gingrich, still riding what he thought was a rising crest of GOP power and influence after storming to victory in the House of Representatives in November 1994. At issue were powerful, often irreconcilable, differences between two budgetary philosophies. Clinton was committed to a broad government role in social and economic growth, while Gingrich was determined to scale back the government's role. Led by two highly articulate advocates, the battle dominated the news, and it led ultimately to a government shutdown affecting the entire nation during the Christmas–New Year holidays of 1995–96. Finally, Clinton emerged triumphant from this political war. The paychecks started flowing again. Clinton regarded his conquest of Gingrich as a big step toward his own reelection.

On the foreign policy front, when the Bush administration had come into office, Yugoslavia, born in the ashes of World War I, had begun to fall apart, with Slovenia, Macedonia, Croatia, and Bosnia-Herzegovina each declaring its independence. Serbia was left, feeling alone, defiant, and righteous, a firebrand of old-fashioned Balkan nationalism. In 1992 a civil war broke out in Bosnia, brutal and ugly, reflecting the religious and nationalistic passions long associated with the Balkans: a hot minority of Orthodox Christians fighting Catholics and then both turning on the Muslims, who represented 44 percent of the population. The war was to last until December 1995.

Once a relatively peaceful, mountainous, multiethnic province of 4.5 million people, Bosnia quickly descended into a bloody hell as Serbian troops crossed the border and swept into the newly independent country, leaving a path of rape, pillage, and destruction behind them. Tens of thousands perished. Serbian sympathizers, inspired by Slobodan Milosevic, a power-mad communist from old Yugoslavia, uprooted Muslim communities in much the same way that the Nazis destroyed Jewish communities in World War II, sending men into concentration camps and women into rape camps.

Muslim villages became killing fields, and "ethnic cleansing," a strangely antiseptic-sounding term used to describe the slaughter of Bosnian Muslims, burst into headlines around the world. When Serbian troops besieged Sarajevo, once the beautiful, cosmopolitan capital of Bosnia, Europe and America could look away no longer. This was genocide impossible to ignore, even by those who had thought the end of the cold war opened a new era of comfort and security in Europe. Bosnia was the lead story on the evening news and the big headline in most newspapers. The North Atlantic Treaty Organization (NATO), at first timidly, later with a show of modest conviction, rose from its usual posture of languid indifference to most challenges and began, however reluctantly, to take limited action. A UN-sanctioned peacekeeping force, composed in part of European troops, was sent to Bosnia with the wispy mandate of separating the warring parties and creating a fair division of the spoils. Details were left to the diplomats. NATO was to provide a small degree of muscle to encourage concessions. After a while, air strikes were conducted against Serbian fuel depots, ammunition dumps, and communication centers, and cruise missiles hit Serbian headquarters at Banja Luka.

Finally, the stench from the Bosnian war—the "horror in the Balkans," as Madeleine Albright put it—reached Washington.[82] Clinton wanted no part of another foreign challenge; yet he was under pressure to act, even from within his own circle of senior advisers. Albright, who, as a young girl, had lived in Yugoslavia when her father, a Czech diplomat, was posted there, argued passionately for U.S. action, even to the point of sending U.S. troops to Bosnia to stop the ethnic cleansing. Christopher, whose position on Bosnia flipped and flopped, supported Albright on this occasion, but both ran up against the firm opposition of General Powell, who feared the United States might soon become embroiled in another quagmire in the Balkans. Albright, exasperated, asked, "What are you saving this superb military for, Colin, if we can't use it?"[83] Powell set conditions on the use of American force that, according to reporter Michael Dobbs, were so "restrictive that they effectively ruled out any kind of intervention in Bosnia."[84] Lake "had the Vietnam bug humming in his ear," wrote Albright. He did not "want to send U.S. forces to fight an unwinnable war."[85]

As Christopher recalled, "That the Balkans had the look and feel of a Vietnam-like quagmire did not help to stiffen spines in our government, especially since General Colin Powell and other top Pentagon officials had been personally involved in the Vietnam conflict."[86]

Lawrence Eagleburger, one of Bush I's secretaries of state, confessed that "when I thought of what might happen if we intervened, what I always feared was Vietnam—the tar baby. Something that started out small but kept growing."[87]

Clinton listened, and then listened some more. He was, on the one hand, instinctively opposed to sending American boots on the ground to Bosnia, but he was, on the other hand, persuaded that the United States ought to do something. He was, Hillary Clinton explained, "frustrated by Europe's failure to act after it had insisted that Bosnia was in its own backyard and was its own problem to solve."[88]

"I . . . didn't want to divide the NATO alliance," Bill Clinton later explained, "by unilaterally bombing Serb military positions, especially since there were European, but no American, soldiers on the ground with the UN mission. And I didn't want to send American troops there, putting them in harm's way under a UN mandate I thought was bound to fail."[89]

Clinton, after many more seminar-style sessions, endless and formless and yet helpful to the president, decided after a while to assign Holbrooke the wildly optimistic task of arranging a cease-fire in Bosnia. It was an assignment the boundlessly energetic diplomat relished; he had won Clinton's backing for the use of an American-led NATO air campaign against Serbian positions, and he believed that a relentless diplomatic and military effort would eventually break Milosevic's capacity to continue the war. Holbrooke, always thinking back to Vietnam, explained to himself and others that "Bosnia was not Vietnam, the Bosnian Serbs were not the Vietcong, and Belgrade was not Hanoi. The Bosnian Serbs, poorly trained bullies and criminals, would not stand up to NATO air strikes the way the seasoned and indoctrinated Vietcong and North Vietnamese had."[90]

Believing he would ultimately prevail, Holbrooke threw himself into a painstaking negotiation with Milosevic. Each thought he could outmaneuver the other. Each ranted and raved, issued threats, and set deadlines, as NATO bombs hit and weakened Serbian positions. Finally, in the fall of 1995, with the United States and Russia applying pressure on Milosevic and with Serbia universally branded a pariah state, Milosevic caved in to Holbrooke's twin demands for a cease-fire and a peace conference. The American diplomat insisted, to everyone's surprise and the media's misery, that the conference take place at the Wright-Patterson Air Force Base near Dayton, Ohio. The base was selected for its inaccessibility to the media. Holbrooke wanted a negotiation without leaks, and he wanted it to be seen as an American diplomatic triumph. He got both.

The negotiations ran November 1–21, 1995, and an agreement was formally signed in Paris on December 14, 1995. Though conservatives condemned the Dayton agreement, others hailed it at the time as a big step out of the Balkan morass. It called for the demarcation of boundaries between the Bosnian Serbs and the Muslims. In addition, an international peacekeeping force under NATO of 60,000 troops, including 20,000 Americans, was to be sent to Bosnia. The Americans were to be there for only one year, beginning on December 20, 1995, and were to operate under a tight set of rules: they were not to engage in combat; they were to be peacekeepers. Many in Congress opposed sending American troops to Bosnia, even for one year and even as peacekeepers.

Not many Republicans believed that the troops would be out in a year. One day, when Defense Secretary Perry stressed the one-year-and-no-more theme during a speech in Chicago, he was cautioned by Donald Rumsfeld, an earlier defense secretary: "Don't say it. Don't say it. You don't know when they are going to be out. You don't know how many people are gonna be killed. You can't know these things—they are not knowable."[91] Rumsfeld was right. U.S. troops remained in Bosnia, though in diminishing number, through the Clinton years, and into the Bush II years as well.

But as 1995 turned into 1996 and as Clinton prepared to launch his reelection campaign, he was now in proud possession of a political and a diplomatic triumph: not bad for the baby boomer from Hope, Arkansas. Clinton had just vanquished Gingrich, Speaker of the House, and Milosevic, president of Serbia. He was on a roll.

Clinton's Republican opponent turned out to be Senator Dole, a seventy-three-year-old World War II veteran, who had won two Purple Hearts and a Bronze Star as an army second lieutenant fighting gallantly in Italy during the concluding months of the war. In one battle, Dole was hit and seriously wounded. After the war, he spent years in rehabilitation hospitals. During his long political career, Dole served conservative causes as a representative and senator in Congress, a chair of the Republican National Committee, a vice presidential candidate in 1976, and now as his party's nominee for president. As he revved up his campaign, Dole entertained illusions that he was a perfect fit for the presidency and that Clinton, an unworthy draft dodger, was beatable; but he should have learned from Clinton's victory over Gingrich that this youthful, fifty-year-old president was a formidable politician, who was determined to win. It was Dole, the "old man," against Clinton, "the kid," as reporter Maraniss described the contest.[92]

Dole had promised in an offhand moment not to compare his war wounds with Clinton's lack of military experience; but, down in the polls, he went negative (no surprise to anyone who remembered Dole as a vice presidential candidate in 1976), stating during his acceptance speech at the GOP convention in San Diego that the Clinton administration represented an "elite who never grew up, never did anything real, never sacrificed, never suffered and never learned."[93] He pounced on every opportunity to underscore his service and his patriotism, by implication suggesting that Clinton was not patriotic because he hadn't served or fought for his country.

On Memorial Day, campaigning in New Jersey, Dole said: "I can't change his record, and he can't change my record. . . . I'm proud to serve my country."[94] The next month, at a Texas convention of the Veterans of Foreign Wars, he made the point that America's role as a superpower beginning in World War II "left its mark on people like Lieutenant John F. Kennedy, Lieutenant Richard Nixon and Lieutenant George Bush. It created a tradition of American leadership, shared by Republicans and Democrats." The former army lieutenant then added: "I want to preserve that legacy as President of the United States."[95] Indirectly, Dole was again suggesting that Clinton did not fit into the post–World War II tradition of Americans electing presidents who had served honorably in the military. Clinton was an aberration, deserving of defeat.

Stephanopoulos worried that Dole might be proven right. He wrote in his memoirs that "Dole couldn't match Clinton as a communicator, but there was still the issue of 'character'—the contrast between the straight-talking war hero of sterling integrity and the slippery draft dodger under an ethical cloud."[96]

But, judging by the polls, the American people were not buying Dole's pitch. On the crucial issue of national security, a *Washington Post–ABC News* poll said that 72 percent of respondents approved of Clinton's handling of the Iraq problem and, if there were to be another war with Iraq, 54 percent favored Clinton as commander in chief and only 35 percent favored Dole.[97] A *CNN-USAToday-Gallup* poll in August 1996 found that, by a margin of 53 percent to 40 percent, the American people approved of the way Clinton was conducting the nation's foreign affairs.[98] Both polls reflected a massive shift in public opinion since the 1992 campaign, when Clinton, realizing his weakness on national security issues, focused almost entirely on the economy. By now the American people were familiar with Clinton's policies and personality, and, putting aside his reputation as a womanizer and a draft dodger, they were prepared to trust him with the weighty problems of war and peace.

"War. Honor. Service. Survival," wrote reporter Maraniss. "The funny thing about the competition between the old man and the kid is that those notions have not always played out in predictable ways during the 1996 presidential campaign."[99] Columnist Richard Benedetto added his slant to this issue: "Republican candidate Bob Dole's World War II service seems to be working against him," Benedetto wrote, "while President Clinton's efforts to avoid service during the Vietnam War seem to matter not a lick. . . . [O]ne would think Dole would be getting at least some credit for his willingness to answer his country's call in time of war and the serious wounds he suffered. He's not."[100]

On Election Day 1996, Clinton easily defeated Dole, getting 49 percent of the vote to Dole's 41 percent. Third-party candidate Ross Perot received only 8 percent, considerably less than he got in his 1992 run.

Finally, the Kosovo Challenge

Clinton's second term was crowded with domestic and foreign challenges. One, involving an insanely foolish fling with a White House intern named Monica Lewinsky, led to his impeachment by the House and trial by the Senate. Though it was often asserted that Clinton had an extraordinary capacity for "compartmentalization"—going from one meeting about the Lewinsky scandal, for example, to another about Middle East negotiations without missing a beat—he lost valuable time first by lying, then by vacillating, and finally by acknowledging his role in this unsavory affair. If there had been no Lewinsky distraction, the president might have been able to anticipate economic problems at home; he might have been able to concentrate on such simmering trouble spots as the Balkans, not to mention the chronic Israeli-Palestinian dispute, to which he devoted his final months in office. By Herculean effort, he brought both parties close to an agreement, but sadly ran out of time, his most precious commodity in the twilight of his presidency.

There was rarely a day, though, that Clinton was not forced to consider the "horror in the Balkans." It ran through his deliberations about foreign policy, and it frequently posed a key question: in light of the ghosts of Vietnam, who floated through the Oval Office as nagging reminders of an earlier debacle, when and how should he use the military might of the United States? His advisers usually split along predictable lines: those who had served in Vietnam urged caution, those whose memories stretched back to World War II and

Munich recommended action. The split was most pronounced when Kosovo, an impoverished, mountainous Serbian province of 2.1 million people, the vast majority of them Albanian Muslims, succeeded Bosnia as the Balkan crisis of the day.

For Milosevic, Kosovo was always an irritant, but it was also a real obstacle in his mad pursuit of a "Greater Serbia." On June 18, 1989, the Serbian leader took an important step toward solving this problem, when he celebrated the 600th anniversary of the Battle of Kosovo at a giant rally near the provincial capital of Pristina. He spoke with passion and pride of a new Serbian nationalism, and, this time, he implied, Serbia would win a decisive victory over all its enemies.

For Bush I, Milosevic was always an unpredictable foe, but at the time he was not a front-burner problem; the Bush administration was preoccupied with the dismantling of the cold war. But at the State Department, a few Balkan experts worried that Milosevic might be on the edge of another dangerous adventure. They rushed to their history texts and found that indeed in 1389 the medieval Orthodox kingdom of Serbia had engaged an advancing army of Muslim warriors from the Ottoman Empire. In a bloody battle, Serbia had been soundly defeated; and with defeat came centuries of humiliation and degradation. Only in the nineteenth century, during the rise of European nationalism, did Serbia again begin to develop a sense of pride and accomplishment, always waving the banner of the Battle of Kosovo as proof that history would one day reserve an honored place for Serbia on the European landscape. Living in this world of illusion, Milosevic, mixing Balkan thuggery with nationalist dreams, had returned to Kosovo, proclaiming that this time Serbia would win.

If Bosnia was the battlefield in the first half of the 1990s, Kosovo was the battlefield in the second half. For most of the decade, it stewed in social, economic, and religious misery, periodically erupting in fights between Serbian troops and loosely organized Albanian radicals and nationalists. When the Dayton Accords were being negotiated in 1995, the issue of Kosovo was not addressed.

Over the next few years, violence erupted and fanned out across Kosovo, a predictable reaction to Dayton's callous indifference. Albanian Muslims took up arms against their Orthodox Serbian masters. Radicals formed the so-called Kosovo Liberation Army (KLA), which the United States at first regarded as a terrorist organization but later as a negotiating partner. From neighboring Albania and other Muslim countries, arms and money flowed into Kosovo. No longer preoccupied with the Bosnian war, which was now, at least temporarily, put to one side, Milosevic saw in the rising conflict in Kosovo a golden opportunity to battle against both the KLA in particular and the Kosovars in general. He dispatched more troops to Kosovo, sent in additional tanks and armored vehicles, and launched a "scorched-earth" policy that had the effect of frightening more than 300,000 Kosovars from their homes. Most fled across the border into Albania and Macedonia. It was a human catastrophe that had the potential for igniting a broader European war, and Clinton, though absorbed with the aftermath of a debilitating sex scandal, had to deal with it.

Among his senior advisers, there were splits on many issues but not on the need to persuade the Europeans to accept primary responsibility for settling the Kosovo crisis. Kosovo was obviously their problem—it was in Europe. And who could forget that a murder in Sarajevo earlier in the century had touched off a world war? It fell largely to Secretary of State Albright and Defense Secretary Cohen to argue the U.S. case to the Europeans. Because Clinton had repeatedly ruled out the use of American combat troops in the Balkans, a questionable decision that severely narrowed his field of options, the secretaries' task became immeasurably more difficult. On one trip after another, Cohen told his European counterparts: "This is your backyard. This is happening [here]. You have got to get involved. This is your responsibility." They listened, but essentially did nothing. Their argument, according to Cohen, was that "unless the U.N. Security Council authorized military action, they could do nothing."

Imagining a Russian veto, Cohen responded: "You know that's not going to take place. The Russians are never going to allow this, and you are going to let these people get 'ethnically cleansed?'"

The European answer: "They were not going to do anything unless we did."[101]

Though there were many on the continent who routinely complained about American hegemony and arrogance, the Europeans usually waited for the United States to take the lead when it came to military action, even if the problem was essentially a European one.

Albright, like Cohen, briefed Congress on a regular basis. Very reluctantly, in 1995 Congress had sanctioned the sending of American peacekeeping troops to Bosnia, but only for one year. When both secretaries began to lay out their options for Kosovo and included the possibility of American troops going there, Congress balked, pointing out that Clinton had not kept his promise about Bosnia; U.S. troops were still there after one year. Cohen remembered one lawmaker after another putting the policy choice in either-or terms: "Either we are going to commit ourselves to something that was endless, or what's the exit strategy?" The lessons of Vietnam permeated congressional questions and concerns.

Cohen was especially proud of the Clinton administration's record of keeping Congress informed about policy deliberation. He always remembered one of Powell's warnings about the importance of winning public and congressional support before any military operation.[102] In reviewing military options, Congress often seemed almost paralyzed by the lingering lessons of Vietnam and the obvious dangers of fighting in the Balkans. But if action was absolutely necessary to prevent further genocide or ethnic cleansing, many members were prepared, as a last resort, to sanction an air war against Serbia, within a NATO context, not on their own. But under no conditions would they agree to send more American troops to the Balkans. To justify their opposition, they frequently quoted the president's own stated opposition.

Within the administration, Albright often led the fight for some kind of U.S. action, later joking that she was "a mere mortal female civilian" taking on both the Pentagon brass and the spooked White House staff. In policy discussions, "'mired' was always the word," Albright noted. "There is no doubt in my mind that they had the Vietnam syndrome, and it did affect people." The Balkans affected her, too, but in a profoundly different way from its impact on many of her colleagues. "Life is very, very weird," she reminisced. "My father had been ambassador to Yugoslavia. This was one part of the world that I really understood. I remember seeing pictures of people being put on railroad cars and taken to concentration camps. So for me it was much more the Second World War [than it was Vietnam]."[103]

Albright ardently believed that something had to be done to stop the ethnic cleansing in Kosovo, examples of which appeared regularly on the evening newscasts in Europe and America. In British prime minister Tony Blair, she found a reliable ally and, as often as possible, arranged for Blair to visit Clinton at the White House or Camp David for long, private talks about a Europe finally free of conflict. Blair had one immediate mission: to persuade the American president to lead an international effort to rid Europe of Milosevic. Ultimately Blair was successful.

Holbrooke was another ally. At Albright's urging, he returned repeatedly to the Balkans, the scene of his earlier triumph. Now, in Kosovo, his task was as formidable as it had been in Bosnia: somehow to persuade Milosevic to accept a modest international force of unarmed verifiers to separate the Serbs from the Kosovars and arrange a cease-fire. Time and again, Holbrooke flew to Belgrade and negotiated with the Serbian leader, warning him of a massive NATO air campaign to be led by the United States if he did not accept the diplomat's modest proposal. Milosevic was not in a buying mood. He believed NATO was not up to the job, and Clinton not up to another Balkan fight. As Halberstam was later to report, "If Dayton had been difficult, Kosovo was even more difficult. Holbrooke found Milosevic not only manipulative as in the past, but furious at the way everyone was now aligned against him. He was angry that the Kosovars were doing to him what he had threatened to do to the West—create a Vietnam on his sovereign soil."[104]

As the fighting spread, a diplomatic contact group was organized: the United States, Britain, France, Germany, Italy, and Russia. They tried to arrange a Kosovo peace conference at Rambouillet, France, to take place in February 1999. A massacre uncovered in the Kosovo village of Racak triggered a terrible upsurge of fighting and added to the urgency of a peace conference. Finally, both belligerents, under steady international pressure, agreed to meet with the contact group at Rambouillet starting on February 6. Albright represented the United States. She shuttled tirelessly between the belligerents, urging, cajoling, pleading with them to accept a compromise formula: wide-ranging Kosovo autonomy within Serbia, to be guarded by an international force of 28,000 troops. Not only did both sides reject her formula—the Kosovars, because they wanted independence, not autonomy; and the Serbs, because they refused to accept an international force—but within the contact group itself differences surfaced that undercut her effort. The Russians, like the Serbs, rejected an international force, and the French and the Italians could not decide on any plan of action. A meaningless compromise was struck; everyone would take three weeks off and then return for another round of talks. Meanwhile, it was understood, the cruel bloodletting would continue.

Albright returned to Washington, and, with stubborn determination, argued for a major air campaign against Serbia and, if necessary, ground action. Cohen at the Pentagon and General Wesley Clark at NATO headquarters threw their support behind Albright. Vice President Gore, who had been meeting quietly with Russia's prime minister, Victor Chernomyrdin, and getting another perspective on Milosevic, believed that only American military action could get the Serb's attention.

From the White House, Clinton provided his justification for an air war against Serbia—an air war only, no troops on the ground—in a televised address. He had to explain why Kosovo was in the "national interest" of the United States, why it required the commitment of American forces. He appealed to the decency and goodwill of the American people. He said that Milosevic had taken away the Kosovars' autonomy and unleashed a brutal campaign of ethnic cleansing: "killing civilians, burning villages, and driving people from their homes, sixty thousand in the last five weeks, a quarter million in all," as Clinton later wrote.[105] His aim was to convince Milosevic to stop the killing in Kosovo. His other aim was to convince the American people that he was doing the right and noble thing.

Clinton inserted the line "I do not intend to put our troops in Kosovo to fight a war" into his remarks, a line that represented, as Halberstam wrote, "a mandatory political step" to appease Congress. "It was the compromise of all compromises," Halberstam wrote. "It would be hard, six years into the Clinton presidency, to think of a sentence more important within the bureaucracy. It summed up with surprising accuracy all the contradictions and the ambivalence of America as a post–Cold War superpower." To the military, "it was not a mere throwaway line; rather it seemed to be carved in stone. . . . It was a reminder of the ambiguity of the Vietnam decision-making, of civilians who were willing to enter a war zone without any of the hard decisions having been made."[106]

Albright, meanwhile, appearing on CNN's *Larry King Live,* was asked how long the bombing campaign would last—"three, four days. . . . Is there a plan?" King wondered. "Wary of criticism that Kosovo might turn out to be another Vietnam," Albright later wrote, "I said I couldn't give details but 'it's going to be a sustained attack, and it's not something that's going to go on for an overly long time.'"[107] Clearly she wanted to send a strong message to Milosevic that he was going to pay a price for his ethnic cleansing, but she also wanted to ease domestic concerns that the United States might be slipping into another long, twilight struggle that was not really in the national interest of the country. In fact, neither she nor Clinton nor Cohen knew at the time how long the bombing campaign would last, but they all hoped that it would bring Milosevic to his senses. For the moment they chose not to think about a ground campaign.

The air war, which began on March 24, 1999, produced devastating bombing and cruise missile attacks on bridges, factories, communication centers, air bases, and government installations in Belgrade and in Pristina, which was occupied by Serbian troops. It seemed like all-out war, the bombing campaign a necessary softening-up of enemy positions preparatory to a ground assault.

As the days stretched into weeks and the weeks into months, and still Serbia battled on, showing no sign of capitulation, Cohen and Clark began to contemplate the need for an American-led ground attack against Serbia. How many troops would be needed? Cohen asked his generals. "One-hundred-and-eighty thousand" was their considered response, if the goal remained the same—to change Milosevic's mind and, if necessary, decapitate his regime. "The only country that would have contributed would [have been] the Brits," Cohen recalled. "They said . . . 20,000. So where would the rest come from? From us."[108] Congress would have strenuously objected to such a commitment, Cohen felt, and so would Clinton and a number of his senior advisers.

Clark, for his part, made it clear to Berger and through him to Clinton that he needed ninety days to prepare for a ground invasion of Serbia. "You've got to give me the green light," he pleaded, because winter was approaching.[109]

In late May American bombing of Serbia intensified. So did all diplomatic efforts to persuade Milosevic to give up the fight. The Russians ultimately withdrew their support from Milosevic, an action that ended up breaking the back of the Serbian leader's resistance. Without Russia, Milosevic was lost.

At issue was more than a civil war in Serbia; at issue, too, were the cohesion of NATO and the credibility of the United States. Everyone understood at the time that if the United States, assisted only by Britain, had to invade Serbia at the head of a force of 180,000 troops, NATO would have split apart. There was powerful pro-Serbian sentiment in Italy and Greece, and little enthusiasm elsewhere in Europe for an American-led expansion of the Balkan wars. "It would have been," Berger said, "a coalition of the willing, sort of a NATO-lite." He said, "American credibility would have been shattered had we blinked." Clinton and Blair were committed. "We cannot lose," they kept saying.[110] Albright admitted that at the beginning of the air campaign "we said we would not use ground troops." Cohen had assured Congress of the same thing: no ground troops in Kosovo. But "because winter was coming," and "if this [bombing campaign] didn't end soon," Albright said, the United States would have had to go to the next step, "the use of ground troops."[111] The prospect, though, was dark and ominous.

"I think we were so committed we would have had to do it," Berger concluded, revealing his own deep reservations, but "it would have taken a long time, and it would have been a very, very costly enterprise." He said, "It would have been a Herculean enterprise, because the terrain there is probably not as bad as it is in northwestern Pakistan, but it sure ain't the plains of Kansas. . . . That would have been the greatest test of the post-Vietnam willingness to use force in an all-out ground war."

Berger was still in his White House office at 3 a.m. one morning, writing a memo to Clinton outlining his options for the next three weeks if Milosevic did not capitulate, despite tremendous pressure, even from the Russians, to do so. The phone rang. It was Talbott calling from the State Department, saying, "Milosevic has put up the white flag. He's calling together his Parliament tomorrow to surrender."[112]

In Kosovo, the United States won and Milosevic lost. The combination of overwhelming air power and powerful diplomatic pressures persuaded the Serbian leader to "put up the white flag." But behind the undeniable victory lurked an unanswered and unanswerable question: what would have happened if Milosevic had not capitulated, if he had continued to fight in Kosovo beyond the cutoff date for a presidential decision to prepare for a ground invasion? Would Clinton have flashed the green light? Or would he have stalled, fearful of another Vietnam-style war and possible debacle? Berger and Albright expressed confidence that Clinton's decision would have been a vigorous nod of the head and a decisive order to invade Kosovo.[113] But in his memoir, Clinton suggests that, in the final analysis, he would not have given his approval to a ground invasion of Kosovo in June 1999.

"Some people argued that our position would have been more defensible if we had sent in ground troops." he wrote. "There were two problems with that argument. First, by the time the soldiers were in position, in adequate numbers and with proper support, the Serbs would have done an enormous amount of damage. Second, the civilian casualties of a ground campaign would probably have been greater than the toll from errant bombs. I didn't find the argument that I should pursue a course that would cost more American lives without enhancing the prospects of victory very persuasive. Our strategy would often be second-guessed, but never abandoned."[114]

Clinton did use American military power, but mostly from 30,000 feet. By the late 1990s, Vietnam was still a force in decisionmaking, but it surfaced in new and odd ways, sometimes as a rip-roaring reassertion of old-fashioned American values, at other times as a cautious response to a series of deadly challenges.

7

Bush II: Boots on the Ground

I am a product of the Vietnam era.
—GEORGE W. BUSH, interview with Bob Woodward, August 2002

You've got to take 9/11 and smack it down right in the middle.
—DICK CHENEY, author interview, January 14, 2010

FOR BILL CLINTON, "boots on the ground" was a military option to be avoided if at all possible, no matter the provocation. A cruise missile attack at a terrorist base, a series of bombing runs from 30,000 feet—these could be sanctioned, however grudgingly, but only if the president had assurances from the Joint Chiefs of Staff that casualties, civilian and military, would be limited to an absolute minimum. But to commit American troops to a dangerous mission of uncertain cost and duration? That was another story. Almost automatically in the Clinton White House, the prospect of boots on the ground conjured up dark memories of Vietnam. Might this be the time when the United States would again be sucked into an unwinnable guerrilla war?

For George W. Bush, after 9/11, however, the option of "boots on the ground" was not only encouraged, it became his favored option. Vietnam be damned, Bush seemed to be telling the world. From now on, the United States would demonstrate its seriousness, its determination to win "the war against terrorism," by committing its troops to battle. And if that meant casualties, civilian and military, then so be it. Bush believed that war was never a dainty business. "The antiseptic notion of launching a cruise missile into some guy's, you know, tent, really is a joke," Bush told reporter Bob Woodward, referring to Clinton's attack on a terrorist camp. "I mean, people viewed that as the impotent America . . . a flaccid, you know, kind of technologically competent but not very tough country . . . that when struck, we wouldn't fight back."[1] With 9/11 firing up his anger, he wanted everyone to know that the days of

Clintonian caution were over, that the United States was again on the move, and let its enemies beware!

Boots on the ground was the president's direct order, recalled Donald Rumsfeld, Bush's secretary of defense. "The president from 9/11 on was saying when are we going to get some people on the ground," Rumsfeld said of plans for an American move against Afghanistan. "Simply firing missiles wasn't good enough," Rumsfeld remembered the president saying. "He felt that the U.S. reaction to the attacks on the Khobar Towers [in Saudi Arabia] and on the USS *Cole* [in Yemen] with cruise missile attacks on mud huts in a training camp [wouldn't do it]." That approach was even worse than meaningless, because not only did it fail to stop the threat, but it also signaled that that was all the U.S. government was capable of doing, Rumsfeld said. It did not take a highly paid analyst to recognize the difference between Clinton and Bush. "It was not to avoid [people on the ground]," Rumsfeld said of Bush's approach, "but to achieve that."[2] The difference between the two presidents was misleading, though, for it suggested that Bush was breaking away from the inhibiting legacy of Vietnam and opening a new and bold chapter in America's national security policy. In truth, Vietnam shadowed him, as it had shadowed Clinton, but after 9/11 the legacy of that lost war took on a new look.

Bush versus Gore: Yale, Harvard, and Vietnam

The candidates were so similar, and yet so different. The 2000 presidential campaign, for the first time, featured two baby boomers for whom the war in Vietnam had played a major role in their younger years. After graduating from Yale in 1968, George W. Bush, born in 1946, ducked service in Vietnam by joining the Texas Air National Guard. Strange, because he supported the war. Albert A. Gore Jr., born in 1948, volunteered and served in Vietnam after graduating from Harvard in 1969. Stranger still, because he fiercely opposed the war. Both were the sons of successful fathers who had been elected to high public office. Both lived in a privileged environment, and both attended elite New England schools. Historians had trouble finding another presidential campaign in which the two candidates, to quote reporter Frank Bruni, were "not only such prominent political heirs but also from such similar stations and members of the same generation."[3]

Bush was born in New Haven, Connecticut, while his father, a World War II hero, was finishing his studies at Yale. The family then moved to Texas. The oldest of Barbara and George H. W. Bush's six children, George W. was not an exceptional student, either at Andover or at Yale. He was best known as a "frat boy" who rarely exhibited an interest in world affairs. Vietnam and the draft hovered over the near horizon for most students, but, according to one of his biographers, Bill Minutaglio, Bush's friends at Yale "wondered if Vietnam was on Bush's mind at all, since he hardly ever spoke about it. He rarely talked about the nuances of the war, the stances his father [then a representative from Texas] and grandfather [Senator Prescott Bush of Connecticut] were taking, the military strategies, the roiling student protests, the way it was all rattling the highest levels of government around the world."[4] Another biographer, Jacob Weisberg, echoed this theme of non-interest. "For most of his life, George W. Bush did not engage with public affairs. Bush basically blew off the 1960s, the Vietnam War, and Watergate."[5] When speakers came to Yale to express their views about the war, pro or con, "my friends and I did not attend the speeches," Bush wrote.[6]

But on rare occasions, Bush would discuss the war with a friend. He was a supporter of the war, as most Texans were, and he was disturbed by "unthinking opposition to the war, just for its own sake," according to Robert Beebe, considering it "knee-jerk." Another friend, Doug Hannah, recalled, "George and I used to talk all the time that there has to be a better alternative than being a lieutenant in the Army." Hannah added, "We didn't know people who were killed in Vietnam. We lost far more friends to motorcycle accidents than we ever did to Vietnam." The war did not seem seriously to intrude into their lives. Bush registered for the draft during a school break in Houston, but, as a student, was deferred. If Vietnam absorbed Bush at all, it was in his desire "not to derail his father's political career." He knew that one day, as he confided to his fraternity brother Ronald Betts, "he had to be in military service of some kind."[7]

But it had to be the kind of service acceptable to the family tradition. "Leaving the country to avoid the draft was not an option for me," Bush wrote in a campaign autobiography published in 1999. "I was too conservative and too traditional. My inclination was to support the government and the war until proven wrong, and that only came later, as I realized we could not explain the mission, had no exit strategy, and did not seem to be fighting to win."[8]

As he approached his graduation from Yale, Bush faced a key decision: should he volunteer for service in Vietnam? He wanted to be a fighter pilot, just as his father had been during World War II. "I wanted to learn a new skill that would make doing my duty an interesting adventure," he later wrote. "I had never flown an airplane but decided I wanted to become a pilot." Here, in his campaign autobiography, drafted to glide past potential problems, Bush said that he had heard from "contemporaries" that "there were openings for pilots in the Texas Air National Guard." He called and learned that there were in fact "several openings." Why? Because, he explained, while others might have been unwilling to devote "almost two years of full-time duty required for pilot training," he was willing.[9] Bush wanted to convey the impression that he, as compared with others, was ready to make this sacrifice for his country—two years of pilot training in Texas, but apparently no more. He saw an opportunity limited in time and scope. He could pick up a "new skill" and wear a uniform.

In late May 1968, when as many as 350 Americans were being killed every week in the Vietnam War, Bush, about to graduate from Yale, applied for service in the Texas Air National Guard. It was May 27, and he was accepted on the same day. His commander, Colonel Walter B. "Buck" Staudt, seemingly overjoyed at the thought of having the son of a member of Congress from Texas in his unit, went through the motions of administering the oath to Bush at a special ceremony, even though he knew that Bush had already been sworn in a few hours earlier. Staudt wanted his picture taken with the son of a celebrity. When Bush was later commissioned a second lieutenant, Staudt held another camera-ready ceremony, with George Bush the father also in attendance.[10]

Did Bush receive preferential treatment? The question was often asked during a number of his political campaigns. The answer: of course he did. To many observers, it seemed that Bush was "moved up" in the National Guard ahead of "hundreds, probably thousands of other young Texas draft age men." Ben Barnes, the Texas House speaker, admitted in a legal deposition years later that "he took a call from a Bush family friend seeking favoritism to move Bush up on the National Guard waiting list. Barnes said no one from the Bush family ever contacted him, but Houston businessman Sid Adger did call and urged Barnes to get George W. Bush a pilot position in the guard. Barnes said he contacted General Rose of the Texas Guard to make the request."[11] According to the *Los Angeles Times,* Bush was able to "jump into the officer ranks without the exceptional credentials many other officer candidates possessed."[12] Bush had scored only 25 percent on an aptitude test for entering pilots, the lowest acceptable grade.[13]

Bush learned to fly an F-102 Interceptor jet, described by Minutaglio as "nimble but increasingly obsolete,"[14] at the Moody Air Force Base in Georgia.

He was then assigned to the 147th Fighter Wing at the Ellington Air Force Base in Houston. For the rest of his service in the National Guard, the closest Bush got to war was news that two pilots from his unit had crashed and died—one over the Gulf of Mexico and the other during a test flight. In his campaign autobiography, he wrote, "It brought a sobering reality to what we were doing. I served, and I am proud of my service."[15] Because campaign autobiographies are not meant to be anything more than the literary equivalent of a political ad, Bush used his book to suggest that during his time in the National Guard, he was preoccupied with more than flying: he was thinking big thoughts. One was about "the lesson of Vietnam."

"Our nation should be slow to engage troops," he explained, reflecting the prevailing GOP updating of the Powell Doctrine. "But when we do so, we must do so with ferocity. We must not go into a conflict unless we go in committed to win. We can never again ask the military to fight a political war. If America's strategic interests are at stake, if diplomacy fails, if no other option will accomplish the objective, the Commander in Chief must define the mission and allow the military to achieve it."[16] It could be argued that after 9/11 Bush pulled the trigger before he gave diplomacy a chance to fail.

However, it was not national policy that absorbed Bush in the fifteen years after his National Guard service. He was, during this time, largely adrift. He lacked his father's focus. He stumbled from one job to another without a fixed goal in mind. With his family's encouragement, he enrolled in, and was graduated from, the Harvard Business School in 1975; and, like his father, he entered the Texas oil business, but he made little of it. In 1977 he met and, a few months later, married Laura Welch, a teacher and librarian. The following year, he ran an amateurish campaign for Congress, and lost. Bush then fell into a deep midlife crisis, which only ended, when, around age forty, he suddenly experienced a religious revival. Born again, infused with a fresh burst of energy and direction, Bush stopped drinking and started thinking seriously about politics, which was, after all, the family business.

In 1988, during his father's first run for the presidency, the younger Bush not only defended Dan Quayle, his father's controversial running mate, he also served as a kind of backstage consigliere. (Any problem? Let George handle it!) He did so well, by all accounts, that he began to think about running for office again, this time for higher office. In 1989 he took a first step. He became the managing general partner of the Texas Rangers, turning the faltering baseball franchise into a financial success and earning goodwill throughout the state. In 1991 he set his sights on the governorship of Texas, then occupied by the popular Democrat Ann Richards, who figured she could easily defeat him. Years later, she confessed in frustration that during the campaign she could not break through Bush's flat-out refusal to go beyond his script.[17] A panelist in a gubernatorial debate asked Bush the predictable question: had he received preferential treatment of any kind? Bush's rehearsed answer: "All I know is that a position opened up, and I got to enlist," he said, adding, "I knew I wanted to learn to fly airplanes, and this was a great opportunity. If there was any influence exercised on my behalf, I sure didn't know about it."[18] Bush was stretching the truth on this point—and one other. He knew when he joined the National Guard that he would almost certainly not be going to Vietnam; yet he asserted: "I know my unit could have been called up at any time and just flying airplanes is dangerous. I could have been killed. You think about that when you turn on those afterburners."[19]

Bush won the Texas governorship in 1994 and again in 1998; and as the 2000 presidential campaign neared, GOP insiders were betting that he would be their standard bearer, and that he would face the incumbent vice president, Al Gore. They were two baby-boomer candidates representing the same generation but differing hugely on a crucial decision they both faced in the late 1960s: service in Vietnam.

While Bush quickly joined the National Guard, which kept him out of Vietnam, Gore acted like a character in a Dostoevsky novel, agonizing deep into the night about his next step. Because he passionately opposed the war, he did not want to serve in Vietnam; and yet if he refused to serve, he would surely damage his father's campaign for reelection as an antiwar senator from Tennessee, a state sympathetic to the war. Gore engaged in many conversations with himself and with others until, finally, he decided to volunteer for U.S. Army service in Vietnam.

Gore from Carthage

Whereas Bush, until age forty, charted an uncertain path, Gore from childhood seemed destined to follow in his father's footsteps. In the Gore household, as in the Bush household, politics was the lingua franca of family conversation. Albert Gore Sr., though of modest means, finished college and law school in Tennessee, as did his wife, Pauline. He then pursued a political career, running first for the House, where he took his seat in 1939, as war clouds gathered in Europe and the Pacific, and then for the Senate, moving to the upper chamber in 1953, as the United States finished one war in Korea and prepared for another in Vietnam. The Gores had two children; daughter Nancy was ten years older than son Al, who attended the posh St. Alban's school, where he was known as a bright, hard-working student.

When Gore enrolled at Harvard in 1965, the campus was already starting to bubble with antiwar agitation. In 1967 one of Gore's classmates quit Harvard, joined the army, and was soon killed close to the Cambodian border in an ambush. Gore was stunned by the news, which raced through the dormitory.[20] The death deepened Gore's personal anguish about the war. At the same time, President Lyndon Johnson declared that as of spring 1968, most graduate school deferments would come to an end, "a seismic event for thousands of young men who had counted on three or four years in the snug harbor of a Ph.D. program to help them wait out the end of their draft eligibility at age twenty-six."[21]

During Gore's senior year, when students occupied University Hall, bringing Harvard to a virtual halt, he was much absorbed with the debates of the day. Like his father in the Senate Foreign Relations Committee, he was arguing the pluses and minuses of American policy, especially as they affected his own decision on whether, and, if so, how to serve. With his high school sweetheart, Mary Elizabeth "Tipper" Aitcheson, Gore reviewed each of his options, as if he were planning a political or military campaign. After a while, she felt he was devoting more time to considering the effect of his decision on his father and mother, his Harvard classmates, and his friends in Carthage than he was on their future as a married couple.[22] Gore wondered, for example, whether he would be able to show up on Carthage's Main Street "without feeling small and guilty."[23]

More than anyone, it seemed, Gore worried about his father. Senator Gore had become a major critic of the Vietnam War, and in Tennessee his antiwar reputation had robbed him of much of his earlier appeal. The senator was vulnerable, and his son wanted to help him.

Finally, Gore enlisted in a two-year program in the U.S. Army. Of the 1,115 Harvard graduates in his class, only about a dozen ended up serving in Vietnam.[24] Gore was one of them. After his basic training at Fort Dix, New Jersey, he was sent to Fort Rucker, Alabama, where he worked in the public affairs office, becoming in effect an army journalist.

Once in the army, Gore volunteered immediately for Vietnam. Being in Vietnam while his father was still running for reelection against GOP candidate Bill Brock could have been proof, if any were needed, that the Gore family was patriotic, even if the senator was against the war. But Gore's departure for Vietnam was held up until after the November 1970 election, which the senator lost. Gore believed his delay was engineered by the Nixon White House.[25] Gore went to Vietnam in January 1971 and stayed for five months, serving in a noncombat role as an army journalist. He was based at Bien Hoa, considered to be relatively safe. He was given the nickname "Brother Buck," and he was assigned an M-16 rifle, which he occasionally carried but never used. "I didn't do the most, or run the gravest danger," he said. "But I was proud to wear my country's uniform."[26]

When Gore returned from Vietnam, he studied for a time at Vanderbilt's divinity and law schools and worked as a reporter for the Nashville *Tennessean*. But in 1976 he followed his father's footsteps into the world of politics. He ran for his father's House seat and won. He was twenty-eight. Six years later, in 1984, Gore ran for a Senate seat and won. Among political reporters, Gore came to be recognized as a serious comer. In 1988 he decided to run for the big prize: the Democratic presidential nomination. During the campaign, he showed a photo of himself carrying an M-16 rifle, suggesting he was a combat soldier during his service in Vietnam. The photo was, as Gore biographer Bill Turque put it, "misleading."[27] More important, though, he was never able to generate enough traction in a crowded field, and he ultimately dropped out of the race. But four years later, he ended up on the national ticket as Bill Clinton's running mate. Elaine Kamarck, who later worked for Gore, described her boss as "a formal politician who often came across as wooden, or, even worse, condescending, in public. But," she added, "he was organized, decisive and wise in the ways of Washington, traits Clinton valued."[28]

Bush and Gore Played to a Draw in 2000, but Bush Won

As the 2000 presidential campaign opened, the smart money was on a Gore victory, largely because the country was enjoying "peace and prosperity," a phrase politicians would spend millions to own. And yet among Bush's closest aides, especially his political guru, Karl Rove, one could not help but pick up a tingling sense of excitement that the next president of the United States was going to be another Bush, not a Gore. Their candidate, always underestimated by his political foes, was a likable, two-term governor of a big southern state. He had not accomplished much, but he had a proper pedigree, lots of money, a tested team of campaign advisers, a lovely wife, and twin daughters: the perfect all-American résumé, except for his failure to serve in Vietnam and his reputation as an inexperienced lightweight. Rove engineered a strong, GOP message of the day: after eight years of Clinton and the Democrats, the White House was left in scandal, the United States was no longer the undisputed world power, and the American people wanted—and needed—a change. Under a Bush administration, America would be revived, its power and spirit restored. A new, muscular toughness would replace the flaccid defensiveness of the Clinton years. Besides, even though the economy had done well in the 1990s, Bush's economists pointed to troubling signs on the near horizon. A-B-C, the Bush campaign seemed to be shouting from every podium, Anything/Anyone-But-Clinton. And wouldn't Gore be just another Clinton?

Three men and one issue stood in Bush's way: John McCain, an attractive senator from Arizona who had not only served in Vietnam but had been a prisoner of war there for more than five years; Walter Robinson, an investigative political reporter for the *Boston Globe*, who dug into Bush's past association with the Texas Air National Guard and came up with damaging and embarrassing information; and, of course, Al Gore, who, as vice president, started the 2000 campaign as the candidate favored to win. The issue that, more than any other, repeatedly connected this trio to Bush was Vietnam, his non-service, and his apparent disinterest. But would the American people care?

The McCain Challenge

Up until February 1, 2000, the Bush cavalcade zipped along from one campaign stop to another, the candidate always smiling, always on time and always on message. He easily won the January 24 Iowa caucuses, beating such opponents as publisher Steve Forbes and former ambassador Alan Keyes. McCain had skipped Iowa, throwing his comparatively limited resources into the upcoming New Hampshire primary on February 1.

For months, McCain had been traveling around New England on a bus called the Straight Talk Express, home on wheels not only to the candidate but also to groups of reporters, who spent hours between campaign stops talking to McCain in a very free-form style about every subject on the news agenda. If the reporters were the only voters, McCain would have won in a landslide: he was the media darling, so different from the more typical politicians, Bush among them, who were controlled by stern handlers who trotted them out only rarely to talk with reporters. Not surprisingly, then, McCain took advantage of his popularity with the press to hit key points of difference between himself and Bush, none more telling than their vastly contrasting histories of military service.

McCain, a graduate of the Naval Academy at Annapolis, came from a family of distinguished naval officers. His father and grandfather had been admirals. While on a mission over North Vietnam in 1967, while Bush was still a frat boy at Yale, McCain was shot down, badly hurt, beaten, and imprisoned in the infamous Hanoi Hilton, often in solitary confinement. Because his father commanded American operations in the Pacific, McCain was offered an early release, which, if accepted, the communists would have painted as a humanitarian gesture in the face of U.S. "aggression." But McCain turned them down, infuriating his captors and opening himself to further punishment.

McCain's story made for compelling copy, and reporters and columnists exploited every angle, so much so that McCain said, unpersuasively, that he was "embarrassed" or "bored" by its repetition. "I mean, Jesus, it can make your skin crawl," he said. One photograph, of McCain and his A-4 Skyhawk fighter-bomber, the very picture of the patriot warrior, acquired an iconic place in the campaign.[29] Inevitably, reporters compared McCain's record with Bush's, and it was rarely a favorable comparison.

Charles Krauthammer, a conservative columnist for the *Washington Post*, was particularly impressed by McCain's stoic but courageous rejection of an early release from captivity. "It is, interestingly, a peculiar kind of courage, a kind that fits perfectly with America's still conflicted feelings about Vietnam," Krauthammer wrote. "He refused because that would have violated the military code of conduct under which one does not accept early release until those who have been captured earlier have been released first."[30]

Even among those Americans who had opposed the Vietnam War, there were many who were fascinated by the McCain candidacy, finding in the open and engaging senator a "reason to acknowledge that there was honor, and enduring value, in his wartime record as a navy pilot and five-year prisoner of war."[31]

The McCain campaign represented an insurgency in the GOP's usually staid ranks. The candidate's life was projected as the stuff of legends; in so many ways, the antithesis of Bush's. With the New Hampshire primary approaching, McCain ran a TV ad in January 2000 called "Commander." A narrator said: "There's only one man running for president who knows the military and understands the world: John McCain." The ad then noted that it was McCain, who was a navy pilot and a prisoner of war, who had suffered for his country. Though McCain would often dismiss the campaign's focus on his Vietnam experience, he never stopped it. He appreciated its potential value.

Wherever he went, McCain stopped at American Legion posts, where he was warmly welcomed. He also visited with the Veterans of Foreign Wars. He was certain he was on to what could be a rewarding strategy.

On February 1, when the independent-minded voters of New Hampshire went to the polls, Bush was still considered the front-runner for the GOP nomination. He had the money, the organization, and the momentum of his Iowa triumph. But McCain stunned the political world with an overwhelming 49 percent to 30 percent victory. Overnight, the Arizona senator became a credible candidate for the GOP nomination. The thinking at the time was that if he won in South Carolina, a state with 375,000–400,000 veterans and four major military installations,[32] on February 19 and then in Michigan on February 22, he would be able to snatch the nomination from the favored Bush. South Carolina suddenly became the battleground state that each candidate felt he had to win.

The Bush campaign pulled out all the stops, determined to beat McCain in South Carolina and salvage their candidate's once-soaring campaign. McCain, for his part, focused on military issues, his presumed strength. Blaming the Democrats, not his opponent, McCain highlighted reports of a downgrading of military preparedness, as the cold war slipped into history, and he bemoaned stories of 12,000 servicemen so poorly paid that they could receive food stamps. As commander in chief, McCain thundered, he would not need any on-the-job training.[33]

At a February 3 rally, Bush shared a platform with J. Thomas Burch Jr., chairman of the National Vietnam and Gulf War Veterans Committee, who accused McCain of opposing legislation dealing with the aftereffects of Agent Orange, a poisonous chemical used in Vietnam, and also of objecting to other legislation designed to help the relatives of servicemen missing in action in Vietnam. "He came home, forgot us," Burch charged. A quintet of senators—four Democratic, one Republican—wrote to Bush, upset by Burch's charges and Bush's decision not to rebut his "surrogate."[34] McCain tried to ride above the Burch fracas. "A little bit of foolishness," he said. "Of all the people they could attack on veterans' issues, they're attacking me?"[35] But he also expressed disappointment with Bush. "I gave him a pass on the National Guard, and now he comes after me on this," McCain grumbled.[36]

On February 15, four days before the crucial primary, McCain and Bush confronted each other in a televised debate hosted by CNN's Larry King. McCain wasted no time attacking Bush for allowing Burch to hit him below the belt. Naively, McCain appealed to Bush's better nature. "Governor Bush had an event, and he paid [for] it, and . . . stood next to a spokesman for a fringe veterans group. That fringe veteran said that John McCain had abandoned the veterans," said McCain. "Now, I don't know if you can understand this, George, but that really hurts, that really hurts. And so five United States senators, Vietnam veterans, heroes, some of them really incredible heroes, wrote George a letter and said, 'Apologize, you should be ashamed.'" McCain should have checked with Ann Richards about how Bush usually responded to a debater's thrust. He might have learned that Bush never yielded ground and always stuck to his position, trying to sound reasonable, even complimenting his opponent. "The man was not speaking for me," Bush responded. "If you want to know my opinion about you, John, you served your country admirably and strongly, and I'm proud of your record, just like you are."[37] At that moment in the King debate, McCain might have heard a hissing sound, like air slowly escaping from his campaign balloon.

The veterans' vote in South Carolina was an estimated 13 percent[38] of the total electorate, and both candidates struggled to capture it. Bush's campaign operated mostly in a netherworld of rumor and slander. Phone banks exploded with calls charging that McCain was a "traitor," because he favored normalizing relations with Vietnam.[39] One rumor, illustrative of the genre, said McCain was gay; another said he had fathered an illegitimate child with a North Vietnamese woman, which got him favored treatment from the communists.[40]

On February 17 McCain ran into controversy when he told a group of reporters on his Straight Talk Express that "I hate the gooks," his North Vietnamese captors. "I will hate them as long as I live."[41] Once uttered, his comment made headlines and forced the North Vietnamese to rebut it. Actually, as was soon to be made clear, the North Vietnamese favored McCain's candidacy, because, as reporter Rajiv Chandrasekaran wrote, "he was an early advocate for reconciliation and the resumption of normal diplomatic ties between the United States and Vietnam. The Arizona senator has made more than a half-dozen trips to Vietnam since 1985."[42] In the end, Bush won the primary by a percentage of 53-42; and though McCain went on to win in Michigan, his insurgent campaign effectively lost its national allure and slowly sputtered to an end. Bush proved in South Carolina, as Clinton had proved in two presidential campaigns, that the American people no longer put much stock in a candidate's wartime service or exploits in Vietnam. Bush and McCain split the veterans' vote.[43]

The Robinson Challenge

Over many years, Walter Robinson, an investigative reporter for the *Boston Globe*, had developed an eye for inconsistencies between what a politician projected to the public and what he or she actually did or said. When it looked like George W. Bush was going to win the GOP nomination for president of the United States, Robinson began to dig into the records of Texas politics to see if the private Bush measured up to the public one. He found problems in Bush's military record. Other reporters found similar problems. Their stories over the next few months portrayed a candidate less than candid about his National Guard service.

On May 23 Robinson rattled the Bush campaign with a story that there was an unexplained gap in the candidate's record as a National Guard pilot. Bush finished his training as a pilot in June 1970. Later, in his autobiography, he wrote: "I continued flying with my unit for the next several years." He was honorably discharged in October 1973. Robinson obtained copies of some of Bush's military records, and they showed that he did not fly during the last eighteen months of his service. For a whole year, according to the records, Bush did not appear for drill duty. When Robinson asked for an interview, Bush's spokesman said that Bush had "some recollection" of attending drills but possibly not on a consistent basis.

Bush worked in Alabama from May to November 1972, helping out with a U.S. Senate race. According to National Guard rules, he was supposed to attend drills at a local Air National Guard unit; however, nothing in his files showed that he did. William Turnipseed, the retired general with an unforgettable name who was in charge of the Montgomery unit at the time, told Robinson that Bush never showed up for duty there. In November Bush went back to Houston. The following May, his superior officers at the Ellington air base could not evaluate his work from May 1, 1972, to April 30, 1973, because, they wrote: "Lt. Bush has not been observed at this unit during the period of this report."[44]

The Bush campaign felt the need to respond to Robinson's story. "I did the duty necessary," Bush said in a careful denial. "That's why I was honorably discharged." Under questioning, though, he was obliged to concede that he did his guard duties, as Robinson wrote, "at irregular intervals."[45] On October 31 Robinson returned to the Bush record and, point by point, disputed the campaign's defense of it. On one point, whether he ever showed up for duty in Houston after his return from Montgomery, Robinson wrote: "There is other evidence that Bush's attendance was so inconsistent that his commanders did not know he had returned to the Houston base."[46]

Robinson's report especially disturbed Democratic senator Bob Kerrey, who had presidential dreams of his own in those years. "It upsets me," Kerrey told Robinson, "when someone says, 'Vote for me; I was in the military,' when in fact he got into the military [National Guard] in order to avoid serving in the military, to avoid service that might have taken him into the war. And then he didn't even show up for duty.'"[47]

Other reporters also dug into the Bush-Vietnam story, but, because it was fuzzy at the edges and inconclusive at its core, it never quite coalesced into a serious embarrassment. It was a story about how a presidential candidate had avoided service in Vietnam, and the American people had already proven during the Clinton years that they were ready to move on. Therefore, even though the story occasionally hit the front pages and made the evening news broadcasts, it lacked the power to derail the Bush campaign. It remained an insight into a candidate's character, but nothing more.

The Gore Challenge

Well before the start of the general election campaign, the magical period from Labor Day to Election Day when the electorate begins to show a real interest in politics, Al Gore would, often enough, wave his military credentials before the electorate, hoping that it would be noted and appreciated that while he volunteered for service in Vietnam, his opponent preferred the sanctuary of Houston, Texas. When he spoke before the American Legion in September 1999, for example, he stressed his devotion to a strong national defense and added, pointedly, "I was honored to wear my country's uniform during the Vietnam War." He also emphasized that his commitment to veterans was "more than a policy position"—it was "a personal and moral standard to bear."[48]

Gore arranged for the leaking of a set of letters he wrote in 1966 about his adamant opposition to the Vietnam War. As a student, he was moved by the "courage and rashness" of a classmate, who quit Harvard and went to Vietnam. "I don't think I was ever the same," he wrote of his experiences returning to Boston in military garb after joining the army. Gore, according to journalist Curtis Wilkie, was also "deeply troubled by the scornful reaction of other students to those who defended the war, or fought in it."[49] Joining the National Guard "didn't feel right," he remembered.[50] Yet defending U.S.

policy in Vietnam didn't feel right either. "Al Gore has a chip on his shoulder about Vietnam," wrote reporter Laurence McQuillan.

> He bristles at suggestions that his days in a war zone don't count, because he was there only a few months and spent that time as an Army journalist. He really gets upset if you think he was given special treatment because his dad was a U.S. senator at the time. . . . And . . . don't get him started on the war itself and the leaders in Washington who "completely screwed up" U.S. involvement there. With his thin skin about Vietnam, it is easy to strike a nerve.[51]

Did an American president have to have military service in a war? "Some distinguished leaders in the past have not had military experience, so you can't say it's essential," Gore asserted in an interview. A moment later, though, he suggested that wartime service was indeed essential. "I can only speak to my own experience in life," he told reporter Scott Shepard on Memorial Day weekend, a period that included a visit to West Point to deliver the graduation speech. "I would find it hard to relate to these cadets today or to the soldiers I meet on duty in the same way that I do if I had not had the experience of serving in uniform and serving my country overseas myself. It gives an extra dimension about what you think and feel when you're talking about the issues that face them."[52]

Whenever he thought it appropriate, Gore stressed his military service. On the campaign trail, he would often ask, "How many other Vietnam veterans are here?" He'd scan the crowd. "Welcome home," he'd shout. "I'm a Vietnam veteran." When he would visit an American Legion post, he would wear his hat at what one reporter described as "a jaunty angle," suggesting he was comfortable with the other veterans in the hall. In campaign advertising, he appeared as a Vietnam-era soldier with his M-16 rifle, though combat was not his thing in Vietnam.[53]

By hitting the theme of his own military service in Vietnam, Gore might have thought that Bush, in embarrassment, would have backed off the issue of military service and national security. But, quite the contrary, Bush seemed to believe that national security was one of his strongest suits. He questioned whether Gore would make a good commander in chief, criticizing what he described as a drop in the military's morale and prowess during the Clinton-Gore administration. There ought to be, he continued, "a new sign on the Pentagon that says 'Under New Management.'" And he would be the new manager.[54]

Bush campaigned as though he and his Republican colleagues were the only ones wise in the ways of national security. Often, on weekends, he would meet at his Crawford ranch with a small team of advisers, including Condoleezza Rice, Robert Zoellick, John Bolton, Paul Wolfowitz, and, on occasion, former secretary of state George Shultz. They would brief the candidate on China, Iraq, NATO enlargement, Iranian and North Korean nuclear development—subjects beyond his sphere of knowledge as a candidate but ones that he would have to deal with as a president. When the Kosovo crisis broke, Bush made the "stupid statement," said one of his advisers, about how he, as governor and therefore commander of the Texas National Guard, had acquired the experience to command the armed forces of the United States. Kosovo was not the place to engage American power, Bush said, dipping his toes into a Washington struggle between the Clinton White House, which favored engagement, and the GOP leadership on Capitol Hill, which opposed it. But Bush listened to Rice and Wolfowitz and changed his mind; he ended up supporting Clinton on this issue, an important show of bipartisanship in foreign affairs during a presidential campaign.

When it came time to select a vice presidential running mate, Bush chose the hawkish Dick Cheney, who had been a member of Congress from Wyoming and his father's secretary of defense. Cheney had not even served in the National Guard, and he had benefited from numerous deferments, as a student and father, during the 1960s. In 1989 he reportedly said with careless arrogance that he had "other priorities in the '60's than military service."[55] "Other priorities well, la-di-da," mimicked Democratic senator Tom Harkin after Cheney's selection as Bush's running mate. "I knew a lot of guys who had other priorities, too, and they didn't come back" from the war.[56] Cheney's pick represented a major departure for the GOP. Ever since Eisenhower, every GOP ticket had included a wartime veteran.[57]

Gore, meanwhile, chose Senator Joseph Lieberman of Connecticut, who made history as the first Jewish American on a national ticket. Like Cheney, Lieberman had avoided military service, receiving a string of deferments in the 1960s as a student and father. Years later, he recalled that he always felt "slightly embarrassed" about his failure to serve but that many of his classmates at Yale had also managed to avoid service, whether by enrolling in medical school or divinity school or skipping across the border into Canada claiming to be a conscientious objector. "Everyone seemed to find a way," he added, with a shrug of discomfort.[58] Everyone, that is, like Lieberman or

Cheney, who used their student status to protect themselves from service in Vietnam, knowing full well that many others would have to serve.

The Final Bush-Gore Exchanges

After the party conventions, Bush and Gore found themselves in a surprisingly tight campaign, each striking traditional chords designed to appeal to the party faithful. Bush benefited from his themes of cutting taxes and supporting the military, and Gore from his proven record of peace and prosperity. During their televised debates, Bush ducked every frontal challenge, while smiling and staying on message, and Gore sighed and came through as a know-it-all smarty pants. As often as possible, Gore returned to his I-volunteered-for-service-in-Vietnam-and-what-did-you-do-governor? theme, but it failed to jar either Bush's genial demeanor or his apparent grip on the national security issue. When moderator Jim Lehrer asked Gore in the first debate who was better prepared to handle national security, he responded, "When I was a young man, I volunteered for the Army. I served my country in Vietnam . . . [M]ost of my peers felt against the war as I did. But I went anyway. Because I knew if I didn't, somebody else, in the small town of Carthage, Tennessee, would have to go in my place."[59] Twice in the third debate, Gore stressed his Vietnam service. "There were plenty of fancy ways to get out of going and being a part of that," he said. "I went and I volunteered, and I went to Vietnam. I didn't do the most or run the gravest risk by a long shot, but I learned what it was like to be an enlisted man in the United States Army." Later in the debate, trying to put distance between himself and Clinton, Gore added, "I keep my word. I have kept the faith . . . I volunteered for the Army, I served in Vietnam. I kept the faith with my family."[60] Apparently, the American people honored Gore for his Vietnam service but gave him no extra points; they also seemed willing to forgive Bush for avoiding service in Vietnam.

A few days before the election, two senior Democratic senators, Daniel Inouye of Hawaii and Bob Kerrey of Nebraska, both with records of impressive military service, tried to make Bush's non-service in Vietnam more of an issue. "Where were you, Governor Bush?" Inouye asked. "What about your commitment? What would you do as commander-in-chief if someone in the Guard or service did the same thing?" Kerrey asked how Bush could have joined the National Guard "even though there were 500 people ahead of him" and at that point in time "350 Americans were dying every single week in Vietnam."[61]

November 7 proved to be a memorable day in the history of American elections. The country was split down the middle. Nationally, Gore won the popular vote; but the vote in Florida was so close that neither he nor Bush could lay undisputed claim to a win, and without Florida's twenty-five electoral votes neither could lay claim to the presidency. For the next six weeks, everyone was fixated on an embarrassing political circus of ballot recounts, legal challenges, and partisan recrimination. The effect was to shrink the lofty image of American democracy to a caricature of a crooked election in a banana republic. Finally, on December 12, 2000, the Supreme Court left its jurisprudential perch, entered the world of politics, and decided 5-4 to give Florida's electoral votes—and the presidency—to Bush. In an election in which tens of millions voted, the final result was decided by a single vote. In this way, the son of the forty-first president of the United States obtained the legitimate right to 271 electoral votes, one more than needed to become the forty-third president of the United States.

The Bush II Presidency

It was to be John Wayne's America, and George W. Bush was in the saddle, scanning the endless Texas horizon of sage brush and cactus and seeing boundless opportunity in what one adviser described as "open spaces [and] open skies."[62] He had not yet become a "war president," but he was already projecting a new militancy in his rhetoric and policy, a new toughness that seemed to place old alliances in a suddenly uncertain status. Critics were beginning to use terms such as "American unilateralism." Bush wanted to break decisively not only with the Clinton era but also with the lingering ghosts of Vietnam, which he saw (or thought he saw) in the exercise of American power. He wanted to resurrect a new Reaganesque optimism in America, a new post-Vietnam appeal to American exceptionalism. His father had boasted, after the Persian Gulf War, that he had "buried" the ghost of Vietnam in the "sands of the Arabian peninsula," but Bush saw the ghost, as though risen from the ashes, in Clinton's policies toward Somalia, Bosnia, and Kosovo—and it was Bush's job, he thought, to kill it. Before 9/11, and even after, living in his world of prairies and illusion, he often thought he could do it with a gesture here and a policy change there, but he was soon to learn that the presidency involved a much more serious approach to foreign policy. Among a number of his senior advisers, most notably Vice President Cheney, Defense Secretary Rumsfeld, and Deputy Defense

Secretary Wolfowitz, there was also a growing conviction, even before 9/11, that the United States would soon have to take action against Saddam Hussein's Iraq. They were waiting for their moment; it was only a matter of when.

The Powerful Effect of 9/11

Bush set an activist course in foreign policy and an unimaginative, conservative, cut-taxes tone in domestic policy. If it were not for 9/11, he would likely have gone down in history as another one-term president, another Bush forced into early retirement. But the historic events of 9/11 changed everything: for him, for America, and for the world. "You've got to take 9/11 and smack it down right in the middle of it," Dick Cheney said. "It was a dominant . . . development that overwhelmed everything."[63]

Years later, Cheney explained his thinking to NBC's Brian Williams. "I was in the bunker under the White House on 9/11, watched as the World Trade Center was destroyed, the Pentagon was hit, 3,000 Americans were killed. Never before [had] I seen an attack like that on the United States. And I was bound and determined, as was the president I then worked for, that that was never going to happen again on our watch."[64]

As a result of al Qaeda's 9/11 attack, George W. Bush became a war president, and the United States suddenly found itself engaged in an unexpected war in Afghanistan and then, a year and a half later, in a long, grinding war in Iraq. Both wars took a terrible toll on the American economy, but so far as the White House was concerned, they exercised a positive influence on American politics; Bush rode the wars to a second term in 2004.

Vietnam, it was said time and again, was not on their minds as Bush, Cheney, and their top advisers considered policy options in Afghanistan and later in Iraq. Vietnam was a lost war, not one to serve as inspiration for post-9/11 conflict. Their model, they insisted, was the Persian Gulf War. Bush's father had been president, Bush's vice president had been secretary of defense, and, more important, the United States had won decisively, something it had not done, except perhaps for its penny-ante invasions of Panama and Grenada, since World War II. Whether Bush considered it or not, his father's strategy in the Persian Gulf War followed the Powell Doctrine, and the Powell Doctrine emerged from the Vietnam experience, as interpreted by President Ronald Reagan and his secretary of defense, Caspar Weinberger. Also, if any in Bush's team had a romantic streak, they might have remembered a line from Irving Berlin: "The song is ended, but the melody lingers on." Vietnam was over, all of its negative connotations stashed away in a fading folder of American history, but its legacy lingered on, often unspoken, but just as often a guiding factor in the evolution of Bush's response to 9/11.

"It was always there," said Condoleezza Rice.[65] As it had been for Gerald Ford, Jimmy Carter, Ronald Reagan, George H. W. Bush, and Bill Clinton, in different ways and at different times, Vietnam would become an unavoidable presence in George W. Bush's decisionmaking. It had become part of the Oval Office DNA.

Vietnam "affected everyone differently, but the memory [has been] lasting," Rumsfeld believed. "I was affected by Vietnam, like [many] others. . . . Those images of Americans leaving in helicopters [from Saigon] worked against us as a country and affected people's judgments. So [the U.S. experience in Vietnam] had to have affected successive leadership levels, military and civilian, to want to try to avoid reinforcing that impression."[66] Translation: henceforth the United States could no longer shilly-shally through a crisis. It could no longer lose another war. It could no longer be humiliated. It had to be tough; and if challenged, it had to meet the challenge and emerge triumphant for the world to see.

Take, for example, two images from recent American history that strongly influenced the Bush team as the president and his advisers plotted the twists and turns of their antiterrorism policy. "They [the images] came up constantly," recalled Douglas Feith, who worked in Rumsfeld's Pentagon during the buildups to the Afghan and Iraq wars.[67] One image, dating back to the late 1960s, was of the hulking figure of President Johnson leaning over a large map of North Vietnam while considering targets for the next American bombing run; the other was of President Clinton ordering American cruise missiles to attack al Qaeda bases in Afghanistan, kicking up lots of sand and dust but apparently accomplishing little else. When it became clear, within hours after 9/11, that the United States was going to retaliate militarily against al Qaeda and its Taliban hosts in Afghanistan, these images popped into the president's mind and helped fashion his response to the terrorist challenge. They soon grew into presidential decisions about what to do and what not to do.

The Johnson image had a particularly powerful effect on Bush. Should a president be the one to select bombing targets? Obviously not, Bush concluded. It seemed to him to violate the delicate balance in civilian-military relations. Johnson had micromanaged the war. Result, according to the GOP catechism, which Bush had studied and absorbed: the United States had lost the war. Therefore, the lesson for Bush was that in wartime, the president should set overall policy, then step back and let the generals run, and win, the war. "I can't recall a time that he [Bush] was ever involved in selecting targets," Cheney said. "To have a White House staff selecting targets for the forces 10,000 miles away was exactly the wrong way to operate. . . . We wanted to make certain that the commanders on the scene, the guys who ran the war, had the opportunity to run the war."[68]

And win the war, it should quickly be added. That was another lesson Bush extracted from the Johnson experience in Vietnam. If the United States was going to fight a war, it had to be determined to win, a policy position first articulated by Reagan. After Vietnam, anything short of victory was, for Bush, unacceptable. (And yet he found a few years later in Iraq that he had to set- tle for a lot less than victory.) He was convinced, looking back on the lost war, that Congress would never have pulled the funding if it had thought the United States was winning. But, after so many years of casualties, escalating cost, and inconclusive warfare, it was no wonder that Congress, reflecting the impatience of the American people, would grow weary of the fighting and cut the purse strings. Given those lessons, what was Bush's plan for Afghanistan?

First, American troops and commanders would be given a clear, unambig- uous mission. Afghanistan would not be another Vietnam, dragging on end- lessly without a clear goal in sight. "Your mission is defined," Bush stressed, as he announced the opening of the war on October 7, 2001. "Your objectives are clear; your goal is just; you have my full confidence; and you will have every tool you need to carry out your duty."[69] Powell had insisted on mission clarity, and Bush complied.

Second, the war would be prosecuted in a new, post-9/11 fashion: no more "bombing pauses" that pockmarked American strategy during the Vietnam War; no more "hit, talk, hit,"[70] which suggested confusion in the American negotiating position. Bush pressed for a military victory over al Qaeda. He didn't use World War II terminology, "unconditional surrender," but at the time he meant just that.

Finally, the war would be clearly explained. Bush believed that Johnson was guilty of two big mistakes: never explaining the war, meaning that he had failed to win popular backing ("the people g[o]t disassociated from their commander-in-chief," he said),[71] and micromanaging the war, meaning that, after a while, Johnson had lost the support of the military brass.[72] Andrew Card, his chief of staff, urged his boss: "Don't be a general, be a president. . . . You have to win . . . but you have to let the generals win." No, Bush assured Card, "I am not going to be a general."[73]

If the Johnson image left a powerful, if negative, imprint on Bush's war plans for Afghanistan and Iraq, the Clinton image left a smirk. The Democratic president, besmirched by scandal, came through to the Bush crowd as a wonky, unprincipled graduate student totally unprepared for presidential responsibilities in an age of terrorism. Their favorite story, repeated endlessly, dealt with Clinton's order to bomb a key facility in Baghdad at night, when no one was there, and his dismay when he learned that a civilian was on duty the night of the attack and was likely killed. Like Carter, he thought, apparently, that war could be bloodless.

Bush, when faced with the prospect of war, considered Clinton to be a chief executive of small vision, frightened by the past and cautious about the future. By comparison, he considered himself to be a president of large strategic plays. He would wage a crusade against "Islamic fascists." He would produce bin Laden "dead or alive." He would create a new Iraq, a thriving democracy in the heart of the Arab world. He would bring freedom to everyone. And through it all, Bush imagined, America and its economy would prosper.

When Bush as a war president welcomed visitors to the Oval Office, he exuded an air of supreme self-confidence. He would, on occasion, point to a portrait of Abraham Lincoln and recall the excruciating times of the Civil War. "He's on the wall," Bush told author Bob Woodward, "because the job of the president is to unite the nation."[74] He added, "The job of the president is to unite a nation to achieve big objectives. Lincoln understood that, and he had the toughest job of all uniting a nation."[75] He turned to Vietnam. "I am a product of the Vietnam era. I remember presidents trying to wage wars that were very unpopular, and the nation split," he said.[76] Asked by Woodward about "big strategic plays" of past presidents, Bush said that Johnson, unlike Lincoln, failed to unite the nation during a difficult time and "couldn't achieve big goals."[77] Bush believed he could win where Johnson had lost, because he, Bush, possessed the toughness, the agility, and the wisdom to lead the nation in the new war against terrorism.

Cheney seemed to derive the most pleasure from belittling Clinton's toe-in-the-water approach to the use of American military power. After 9/11, Cheney stressed, "we had to be serious." Clinton's "half-hearted symbolic response" to terrorism "was not going to do the job. . . . We've seen Clinton firing off cruise missiles at training camps [in Afghanistan] with virtually no results." Part of the explanation, according to Cheney, lay in the awkward Clinton-Pentagon relationship.[78] Many of Clinton's advisers, critics of the Vietnam War from their student days, had never served in the military. They distrusted the military. Now, in power, they brought a heavy dose of skepticism to the advisability of using military force. Almost immediately, they recalled the bitter experience of Vietnam and concluded that there had to be a better way. For its part, the Pentagon brass felt uncomfortable with the Clinton White House. "There was a degree of distrust from both sides that sort of permeated the Clinton years," Cheney remarked. Under Clinton, the United States used military force with extreme reluctance, one small step after another. Incrementalism was the desired mode of operation, even when the Pentagon was recommending stronger action. "If you are serious about using military force, you have got to be prepared to go that extra step," Cheney said.[79]

The War in Afghanistan

In Afghanistan, the "extra step" was the unprecedented hookup between new sharpshooter aircraft and a small ground force of CIA and Special Forces. For years, U.S. military strategy had been based on the deployment of massive ground power. "If you wanted to do anything significant," Feith explained, only half facetiously, "you had to do it in multiples of 300,000."[80] But Rumsfeld demanded new options. "Get a group functioning fast," he urged. "Lift out of conventional mindset."[81] Bush had been applying heavy pressure on Rumsfeld to get the U.S. military ready for swift retaliation.

The group, consisting of Rumsfeld, the CIA's George Tenet, and Generals Richard Myers and Tommy Franks, recommended a drastic change in America's war strategy. Instead of deploying a large division, which could take months, deploy a small brigade, it urged. Quickly establish contact with local, friendly militias. Target the enemy. Relay relevant coordinates to airplanes circling overhead and equipped with highly accurate bombs and missiles, and then get out of the way. "The combat power [of the new brigade] is enormous," explained Feith. Whereas it took hundreds of sorties in World War II to destroy a bridge, "now we can send a single plane up, and it will have 10 to 20 missiles or bombs on it—and that one plane can destroy 20 bridges. It is a revolution that you can hit what you aim at."[82] Rumsfeld was proud of the results, too. The effort would enable U.S. forces to push al Qaeda out of Afghanistan and overthrow the Taliban, he said. "[That was] what was accomplished, thanks to the remarkable relationship between the [CIA] and our Special Forces."[83]

Unlike in Vietnam and in the Persian Gulf War, the United States would use a "light footprint" in Afghanistan, at least at the beginning of the war, which started on October 7. Rumsfeld remembered the failed strategy of

Vietnam, where hundreds of thousands of troops were deployed. The new warfare of the twenty-first century demanded a smarter strategy. It was ad hoc, fashioned in the hothouse environment of 9/11, and for a time it worked, or seemed to. This was all part of a broader Rumsfeld plan to change the U.S. armed forces from what analyst Susan B. Glasser called "a lumbering Cold War conventional force into a leaner, meaner, high-tech military capable of lightning strikes."[84]

At a televised October 11 news conference four days after the start of the Afghan War, Bush was asked how he could "avoid being drawn into a Vietnam-like quagmire in Afghanistan." Bush had been carefully prepped for a Vietnam question. "We learned some very important lessons in Vietnam," he replied. First, "you cannot fight a guerrilla war with conventional forces. . . . [W]e're engaged in a different type of war" in which conventional forces would be just one piece of the puzzle. Second, "we've got a clear plan." And, third, there was no telling how long the battle would last. Al Qaeda might be "brought" to "justice" "tomorrow . . . a month from now . . . a year or two" from now. "But we will prevail . . . I am determined to stay the course." He was to repeat these lessons many times: this was not a conventional war, we had a clear strategy, and we were in it to win.

Another question concerned al Qaeda leader Osama bin Laden. Bush had once boasted that the United States would capture him "dead or alive," using the colorful language of a Texas sheriff. Again Bush spoke with absolute self-confidence, as though for this president an American failure to nab the terrorist leader was unimaginable. "We'll get him running," he said. "We'll smoke him out of his cave and we'll get him eventually."[85] In fact, bin Laden slipped through a sloppy U.S. military operation in the mountainous region of Tora Bora in December and was not caught.

Here was a strategic blunder of lasting consequence. The Bush administration was already shifting its military focus from Afghanistan to Iraq, surprising even General Franks. If Bush could have captured or killed bin Laden at Tora Bora, which was then possible, he would have changed the dynamic of the war on terror, saving American lives and treasure in both Iraq and Afghanistan.

Time and again, Bush stressed the special nature of the Afghan conflict, something America was not "used to." "The Greatest Generation was used to storming beachheads," he said at the October 11 news conference. "Baby boomers such as myself were used to getting caught in the quagmire of Vietnam, where politics made decisions more than the military sometimes."[86] In fact, Bush never stormed a beachhead, and he was never himself "caught" in "the quagmire of Vietnam." He was, though, obsessed by the image of Johnson micromanaging the war, and he promised himself that he would never micromanage the Afghan War.

In the first few weeks of the war, success seemed assured. America and its allies swept toward Kabul, overrunning Taliban positions, and scoring significant military gains; and then, suddenly, without explanation, an odd quiet seemed to settle over the battlefield. A skirmish here or there, but no sustained attacks anywhere. The Taliban remained in control of Kabul. Questions erupted at news conferences in Washington and Islamabad. What was happening?

Bush tried to keep official spirits high. He told an October 26 National Security Council meeting, as he later wrote, that "we shouldn't give in to second-guessing or let the press panic us."[87] But in a front-page story on October 31 titled "A Military Quagmire Remembered: Afghanistan as Vietnam," R. W. Apple Jr., an experienced *New York Times* reporter, shook up the Washington establishment. "Could Afghanistan become another Vietnam?" Apple asked. "Is the United States facing another stalemate on the other side of the world?" Apple had covered the Vietnam War. "Premature the questions may be," Apple admitted. "Unreasonable they are not." Apple acknowledged that there were "differences" between the two wars; but the "echoes of Vietnam" were "unavoidable," he wrote, and the "ominous word 'quagmire' has begun to haunt conversations among government officials and students of foreign policy."[88] Apple was not the first to compare Afghanistan to Vietnam, but his commentary in the *Times* had a stunning impact on Bush's advisers, who began to question their war strategy.

Columnists Charles Krauthammer and Bill Kristol, both pro-Bush hawks, also contributed to White House dyspepsia. "It's a flawed plan," Kristol wrote.[89] "Half-measures" were doomed to fail, Krauthammer insisted. The commentators suggested strongly that Rumsfeld's light footprint strategy was wrong. More troops were needed, perhaps lots more. "To restrain our military now in order to placate the diplomats is a tragic reprise of Vietnam," Krauthammer wrote.[90]

Their criticism was triggered at least in part by Sunday talk show appearances by Vietnam veteran John McCain on October 28. The Arizona senator urged the president to deploy "significant" numbers of additional American troops to Afghanistan, "in force," he stressed. He was not specific about how many. Air power alone, no matter how skillfully applied, could not do the job, he argued.[91] At the White House, Bush asked Rice, "What's up?" Rice answered: "You could use more Americans in this."[92] But for Bush "more

Americans" reminded him of the creeping and ultimately unsuccessful escalation in Vietnam, and he waved off the idea. "More Americans" would also
have meant more news stories about policy haggling among cabinet officials
and congressional questions about the efficacy of his Afghan strategy, and that
would surely have poisoned the post-9/11 atmosphere of patriotism and pride
and, worse, suggested irresolution on his part—all, in Bush's mind, an echo
of Vietnam he did not want to hear. No, he decided, he would stick with the
strategy Rumsfeld and the Joint Chiefs had presented to him. He had considered other options, including one that recommended a ground invasion by
hundreds of thousands of American troops. Under increasing pressure for
action, a nonstop barrage of calls, e-mails, and inspired opinion pieces, Bush
and Rumsfeld rejected the army's advice and chose the controversial light
footprint approach. It had the advantages of quick engagement, limited casualties, and the headline-grabbing virtue of a post-Vietnam military doctrine.

At the time, what was central in Bush's mind was decisive action. He wanted
the glory of the Persian Gulf War but none of the anguish of the Vietnam
War. America was back from Vietnam, he insisted. It was a consoling theme
"articulated" in all of their meetings, national security adviser Rice recalled.
"If you are going to do something, do it decisively. . . . The president was very
much a believer in that."[93]

By mid-November, to the administration's delight, the gnawing fear of
the Vietnam specter faded, as troops from the Northern Alliance, supported
by only a few hundred American troops, smashed their way through Taliban
positions on the outskirts of Kabul, and reporters began to see signs of Taliban
flight from the capital city. The Northern Alliance (and its American and British allies) soon rolled triumphantly into Kabul. In December the Taliban force
was routed, with many Islamists including Osama bin Laden and his al Qaeda
followers fleeing across the mountainous border into Pakistan. The sigh of
relief among Bush advisers (the United States won decisively, a Vietnam-style
quagmire averted) could be heard years later, as they laughed off "the Apple
exclusive" and enjoyed memories of a victory in the early phase of the long
Afghan marathon. Maybe, they felt, the United States had finally turned its
back on Vietnam. Maybe.

And Then, Iraq

No sooner had Bush & Co. "won" in Afghanistan than they turned their sights
on Iraq, still the unfinished business of the Persian Gulf War for a number of

key officials. Bush had not been an early advocate of American action against Saddam Hussein, the brutal dictator of the Mesopotamian basin; but flush from his victory over the Taliban, Bush saw a glorious opportunity to rearrange the Middle East landscape. He joined Cheney, Wolfowitz, and others in believing that the time had come for dramatic action against Saddam Hussein. Overnight, it seemed, "regime change" in Iraq became his administration's top priority, even though during his presidential campaign he had disparaged the very notion of "regime change" as an appropriate job for the American army.

Through much of 2002, the Bush administration was on a war footing. On one level, it was an ongoing war against the global terror network of al Qaeda, which had started on 9/11. On another level, it was to be a war against Saddam Hussein, who was repeatedly accused of collaborating with al Qaeda, building weapons of mass destruction, and threatening America's allies in the Middle East. He was also accused of masterminding an assassination attempt against the president's father, former president George H. W. Bush, during a 1993 visit to Kuwait. The twin wars against al Qaeda and Iraq allowed Bush to claim the mantle of war president, which yielded enormous political benefits for the Republicans during the 2002 and 2004 election campaigns. Democratic critics were regularly denounced as being "soft on terror," just as earlier Republicans had denounced Democrats as being "soft on communism." In addition, as a war president, Bush could, and did, take liberties with the legislative process to advance his antiterror program. More than anything, the wars sharpened the policy focus of the administration, playing to the nation's patriotism and strengthening Bush's political base while cutting into critics' ability to point out inaccuracies and inconsistencies in the president's war policies.

In preparation for the Iraq War, Rumsfeld paused in mid-October 2002 to draft what Feith later called the "Parade of Horribles" memo.[94] He listed two dozen "horrible" possibilities, one of which was that the United States might lose. "Vietnam stood for the proposition," Feith explained, "that maybe after 200 years of winning, people may not weigh as heavily as they should the danger of losing. . . . Vietnam was certainly an argument for giving serious consideration to the possibility that wars can go badly."[95] Rumsfeld might have been paying homage to an old rule of thumb in Washington, known by three letters: CYA, or cover your ass. He summoned Wolfowitz, Feith, and Generals Myers and Peter Pace to a "drop everything" meeting in his office. What could go wrong? They discussed everything from not finding weapons of mass destruction to losing the war. Then, in bullet fashion, Rumsfeld listed everything that could go wrong. And over the next few years, many of them did go wrong.

On March 19, 2003, after months of military maneuvering and diplomatic justifications before the UN Security Council, the United States bombed Baghdad. The war against Saddam Hussein had begun.

Once again, the administration's military strategy was questioned, this time not only by a chorus of political and journalistic critics but also by high-ranking army officers, who vented their misgivings to selected reporters and columnists. Despite the U.S. experience in Afghanistan, which went well, the army brass refused to budge from classic doctrine formed in the aftermath of Vietnam: an invasion of Iraq would require a clear strategic goal and a heavy footprint of troops supported by tanks and planes. Rumsfeld, though, favored the light footprint approach. It had worked in Afghanistan, he believed, and it would work in Iraq. If Rumsfeld had looked through his predecessor's files, he would have learned that the former secretary, William Cohen, had concluded that, for a successful invasion and occupation of Iraq, the United States would need between 350,000 and 450,000 troops.[96] Cohen had planned for an invasion and an occupation; Rumsfeld planned only for an invasion. One of his big mistakes in Iraq was to ignore the cost and responsibilities of an occupation that he had not anticipated.

On both policy and doctrine, therefore, Cohen and his army brass were in sync; Rumsfeld and his army brass were out of sync—an embarrassing fact that came to the public's attention when army chief of staff Eric Shinseki broke ranks with his defense secretary and told congressional panels in February and March of 2003 that "several hundred thousand" troops would be needed in Iraq, an estimate consistent with the Cohen judgment but at odds with the Rumsfeld approach. Wolfowitz dismissed Shinseki's estimate as "wildly off the mark," but it touched off a rumble of criticism of Bush's policy in Iraq, which the president and his defense secretary deeply resented. In a short time, Shinseki, a respected and experienced general, was forced to retire.

Shinseki was clearly a scapegoat. He was only telling the truth about standard army doctrine, which anticipated the need for an occupation strategy after a successful invasion. By removing members of Saddam Hussein's Baath Party from the Iraqi government and disbanding the Iraqi army, the United States lost the expertise it needed to run the country effectively. Bush and Rumsfeld ignored the advice and experience of their own military chiefs, precipitating the mess that was shortly to ensue. They also ignored the advice of Secretary of State Colin Powell, who diplomatically recalled that "there was not unanimous agreement" among the president's senior advisers. He said that "when you take out a government, which is what we did, you become the government."[97]

In his memoirs, Rumsfeld described a less-than-ideal situation among Bush's top advisers. "There were far too many hands on the steering wheel, which, in my view, was a formula for running the truck into a ditch," he wrote. The president "did not always receive, and may not have insisted on, a timely consideration of his options before he made a decision, nor did he always receive effective implementation of the decisions he made."[98]

Renovating Army Doctrine: Hearts and Minds

Meanwhile, Shinseki did not know at the time, nor did many of his colleagues, that army doctrine was on the edge of a major renovation. When hostilities started in Iraq, army generals were still living in a pre-9/11 world. By training and habit, they clung to their vision of traditional warfare. They knew more about the "Kraznovians," for example, a mythical enemy created for war games, than they did about the Iraqis, their new, real enemy. The Kraznovians were patterned after the Soviet Army, which had in fact dissolved a decade earlier when the Soviet Union disintegrated. But, in a large mock tank battle at the National Training Center in the California desert in the winter of 2002, they were still seen as the enemy, and the mock battle was still being fought in central Europe rather than in the deserts of Arabia. According to *New York Times* reporter Dexter Filkins, "The American Army found itself disastrously unprepared for the conflict that unfolded."[99] The troops were not trained for the brewing insurgency they were soon to face in Iraq, and it took several years for the army to resurrect the doctrine of counterinsurgency. In South Vietnam, U.S. forces had faced an insurgency and lost, and the military did not want to look back. Only the building catastrophe in Iraq and the trailblazing work of a new cadre of younger officers taught the army to "eat soup with a knife."

General David Petraeus led the way. Very much on his mind was the counterinsurgency experience in Vietnam. It was no accident that his Princeton doctoral dissertation was called "The American Military and the Lessons of Vietnam."[100] One such lesson was that in the new irregular warfare challenging American interests around the world, the army had to do more than kill the enemy; it also had to "win hearts and minds," a phrase reminiscent of Vietnam. This emphasis would mean less tank training and more language training, more cultural sensitivity, more nation-building skills—all the skills that Bush, in his presidential campaign, had brushed aside. It would mean a fundamental readjustment of army training and outlook. If Powell was the military hero of the 1990s, Petraeus became the hero of the early twenty-first century.

In an article in the *Atlantic*, Andrew J. Bacevich outlined a major split in the army between the "Crusaders"—those trailblazing officers who focused on counterinsurgency—and the "Conservatives," who feared that the new emphasis would leave conventional forces depleted. "Back in the 1960s an earlier experiment in changing entire societies yielded unmitigated disaster— at least that's how the Army of the 1980s and 1990s chose to remember its Vietnam experience," Bacevich wrote. "Crusaders take another view, however. They insist that Vietnam could have been won—indeed was being won, after General Creighton Abrams succeeded General William Westmoreland in 1968 and jettisoned Westmoreland's heavy-handed search-and-destroy strategy, to concentrate instead on winning Vietnamese hearts and minds. Defeat did not result from military failure; rather, defeat came because the American people lacked patience, while American politicians lacked guts."[101]

John Nagl, a West Pointer and author of the 2002 study *Learning to Eat Soup with a Knife: Counterinsurgency Lessons from Malaya and Vietnam,* was the perfect example of a Petraeus protégé. According to Bacevich, "For Nagl, the imperative of the moment [wa]s to institutionalize the relevant lessons of Vietnam and Iraq, thereby enabling the Army . . . 'to get better at building societies that can stand on their own.' . . . An Army that since Vietnam has self-consciously cultivated a battle-oriented warrior ethos will instead empha- size, in Nagl's words, 'the intellectual tools necessary to foster host-nation political and economic development.'"[102]

Clearly, the Vietnam experience, in one way or another, was never far from the American officer running the war or the reporter covering it. Shortly after hostilities erupted, a severe sandstorm hit Iraq, no different from hundreds of others in that part of Arabia, and it slowed down the American advance from Basra to Baghdad. Within days, reporters were writing gloomy stories about the American army getting "bogged down" in the sands of Iraq and about an enveloping "quagmire." Vietnam did not specifically have to be mentioned, though it often was, but fears rose that once again the United States was get- ting stuck in a faraway war.

When at least fifteen Iraqis were killed by an errant American missile in late March, stories appeared about "collateral damage," the continuing nightmare of policymakers engaged in irregular warfare. Just as Clinton had worried about the night watchman caught in an American bombing run in Baghdad, so Bush and his aides worried about civilian casualties as the fighting intensified. If one point of counterinsurgency was to win hearts and minds, then the United States could not kill innocent civilians in its attempts to knock out the enemy. News organizations were quick to pick up the twin themes of innocent civilians being hit by American attacks and the American army getting bogged down in the Iraqi desert.

"Welcome to hell," wrote James Webb, then a writer and now a Democratic senator from Virginia. In a *New York Times* opinion piece on March 30, which was highly critical of Bush's decision to invade Iraq, Webb invoked the memory of Vietnam, where he had served as a marine officer: "Many of us lived it in another era. And don't expect it to get any better for a while."[103]

Apple of the *Times* turned his critical eye on Iraq, just as he had on Afghanistan, and concluded once again that U.S. military strategy was dead wrong. In a March 30 article, he wrote: "With every passing day, it is more evident that the allies made . . . gross military misjudgments. . . . The very term 'shock and awe' has a swagger to it, no doubt because it was intended to discourage Mr. Hussein and his circle. But it rings hollow now."[104] Apple always seemed gloomy about America's adventures in Arabia, conveniently finding parallels with Vietnam. But a postscript is appropriate here: Apple's critique appeared just as the U.S. military was emerging from the sandstorm and resuming its push toward Baghdad, which fell soon thereafter.

Nothing seemed to please Rumsfeld more than catching media mistakes or misjudgments. He briefed the Pentagon press often and loved the attention, perhaps at no time more than when the people of Baghdad, liberated from Saddam Hussein's tyrannical rule and helped by American troops, pulled down a large statue of the Iraqi dictator in a main square and joyfully defaced it, signaling the end of a dark era in Iraqi history and the beginning of a more hopeful one. No one at a senior level in the Pentagon anticipated a rising, widespread insurgency, but at least one official was jarred into raising questions.

On April 2, 2003, an opinion piece in the *Washington Post* by a retired marine colonel named Gary Anderson warned that the fall of Baghdad was not going to end the war. Saddam Hussein, who admired the Vietnamese revolutionary Ho Chi Minh, had, according to Anderson, a "greater game" in mind. Assuming the fall of Baghdad, Hussein wanted to draw American forces into a "protracted guerrilla war" and then, when the moment was right, stage a "Black Hawk Down" event, followed by a 1975 North Vietnamese–style assault on the tired and weak-willed Americans, who would finally leave in disgrace.[105]

Feith added another spin to the Hussein-Vietnam connection: that the Iraqi leader, a student, in his way, of the Vietnam War, might have believed that the U.S. buildup was a bluff and that the United States was never serious about launching a war it suspected it could not win.[106] Here the Vietnam experience again affected the thinking of an American adversary. Just as the Soviet Union had read the American defeat in Vietnam as an Open Sesame for mischief-making in Africa and Asia, Hussein might have misread the American defeat as reason to doubt that the Americans still had the will to undertake another dubious adventure in Arabia.

After reading the Anderson piece, a friend called Wolfowitz in his Pentagon office and insisted that, busy though he might be, he glance at it. Wolfowitz was genuinely impressed by Anderson's analysis, so much so that he invited him in for a talk and then dispatched him to Baghdad to work as a consultant to L. Paul Bremer, head of the Coalition Provisional Authority. One day, Anderson briefed Bremer on what he took to be mounting evidence of urban guerrilla warfare in a number of Iraqi cities. That was not what Bremer wanted to hear. That sounds like Vietnam to me, Bremer said, adding, this is not Vietnam. He showed Anderson the door.

Wolfowitz discussed the Anderson thesis with Rumsfeld but got nowhere. It was not what the defense secretary wanted to deal with at this point. Rumsfeld already had tried to persuade his top generals to adopt his light footprint strategy but had not succeeded, and now a "big battle" strategy, cleared by the generals, was set. General John Abizaid, the U.S. commander in Iraq, like so many of his colleagues, did not believe in an insurgent Iraq and pursued the "big battle" strategy, even as the battlefield was changing in front of his eyes. As reporter Filkins observed: "Instead of planning how to fight the next insurgency [in the wake of Vietnam], the Army went right back to preparing for what it loved to do: fight big battles against big, uniformed armies just like itself. Training in guerrilla war . . . was banished from the Army's curriculum."[107]

But it was not banished from Petraeus's thinking, or from Nagl's, or from the thinking of others in the army who believed that Iraq was turning into a counterinsurgency challenge, and that American policy had to change. In June 2004 Bush replaced Abizaid with General George Casey, son of a general who had been killed in Vietnam. Casey, like Abizaid, was of the old school, but in Washington and Baghdad the winds of change were blowing. Proof was on the cover of the July 5, 2004, edition of *Newsweek*, a large color photo of Petraeus in battle gear. "Can This Man Save Iraq?" the magazine asked. Petraeus "is the closest thing to an exit strategy the United States now has," wrote reporter Rod

Nordland. Rumsfeld was furious. Casey was told "to shut down the Petraeus publicity machine," as writers David Cloud and Greg Jaffe put it. "From now on," Casey told Petraeus, "I'm your PAO," or public affairs officer.[108] Petraeus stubbornly stuck to his belief that Iraq was an insurgency and that the United States had to shift strategy from counterterror to counterinsurgency as quickly as possible before Iraq disintegrated into a bloody civil war.

Throughout the 2004 presidential campaign, Democrat John Kerry, a senator from Massachusetts who had served in Vietnam, raised the issue of Vietnam time and again but gained little traction. Bush was focused on the war against terror, and he ultimately won his second term, something his father was not able to accomplish. In December 2004, his reelection behind him, Bush started to change policy and personnel. At the State Department, Powell was out and Rice was in. The president chose Rice's deputy, Stephen Hadley, a trusted and experienced official who had maintained a low profile while working for a succession of Republican presidents, to replace her as national security adviser. Though flattered, Hadley had a big problem, which he felt had to be addressed before he could accept the job. The Iraq War was at that time sliding ominously toward civil war, and Hadley wondered whether the United States would be "going through Vietnam all over again." Would Iraq become another Vietnam? Would it lead to another "failure of policy, shattering our Army, and result in all the self-doubt?" Hadley was not usually one to turn down a presidential offer, but he had to hear from Bush that he would not be facing another Vietnam in Iraq. He raised his questions directly with the president.

"We are not going to go there," Bush stated flatly. Time and again, with the unsettling legacy of Vietnam on his mind, too, Bush insisted, "We have to have victory" in Iraq. He shared Hadley's deep concern about the consequences of failure. Bush repeatedly told Hadley, "We have to win, we have to have victory." Hadley accepted his new job, in part because he had been persuaded over the years that Bush was a stubborn man who "never gives up" and one day would achieve "victory," however that might be defined. Both Bush and Hadley had come to conclude that another failure, like Vietnam, could not be allowed to happen. Failure in Iraq was simply an unacceptable outcome for the United States.[109]

But how to win? Hadley had been an early supporter of what came to be called the Petraeus Doctrine, and he discussed it often with the president. But changing American policy, he was to learn, was a lot like changing a giant corporation like General Motors: it took time. Eventually, though, the embattled president came to appreciate the value and timeliness of "eat[ing] soup with a knife."

The reason, Bush acknowledged: "I worried we might not succeed." Vietnam suddenly flashed through his mind. "We could be looking at a repeat of Vietnam," he later wrote in his memoirs, "a humiliating loss for the country, a shattering blow to the military, and a dramatic setback for our interests. If anything, the consequences of defeat in Iraq would be even worse than in Vietnam."[110]

In early 2007 Petraeus took over the job of saving the U.S. gamble in Iraq, and almost immediately began to benefit from a major shift in Iraqi politics. Sunni militants, who had worked closely with al Qaeda insurgents, changed sides and began to cooperate with the American army and with Shia leaders in Baghdad. Petraeus took quick advantage of the change. He pressed the White House for thousands of additional troops, popularly referred to as "the surge," as he readjusted his strategy to meet the requirements of "nation-building" and counterinsurgency.

Though Bush was philosophically opposed to "nation-building" and objected to anything that smelled of Vietnam, he bought into the controversial "surge" and readjustment of strategy. It was a risky move; at times it seemed to Bush like the incrementalism that he associated with Vietnam. Moreover, there was no guarantee of victory. Soon, however, the violence ebbed to acceptable levels, acceptable enough so that, finally, neither Bush nor Hadley had to worry any longer about losing the war.

Bush could leave the White House in January 2009 knowing that he had arranged for a gradual shift of security responsibilities from the American army to the new Iraqi army. He could leave with a small degree of honor. He had not won in Iraq, but he had not lost, either.

8

2004: The Swift Boat Campaign

How do you ask a man to be the last man to die for a mistake?
—JOHN KERRY, Testimony, Senate Committee on Foreign Relations,
April 22, 1971

I said I wasn't the smartest guy in the world, but I know that there were only
three of us.
—PAT RUNYON, interview, April 9, 2006

WITH ONLY A small leap of imagination, one could argue that the 2004 presidential campaign began on April 22, 1971, when a twenty-seven-year-old veteran of the Vietnam War, dressed in khaki fatigues with four rows of ribbons over his left pocket, delivered a blistering attack on America's war policy before the Senate Foreign Relations Committee. The veteran was John Kerry, a Yale graduate from Massachusetts who had volunteered for duty in Vietnam and won two medals for bravery and three Purple Hearts. His testimony, memorable for its force and eloquence, stunned the senators and silenced the impressive chamber, filled with a standing-room-only crowd. It also personalized a war seemingly without end. Kerry became, with this special speech delivered at this special time, a national celebrity.

Kerry demanded "an immediate withdrawal from South Vietnam." He had come to Congress, and not the White House, he said, because only "this body can be responsive to the will of the people, and . . . the will of the people says that we should be out of Vietnam now."[1] Had Kerry stopped with this demand, and not continued with accusations of American atrocities in Vietnam, he probably could have avoided the devastating criticism that hounded him throughout his political career, criticism that morphed into ugly, unsubstantiated charges of treason and treachery, deception, lies, and cowardice and led thirty-three years later to the formation of the Swift Boat Veterans for Truth (SBVT), whose sole purpose was to destroy his presidential ambitions. But Kerry did not stop. He told the senators about the Winter Soldier Investigation, a Detroit gathering a few months earlier of about 150 "honorably discharged" veterans. In 1776, he said, the pamphleteer Tom Paine had written about the "sunshine patriot," who had deserted at Valley Forge "because the going was rough." Now, Kerry continued, the going is rough again, and veterans who opposed the war felt they had to speak out against "the crimes which we are committing."

Quoting the "very highly decorated veterans" in Detroit, Kerry plunged into rhetoric unusual for the halls of Congress. "They told the stories at times they had personally raped, cut off ears, cut off heads, tape[d] wires from portable telephones to human genitals and turned up the power, cut off limbs, blown up bodies, randomly shot at civilians, razed villages in fashion reminiscent of Genghis Khan, shot cattle and dogs for fun, poisoned food stocks, and generally ravaged the countryside of South Vietnam," Kerry said slowly, his unmistakable New England accent registering both disappointment and disgust. "The country doesn't know it yet," he continued, "but it has created a monster, a monster in the form of millions of men who have been taught to deal and to trade in violence."

Kerry paused for a moment before asking a question that was to reverberate beyond the antiwar movement. "How do you ask a man to be the last man to die in Vietnam? How do you ask a man to be the last man to die for a mistake?" Every now and then a question has the power to crystallize a national debate. Here was such a question. If the war was a mistake, why pursue it?

Then, more with a dignified sadness than any pumped-up pomp—though maybe with a bit of both, since Kerry was an accomplished orator and knew it—he finished his testimony with these words:

> We wish that a merciful God could wipe away our own memories of that service as easily as this administration has wiped their memories of us. But all that they have done and all that they can do by this denial is to make more clear than ever our own determination to undertake one last mission, to search out and destroy the last vestige of this barbarous war, to pacify our own hearts, to conquer the hate and the fear that have driven this country these last 10 years and more and so when in 30 years from now, our brothers go down the street, without a leg, without an arm or a face, and small boys ask why, we will be able to say 'Vietnam,' and not mean a desert, not a filthy obscene memory but mean instead the place where America finally turned and where soldiers like us helped it in the turning.[2]

The Senate chamber, which had been still, erupted in wild cheers and applause. Outside, where hundreds of antiwar veterans had gathered to express their opposition to "this administration's" war, many got down on one knee, clenched their right fists, and pointed them to the sky.

The next day at the White House, Richard Nixon, Henry Kissinger, and White House chief of staff Bob Haldeman reviewed reports of Kerry's testimony. They acknowledged reluctantly that he had done "a hell of a great job," as Haldeman put it. "He was extremely effective," Nixon added. "A Kennedy-type guy; he looks like a Kennedy, and he talks exactly like a Kennedy," Haldeman said.[3]

Still, it was not hard for them to submerge their admiration in the cool political waters of a get-John-Kerry campaign. White House aide Charles Colson took charge of it. "Destroy the young demagogue before he becomes another Ralph Nader," he wrote. But it was hard to find any dirt. "I don't ever remember finding anything negative about Kerry or hearing anything negative about him," Colson recollected. "If we had found anything, I'm sure we would have used it to discredit him."[4] Colson then came up with the idea of sponsoring another "John Kerry" to destroy the real John Kerry. He found John O'Neill, a Swift Boat veteran who supported Nixon's policy in Vietnam and was angered by Kerry's testimony. "He forced us to create a counterfoil," Colson told writer Joe Klein. "We found a vet named John O'Neill and formed a group called Vietnam Veterans for a Just Peace. We had O'Neill meet the President, and we did everything we could do to boost his group."[5] O'Neill, for his part, said the group had been formed before the White House got in touch with him.[6]

A joint appearance on the popular *Dick Cavett Show* was arranged, pitting one Vietnam vet against the other. Kerry emerged the victor. He looked cool, almost scholarly, clearly adept at using the lights and cameras to fashion an image and project a message. O'Neill, on the contrary, sounded strident. "We knew that when he [Kerry] left the set . . . it wasn't the last we were going to hear from him," Cavett said.[7]

Kerry carried his antiwar message from one end of the country to the other, selling himself in the process. His Senate testimony had fired up his political ambitions, which were never far from the surface in any case. But his testimony also aroused powerful currents of anti-Kerry sentiment, including among other Swift Boat veterans. Kerry had suddenly become radioactive, and from then on, his political opponents, especially O'Neill's Swift Boat buddies, portrayed him as unpatriotic, arrogant, lying: perfectly capable, in fact, of betraying his country in collaboration with the Vietnamese communists.

At the beginning, Kerry and his more like-minded colleagues considered these vindictive portrayals to be a sick joke. David Thorne, once his brother-in-law and now a dear friend, remembered the initial Nixon salvos. "We both laughed at the fact that the President of the United States was after John," he said. "It was just unbelievable. He was as patriotic a guy as Yale University and the U.S. Navy ever produced."[8] After a while, though, the attacks stopped being a sick joke; they became personally offensive. Although Kerry saw his service in Vietnam as a shining example of selfless patriotism, many of his Swift Boat colleagues saw him as boastful, egotistical, and politically driven. To such critics, not one but two Kerrys snapped into focus: the Kerry in Vietnam, who was seen as obnoxious but in the final analysis acceptable; and the Kerry after Vietnam, who was seen as totally unacceptable, a lying leper ready to sell his soul to the enemy. Steve Hayes, a thoughtful Virginian and former Swift Boater, tried to explain the hurt feelings of his comrades. "If Kerry had not appeared before the Fulbright Committee," Hayes believed, "there would be no Swift Boat drama. Nothing." He added, "I felt deeply wounded, like he was attacking me personally, and I carried that feeling against him for a few decades. This was not an overnight feeling. I disliked him intensely."[9] The Swift Boat Veterans for Truth, formed in 2004 out of such powerful emotions, had but a single goal: to demolish Kerry, his reputation, and his presidential ambitions.

Latch's Legions

On May 4, 2004, shortly after John Kerry emerged from a pack of Democratic contenders as the clear front-runner for his party's presidential nomination, eighteen Vietnam veterans gathered at the National Press Club in Washington, D.C., to announce the formation of the Swift Boat Veterans for Truth. The leader was retired Admiral Roy Hoffmann, a short spark plug of a naval officer, patriotic and pugnacious, whose nom de guerre was Latch. In Vietnam, in the late 1960s, he had been Kerry's commanding officer. Now he was Kerry's enemy. Before a bank of television cameras and a gaggle of journalists, Hoffmann released a letter to the public, alleging in a point-by-point denunciation that Kerry did not have the "right stuff" to be president and ought to withdraw from the race. The newly formed Swift Boaters believed their demand was hot news, sure to make a big splash on the evening newscasts and dominate the next morning's headlines. After all, they thought, they were the ones who really knew Kerry. They had served with him on dangerous Swift Boat missions in the Mekong Delta of South Vietnam. Who better to judge his strength of character, his judgment, his leadership? In the evening, they were disappointed to learn that only C-Span broadcast their news conference.

Down the hall, Kerry loyalists, tipped off to Hoffmann's plans, staged a competing news conference refuting the Swift Boat allegations. They seemed to regard these Swift Boaters as an irritant, a group to be watched, but not a serious threat to the campaign. They, too, attracted cameras but little coverage.

While the Kerry operatives then returned to campaigning as usual, Hoffmann sounded general quarters and prepared for a big battle. Hoffmann regarded his anti-Kerry organization, at the time embryonic in form, as a military operation requiring an infusion of political expertise if it was to be taken seriously. And he set about finding talent sympathetic to his cause.

If Hoffmann was commanding officer of the Swift Boat group, its executive officer was William Franke, a burly Virginia businessman with extensive operations in postwar Vietnam. They invited John O'Neill to join their anti-Kerry crusade. By this time a highly successful Texas lawyer who had graduated first in his class from the University of Texas Law School and then clerked for Supreme Court justice William Rehnquist, O'Neill accepted with alacrity.

The triangle of Hoffmann, Franke, and O'Neill then hired Chris LaCivita, an experienced Republican consultant, to manage their Swift Boat campaign, who in turn pulled together a team of top public relations experts. Leaning heavily on LaCivita's political instincts, contacts, and experience, the SBVT leaders planned for open and aggressive warfare.

A bit of luck then dropped into Hoffmann's lap. He stumbled upon a copy of scholar Douglas Brinkley's adoring biography of Kerry, *Tour of Duty: John Kerry and the Vietnam War*, and the book infuriated him. Hoffmann resented Brinkley's description of the admiral as a "hawkish" commander with a "genuine taste for the more unsavory aspects of warfare," comparable to the "rough-hewn colonel in the movie *Apocalypse Now* who boasted that he 'loved the smell of napalm in the morning.'"[10] In addition, the book, in Hoffmann's judgment, was full of errors and misjudgments, inflating Kerry's stature as a war hero.

Hoffmann urged his Swift Boat supporters to read the book and check the index. He wanted them to find mistakes. Veteran Joe Ponder found one of painful significance to him. Brinkley had written that in one particular battle—which mangled one of Ponder's knees—seventeen Americans were wounded. "I was on that mission," Ponder recalled, "and there were three of us wounded, only three."[11] That was hardly a mistake of historic consequence, if indeed it was a mistake, but Hoffmann put it in his Kerry file. Other veterans reported finding far more meaningful mistakes, suggesting on many occasions that Kerry was a liar.

Through June and July, Hoffmann diligently dug into his Vietnam network of Swift Boat veterans, encouraging 295 of them, according to Franke, to join his new outfit.[12] Most could not shake off their feelings of outrage and anger at Kerry's 1971 testimony before the Fulbright committee. O'Neill during this time undertook fund-raising in Texas, where he collected money from oil and business executives, such as T. Boone Pickens and Harold Simmons, who were also giving generously to George W. Bush and the GOP. Working with a conservative scholar, Jerome R. Corsi, he also found the time somehow to coauthor an anti-Kerry screed, called *Unfit for Command: Swift Boat Veterans Speak Out against John Kerry.* Franke helped LaCivita organize the anti-Kerry campaign. He claimed in numerous conversations that he was not a political operator, certainly not wedded to one party or the other, but Franke performed in 2004 like a committed member of the Bush team.

From the beginning, mindful of campaign laws, the Bush strategists kept a safe, respectable distance from Franke and his Swift Boaters, constituted as an independent "527" group. But they did nothing to discourage its growth in number or fund-raising; nor did they discourage their supporters from joining the Swift Boat campaign.

"I'm John Kerry, and I'm Reporting for Duty"

The Democratic National Convention opened in Boston on July 26, 2004, and closed on the 29th, when John F. Kerry, saluting crisply to the cheering delegates, deliberately invoked his military experience in Vietnam to prove that he could lead the nation in war. He could be as tough as any Republican, he seemed to be saying, especially one, like President Bush, who had never served in Vietnam. Bush, running for reelection as a war president, had been wrapping himself in the American flag and promising, with steely determination, to win the war against terrorism.

When the Democrats left Boston in late July, they were a happy band of warriors, many confident that Bush could and would be beaten. The convention themes had been decidedly upbeat, producing encouraging poll projections. The delegates had heard a rousing speech by their presidential candidate, in which Kerry had charged that in Iraq, more than a year after the U.S. invasion, there were still no signs of "weapons of mass destruction," the discovery and destruction of which were among the stated reasons for the invasion. This was bad for the nation, the delegates understood, but good for their political prospects.

At the top of the Kerry campaign sat two political strategists, Bob Shrum and Mary Beth Cahill, who had been through many political campaigns. The convention had gone well, in their view, and Kerry's election was now a distinct possibility. Their working assumption was that August would be a "dark" month, meaning in political terms that neither side would run any political ads until after the GOP convention in late August and the Labor Day weekend in early September. In one sense, their assumption was right: they went dark, and so did the Bush campaign. In another sense, the Shrum-Cahill duo was embarrassingly wrong, so wrong, in fact, that when the Swift Boat loyalists attacked Kerry in the first week of August, the Kerry high command was taken totally by surprise, as if Latch's legions had just arrived on an uncharted flight from Mars.

Shrum and Cahill could have answered the Swift Boat charges with a television blitz of their own, but they refused to alter their original campaign strategy. Kerry essentially did nothing to respond to the charges until August 19. But by then the group had gained precious momentum, he was thrown on the defensive, and Bush could observe and enjoy the fratricide from his safe perch at the White House.

Behind the Shrum and Cahill calculation was money, the mother's milk of American politics. Kerry had the money for a counterattack against the group, if he wished, but his senior advisers did not want to repeat the Dukakis mistake of 1988, when the Democratic candidate ran out of money for political advertising in October, the crucial month of any campaign. Kerry believed at the time that he could survive the initial Swift Boat attack by living off the so-called "free media," doing interviews on radio and television while creating enough political buzz to generate a flow of newspaper stories to keep him in the public eye. Then, after Labor Day, he would open a major TV blitz designed to blast Bush and squelch the Swift Boaters, and still have enough money left for the final October rush to Election Day. But, according to Kerry's brother, Cameron, a Boston lawyer, Kerry, like Shrum and Cahill, underestimated the force of the Swift Boat onslaught.[13]

The Swift Boats Return to War

Anticipating a "dark" month in August, LaCivita went on the attack. On the evening of August 4, Sean Hannity, the politically conservative star of the

Hannity and Colmes broadcast on Fox News Channel (FOX), got a jump on all his competitors; he was given a copy of the first anti-Kerry ad from someone on LaCivita's staff. "Let's take a peek," Hannity said, playing the teasing host.[14] Across a dark screen came one unidentified Vietnam veteran after another, dressed conservatively, speaking in somber tones. Each ripped into Kerry's record. Kerry "has not been honest about what happened in Vietnam," one intoned. From the lips of another: "He is lying about his record." A third veteran added, Kerry was "lying about his first Purple Heart." A fourth piled on, "John Kerry lied to get his Bronze Star." Thus was the essential Swift Boat theme struck, and it would be repeated with metronomic regularity throughout the month: Kerry was a liar who did not deserve a Purple Heart, Bronze Star, or the presidency. The next day the same ad started running in three battleground states: Ohio, Wisconsin, and West Virginia.

In the evening, Hannity upped the ante. He again ran the Swift Boat ad on his primetime FOX broadcast, and he opened a relentless attack on Kerry's wartime service during his program, sometimes inviting both pro- and anti-Kerry veterans into the debate. The subject of Kerry's wartime record became a frequent topic on FOX. One FOX reporter remembered that in the month of August alone, his network had broadcast 149 reports on Swift Boat criticism of Kerry.

According to a University of Pennsylvania survey released on August 20, 2004, 57 percent of the respondents, who were polled between August 9 and 16, had already seen or heard the Swift Boat attack ad.[15] "Once you put it out," said the late ABC News producer Leroy Sievers, "it gains that credibility and reaches that audience, and then the rest of the media does follow. You know it's that 'pack mentality'—that 'oh, they're covering this, [so we must].' ... It's seen on FOX, it's seen somewhere else, and it's very effective, but also very troubling."[16]

Suddenly, it seemed, the Swift Boat message was everywhere, not just on FOX, but also on CNN and MSNBC, on talk radio, on the Internet, on cell phones. LaCivita added another arrow to his quiver: the book of anti-Kerry charges and allegations by O'Neill and Corsi, which caught fire on the talk shows and, before long, leaped onto the best-seller lists all over the country and remained there through the campaign. *Unfit for Command* compiled evidence, it said, that Kerry was a chronic liar about his wartime record in Vietnam. Finally, LaCivita set up a website as part of the Swift Boat attack. Much to Hoffmann's delight, it, too, was a significant success. During the week ending August 8, according to the *Washington Post*, "966,000 people visited the anti-Kerry group's Web site"—almost as many as visited the Kerry website, which had been in operation for a much longer period of time.[17]

On August 19, when Kerry finally burst out of his August cocoon, blasting the Swift Boaters and charging that Bush "wants them to do his dirty work,"[18] the mainstream media began to pick up the story. PBS's *NewsHour with Jim Lehrer* was among the first to treat the Swift Boats as a legitimate story. O'Neill was invited to debate *Boston Globe* columnist Tom Oliphant, one of Kerry's old friends, on August 19. The *New York Times* ran a long story on August 20 questioning a number of the Swift Boat allegations.[19] Other major newspapers ran similar stories. What started as a favorite conservative nugget in early August became a mainstream story by early September.

A question cutting to the heart of journalistic responsibilities arose at this time: was it the media's role to see if there was any truth in the SBVT charges? Kerry, months later, was still arguing that it was. "Why are they allowed to lie by the media?" he asked. "That's the real question. What's happened to the gatekeepers? What's happened to the truth standard in the media? What's happened that allowed people to repeat lies? . . . [T]he lies were allowed to continue."[20]

He admitted, "Look, are you asking me should it have been responded to immediately? I've said it a hundred times—yes." But with characteristic New England reserve, he added: "I'm not going to get into pointing fingers at anyone,"[21] meaning that he was not going to blame Shrum and Cahill. No, Kerry was not obliged to listen to his advisers; he was the candidate, and he should have called the shots.

Xmas '68, a Boston Whaler, and a Mysterious Purple Heart

In 1979, four years after the United States fled from its Saigon misadventure, the movie *Apocalypse Now* premiered to wide acclaim. It was producer Francis Ford Coppola's vision of the Vietnam War. An editor at the *Boston Herald-American* had a good idea: why not ask John Kerry, a prominent local veteran, to review the movie? Coppola's image of the war, judging by the movie, was that it was a giant drug party where Swift Boating sailors careened through the Mekong Delta listening to loud rock music and shooting indiscriminately at communist guerrillas. Kerry wrote in his review that this "hallucinatory image" was way off the mark. "Somewhere, just like the country in its involvement in Southeast Asia," he wrote, "Coppola got lost." Then, in a sense, Kerry got lost; in his review, he allowed his imagination and his rhetoric to wander into a field of dreams. "I remember spending Christmas eve of 1968 five miles across the Cambodian border," he said, "being shot at by our South Vietnamese allies, who were drunk and celebrating Christmas. The absurdity of almost being killed by our own allies in a country in which President Nixon claimed there were no American troops was very real."[22]

This vision appealed to Kerry, because, seven years later, on March 27, 1986, he described it once again on the floor of the U.S. Senate. "I remember Christmas of 1968 sitting on a gunboat in Cambodia," he said. "I remember what it was like to be shot at by Vietnamese and Khmer Rouge and Cambodians, and have the President of the United States telling the American people that I was not there; the troops were not in Cambodia." He then used a verb that the Swift Boaters would not let him forget. "I have that memory, which is seared," Kerry stressed, "seared in me, that says to me, before we send another generation into harm's way we have a responsibility in the U.S. Senate to go the last step, to make the best effort possible in order to avoid that kind of conflict."[23] Back then, Kerry's rhetoric was ideal for his political supporters, but in 2004 it got him into trouble.

Hoffmann seized on the word "seared" as one more bit of proof that Kerry was a liar. First, he said, Kerry was not in Cambodia on Christmas Eve 1968, and, second, Nixon was not president at the time. (He was, in fact, president-elect.) With a dismissive wave of his hand, Hoffmann said: "That business about 'it seared in my mind,' 'I was in Cambodia, being fired on by the Cambodians, by the Khmer Rouge . . . or by the Vietnamese' . . . he wasn't even close." The admiral frowned. "He was at least fifty miles away. . . . He wasn't there. Even his own crew people . . . have said, 'No, we weren't in Cambodia.'"

Could it have been an honest mistake? he was asked. "No, I don't think so," Hoffmann replied. Clearly, the admiral had made up his mind.[24]

O'Neill, in his best-selling book, reinforced Hoffmann's view. He and Corsi, his coauthor, wrote that the zone of operations of Kerry's division extended to Sa Dec, which was "55 miles from the Cambodian border"; that he could not operate any closer to the border even if he had wanted to. "A large sign at the border prohibited entry," the book said, quoting Tom Anderson, the naval commander in the region, as confirming that "there were no Swifts anywhere in the area." The book then claimed that "at least three of the five crewmen" on Kerry's boat denied they were ever in Cambodia,[25] leaving the distinct impression that the authors had talked to the crewmen and the crewmen had confirmed this account.

Bill Zaladonis, identified as one of the crewmen, told a completely different story. He said that O'Neill had not contacted him before writing that at least three of the five crewmen denied being in Cambodia, and that he did not remember exactly where he was on Christmas Eve 1968. But he left no doubt that, on a number of occasions, he was either close to Cambodia or in Cambodia. At the time U.S. Special Forces were often conducting secret cross-border operations in Cambodia. The Swift Boats would carry them to the border, sometimes across the border, and then beat a hasty retreat; Cambodia was supposed to be a neutral country. Zaladonis participated in these secret missions. "When we went up that river from Ha Tien, which we did from time to time," Zaladonis said, "we were right on the border. If you beached on the left bank, that was Cambodia. If it was the right bank, it was Vietnam."[26]

It was left to Kerry, during the 2004 campaign, to refute both Hoffmann and O'Neill, which he effectively did, except that he came late to his own defense and he made one understandable mistake, which cast enough of a doubt over his argument to allow the O'Neill allegations to survive his counterattack. After a detailed check of his personal records and U.S. Navy records, Kerry told NBC's Tim Russert a few months after the election, "We were on the Cambodian border on Christmas Eve, absolutely." Kerry said, "We were right on the Cambodian border that night. We were ambushed there, as a matter of fact. And that is a matter of record . . . it's part of the Navy records."[27] A Kerry spokesman, Michael Meehan, had contributed some details the previous summer: "John Kerry and his crew were on patrol in the watery borders between Vietnam and Cambodia deep in enemy territory," he said. "In the early afternoon, Kerry's boat, PCF 44, was at Sa Dec and then headed north to the Cambodian border. . . . Kerry and his crew along with two other boats were ambushed, taking fire from both sides of the river, and after the firefight were fired upon again."[28]

On one other occasion, Kerry actually was in Cambodia—five miles across the border—a fact that helped explain his misstatement. It was in February 1969, a few months after his Christmas adventure near the Cambodian border. This time, "We went up on a mission with CIA agents—I believe they were CIA agents—CIA special ops guys," Kerry said. "I even have some photographs of it, and I can document it. And it has been documented."[29] The person responsible for Kerry's records, David Stone, recalled that Kerry went "across the Cambodian border, to deposit some CIA types, or Special Forces, or something like that."[30] Clearly, Kerry was near or in Cambodia twice; but in relating his two visits, he confused one visit with the other, saying he was *in* Cambodia on Christmas Eve when, in fact, he was only near Cambodia at that time. "What I did was conflate [both] into one event," he explained, "'cause I was speaking very quickly on the floor of the Senate and talking for about two minutes. But the fact is, both of those events were accurate. We were ambushed. We were ambushed by folks on the Cambodian border. On another occasion, I went in, and, as I said [to] Tim Russert, conflated them into one event. But the simple fact is, there was no untruth in either thing that happened."[31]

Hoffmann was not persuaded, nor were many of the other Swift Boaters. No, "not when you stand before the Senate of the United States and make these outrageous statements," the admiral asserted vigorously. "This is in the Congressional Record. This is in 1986—he's standing before the Senate Armed Services Committee, and he's making these statements. That's how I know it."[32] Neither Hoffmann nor O'Neill was prepared to cut Kerry any slack, not in the midst of the 2004 campaign. In O'Neill's book, in various TV ads, on their website, and during broadcast interviews, they continued to hammer away at Kerry, leveling a series of charges against him. Some were very damning, amounting to accusations of treason and collusion with the enemy. Others were ludicrously exaggerated, distorting the candidate's record beyond recognition. Through it all, though their charges were cutting, bitter, and ugly, the accusers conveyed an impression of political innocence and independence. They were only telling the "truth," they insisted, and they had nothing to do with the White House. Kerry had his own definition for their "truth." "They lied and lied and lied about everything," Kerry told the *New York Times* in 2006.[33]

Kerry also faced criticism from the Swift Boaters for having departed from Vietnam after a relatively short time. "He left in about four months, much short of the twelve-month normal tour of duty that people serve," O'Neill said. "He did that on the basis of having three Purple Hearts."[34]After getting his third Purple Heart, Kerry did in fact request an early exit from Vietnam and got it.

Schachte versus Kerry: Who Was Telling the Truth?

Among Latch's most prominent legionnaires was William Schachte Jr., a native of Charleston, South Carolina, who wanted no part in the 2004 presidential struggle for power but ended up playing a major role, though he did so with extreme reluctance. His story in itself was not important; but because it portrayed him saying one thing and Kerry another, it was used by the Swift Boaters as another example of Kerry as a finagling liar to be distrusted.

Schachte, a gentleman of the South who had enjoyed a distinguished career in the U.S. Navy, was, for Hoffmann, a perfect foil. After serving honorably in the Mekong Delta, Schachte rose to become judge advocate general, the top uniformed lawyer in the navy, an assignment carrying the rank of admiral. When he retired, he returned to Charleston and pursued an active legal practice. Described as a "reflective and spiritual man," Schachte was never far from his lifelong study of the Bible; he took his faith seriously.[35] Almost by accident, he became a supporter of the Swift Boat group, an advocate for a political cause.

In the spring of 2003, when reporters first got wind of a Kerry campaign for the presidency, and when the SBVT was still only a whimsical glimmer in Hoffmann's eye, the *Boston Globe* began digging into Kerry's past role not only as an antiwar critic but also as a wartime winner of medals and Purple Hearts. The paper came upon Schachte while looking into conflicting recollections of an incident on the Mekong on the night of December 2–3, 1968. Schachte had been there, and so had Kerry. Wartime memories live in aging corners of the mind; seldom are they reliable affidavits of truth. Still, Schachte said in April 2003 that he remembered the night: there had been a "firefight," he said. "He got hit," Schachte said of Kerry, describing it as "not a very serious wound at all."[36] Schachte's remembrance tended to confirm Kerry's account; and there it would likely have rested, if it were not for Hoffmann's stubborn determination.

Like so many of Latch's legions, Schachte was contacted by his former commanding officer; Schachte, always the gentleman, obliged Hoffmann by looking at Brinkley's book. He saw what Brinkley had written about him, or not written about him. On August 27, he produced a sharply critical and public response to the book's account of what happened on December 2–3. No longer was he calmly recollecting the events of a night many years before, as he had been to the *Boston Globe*'s reporter; now he was outraged and as such changed his story. "I was astonished by Senator Kerry's rendition of the facts of that night," he wrote in a statement that was published in the *National Review*. "Notably, Lt. (jg) Kerry had himself in charge of the operation, and I was not mentioned at all. He also claimed that he was wounded by hostile fire."[37]

Questions quickly arose. Which Schachte was the real Schachte: the benign source of 2003 or the clearly hurt source of 2004? If there was "no hostile fire," as Schachte's 2004 statement said, then there was no "firefight"; but if there was a "firefight," then there was "hostile fire." And how could Kerry be "in charge of the operation," as Schachte wrote that the Brinkley book alleged, when he, Schachte, said he was in charge? He had commanded every mission, he insisted. Was it possible that Schachte had been offended by Brinkley's account and was now seeking his own revenge?

A bit of history: In the fall of 1968, the new commander of naval forces in Vietnam, the admired and respected Vice Admiral Elmo R. Zumwalt Jr., decided to change U.S. policy in the Mekong Delta by going on the offensive and sending Swift Boats into the Delta in hot pursuit of enemy troops and supplies. Their mission was called Operation Sealords. These fifty-foot aluminum boats moved noisily but effectively through the narrow waterways, but could suddenly be exposed to ambush attack by camouflaged guerrillas. "People started getting wounded, and boats were getting shot up," remembered Steve Hayes. "They needed a steady stream of replacements."[38]

Kerry was one of the replacements. "When I signed up for the swift boats," he wrote in a contribution to a 1986 book about Vietnam, "they had very little to do with the war. They were engaged in coastal patrolling, and that's what I thought I was going to be doing."[39] In fact, according to Brinkley's book, Kerry arrived in Saigon on November 17, 1968, and then spent the first couple of weeks patrolling the Cam Ranh coastline, fighting Monsoon Mamie, a storm of memorable dimension, and searching for guerrillas among the fishermen in sampans and junks.[40] Kerry was a green, inexperienced lieutenant, and he was just killing time on routine patrols while waiting for his own command.

Enter Lieutenant Schachte, the imaginative commander of a special mission called Skimmer OPS. To advance Zumwalt's new approach, Schachte designed a perilous but effective nocturnal mission using a skimmer, or Boston Whaler, a foam-filled, fiberglass boat about fifteen feet long, powered by an outboard motor and manned by a crew of three. The Boston Whaler would approach a "hot" zone, cut its motor, and drift silently toward a suspected enemy position. Its purpose was deliberately to attract enemy fire, thereby exposing the enemy to the superior firepower of Swift Boats that were pre-positioned to be near the exposed skimmer. It was a game of bait-and-destroy. It was never designed to take and hold territory. It was, according to writer David Halberstam, who had covered the war, "terribly, unbelievably dangerous stuff." The Vietcong would go underwater for hours, waiting for a Whaler or a Swift Boat, and then ambush the Americans.[41]

Kerry heard about Skimmer OPS, and he volunteered for a Boston Whaler mission. Schachte gave him the chance. Here the narrative splits in two directions.

First, the Schachte version of what happened. (The lawyer in Schachte understood the value of a good witness; he was, unfortunately, his version's only witness.) "I was in command and physically in the skimmer on each of the missions, up to and including the one of December 2/3 on which Lt. (jg) Kerry served under my command," Schachte recalled. "I . . . have a crystal clear recollection of the events."[42] Schachte wrote that on the night of December 2–3, 1968, there were two officers, himself and Kerry, and one crewman, whose name he said he forgot.

"During the early morning hours, I thought I detected some movement inland," Schachte wrote. He fired a hand-held flare, which lit up the area; and he "immediately opened fire," or tried to, but his weapon jammed. According to Schachte, Kerry then opened fire, but his gun also jammed. "As I was trying to clear my weapon," Schachte continued, "I heard the distinctive sound of the M-79 [single-shot grenade launcher] being fired and turned to see Lt. (jg) Kerry holding the M-79 from which he had just launched a round. We received no return fire of any kind nor were there any muzzle flashes from the beach."

"Upon returning to base," Schachte informed Lieutenant Commander Grant Hibbard, his commanding officer, that "we had received no enemy fire" and, for that reason, he went on, "I did not file an 'after action' report." Schachte wrote that Kerry "requested that he be put in for a Purple Heart as a result of a small piece of shrapnel removed from his arm." "Because there was no hostile fire," Schachte said he "could not support the request because there was no hostile fire. The shrapnel must have been a fragment from the M-79 that struck Lt. (jg) Kerry, because he had fired the M-79 too close to our boat."[43]

Schachte's story was repeated endlessly during the 2004 campaign as further proof that Kerry could not resist a self-promoting lie to advance his political career. The Swift Boat leaders latched on to Schachte's story, because he appeared to be such an authentic, believable source; "unassailable," one of them said.

Now the Kerry version of what happened on December 2–3, supported by the recollections of two crewmen and the navy's own record. Brinkley's account did not mention Schachte at all, which offended him deeply; it highlighted only Kerry. "It was a half-assed action that hardly qualified as combat," Kerry told Brinkley, "but it was my first, and that made it very exciting." He was not talking about one of the great battles of the war, clearly. "Three of us, two enlisted men and myself, had stayed up all night patrolling the shore . . . north of Cam Ranh." A couple of "innocent fishermen" appeared around a bend in the river. One of the crewmen tried to open fire, but he could not; he had failed to remove the safety on his machine gun. Otherwise, Kerry noted, the fishermen would have been killed, "blown to bits and scattered in the water." The next few hours were uneventful. Kerry picked up a number of fishermen and brought them to a nearby Swift Boat. But "most of the night had been spent being scared shitless by fishermen whom we would suddenly creep up on in the darkness." At about 2 or 3 a.m., "while it was still dark," Kerry said he steered his skimmer into an inlet "designated as our [ultimate] objective." He remembered, "It was scary as hell. You could hear yourself breathing."

Suddenly, in the darkness, Kerry thought he saw "a group of sampans" heading toward the shore. He had been briefed, he said, that "this was a favorite crossing area for VC trafficking contraband." Like Schachte, he fired a flare into the sky. The men on the sampans "bolted erect, stiff with shock," and they moved quickly for cover. "We opened fire. . . . My M-16 jammed [as Schachte had also reported], and as I bent down in the boat to grab another gun, a stinging piece of heat socked into my arm and just seemed to burn like hell." Kerry made no mention of attempting to fire an M-79. "Then it was quiet."[44]

Kerry added, "Without any knowledge of what kind of force was there, we were not all about to go crawling on the beach to get our asses shot off. We were unprotected; we didn't have ammunition, we didn't have cover, we just weren't prepared for that. . . . So we first shot the sampans so that they were destroyed and whatever was in them was destroyed."[45] Kerry said that the commander of the nearby Swift Boat warned him of a possible ambush. He decided then to clear the area, slipping past the danger zone without further incident. And with that maneuver the events of December 2–3 ended.

But during the 2004 campaign, the controversy between Schachte and Kerry became a serious problem of credibility for the Massachusetts senator. If Schachte was commanding the Boston Whaler on that night of December 2–3, as he claimed, then obviously Kerry could not have been. But if Kerry was commanding the Boston Whaler, then Schachte could not have been. On this one issue, Kerry left little room for doubt. "He wasn't with me on the skimmer," he said. "I went in on the skimmer, not him."[46]

Kerry then added two witnesses to his story, and they were very persuasive. Bill Zaladonis and Pat Runyon were navy crewmen of modest background, who swore they were Kerry's crewmen on the Boston Whaler on December 2–3, 1968, and Schachte, they insisted, was not on the skimmer. "There's a lot of things I'm not certain about that night, what happened in different events," Zaladonis said, "but I do know it was us three on the boat—John, Pat, and myself." Runyon was asked the same question: who was on the boat? "I said I wasn't the smartest guy in the world," he replied, "but I know that there were only three of us." He then said, "That night was so special you are going to remember who's with you. You might not remember what boat took you there or the time of night or whatever, but you're going to remember something you've only done once. And it's a night that scared the hell out of you. You're going to remember who was with you. It's just impossible to lose one person in a small boat" that was, he indicated, about the size of a dinner table. "It was no man-of-war."[47]

When a *Globe* reporter contacted Michael Voss, the skipper of the Swift Boat, asking for confirmation, Voss said he remembered the mission but did not remember whether Schachte was on board with him. "I am not certain who was on a skimmer on a certain night thirty-six years ago," he stated, avoiding any entanglement in the Schachte-Kerry flap.[48]

Zaladonis and Runyon met in the navy, which they joined in 1966. They were assigned to the USS *Paul Revere*, then on its way from San Diego to Cam Ranh Bay. They became close friends, "steaming buddies," according to navy slang. Zaladonis, from Pennsylvania, was big, talkative, decidedly outgoing. Runyon, from Ohio, was short, quiet, a man of few words with a gentle smile. In the summer of 1968, after a tour of coastal patrolling, they put in for a change of duty. "They [the navy] asked for two volunteers [for Swift Boat duty], Runyon recalled. "Bill and I were always friends and decided to go over together."[49]

On December 2–3, 1968, they remembered being on a secret skimmer mission with Kerry in command. "I got Pat involved," said Zaladonis. "He . . . was complaining that he hadn't seen any action, been in any firefights, or anything like that. And I said: 'Well, I'm doing this thing with Kerry tonight. You ought to join us. We need somebody else.' I brought it up with Kerry, and he approved it. So [Pat] got involved in it." Zaladonis knew little about the purpose of the mission. "As far as I know, we were just going to some bay that they knew the VC were using as a staging area, or a crossing area and stuff like that, and we just had to go in there and see what was going on. And a Swift Boat towed the skimmer up there."

It was in the dead of night, when the skimmer cut its power and slipped silently into a "staging area." No one on board the skimmer knew whether VC guerrillas would be there to greet them. "Unfortunately, when we got there," Zaladonis continued, "they were [there]. . . . There was a lot of small sampans and basket boats in there fishing, which they weren't supposed to be there." The reason was that this "staging area" was in a "free fire zone," meaning anyone caught in a "free fire zone" would be considered an enemy combatant and would either be captured or killed. "They weren't supposed to be there after nightfall," Zaladonis said. "So we started yanking these people out of there, taking them back to the Swift Boat to be interrogated."

At one point, Kerry saw "a couple of sampans crossing in front of us," Zaladonis recalled. Were they VC? Kerry suspected they were. Zaladonis manned the M-60 gun. He was seated on the bow of the skimmer. Runyon ran the small, occasionally unreliable engine in the rear. Kerry "wanted to pop a flare," Runyon recalled. He also wanted Runyon to start the engine, "because we don't know what we're going to get. 'Cause once you pop a flare, you light them up, [but] you light yourself up [too]." Once Kerry popped the flare, "people of age, young men—they started scrambling." Zaladonis remembered the scene. "John told me to open up. I didn't have to be encouraged. Once he said open up, I opened up, because I wasn't sure for my life. But yes, he told me to fire. I wouldn't have fired if he hadn't told me to, unless they were firing at us." Runyon was struck by one odd fact. "They were the only ones moving," he recalled. "The others we come up on were always setting. These were moving. They weren't fishing." Zaladonis said the shooting stopped after "ten seconds or so." "We just got out of there, because we didn't know what the heck we were getting into. We weren't armed that well, and we headed back to the Swift Boat."

Somehow Kerry got hurt. Exactly how was not clear. Zaladonis recalled, "I don't know if they even fired back at us. I had an M-60, and I was firing at them. The muzzle flash is kind of like getting your picture taken with a flash camera at night—you can't see. . . . I opened up at these people, right in front of me. John didn't like where I was shooting, so he directed my fire more to the right. And I followed around with the M-60."

It was not unusual for Americans to open fire on an enemy, or a supposed enemy, they actually saw, or thought they saw, an enemy who returned fire or just as often an enemy who did not return fire. Schachte acknowledged that he fired at the enemy, or tried to, but told his commanding officer a few hours later that there had been no return fire.

Another question surrounding the night of December 2–3 was whether Kerry deserved the Purple Heart medal that he received for this action. The Swift Boat group argued that he did not.

Years later, Admiral Zumwalt's son, James Zumwalt, a retired navy and marine officer otherwise sympathetic to the Swift Boat attack on Kerry, remembered that his father "viewed all who answered their country's call to duty in Vietnam as heroes. . . . [M]y father would have taken the position that one does not question the medals a Vietnam veteran received, or did not receive, for his actions on the battlefield. As long as one served and did so honorably, he was a hero whose courage was not determined simply by a piece of metal being placed on his chest. Therefore on the issue of the Purple Hearts, I believe my father, absent further evidence, would have disagreed with the position taken by the [Swift Boat Veterans for Truth]."[50]

What happened, according to navy records, was that Kerry was hit by shrapnel, a very common injury. Rarely was the wound considered serious; rarely did it prevent the officer from returning to duty the next day. Kerry was treated shortly after his skimmer returned to base in the early morning hours of December 3. "Shrapnel in left arm above elbow," read the navy record of the day. "Shrapnel removed and appl[ied] bacitracin dressing. Ret[urned] to duty." The signature of a J. C. Carreon, either the doctor on duty or a medical crewman, was on the "sick call treatment record." O'Neill and Corsi wrote that a Dr. Louis Letson treated Kerry, using "tweezers to remove the tiny fragment," which the authors described as "barely embedded in his arm."[51]

During the last three months of Kerry's Vietnam tour, according to a *Los Angeles Times* investigative report, forty-six Swift Boat personnel were wounded. "Most were hurt by shrapnel and all but five of the cases earned Purple Hearts," the newspaper noted. About half of the men had shrapnel injuries described as light or minor, and about half of these wounds "could not clearly be traced to enemy fire."[52] George Elliott, who was Kerry's commanding officer at An Thoi base, and no friend, described the sad ordinariness of Purple Hearts being awarded to troops with shrapnel wounds. "There were an awful lot of Purple Hearts—from shrapnel, some of those might have been M-40 grenades," he said. "The Purple Hearts were coming down in boxes. Kerry— he had three Purple Hearts. None of them took him off duty. Not to belittle it—that was more the rule than the exception."[53]

Kerry's friend David Thorne was a Vietnam veteran who received a Purple Heart, in his case for an injury sustained in April 1969. He said he never put in for a medal and did not know he had received one until after his discharge from the military a year or so later. "[What] bugs me," he stated, was the questioning of Kerry's patriotism by the Swift Boat group:

> What they are saying is that the blood that John Kerry shed for his country is less honorable than the blood others have shed for their country. I don't understand it. . . . Because if you call that into question, what they question is all the Purple Hearts that have ever been issued. They call

into question all the medals that have ever been issued. Because it's all on the basis of "was he acting honorably?" and "was he less worthy of receiving these things?" And who is to sit there thirty-five years later and make that judgment? It just boggles my mind.[54]

When questioned about Swift Boat criticism of his Purple Heart medals, Kerry often took the high ground, using a very interesting word to describe his feelings: "graced." He said he had been "graced," and he returned to the word time and again. "A Purple Heart is given under navy regulations," he explained, "based on whether or not you are wounded in action—they don't measure the size [of the wound]. . . . I never claimed on anything, never said in an interview—from the day I came home, I said I was one of the graced. I was one of the lucky ones. I never ever suggested—other than the fact that I was very lightly wounded, a very, very lucky human being." One day, Kerry related, he emerged from the cabin on his Swift Boat and saw evidence of his good fortune. He looked up and saw "three bullet holes right in a row, straight up above my head." Had the bullets been fired a few inches lower, he would have been killed. On another day, a B-40 rocket "blew out all the windows, it hit the boat. I could have been knocked out." He paused. "I mean, it's luck, okay, and you're graced to come home."[55]

Finally, there was the matter of code names, usually used to facilitate communication between officers, or ships, or units, and to confuse the enemy. On the December 2–3 issue, O'Neill in his book made a small but revealing point when he and Corsi wrote that Kerry, for this mission, was code-named "Robin" and Schachte was code-named "Batman."[56] But the code names made little sense. Why, asked Zaladonis in bewilderment, "why would Schachte be on the skimmer if he was 'Batman' and Kerry was 'Robin'? Did they have radios to talk to each other while they were on the skimmer? No! The boat was fourteen feet long." If they had code names, he implied, the reason was that they had to be on different boats. On the skimmer, they just talked to each other.[57]

Schachte seemed to be a thoroughly honorable man who got caught in the swirl of political controversy during the 2004 campaign. Reluctantly or not, he became an important part of the Swift Boaters' effort to upend Kerry's presidential hopes, cited dozens of times as proof that Kerry was a liar. But a very careful examination of the existing evidence shows that Kerry was telling the truth, as best he remembered it, and Schachte, perhaps unintentionally, was projecting an inaccurate picture of what happened on the night of December 2–3 in the Mekong Delta.

On a few of the contentious issues separating Kerry from the Swift Boat supporters, it may never be possible to determine the absolute truth. But on most of the issues, and certainly on this one, the weight of truth falls heavily on Kerry's side. Schachte was somewhere on the night of December 2–3, 1968, but he was not on the skimmer with Kerry. He should never have allowed himself to be seduced into Hoffmann's crusade of hate. He should have followed his instincts and risen above the fray.

Kerry lost the election, and the Swift Boaters emerged from their deep, quick immersion in presidential politics with the pleasure of denying Kerry the White House but with their honor and reputation forever sullied by their vicious, negative campaign. They gave birth to a new political phenomenon called "swiftboating," which worked its way into the political lexicon and which came to represent the worst in American politics. Any politician could lose an election, but to lose as a result of having been "swiftboated" was only to add insult to injury.

Meanwhile, some Swift Boat veterans, offended by the Hoffmann-style assault of 2004, refused to allow their Vietnam experience to be tainted by immersion in angry political warfare. "We've all been attributed to the sleaziness that those guys assigned to Kerry," said veteran Stan Collier. "I think we've all been demeaned." Another Swift Boat veteran who chose to be identified as "Carlo" opined on a Swift Boat–related website, "I think it's disgraceful that a handful of people have managed to turn 'Swift boat' into a synonym for 'To smear somebody with lies.' . . . I hope you guys can take the term back to connote bravery, courage and sacrifice, like it always has."[58]

Latch's legions thought of themselves as pure patriots, independent of politics and loyal only to flag and country. They wrapped themselves in the red, white, and blue and argued that anyone who disagreed with their understanding of honor and truth was unpatriotic. Once, asked directly whether Kerry was unpatriotic, Hoffmann nodded but would not utter the word.

By invoking the war in Vietnam, Hoffmann demonstrated its lingering lethality; and by recalling Kerry's April 1971 testimony suggesting that American warriors in Vietnam were guilty of war crimes, he proved that Vietnam still aroused powerful emotions more than thirty years after most of the fighting had ended and the troops had come home.

9

Obama: "Afghanistan Is Not Vietnam"

Vietnam walked the halls of the White House.
—BRUCE RIEDEL, interview, April 15, 2010

The Vietnam conflict was a life-defining experience . . . and it continues to
impact us all—the pain, the conflict, the healing.
— MIKE MULLEN, Washington, D.C., May 31, 2010

IT WAS LATE January 2009, and Barack Obama, the newly inaugurated president, young, vigorous, as ambitious as he was inexperienced, was presiding
over his first review of national security policy. Confronting a historic economic crisis as well as two wars, Obama had the air of a natural leader, cool
under the circumstances. He was determined to be intimidated by no one, not
even the Pentagon brass.

Obama saw the American war in Afghanistan as a twenty-first century
example of asymmetrical warfare. It was an insurgency, not a "war on terror," as his predecessor had labeled it, and American policy had to be revised
to confront the spreading Taliban threat. For the past few years, the George
W. Bush administration had effectively ignored Afghanistan, focusing instead
on the controversial troop surge in Iraq. One result was that the Taliban took
advantage of that benign neglect to strengthen its position throughout the
south and to undermine the authority of the Karzai regime in Kabul. For the
first time, according to intelligence from Afghanistan, a Taliban victory was no
longer regarded as a fantasy; it was now a real possibility.

After Vietnam, no American president could tolerate another defeat: certainly not a Democrat and certainly not Obama, who had never served in
the military. He had, during the presidential campaign, spoken about sending more troops to Afghanistan (two brigades, he had promised); now, as
president, he wanted to act on his promise. Afghanistan was the war that the
United States had to fight and win, he repeatedly stated; Iraq was the war that

the United States had to bring to a speedy end. His campaign rhetoric now shaped his war policy. Unless he was prepared to abandon his rhetoric, he was going to have to make his stand in Afghanistan. Troops alone would not do the job, he knew, but without more troops, the job could not be done. But how many more troops, for what specific mission, and how long would they stay? Now, delving for the first time into the practical problems of policymaking, Obama was quickly to learn that any discussion of troop deployments resurrected old, nagging doubts about another war, lost years ago.

In fact, Obama wanted no part of Vietnam; he thought he had made that clear more than once. He was, as he had said repeatedly during the campaign, post-Vietnam and post–cold war. He was a small child when Lyndon Johnson escalated the war in Vietnam and only thirteen when it ended. "He's really the first generation of recent presidents who didn't live through that," said David Axelrod, a senior adviser. "The whole debate on Vietnam, that was not part of his life experience."[1] Yet the ghosts of the Vietnam War seemed to be everywhere, a dark memory none of his top advisers seemed able to shake as they pondered the Afghan situation.

Vice President Joe Biden, whose long service on the Senate Foreign Relations Committee had sharpened his dovish instincts about putting more "boots on the ground" in Afghanistan, was of the Rumsfeld school, opting for the "small footprint" on the ground linked to super-sophisticated aircraft hovering over the battlefield.

Secretary of State Hillary Clinton, who, during her time as senator and in her run for the presidency, had occasionally flown with the hawks to cover her natural caution about putting more troops into Afghanistan, favored a realistic political compromise, believing no military solution was possible.

Secretary of Defense Robert Gates, a Republican with vast CIA experience who had labored for President George W. Bush, brought a flinty credibility to his controversial conviction that Afghanistan was stretching America's military to the breaking point (as he wrote a year later in *Foreign Affairs*, "The United States is unlikely to repeat a mission on the scale of those in Afghanistan and Iraq anytime soon").[2]

National Security Adviser James Jones, a former Marine Corps general who had served nobly in Vietnam in 1967–68, later concluded that the United States had made major mistakes, the biggest being that it might have wanted freedom for South Vietnam more than the South Vietnamese did, a surefire formula for failure.

Richard Holbrooke, who had just been appointed Obama's "special representative" for Afghanistan and Pakistan (AfPak, as it was called), carried with him ineradicable memories of America's tragic experience in Vietnam, where he had served as a young Foreign Service officer in the early 1960s.

Admiral Mike Mullen, chairman of the Joint Chiefs of Staff, Annapolis graduate, and Vietnam veteran, later came to believe that American military power could only be used in a "precise and principled way."[3]

In one way or another, these officials had been powerfully influenced by the Vietnam War. They hoisted a yellow flag of caution whenever the president raised the subject of sending more troops to Afghanistan. Vietnam did not mean that the United States could not fight another war, but it did mean that any war would now have to have a clear purpose, congressional backing, and an exit strategy.

"We remain the strongest country in the world," Secretary Clinton said, "but the way we exercise that leadership has changed dramatically."[4] The Vietnam war had left a long shadow.

If Obama's principal advisers could not escape the memories of Vietnam, neither could the media. Columnist Jeffrey T. Kuhner, writing in the *Washington Times* on January 25, 2009, warned, "Afghanistan threatens to destroy Barack Obama's presidency." Under the headline "Obama's Vietnam?" Kuhner told his readers that nation building would not work in Afghanistan, and more troops would only ratify a "massive strategic military blunder."[5]

The same headline, "Obama's Vietnam," was splattered dramatically across the January 31, 2009, cover of *Newsweek*, cautioning that the war in Afghanistan was beginning to look "disturbingly familiar" to the war in Vietnam. Writers John Barry and Evan Thomas carefully cited "important differences" between Afghanistan and Vietnam and noted General David Petraeus's impatient dismissal of "history by analogy." But the authors concluded that "we may now be facing a situation where we can win every battle and still not win the war—at least not within a time frame and at a cost that is acceptable to the American people." It quoted Secretary Gates: "My worry is that the Afghans come to see us as part of the problem, rather than as part of the solution," he said. "And then we are lost."[6]

Foreign crises have been analyzed by a generation of American presidents, cabinet officers, and generals through the hypnotic lens of Vietnam. Obama felt it was his responsibility as the first post-sixties generation president to break the link between Vietnam and Afghanistan. The word filtered through the new administration: the president does not want to hear about Vietnam! During one meeting, when Holbrooke reminded everyone that decades earlier, Lyndon Johnson, sitting in the same room, had grappled with a similar set of problems, Obama interrupted him and asked, "Richard, do people really talk like that?"[7]

"People are going to try to analogize," explained James Steinberg, Obama's number-two man at the State Department, but "Obama [is] trying to break the analogy."[8] He had drawn a sharp distinction between Iraq, which he considered a "war of choice," and Afghanistan, which he considered a "war of necessity." Why the distinction? Because, as Steinberg put it, "Afghanistan was the place from which they killed Americans, and therefore, that's why this wasn't Vietnam."[9] Obama wanted his advisers to focus on what is, not what was.

Chuck Hagel, a former GOP senator from Nebraska and cochair of Obama's National Intelligence Board, spent a good bit of time with the new president and thought he understood Obama's vision of a changing world. "His point was," Hagel said, paraphrasing Obama's words, "'we're not going to be held hostage to what happened in Vietnam. . . . This is a new ball game, a new day, a new world. We're going to roll forward.'"[10]

The United States was fighting in Afghanistan, Obama believed, not out of pique or pride but out of a cold reading of its national interest: al Qaeda had used Afghanistan as a terrorist base for its surprise 9/11 attack on the United States, and the United States was going to make sure that Afghanistan would never again be used in the same way. There was another reason, too, equally meaningful to him. Neighboring Pakistan was nuclear-armed, it was unstable, and it served as a sanctuary for Islamic extremists and al Qaeda terrorists who dreamed of getting their hands on nuclear weapons. Hence the strategic link between Afghanistan and Pakistan. If the United States could construct a relatively stable Afghanistan, then it would be easier to protect a shaky Pakistan (and its nuclear weapons) from falling into fanatical hands. Even though at the time Obama's national security experience might fill a thimble, he spoke with supreme self-confidence about his AfPak strategy, as though he had been a president or a general for years, as though he had faced—and conquered— similar challenges in the past.

Flashback

Barack Obama was born on August 4, 1961, in Honolulu, the biracial son of a Kansan mother, Ann Dunham, and Kenyan father, Barack Obama Sr.

Although technically part of the baby boom, which ran from 1946 to 1964, the experience of his generation, born in the 1960s, was far different from that of the baby boomers born in the 1940s, like Bill and Hillary Clinton, Al Gore, John Kerry, and George W. Bush. For Obama's cohort, Vietnam was a fuzzy childhood memory rather than a life-and-death issue.

"In the back-and-forth between Clinton and Gingrich, and in the elections of 2000 and 2004, I sometimes felt as if I were watching the psychodrama of the Baby Boom generation—a tale rooted in old grudges and revenge plots hatched on a handful of college campuses long ago—played out on the national stage," Obama wrote. He wanted to move the country beyond that dynamic, toward something new.[11]

Obama, a graduate of Columbia University and Harvard Law School, ended up in Chicago. He taught at the University of Chicago Law School and won a race for the Illinois Senate in 1996. In 2004 the ambitious young politician claimed a seat in the U.S. Senate, becoming the only African American senator.

By this point, Obama already was a national star owing to his keynote address at the 2004 Democratic convention in which, in stirring oratory, he called for unity and asked the country to put aside its red-state and blue-state differences. He continued his upward trajectory in the Senate, and the White House loomed as the next prize, despite a big obstacle standing in Obama's path: Senator Hillary Clinton from New York. Clinton, fourteen years Obama's senior, also had four more years of Senate experience than Obama, had been on the national stage for almost two decades, and had the Clinton political network at her disposal. She was seen as the likely Democratic presidential nominee for 2008. But Obama plunged into the race, as did several other candidates, including 2004 vice presidential nominee John Edwards and Senator Joe Biden of Delaware, whom Obama eventually selected as his running mate. Clinton and Obama generated the most enthusiasm, operating in a stratosphere way above the others.

What distinguished Obama from Clinton, and helped him at a time when the Iraq War was growing increasingly unpopular, was a speech he had given back in October 2002 at a Chicago rally, opposing the move toward war in Iraq. At that point, criticizing the as-yet-unstarted war was not a slam-dunk, even for a Democrat; it represented a risk, as writer Richard Wolffe noted: "The political calculation was not clear for Democratic officials across the country, including an aspiring Chicago politician who was preparing to enter the party's crowded primary field for the United States Senate. So when Barack Obama took the microphone at Federal Plaza, the text of his speech rolled up in his right hand, he was taking a significant gamble."[12] And for an African American candidate running for statewide office in Illinois, the calculations were even more complex, as Obama aide Pete Giangreco recalled:

> His name, Barack Obama, was *different* and not very helpful, and while Roland Burris and Carol Moseley Braun had won statewide races, it's always a challenge for an African-American. So I said, "You might be able to capture the folks on the left who are against this war, and against *any* war, frankly, but there were all the others to take into account." He just took it all in. He finally said, "Well, my instinct is to do this." And my reaction was, "If this is what you really believe, you'll score huge points for courage and saying what you think."[13]

Giangreco was proved right; those "huge points" eventually scored Obama the Democratic nomination and the White House.

It was a sunny day in Chicago on October 2, 2002, and somewhere between 1,000 and 3,000 people turned out for an event that had overtones of the Vietnam era, causing the post-1960s-generation candidate to wince a bit, as biographer David Remnick noted: "Some of the trappings of the demonstration were comically reminiscent of earlier times. While the old John Lennon tune 'Give Peace a Chance' played on the public-address system, Obama leaned over to [rally organizer Bettylu] Saltzman and said, 'Can't they play something else?'"[14]

Obama, in his remarks, was careful not to come across as a pacifist. "I stand before you as someone who is not opposed to war in all circumstances," he told the crowd, citing the Civil War and World War II—in which, he mentioned, his grandfather had served—as examples of worthwhile fights. "What I am opposed to is a dumb war. What I am opposed to is a rash war. . . . A war based not on reason but on passion, not on principle but on politics. . . . I am not opposed to all wars. I'm opposed to dumb wars." Saddam Hussein, he said, was "brutal" and "ruthless," but "poses no imminent and direct threat to the United States, or to his neighbors."[15]

Obama later told biographer David Mendell that this 2002 speech was his favorite. "That's the speech I'm most proud of," Obama said. "It was a hard speech to give . . . because I was about to announce for the United States Senate and the politics were hard to read then. Bush is at sixty-five percent. . . . You didn't know whether this thing was gonna play out like the first Gulf War, and . . . suddenly everybody's coming back to cheering."[16]

But Iraq proved far different from the first Gulf War; indeed, it seemed by the middle of the decade to be looking more like Vietnam. "Iraq looked to be a quagmire, not on the scale of Vietnam, but one that was heading to the same conclusion: withdrawal followed by collapse of the government in power," wrote scholars James W. Ceaser, Andrew E. Busch, and John J. Pitney Jr. "Put more simply, it was defeat, and many asked, 'Why prolong the inevitable?'"[17]

The 2002 speech, then, was a central building block for Obama's campaign, which officially began in February 2007. "This speech had cemented his opposition to the invasion that all of our main primary opponents had supported; it had been a huge engine for our candidacy since Day One, and we often distributed copies of the speech at events," wrote Obama's presidential campaign manager, David Plouffe. "It wasn't simply that Obama spoke out against the war, but that he had delivered a well-constructed and remarkably prescient overview of what he feared would happen down the line if we invaded Iraq—a lengthy occupation, great human and financial costs, and a burden that America would have to bear for a very long time."[18] It propelled Obama to a win in the Iowa caucuses, relegating Clinton to a disappointing third-place finish behind Edwards. But Clinton came back to win the New Hampshire primary, and the two fought a drawn-out battle in which Obama eventually prevailed.

Obama's Seminar

It was like a "long, long lunch where you never stop eating or talking for days and days," Senator Jack Reed, a Democrat from Rhode Island, recalled.[19] He was describing a remarkable seminar on American foreign policy, starting with memories of Vietnam and ending with fears about Afghanistan and Pakistan. The setting, though, was not a classroom in a New England college; it was an American military plane in July 2008, heading toward Kuwait City. From Andrews Air Force Base near Washington, D.C., the flight would take fourteen hours. It was carrying a troika of consequential senators, including the next president of the United States.

Obama had asked Reed, a respected colleague, to arrange a visit to the Iraqi and Afghan battlefields, essential eyewitness experience for any presidential candidate. He had also asked Chuck Hagel, a maverick Republican from Nebraska, to join them. Obama had chosen his travel companions with care. Both had been mentioned as possible vice presidential running mates, Hagel even as a possible GOP presidential candidate. Reed, a West Point graduate, had journeyed frequently to Iraq and Afghanistan. He was a soldier-scholar, for whom public service in the form of politics was a career choice. Hagel was a Vietnam veteran, wounded in battle in 1968, winner of two Purple Hearts, who broke ranks with his party by criticizing the Bush administration's handling of the Iraq war. "To question your government is not unpatriotic—to not question your government is unpatriotic," Hagel had stated.[20]

Shortly before takeoff, Obama told reporters that he wanted to get a sense of the U.S. military's biggest concerns. "I'm more interested in listening than doing a lot of talking," he said.[21] On the plane, the three senators discussed Vietnam. What had this war wrought? Obama was on his way to Afghanistan, but he wanted to talk about Vietnam: not so much the history of the war, which he thought he knew, but the powerful legacy of the war, which he sensed at every turn in his rising career.

When Reed thought about Vietnam, he was reminded of the Japanese movie *Rashomon*. "Everybody has a different take on it," he said.[22] General Westmoreland's take was still victory by attrition; Reed's was that of a young West Point cadet, year 1967, when "Vietnam was the issue of the time." What worried him was that Vietnam was "not only not a winning proposition . . . it was going to destroy the army—[no] discipline, drug abuse, fratricide, the complete lowering of standards. . . . This was a loser." Reed did not serve in Vietnam, but he saw its devastating effect on troops returning from the war and came to appreciate the effort of a small group of bright and imaginative officers to transform the post-Vietnam army's approach to war. Citing the Powell Doctrine, Reed explained: "They understood that you can't fight without popular support, and if you are going to fight, it has to be overwhelming—quick, decisive . . . and short."[23]

Obama did not take notes; he listened, and Reed and Hagel both later remarked that Obama was a great listener. Continuing his recounting of the Vietnam legacy, Reed heaped praise on Bush I and Brent Scowcroft, whom he described as "smart . . . shrewd, tough." He admired their "extraordinarily shrewd use of military force" in the Persian Gulf War. Because of what they "learned from Vietnam," Reed said, Bush I and Scowcroft, "these two very gifted people," decided not to attack and occupy the Iraqi capital of Baghdad. It could have been done; they chose not to do it. "Too complicated—culture, history, politics; we don't know any of that stuff," Reed explained.

But if Reed gave high marks to Bush I, he did little to suppress his disapproval of Bush II, whom he described as a "not particularly introspective personality," who fell for the "notion" of using "unilateral military power from an ideological standpoint." Of course, the notion arose in response to 9/11, but Reed regarded Bush II's overall approach to military force as "totally flawed." In Afghanistan in 2001 and 2002, the United States won a "convincing conventional victory," defeating the Taliban, but "we missed the strategic objective" of destroying the al Qaeda "network" by allowing Osama bin Laden to escape across the border into Pakistan.[24]

As the airborne seminar continued over dinner and then breakfast and lunch, the conversation flowing effortlessly from one topic to another, it was clear that Obama was absorbing Reed's central message: Vietnam might not be the only reason why the United States would, or would not, act in a crisis, but its continuing relevance forced every president to consider the lessons of Vietnam when he prepared for war.

Reed shifted subjects from Afghanistan to the American invasion of Iraq, which he called a "strategic misstep of huge proportions."[25] Hagel used even tougher language, not just in the privacy of the airplane seminar but in public. In January 2007 he had labeled Bush's decision to send more troops to Iraq as "the most dangerous foreign policy blunder in this country since Vietnam."[26] And he went on to describe the Bush administration as "one of the most arrogant" in recent history, "the lowest in capacity, in capability, in policy, in consensus."[27] It was no surprise that Bush dismissed Hagel almost as much as Obama prized him as a great friend, a person with whom he could share his most private concerns.

Obama continued to raise questions, and Reed and Hagel tried to answer them. How do you apply the lessons of Vietnam? Are they relevant to Afghanistan? What are our interests there? Why are we there? It was, Hagel recalled,

> a strategic and tactical conversation, it was a personal conversation. . . . I think it was probably the first time he'd ever had an opportunity to sit and talk in a confined way to a person you can trust and really go down deep, and we had the time to do that . . . without anybody peering in, or cameras, or [reporters asking questions like] "Why is he doing this?" or "What is his motive?" So my guess is, probably for him it was the first time that he really had some time to do that.

All three senators found themselves especially fascinated by the way presidents handled the pressures of war; in Hagel's words, "how leaders can get so caught up in the heat, in the passion, in the political environment of the moment on these issues, where you can't get yourself up over the trees to see where this is all going, to get some strategic thinking." Obama was clearly trying to get himself "up over the trees," and he was not yet president. Hagel sympathized: "You get sucked down into the swamp of this town, the pressures, the media, left, right, everybody hammering at you."

On Afghanistan, Hagel was certain that Obama was going to inherit a "no-win" situation. "He was left with a mess," Hagel said. "'Do you pull out?' 'Do you not pull out?' . . . What the hell—there was no end, no good options." But Obama faced even more formidable problems than Afghanistan. Obama "inherited the biggest inventory of problems of any president since Franklin Roosevelt," according to Hagel. "Maybe worse, since Roosevelt didn't have two wars."[28]

The three senators were all singing from the same sheet of music. "We sort of tend to think alike," Reed said. They all agreed that the underlying challenge of the Afghan War was Pakistan, an unstable country with nuclear weapons and terrorist sanctuaries. "As long as they have those strategic weapons, they are very dangerous to the world." Reed was deeply worried. In order to stabilize Pakistan, he felt, "we had to stabilize Afghanistan."[29] And to stabilize Afghanistan, the United States had to fight a very smart counterinsurgency war, in which the civilian side of the overall effort would be seen by Washington as being just as important as the military side. It was this linkage of Afghanistan to Pakistan that became the key to Obama's new AfPak policy, hatched on a long flight from Washington to Kuwait in July 2008, when most of the conversation centered on the legacy of the Vietnam War.

Obama versus McCain

Obama's general election opponent, John McCain, had started the GOP primaries as his party's front-runner, only to fall behind and then gradually claw his way out of the heap to regain the front-runner's mantle and the nomination. A hawk on the Iraqi troop surge, McCain benefited politically from its apparent success.

McCain's support for General Petraeus's approach emerged from McCain's own life history, particularly his ongoing relationship with the Vietnam saga. In a lengthy piece about McCain in the *New York Times Magazine* on May 18, 2008, reporter Matt Bai wrote:

> The lesson McCain drew from Vietnam all those years ago is that you cannot turn your back on a war when at last you figure out how to win it, and he is determined not to let that happen again. Far from having failed to internalize the legacy of Vietnam, as some of his friends in the Senate suspect, he is, if anything, entirely driven by it. "I don't think you can isolate John's views in Iraq from his experience in Vietnam," Gary

Hart told me. "Whether he is aware of it or not—and I want to tread carefully here, because I don't like psychologizing people—I don't think he can separate those things in his mind. In a way, John is refighting the Vietnam War."[30]

McCain used his war-hero credentials to his advantage with sympathetic audiences, such as the Veterans of Foreign Wars, which held its August 2008 convention in Orlando, Florida. Obama, back from his trip to Iraq, also spoke to the group. Because he had not served in the military, Obama assumed correctly that he would be received with little more than polite applause. McCain accused Obama of pushing a "retreat and failure" policy in Iraq and Afghanistan, while Obama argued that the real question was who would exercise the best judgment. He outlined his policies for Iraq and Afghanistan, the same policies he was to carry with him into the White House.

In Iraq, Obama said, military power alone would not lead to victory. Only a political reconciliation among the competing Iraqi forces would open the door to a long-term solution. In the interim, the United States should begin a redeployment, another way of saying a gradual withdrawal. Remove U.S. combat brigades in sixteen months (as president, he would do the job in nineteen months), retain a residual force to battle al Qaeda, train Iraqi troops and police, and transfer responsibility for security to the Iraqi government. Assuming a degree of success in Iraq, Obama had his eye on two other targets: first, redirecting the $10 billion monthly cost of the Iraq war to the sluggish American economy; and second, turning everyone's attention to "the fight against al Qaeda and the Taliban in Afghanistan and the border region of Pakistan."

Afghanistan, Obama emphasized, was the "central front in the war on terrorism," and he pledged that "this is a war that we have to win." As president, Obama added, "I will have no greater priority than taking out these terrorists who threaten America, and finishing the job against the Taliban." He promised to add "at least two additional U.S. combat brigades and an additional $1 billion in non-military assistance" to the anti–al Qaeda/Taliban campaign in Afghanistan. He then directly linked the war in Afghanistan to the dangerous border regions of Pakistan, where al Qaeda and the Taliban enjoyed a privileged sanctuary. So long as there was a "terrorist safe-haven in northwest Pakistan," Obama warned, the United States could not "succeed in Afghanistan."[31] Here was an example of a presidential candidate feeling the need to play down his "dovish" approach to Iraq with a "hawkish" policy on Afghanistan.

As in his 2000 bid, McCain's experiences as a prisoner of war in Vietnam played a key role in his campaign. At one point, when his advisers talked him into running an ad using stark footage of the imprisoned McCain—"prone and in excruciating pain, his broken bones encased in slipshod dressing," as reporters John Heilemann and Mark Halperin described it—senior aide Steve Schmidt was blunt: "You don't have an option of not talking about who you are and what made you who you are," he told the candidate. "That decision got made the day you decided to run for president of the United States. Whether you like it or not, that's reality, and if you don't do it, we don't have a prayer."[32]

McCain hit home with a quip during a GOP candidates' debate in October 2007 in Orlando. "In case you missed it," he told the audience in response to a question about how he and Clinton would match up in a potential general election contest, "a few days ago Senator Clinton tried to spend one million dollars on the Woodstock Concert Museum. Now, my friends, I wasn't there. I'm sure it was a cultural and pharmaceutical event." Laughter from the onlookers. "I was tied up at the time." As reporters Dan Balz and Haynes Johnson portrayed the scene, "As the audience got the full impact of his words referring to his torture in Vietnam, they rose and gave him a sustained ovation. The other Republican candidates on the stage joined in the applause."[33]

But in the 2008 general election race against Obama, McCain faced a problem similar to that faced by Bob Dole in 1996. McCain, who was born in 1936, was a war hero in his early seventies facing a forty-something opponent with no military service. The question was whether invoking Vietnam would make voters admire McCain, or just think that he was old. McCain, like Dole, was "a septuagenarian senator more comfortable in Washington than anywhere else, a dark-humored war hero with a distinctly premodern sensibility," according to Heilemann and Halperin.[34]

In the second presidential debate between Obama and McCain, a town hall format that would seem to play to McCain's strengths, his war-hero past was not helpful. "Unfortunately for McCain, the town hall debate merely spotlighted differences in style and appearance that worked in Obama's favor," one campaign book explained. "Because of the torture he endured as a prisoner of war in Vietnam, he limped and had difficulty moving his arms. These limitations became obvious when he walked around the debate floor. In a just world, television viewers would have watched him and thought 'war hero.' In the real world, many probably thought 'elderly man.' Obama, as a relatively young man in apparently good health, gained from the visual contrast."[35]

All of this worked to Obama's benefit, as it had to Bill Clinton's in 1996. No military service, no problem. Still, the discrepancy between the two candidates' backgrounds was on the Obama team's mind as they got ready for the nationally televised debates. Obama adviser Greg Craig played the part of McCain. "The expectation was that McCain would condescend to Obama as a wet-behind-the-ears rookie, so Craig played his role accordingly," journalist Evan Thomas wrote. "'Do not lecture me about the war,' Craig-as-McCain said, glowering at Obama, in debate prep. 'Do not tell me how to deploy men in combat. I was flying a jet over Vietnam when you were in grade school.'"[36]

But by the autumn of 2008, when the candidates were debating, the U.S. economy was in free fall. Iraq and Afghanistan had faded as issues. Obama, with his messages of hope and change, roared ahead in the polls, while McCain, tethered politically to the unpopular President Bush, could gain no traction. Even the addition of conservative Alaska governor Sarah Palin, a political unknown with natural charisma, as McCain's running mate gave the GOP ticket only a temporary lift.

Palin, for her part, was all too eager to jump into the fray. One of the issues on which she gleefully attacked Obama was his connection to Bill Ayers, a founder of the Vietnam-era radical Weather Underground group linked to antiwar bombings. Ayers, now an education professor in Chicago, had hosted a coffee for Obama in 1995 when he was first running for the Illinois Senate. The two had worked on an education project together and had occasionally crossed paths. It was red meat for Obama's detractors, who were eager to paint Obama, too, as a radical. The Ayers issue, which had bubbled along as a minor distraction for months, came to the fore when the *New York Times* ran a long piece on October 4, 2008, looking into the ties between the two men. "A review of records of the schools project and interviews with a dozen people who know both men, suggest that Mr. Obama, 47, has played down his contacts with Mr. Ayers, 63," author Scott Shane wrote. "But the two men do not appear to have been close. Nor has Mr. Obama ever expressed sympathy for the radical views and actions of Mr. Ayers, whom he has called 'somebody who engaged in detestable acts 40 years ago, when I was 8.'"[37]

The morning that the *Times* piece ran, McCain's campaign sped up its plans to go after Obama on the Ayers issue. Palin, it was suggested, would use a prepared script that included the following: "This is not a man who sees America as you or I do—as the greatest force for good in the world. This is someone who sees America as imperfect enough to pal around with terrorists who targeted their own country." Palin was thrilled, as writers Dan Balz and

Haynes Johnson described. "'Yes yes yes,' she replied in an e-mail response. 'Pls let me say this!!!' Palin delivered those 'pal around with terrorists' lines almost exactly as scripted at a Colorado fund-raiser. When she finished, she sent another e-mail back to McCain's high command, 'It was awesome,' she said in the message."[38] The Obama campaign had been nervous about the Ayers issue, as Plouffe recalled: "[Strategist David] Axelrod in particular had been obsessing for months about Ayers and the challenge of dealing with this in a media world that would likely oversimplify the story; the specter of swift-boats had been dancing in the political community's head for months."[39]

But the Ayers charges did not have the impact that the Swift Boaters had had in 2004, and Obama steamed ahead toward victory. Not only was Vietnam off the table as far as he was concerned, but Iraq was yesterday's business as well. The focus, he believed, should be on Afghanistan, as he had said repeatedly during the campaign. Once Obama became president, he was faced with the reality of implementing that focus.

Afghanistan: Decision One

Bruce Riedel, a tall, intensely cerebral expert on Middle East terrorism, who had recently retired after twenty-nine years at the Central Intelligence Agency (CIA) and the National Security Council (NSC), was relaxing at his weekend cottage on the Eastern Shore of Maryland's Chesapeake Bay. It was Friday, January 23, 2009, three days after Barack Obama's historic inauguration as the first black president in American history, and Riedel needed a break from the exhausting campaign. He had not played a prominent role—for a time he wrote speeches and press guidance—but he had earned Obama's respect for his detailed knowledge of Afghanistan's competing tribes and personalities. While many of his colleagues angled for jobs in the new administration, Riedel had his sights on returning to a scholar's slot at the Brookings Institution. "I want[ed] to help him get elected," he explained, "I [didn't] want another job. I've been in government enough. . . . I've got the pension plan. I've got the health insurance system. I got a medal. There's nothing else to provide."

Riedel treasured his time on the Eastern Shore. "It was very quiet, lovely," as he remembered the scene. On this special day, the phone rang, as he picked up his morning newspaper. "Please hold for the president," a White House operator said. A second or two later, Riedel heard a familiar voice. "Hi, Bruce, it's Barack." Wasting no time, Obama proposed that Riedel take charge of an NSC review of American policy in Afghanistan. "I know you don't want to come back in the government," the president said. Riedel was relieved. Obama told him that the assignment would be for sixty days; he needed a review and recommendations before the North Atlantic Treaty Organization (NATO) meeting in early April. "Report on Monday to General Jones," Obama concluded.[40]

At this time, Obama did not yet fully recognize the many challenges Afghanistan would pose for his administration. He did know that he did not have a great deal of time. The war was going badly, and the American people were impatient. He told one NSC meeting: "I think I have two years with the public on this. They'll stand by us for two years. That's my window."[41] That would mean the spring of 2011.

Between his election and his inauguration, Obama had been given increasingly pessimistic reports about Afghanistan and its history. Two thousand years ago, Alexander the Great could not conquer Afghanistan, nor could the British in the nineteenth century, nor the Russians in the twentieth. Now it seemed to be America's turn, and the esteemed General Petraeus was warning that only a "sustained, substantial" American commitment could head off a Taliban victory.[42] The Pentagon was floating the urgent need for thousands of additional troops, and the *New York Times,* under the headline "Obama's War: Fearing Another Quagmire in Afghanistan," called attention to a quotation from an 1892 poem by Rudyard Kipling about what awaited the foreign soldier:

> When you're wounded and left on Afghanistan's plains
> And the women come out to cut up what remains
> Jest roll to your rifle and blow out your brains
> An' go to your Gawd like a soldier.[43]

"There has been nothing easy about Afghanistan," Petraeus warned.[44] "This is going to be a long slog," echoed Defense Secretary Gates. If Congress was thinking that the United States could somehow build a "central Asian Valhalla" in Afghanistan, "we will lose." Gates added, "Nobody in the world has that kind of time, patience and money."[45]

From the very first day of the review, Riedel found himself beset by policy and personnel problems, none more sensitive and potentially damaging to the new president than his relations with Gates, the Joint Chiefs of Staff, and his commanding generals. Obama's Chicago Mafia worried that the military establishment might not fully support a president who had never served in uniform. Clinton redux, they feared, only worse. Clinton had had his problems with the "don't ask, don't tell" policy and his own draft issues, but Obama had the additional problem, real or imagined, of David Petraeus, who was not only the extraordinarily popular general who had "saved" Iraq but who also seemed, at least to these guardians of Obama's political fortunes, to be positioning himself for a possible presidential run in 2012. Why else, they wondered, would he be accepting so many public-speaking engagements? Why else had he met with a string of members of Congress? Why else had he opened his doors to the columnists and talk-show pundits?

Still novices to the nuances of Washington's power grid, they found it hard to accept a more obvious explanation: that Petraeus was, in fact, a huge asset to the president. A bemedaled patriot, he engaged in nonstop briefings and appearances for a very good reason: he knew that the war in Afghanistan, like the war in Vietnam, was going to be a long, costly effort requiring patience, support, and understanding from the public and from Congress. Even with the best of armies, Petraeus knew that it would be difficult to defeat the Taliban. It might take ten years, maybe more. Though Petraeus repeatedly fought the Vietnam analogy, he knew that, as casualties mounted, the American people might lose heart in the war, the media might turn hostile, and Congress might then decide to cut funding, especially during tough economic times. It had happened before; it could happen again.

Obama had to show his "national security credentials," Riedel mused, "and if you are going to have a problem with the military, who better to have on your side than a 6'4" U.S. Marine . . . general?"[46] General James Jones, whom Obama selected as his national security adviser, had an excellent reputation and a stellar military career: a Vietnam veteran, he had worked his way up the chain of command until he became the Supreme Allied Commander in Europe in 2003. Obama needed his counsel and experience; he also needed the political protection afforded by a soldier of his stature, integrity, and reputation. "If it comes down to dueling generals," one image-conscious White House official said with a mischievous smile, "a 6'4" Marine on my side, and a rather short, nerdy professorial-looking David Petraeus on the other, I've got the image battle [won]."

"One of the reasons I took the job," Jones said, "was to try to help him . . . decode the military."[47] With his deputy, Thomas Donilon, a Washington lawyer who had worked for a few years in Clinton's State Department, Jones organized a "21st century National Security Council," which was to be not only a dramatic departure from the past but also a disciplined system marked by what he termed "regular order," to be used to develop strategic options requiring presidential decisions.[48] Bush II had allowed his vice president, Dick Cheney, to run a parallel NSC system, which led to back-channel confusion and mis-understandings. Under Obama, there was to be one NSC run by Jones out of the White House; the system worked well, but not as well as Jones had hoped.

"If you'd have had [a better system] in respect to Vietnam," Donilon said, "you would have a better result." During that war, he noted, "fundamental questions . . . were not engaged; . . . fundamental assumptions" were not chal-lenged. It was an ad hoc system, and that was why it failed.[49] Only twice, in Jones's opinion, did his own system come up short: once on Guantánamo Bay (it "was taken out of regular order, and had we not gone too fast with it, we probably wouldn't be in the fix that we're in right now," Jones reflected), the other on the Middle East.[50]

On one issue, the Jones system worked, but ironically produced a totally unnecessary confrontation between Obama and Gates. Shortly after Janu-ary 20, Gates requested more troops. He was the one cabinet officer Obama could least afford to offend. During his presidential campaign, Obama had promised to send more troops to Afghanistan, and he wanted to act quickly, in part to demonstrate that though he lacked military experience, he was ready to flex America's military muscle. But the "regular order" dictated that first Obama had to go through a process of policy review; the president had to see the results of Riedel's study (not expected until late March) before he could act on the defense secretary's request. No, no, Gates objected. "We can't wait two months. We need your decision right now. We need to have the troops in theater before the August presidential election." It was, according to Riedel, a "very unpleasant beginning"—an example of "totally . . . absolutely screwed up" miscommunication at the highest level of government.[51]

Obama, remembering the lessons of Vietnam, wanted exact numbers of additional troops and a clear explanation of their mission. Initially, the Pen-tagon could not satisfy his request when it came to exact numbers, which exasperated the president. The Joint Chiefs knew Obama wanted to send two, possibly three brigades, or roughly 10,000 or 15,000 troops, but they had not yet figured out how many "enablers" would accompany the troops. "Enablers" was Pentagonese for "support" personnel, and this number varied depending on mission. For a few anxious days, an awkward standoff ensued.

On February 17, four weeks after taking office, Obama ordered that 17,000 additional American troops be sent to Afghanistan. He was fulfilling a campaign promise and, at the same time, acceding to a Pentagon need. He described the deployment as "necessary to stabilize a deteriorating situation in Afghanistan, which has not received the strategic attention, direction and resources it urgently requires": Obama's way of criticizing his predecessor's mismanagement of the Afghan War. "Urgent attention and swift action" were required, the president explained, because "the Taliban is resurgent in Afghanistan, and al Qaeda . . . threatens America from its safe-haven along the Pakistani border."[52]

It was left to General David McKiernan, commander of NATO forces in Afghanistan, to add a sobering note of context. At a Pentagon news conference the next day, he bluntly cautioned: "For the next three to four years, I think we're going to need to stay heavily committed and sustain in a sustained manner in Afghanistan." The Taliban insurgency, he said, was "very resilient," fueled by funding, weapons, training, and suicide bombers sent from the tribal areas of Pakistan.[53] McKiernan was projecting a Pentagon time line, not the president's.

Riedel, under Pentagon pressure to finish his review, ran into "the ghost of Vietnam" in the "halls of the White House." He bumped into many liberal Democrats worried about sending troops to fight an insurgency in Asia; worried, too, about whether Obama was following in Lyndon Johnson's footsteps, going into a quagmire. Riedel spoke of one anxious adviser after another: Holbrooke ("You can barely have a conversation with Richard when he doesn't talk about Vietnam"), Nancy Pelosi (she knew "people back home in San Francisco were going to start saying this is another Vietnam"), Biden ("I'm not going to be Hubert Humphrey . . . [going] along with it when I think it's wrong"). "The ghosts of the Vietnam War were there," Riedel summed up.

Three issues dominated Riedel's review. The first was obvious: how to define the essential purpose of the American involvement in the Afghan War. "If you don't define that well," Riedel said, "you're in a lot of trouble."[54] Caspar Weinberger and Colin Powell, thinking back to Vietnam, had always warned that a clearly stated mission was the essential prerequisite for a successful military engagement.

The second issue was Pakistan. "That's where the nukes are, that's where most of the terrorists are, that's where the problems are." Pakistan was the "strategic prize," or, as Riedel put it, the "strategic booby prize." The United States did not have boots on the ground there, and "we shouldn't put" them there, Riedel said, adding that the U.S.-Pakistan relationship has been "very, very difficult" for the past sixty years. "We don't trust them, and they don't trust us. And we are both right—we shouldn't trust each other."[55]

The third issue was the headline grabber: how many troops should the United States send to Afghanistan? This was a question on a slippery slope, the question that always conjured up "the ghost of Vietnam." Obama's primary responsibility was the protection of the American people, but, as Riedel said, "he also doesn't want to get into a quagmire which is going to drain resources and may lead to hopeless conflicts."[56]

By day forty of the sixty-day review, Riedel had a policy draft. Everyone had read it except Obama. Not everyone had agreed on every point, but they all knew they had a workable draft. It was then that White House chief of staff Rahm Emanuel weighed in. "Okay, we need to get the president's head into this now. So tomorrow he's leaving for California. And, Bruce, you're going with him. That's the one time I can guarantee you face time with the president where he is not going to be interrupted is on Air Force One."

By the time Riedel boarded Air Force One, it was already clear that Obama had read the draft, absorbed it, and had questions. It was no surprise, given the deep recession then overwhelming the country, that the cost of the Afghan War was very much on the president's mind. "Remember," Riedel recalled, "we were broke." How much did it cost to send one American soldier to Afghanistan? How much did it cost to train one Afghan soldier or policeman? Could the Afghan replace the American? And how much time would that take? There was one other question, and it brought Obama back to Vietnam. Since he suspected that the Pentagon would one day soon request more troops, above and beyond the recently announced 17,000 deployment, how could he be sure that, despite his best intentions, he would not find himself sliding "into a swamp,"[57] leading the nation gradually, incrementally, into a deeper involvement in an insurgency the United States might not be able to win.

The Johnson example, more than the Kennedy or Nixon examples, was often on Obama's mind. On more than one occasion, he would duck into the office of a senior aide and ask whether he was at risk of becoming another LBJ. Because Obama could never be sure, he worried about another Vietnam, even as he and others fell back on the oft-repeated mantra that Afghanistan is not Vietnam.

Afghanistan: Decision Two

On the morning of March 27, 2009, President Obama's report to the nation on his new strategy for Afghanistan and Pakistan hit all the right notes. If you needed a perfect example of post-Vietnam policy, sensitive to lessons learned in a lost war, this was it.

First, the report was the result of a "careful policy review" of all options. This was pure Obama: no rush to judgment, no matter how perilous the problem.

Second, the United States now had a "clear and focused goal" in the war: "to disrupt, dismantle, and defeat al Qaeda in Pakistan and Afghanistan, and to prevent their return to either country in the future."

Third, the extremist and terrorist challenge resided in both countries. If earlier, the United States focused its efforts only, or principally, on Afghanistan, it would now tackle the problems in Pakistan as well. Obama called on Congress to provide an aid package for Pakistan, stretching it out over the next five years, but no one should get the wrong idea: the days of the "blank check" were over. Referring to the deepening recession, Obama added, "These are challenging times."

Fourth, the United States and NATO had to "reverse the Taliban's gains." Only then could the United States reach out to moderate Taliban in hopes of negotiating a political compromise with them. Obama was not seeking to democratize Afghanistan, which had been a hazy Bush aim; it was now narrowing its ultimate strategic goal to blocking the Taliban and al Qaeda challenge, by training the Afghan military and police, eliminating widespread corruption, and helping to modernize the Afghan economy.

Finally, for the first time, the United States was committed to providing the troops needed to do the job. For six years under his predecessor, Obama stated, "Afghanistan has been denied the resources" because of the demands of the war in Iraq. Now, Obama promised, they would get what they needed: the 17,000 more troops, as announced on February 17, plus an additional 4,000 troops for the training of the Afghans, building toward an Afghan army of 134,000 and a police force of 82,000 by 2011.

Underlying all of the lessons learned from Vietnam was the need for popular and congressional support for the war. Just as the "blank check" days of American aid were over, so, too, were the glory days of imperial power, when a president could act like a king. Obama tried to explain why, in his judgment, the Afghan War was necessary, why it had to be fought, why it had to be won. "The United States of America did not choose to fight a war in Afghanistan," Obama said. "Nearly 3,000 of our people were killed on September 11, 2001, for doing nothing more than going about their daily lives." The United States was attacked, and the United States must now defend itself. "The road ahead will be long. There will be difficult days," he continued. "But we will seek lasting partnerships with Afghanistan and Pakistan that serve the promise of a new day for their people. And we will use all elements of our national power to defeat al Qaeda and to defend America, our allies, and all who seek a better future."[58]

Within days, Admiral Mullen emphasized a shift in military priorities: the war in Afghanistan would now become the "main effort" in American operations abroad. No longer was it to be Iraq, from which the United States was beginning to withdraw.[59] He had sent thirteen recommendations to Obama, among them a reminder that even more troops would be needed in Afghanistan. Petraeus, appearing before the Senate Armed Services Committee, then disclosed that he and his commanders had asked the president for another 10,000 troops. "If you assume that there is an insurgency throughout the country," Petraeus said, "you need more forces."

According to his own counterinsurgency manual, the United States needed 20 soldiers to protect 1,000 Afghan civilians, and in a country the size of Texas with a population of roughly 33 million, it would obviously be years before the United States reached the proper balance. Petraeus warned that if the United States intended to reverse recent Taliban gains, it could only happen with a "sustained, substantial commitment" of additional forces.

Occasionally, Obama offered a note of genuine skepticism regarding the question of whether more troops guaranteed more success, as Petraeus seemed to believe. The president insisted on a Sunday TV interview program, for example, that he was sending enough troops to do the job. "What I will not do," he said, was "to simply assume that more troops [will] always result in an improved situation. . . . There may be a point of diminishing returns."[60]

On another occasion, he used different words but his message was the same. "My strong view," he said, "is that we are not going to succeed simply by piling on more and more troops,"[61] From his own reading of history, Obama knew that the United States had more than 500,000 troops in Vietnam and still lost. What was needed was a program of economic development and political reform. Jones told reporter Bob Woodward: "This will not be won by the military alone. We tried that for six years." He added, "The piece of the strategy that has to work in the next year is economic development. If that is not done right, there are not enough troops in the world to succeed."[62]

The scratchy, occasionally irritating tension between the president and his generals persisted through the year. Obama respected the brave men and women in uniform, most especially the generals and the admirals who led them, but, as he often noted, they had their jobs, and he had his, and they were not the same. His as president were broader, taking into account the needs of the entire nation; theirs were narrower, protecting the nation in accordance with presidential directives.

In late March Obama met with his principal advisers on AfPak policy. Biden insisted that any additional troops have a very clear and specific mission. In this respect, he was a student of the Powell Doctrine, which grew out of the Vietnam War experience. He recalled from his last visit to the region that if you asked ten people in Afghanistan why the Americans were there, you would get ten different answers. Nobody knew. The military chiefs, in their arguments, retreated to one key point, from which they never budged: without further troop deployments, the Afghan War would be imperiled and probably lost. Obama, sympathetic to the Biden view but concerned about the political risks of losing Afghanistan, compromised. He would send more troops, and did, but he would not send as many as the military felt it needed.[63]

Afghanistan: Decision Three

Finally, on May 11, 2009, the brass moved. For months, the governing military troika of Gates, Mullen, and Petraeus had become increasingly unhappy with the performance of the four-star general running the U.S. and NATO military operation in Afghanistan. David McKiernan was the highly experienced commander who had led the armored assault on Saddam Hussein's Iraq in 2003. He hardly deserved to be fired, to be abruptly and publicly humiliated, as though he had botched an important assignment. Yet, in their view, McKiernan seemed somehow out of place in the new cockpit of the Afghan crisis, lacking the imagination, public relations flair, and political skill this command now obviously required. He was a soldier who believed it was his job to fight wars, not to win a popularity prize. In his thirty-seven-year career, he had spent more than twenty years overseas, but less than one year at the Pentagon.[64]

"Blame General Petraeus," explained one Pentagon official. "He redefined during his tour in Iraq what it means to be a commanding general. He broke the mold. The traditional responsibilities were not enough anymore. . . . When you judge McKiernan by Petraeus's standards, he looked old-school by comparison."

In March, after Gates and Mullen had a routine video conference talk with McKiernan about reconstruction and counternarcotics operations in Afghanistan, they both concluded that he did not grasp the essence of counterinsurgency and probably never would. They decided they needed a new general. In April Mullen spoke to McKiernan in Kabul and suggested that he retire. Why? McKiernan objected. He had never disobeyed an order, never questioned the new strategy; besides, he had been led to believe that he was doing exactly what Gates and Mullen wanted him to do. No, he argued, if you want to get rid of me, you are going to have to fire me. If, by this show of bravado, he thought he could avoid being sacked, he was wrong.

By early May, as the situation in Afghanistan worsened, Gates decided he could wait no longer. New leadership was urgently needed, he felt. Mullen fully agreed. "There are those who would have waited six more months," he said. "I couldn't. I'm losing kids, and I couldn't sleep at night. I have an unbounded sense of urgency to get this right."[65] Gates checked with Obama, who raised no objection. Apparently he shared Gates's judgment that a change was in order. The defense secretary announced on May 11 that McKiernan was being fired and a three-star Petraeus protégé named Stanley McChrystal was being assigned to the Afghan post. When McKiernan left Kabul, he told U.S. and NATO troops assembled in the courtyard near his office: "I don't want to leave." He added, "There's work still to be done here. . . . But I'm a soldier and I live in a democracy and I work for political leaders, and when my political leaders tell me it's time to go, I must go."[66] Though disappointed, he tried not to sound bitter.

Interestingly, during the Vietnam War, it was only after President Johnson decided in March 1968 not to run for reelection that he summoned the courage to replace a commanding general, William Westmoreland, who favored an obviously failing strategy of victory through attrition, with another general, Creighton Abrams, who represented a more promising strategy of counterinsurgency. Question: did the McChrystal for-McKiernan switch represent a similar change in strategy, or was the Pentagon simply playing musical chairs?

Gates attempted to answer the question. "We have a new strategy, a new mission and a new ambassador," he told reporters. "I believe that new military leadership is also needed." Gates made a point of stressing McChrystal's "unique skill set in counterinsurgency."[67] From 2003 to 2008, McChrystal had been commander of the Joint Special Operations Command, an elite, top-secret unit whose responsibilities included targeting terrorist leaders.

McChrystal, a West Point graduate, class of 1976, was one of the young Turks determined to rebuild the army into a modern fighting machine staffed by a well-trained volunteer force, and he succeeded. He was a Green Beret, an Army Ranger, and a combat officer in the Persian Gulf War before taking over the Joint Special Operations Command, where he ran the dark side of U.S. operations in Iraq. "He's lanky, smart, tough, a sneaky, stealth soldier," said an old friend, retired General William Nash. "He's got all the Special Ops attributes, plus an intellect." McChrystal had also spent time at Harvard and the Council on Foreign Relations, typical of the new army commander who supplemented his military skills with injections of academic learning.[68]

McChrystal in Command

In early June the Senate Armed Services Committee held McChrystal's confirmation hearings. "I expect stiff fighting ahead," McChrystal said, holding nothing back. He predicted an increase in violence and combat deaths as more U.S. troops arrived in Afghanistan, but he assured committee members that he was not going to Afghanistan for the sole purpose of killing al Qaeda and the Taliban. He stressed balance: killing the enemy, yes, but, more important, protecting the population, the essence of counterinsurgency. What Abrams had attempted to do in Vietnam, for a time successfully, McChrystal would now attempt to do in Afghanistan. "The measure of effectiveness will not be the number of enemy killed," he said. "It will be the number of Afghans shielded from violence."

McChrystal was asked what success would look like. He offered only half an answer: "Success will not be quick or easy," McChrystal said. "Casualties will likely increase. We will make mistakes. . . . But with the appropriate resources, time, sacrifices and patience, we can prevail."[69] McChrystal was sharing the Gates-Mullen-Petraeus catechism with Congress, a political-military catechism steeped in the lessons of Vietnam. It was that the United States can prevail, if (a big if) this Congress, unlike the disengaging Congresses of the early 1970s, continued to provide the resources, accept the sacrifices, and stop asking so many questions.

Gates and Mullen gave McChrystal sixty days to study the problems in Afghanistan and then come up with his own judgment on how to solve them. They hit one point again and again: we don't have much time.

"Silent and Not-So-Silent Reminders"

An office is often a portrait of its occupant, and Richard Holbrooke's small, first-floor office at the State Department was cluttered with memories of Vietnam, the war Henry Kissinger called "the traumatic event of the second half" of the twentieth century.[70] Certainly, Holbrooke seemed to agree. On the wall near his desk was a frayed photograph of a young Foreign Service officer walking the streets of Saigon with General Maxwell Taylor. "That's me," Holbrooke said proudly, pointing to a lanky young man hiding behind sunglasses.

On a bookshelf was an old Zippo lighter, sporting a slogan typical of the 1960s: "I love fucking the army, and the army loves fucking me." Holbrooke handled the Zippo as if it were a precious work of art, returning it carefully to the bookshelf. "These are silent and not-so-silent reminders," he explained. For a moment, Holbrooke, whom friends often called "larger than life," seemed sad, and far away.

Holbrooke loved telling Vietnam stories, even as he was maneuvering the slippery slopes of the AfPak crisis. Fifty years after the end of the Vietnam War, he said, beginning one of his favorite stories, NBC's *Today Show* will host the "last surviving veterans" of the war. "They would come in on their wheelchairs, and they'd immediately start screaming at each other," Holbrooke said, unable to resist a silly grin. "John Kerry and the Swift Boat veterans, and by that time they'd be ninety . . . and the Americans watching would say, 'What the hell was wrong with that generation of Americans?'"

Holbrooke the diplomat chose to deflect this question by answering another that was not asked. "Because the lessons of the war were ambiguous," he said, "each side can choose its own myth."[71] One myth: the military did not lose the war, Congress did. Another myth: the North Vietnamese, armed with a defiant nationalism, won the war, wearing down the American military, Congress, and the public until, in disgust and frustration, the United States just left Vietnam. Still another myth: the American media, espousing liberal, pro-Hanoi sentiments, poisoned the well and lost the war. Holbrooke had his own myth: "The right wing likes to believe," he said, "that Vietnam was lost at home, because of the [media] . . . [but that's] all bullshit. The military was given all the time and resources imaginable, but they had a strategy and a set of tactics which couldn't succeed in that environment." Holbrooke listed four lessons of Vietnam:

1. Know the territory. We didn't know shit about Vietnam.

2. Match the resources to the mission. If it is so damn important, give it enough resources; if it isn't that important, don't do it.

3. Define your objectives clearly.

4. You can't succeed without the understanding and support of the American people as to why you are there. . . . We could never explain [the reason], but still it's truly astonishing that the American people supported [the war] for fourteen years, from 1961 to 1975 . . . the longest war in American history, up to now in Afghanistan. [Holbrooke seemed to forget the massive antiwar demonstrations in Washington and on college campuses.]

In terms of how these lessons related to Afghanistan, Holbrooke said, "History will judge that."

Can we make a judgment now? he was asked.

"You can," he said. "I can't."

Holbrooke's "myth" tended to focus primarily on the similarities and differences between Vietnam and Afghanistan. First, the similarities. In each war, the insurgent enemy enjoyed a sanctuary: the Vietcong had North Vietnam, in addition to slices of Laos and Cambodia, while the Taliban had the mountainous border regions of Pakistan. Just as the Saigon government was weak and corrupt, so, too, was the Kabul government. Both the Vietcong and the Taliban tried to capture and exploit the fire and passion of nationalism. Next, the differences. In Vietnam, the enemy represented a single, united political force, running from Ho Chi Minh in the north to the communist cell leader in the south, while in Afghanistan, the enemy was "totally fragmented" with many internal divisions. In Vietnam, the "Vietcong and the North Vietnamese posed no threat whatsoever to our homeland," while in Afghanistan, al Qaeda used its bases there to prepare its deadly 9/11 attack on the United States— meaning, in Holbrooke's view, that "there is a legitimate reason for us to be in Afghanistan."[72] The question was, once there, what was the best strategy for the United States? Who was the enemy: al Qaeda or the Taliban? How could Obama "win" without getting trapped in another endless war?

Although Vietnam did not provide all the answers, for Holbrooke it was often the touchstone of any serious analysis. Obama wanted to bury Vietnam, just as Bush I had tried to bury it in the sands of Arabia. But it kept popping up, often because Holbrooke reminded his colleagues of its relevance. Obama was tired of hearing about Vietnam. Enough, the president insisted on more than one occasion. There were rumors in Washington that Obama had had it with Holbrooke and intended to drop him. Yet during the summer of 2009 the issue of Vietnam arose with stubborn frequency, and again it was Holbrooke who drew the comparisons, like an impatient teacher alerting his students to the pitfalls of a superpower trying to contain an insurgency.

It's Vietnam, Stupid!

Holbrooke was a footloose diplomat, constantly on the move. One day he was in the Afghan capital discussing Obama's AfPak policy with General McChrystal, who had been studying the complex insurgency in Afghanistan ever since he took up his new job commanding NATO and American forces there. Holbrooke had Vietnam in his bloodstream, and he noticed, almost immediately, that McChrystal was rereading Stanley Karnow's classic study of the Vietnam War.[73] Obama might have been insisting that Afghanistan was not Vietnam, but his commanding general in Afghanistan was delving into a serious report on the Vietnam War to see whether there might be parallels between the two wars, lessons he could apply to his current responsibilities, and his chief AfPak negotiator was encouraging the general to see how the lessons of Vietnam could be applied to Afghanistan.

"Stan Karnow is a very dear friend of mine for forty years," Holbrooke said. "Would you do me a favor and talk to Stan?"

"Sure," McChrystal replied.

Holbrooke knew Karnow's phone number by heart. "Hey, Stan . . . I'm here in Kabul," Holbrooke said when Karnow answered. "Can I put the commanding General McChrystal on the line?" Karnow agreed.

"Hello, sir," said McChrystal. "It's a great honor to talk to you."

Their conversation was brief. According to Holbrooke, it ended abruptly with Karnow asking, "What the hell are you doing in Afghanistan? Get out!"[74] According to Karnow, McChrystal asked him what he could learn from Vietnam that he might be able to apply in Afghanistan, and Karnow responded, "I don't know very much about Afghanistan, but what I learned in Vietnam was that we shouldn't have been there in the first place."[75] The clear implication was that the United States should get out of Afghanistan, not exactly what the new American commander was hoping to hear. Later, Karnow was more blunt, telling an Associated Press reporter: "Obama and everybody else seem to want to be in Afghanistan, but not I."[76]

Holbrooke wanted to play the role of the good mediator, bringing McChrystal and Karnow together, two of his friends who at the time shared a common interest in Vietnam, but his effort backfired. Holbrooke was to have better luck a few weeks later, when he told Tom Donilon about another Vietnam book called *Lessons in Disaster*, written by Gordon Goldstein, who had worked for the secretary-general of the United Nations.[77] At the time Holbrooke could not have known that unintentionally he would be sparking a fierce policy debate about Afghan policy between, on the one side, Obama and his team of White House advisers and, on the other side, Gates and his team of Pentagon chiefs. The discussion would all be cloaked in the garb of a history lesson, nothing more; but in fact it sharpened the differences between Obama and the military, and it lasted until late November, when the president, who had once taught constitutional law, finally imposed on the Pentagon a "contractual clarity"[78] on Afghan policy, to quote Donilon, that left the Pentagon squirming and fuming but in the final analysis ready—what else could it do?—to recognize and respect the president's authority to decide matters of war and peace. Then, to salute and get on with the job.

Holbrooke had a warm spot in his heart for the Goldstein book, and for good reason. A year before, in the final stages of the Obama-McCain presidential struggle, Holbrooke had been asked to write a blurb for a new book focusing on McGeorge Bundy's role in the American military buildup in Indochina during the Kennedy and Johnson administrations. The book would likely have generated a few polite reviews in academic journals, but Holbrooke "saved" it, as he put it, for bigger things. He found the book "really interesting," and sent an e-mail to Sam Tanenhaus, the book review editor of the *New York Times.* "If you don't have anyone doing a review," Holbrooke volunteered, "I'd be happy to do it."

Tanenhaus shot back a reply. "We didn't even notice the book," he admitted. "We'll give you as much space as we can."[79]

Holbrooke, as it turned out, wrote more than a review; he wrote a thoughtful essay powerfully evocative of the early days of the American involvement in Vietnam, when he was a young Foreign Service officer based in the Mekong Delta, and McGeorge Bundy, surely among the "best and the brightest" in America's intellectual arsenal, was President Kennedy's national security adviser. For many years, Bundy had refused to disclose his true feelings about the war, but the book, using interviews and secret memos, revealed Bundy's blunders on Vietnam. It made for sobering reading, especially as Obama was preparing to expand the American commitment to Afghanistan. Holbrooke praised the book for its "power, authenticity and, yes, poignancy," and then he raised the key question: how could Bundy, a man so bright and accomplished, so supremely self-confident, have been so wrong about Vietnam, a war Holbrooke described as a "tragic failure"?

Holbrooke concluded his essay by linking Vietnam to the uncertainties of the Afghan War: "With the nation now about to inaugurate a new president committed to withdraw combat troops from Iraq and succeed in Afghanistan, the lessons of Vietnam are still relevant. McGeorge Bundy's story, of early brilliance and a late-in-life search for the truth about himself and the war, is an extraordinary cautionary tale for all Americans."[80]

Donilon, like a number of Obama's close advisers, had never served in the military and had no personal experience with Vietnam. He was a smart Washington lawyer with limited foreign policy experience. He was focused on ending the Iraq war and turning the corner in the Afghan War. The Goldstein book opened his eyes to the relevance of Vietnam. "I learned a tremendous amount from that book," Donilon recalled. "It had a fairly substantial impact on me."[81] Very quickly, *Lessons in Disaster* zoomed to the top of the best-seller list at the White House.

One evening, Rahm Emanuel brought his children over to Donilon's house for dinner. He asked Donilon's wife, Cathy Russell, chief of staff to Joe Biden's wife, Jill, "What should I be reading?" and Russell mentioned the Goldstein book. Emanuel was so impressed by its striking relevance to the Afghan review that he recommended the book to the president. Everyone was impressed with it. But why?

One likely explanation was that just as Bundy had been advising Kennedy and then Johnson to bite more deeply into the Vietnam apple, setting up not only a 500,000 U.S. troop commitment but also a humiliating U.S. military defeat, so, too, were Obama and his advisers on the edge of making major decisions that they feared might lead to a similar outcome in Afghanistan. They saw a direct link between Vietnam and Afghanistan, and they worried that they might end up making the same mistakes Bundy had made, especially in relations between the president and the military. The McNamaras, the Westmorelands, and the Bundys were all intelligent men, but they knew next to nothing about Vietnam's history and culture. Yet in the pressure-cooker environment of the cold war, they plunged into Vietnam with a mix of gusto, arrogance, innocence, and ignorance. As Bui Diem, Saigon's former ambassador to Washington, wrote: "Vietnamese knew almost nothing about America, and Americans knew even less about Vietnam."[82] Many years later, he said: "[Secretary of State] Dean Rusk used to tell me that when the United States decided to do something, you just did it. No question about the result. You assumed you'd win. You were all . . ."—here the Vietnamese diplomat paused, searching for a polite word of criticism—"You were all . . . so arrogant."[83]

After the war, when Rusk was asked what distinguished North Vietnam's warriors, he provided a one-word answer. "Tenacity," he said. "Tenacity."[84] And when Bundy pondered what surprised him most about Vietnam's warriors, his answer was their "endurance."[85]

For Donilon and his national security team, the Goldstein book was a crash course in presidential decisionmaking during the early 1960s. In the book, Bundy emerged as a smug national security adviser, Johnson as a wildly irrational and secretive leader, and Kennedy as the only one with a cautious view of American interests in Indochina. Indeed, in Goldstein's view, if Kennedy had lived and been reelected, he never would have increased the American commitment to South Vietnam; just the opposite, he would have cut it, and then left. The book was also, to quote Holbrooke, a "cautionary tale" about what decisionmaking in the Obama administration ought not to be.

At the Pentagon, however, the chiefs were not reading Goldstein's book about a war that failed, though they knew of its best-seller status at the White House; they were reading Lewis Sorley's *A Better War,* about a war that, in his view, the United States could and should have won if only Washington had not abandoned its support of South Vietnam.[86] The differences between the two Vietnam books reflected the differences between the White House and the Pentagon about Afghan policy.

Sorley was a West Point graduate and military historian who believed that the U.S. military reacted to the Tet offensive in early 1968 by dramatically improving both its leadership and its strategy. The new commanding general, Creighton Abrams, switched from a policy of attrition to one of counterinsurgency. According to Sorley, Abrams could actually have won the war if it hadn't been for Congress and the media. His book had been floating around the Pentagon for several years, ever since the surge of American forces in Iraq in 2007. It made for interesting, and for some generals, required, reading.

General David Barno, who commanded U.S. forces in Afghanistan until 2005, insisted "first thing" that his staff read Sorley's book, said General Bernard Champoux, a Barno subordinate.[87] Barno's reason, as he later explained, was that he was trying to do in Afghanistan what General Creighton Abrams had done in South Vietnam in the early 1970s: "Abrams fought the war in the last several years with a modest force focused less on big sweep operations and more at working at village levels, with . . . the Vietnamese and in close concert with the US embassy and civilian efforts. . . . I found Abrams' approach fascinating and [thought] it held great parallels for what I was trying to do—thus my enthusiasm."[88] Barno said that during his time commanding U.S. forces in Afghanistan, he often found parallels with Vietnam. It was on their minds all the time, at almost every meeting they had on Afghanistan, he told a gathering of scholars.[89]

For Barno and many of his colleagues, Afghanistan, though a huge challenge, was not a doomed war. With proper support from Congress, they believed, the United States could have won in Vietnam. Like Sorley, many generals were of the view that Vietnam was lost for one reason: the politicians and the pundits in Washington had pulled the plug on the war. A fear permeated the Pentagon that one day Obama would scale back the American commitment in Afghanistan, aware that the American people were more absorbed with the agony of lost jobs than with a faraway war. Then, after a respectable period of time, Obama would simply abandon the fight.

This was a fear in some respects justified but in other respects not so. Obama now owned the war and could not walk away from it without severe political consequences. But as he got accustomed to the complexities of a counterinsurgency struggle, he saw that he was not always in sync with the Pentagon on all aspects of American policy, and he did not want to become another Lyndon Johnson, forced to shelve parts of his domestic agenda for the sake of an increasingly unpopular war.

Obama had invited a group of the nation's top historians to the White House in June 2009 for an off-the-record seminar on what he could learn from recent American history. More than one of the historians spoke about the legacy of Vietnam and warned the president that if nothing else, Vietnam proved that a president's most cherished domestic programs often died on a foreign battlefield. Robert Caro, an LBJ biographer, said: "All I could think of when I was sitting there and this subject came up was the setting. . . . Any president with a grasp of history—and it seems to me President Obama has a deep understanding of history—would have to be very aware of what happened in another war to derail a great domestic agenda."[90] Another historian, Garry Wills, went further. "Four or five" of the historians, he wrote, breaking the off-the-record ground rule, made the point that "pursuit of war in Afghanistan would be for him what Vietnam was to Lyndon Johnson." Wills continued: "I said that a government so corrupt and tribal and drug based as Afghanistan's could not be made stable. He replied that he was not naïve about the difficulties but he thought a realistic solution could be reached. I wanted to add, 'when pigs fly,' but restrained myself."[91]

The Report That Produced the Famous Review

The war between the two Vietnam books—Goldstein's demonstrating through the sorry story of Bundy that the war was poorly understood, badly managed, and thus lost, and Sorley's arguing that it actually could and should have been won with proper support from Congress—ended in a sullen and unsatisfactory draw. In terms of influencing Afghan policy, though, it did not matter, for both were unceremoniously upstaged by a much shorter book; in fact, a sixty-six-page report on the state of the Afghan War drafted by General McChrystal, one of whose first responsibilities was to survey the Afghan battlefield and produce a totally candid assessment for the president. It was to be super-secret, a limited number of copies to be distributed first to Secretary Gates, Admiral Mullen, and General Petraeus and then to Obama. Everyone knew the situation in Afghanistan had worsened since Obama's springtime decision, months ago, to expand the American troop presence there—but how badly? The president's team was anxiously awaiting the general's ground-eye view. The last place in the world they expected to see it, though, was on the front page of the *Washington Post,* but that was where it was splashed on September 21, 2009. Bob Woodward, the *Post's* scoop specialist extraordinaire, had struck again.

"McChrystal: More Forces or 'Mission Failure,'" the headline read. "Top U.S. Commander for Afghan War Calls Next 12 Months Decisive." In McChrystal's words, as reported by Woodward, the situation had gone from grim to grimmer. "Failure to gain the initiative and reverse insurgent momentum in the near term (next 12 months)," the general wrote, "risks an outcome where defeating the insurgency is no longer possible." Although McChrystal concluded his five-page summary with some optimism—"while the situation is serious, success is still achievable"—the thrust of his whole report was decidedly negative.

Without "adequate resources," McChrystal warned, the United States ran the serious risk of "a longer conflict, [with] greater casualties, higher overall costs, and ultimately, a critical loss of political support," adding up to "mission failure."[92] Bottom line: without more troops and a genuine counterinsurgency strategy, McChrystal believed, an American defeat in Afghanistan was likely. In his view, more troops and counterinsurgency went hand in hand. Without more troops, counterinsurgency would fail. Without counterinsurgency, more troops would be a waste. But how many more troops?

There was never a doubt that McChrystal would ask for more troops. He sent his formal request to Gates on September 24. He listed three options. On the top side, 85,000 more troops to ensure a robust counterinsurgency program. On the bottom, 11,000 more troops for the sole purpose of training Afghan forces. In the middle, 40,000 more troops to support a balanced counterinsurgency program. Because most government officials often chose a middle option, thinking it was safer than either extreme, McChrystal, predictably, recommended the 40,000-troop option to Gates. "After careful military analysis of the current situation," McChrystal wrote, "I recommend the addition of four combat brigades with enablers," meaning in Pentagonese roughly 40,000 more troops.[93]

If McChrystal had done nothing more than make this troop recommendation, he would have had the president's attention. Now, though, he had much more: a president, already skeptical about Pentagon requests, was getting angry, too. Obama had been warned by friends that the military was preparing to box him into a corner where he would have no option except to agree with Gates and McChrystal and send more troops to Afghanistan. Colin Powell, though a Republican, had supported Obama in the 2008 election. He was reportedly furious with his old army colleagues for cornering the president. During one of his private visits to the White House, Powell told Obama: "Don't get pushed by the left to do nothing. Don't get pushed by the right to do everything. You take your time and you figure it out."[94]

Over the summer, General Jones had visited the Afghan front and heard one American officer after another express the need for more troops. The war was going badly, and it was underresourced, they informed Jones. By the time Jones returned to Washington, "mission failure" was in the air. Jones, a great believer in "regular order," decided to organize a series of high-level meetings designed to update the president and his advisers on the deteriorating situation in Afghanistan and to decide what to do next. In Kabul, corruption was painfully obvious. U.S. military efforts were stymied. In other words, McChrystal's report only confirmed the obvious: things were bad and getting worse.

The first meeting took place on September 13, a Sunday. It was not listed on the president's official schedule. The maps and other intelligence reports made for depressing reading. Obama, acting as if he were again a professor engaging his students in a Socratic examination of a tough problem, posed a series of basic questions, similar to some of those he had raised a year before with Reed and Hagel on their flight to Kuwait. Is our main enemy the Taliban or al Qaeda? Are they one and the same enemy? Can a counterinsurgency strategy defeat al Qaeda? Are there moderates within the Taliban willing to cooperate with the Karzai regime? What effect would a Taliban victory have on nuclear-armed Pakistan?

On this Sunday, there were no immediate answers, no snap decisions, but Obama could see in the Jones seminars another way of reviewing his Afghan policy before he had to decide on new troop deployments. No one could have anticipated that there would be nine follow-up meetings running into late November before Obama finally decided on his next move.

It was in many ways a remarkable review of national policy. Obama and his senior advisers analyzed dozens of studies, delved into hundreds of pages, and devoted countless hours to a bureaucratic seminar that some thought a waste of time. They explored new approaches to the Afghan War. They challenged their own fundamental assumptions about Afghan and Pakistani societies. It was an ad hoc, wide-ranging process, unusual in its length and depth, and in time it revealed an extraordinary chasm between the president and his military chiefs on U.S. policy toward the AfPak region.

The Obama administration split into two opposing camps. Each leaked damaging and embarrassing information about the other. It was a fascinating example of internecine warfare by headline and anonymous source. It also forced Obama, determined to govern in a post-Vietnam style, to double down on a number of policy positions that were, ironically, the lessons of the Vietnam War—namely, that the president must give the military a clear set of orders, meaning that no "mission creep" was allowed; that military operations had to be fully resourced; that Congress and the public had to be supportive; and that an "exit strategy" had to be in place before the battle even began. Obama would never admit to being an adherent of the Powell Doctrine, but what he proposed, as Leon Panetta at the CIA described it, was the Obama version of the Powell Doctrine.

"You don't deploy a lot of troops unless you know how the hell to get them out," the CIA director said. "What does it take to make sure that there is an endgame here, and when is that mission going to be accomplished, what is the timeframe [for] accomplishing the mission, and what do we do at that point?"[95]

"Exit strategy" was key. As Robert Gibbs, Obama's spokesman, put it: "It's important to fully examine not just how we're going to get folks in but how we're going to get folks out."[96] But, on one substantive issue, Obama departed from the Powell script: although the president was still not sure how many troops he would send to Afghanistan, it would not be of the magnitude of Bush I's effort in the Persian Gulf War.

It was not McChrystal's fault that his secret report fell into Woodward's hands, but the general suddenly found himself in the crosshairs of White House marksmen. During a *60 Minutes* interview in late September, he said matter-of-factly that he had spoken to Obama only once in the past seventy days, and that by secure video.[97] His comment agitated the White House. What was McChrystal up to? wondered Obama's brain trust. Was he suggesting that Obama was a detached leader, a president unconcerned about an ongoing war? A meeting was arranged between the president, then on his way to Copenhagen, and McChrystal, who by chance happened to be in Europe, to set the record straight. McChrystal was in London, addressing the

International Institute for Strategic Studies, a prestigious think tank, and once again he got into hot water, before even meeting with the president.

In the question-and-answer period following his prepared remarks, which focused on his call for a broad counterinsurgency strategy, the general was asked if he thought the strategy in Iraq might also succeed in Afghanistan: that is, focusing on a more limited offensive against al Qaeda–inspired terrorism. McChrystal could have easily sidestepped the question, or waffled in his reply, but he responded with blunt candor. "The short answer is No," he replied. "You have to navigate from where you are, not where you wish to be. A strategy that does not leave Afghanistan in a stable position is probably a short-sighted strategy."

For the past week, ever since Woodward had broken the story of the McChrystal report, Washington had been awash in leaks about policy options. One such option was Biden's: he believed in a minimalist counterterrorism strategy involving a limited number of American troops in Afghanistan, many drone strikes into the Pakistan sanctuaries, and a heavy reliance on special operations. If McChrystal had not known about the Biden option, clearly he should have, because his London answer hit the already uneasy White House like an enemy rocket. Jones, Emanuel, Donilon, and the others were stunned. The president, en route to Copenhagen, reacted coldly. "We got to stop this," he said. "This is not helpful."

The meeting between Obama and McChrystal, aboard Air Force One at the Copenhagen airport, lasted only twenty-five minutes, enough time for McChrystal to apologize and promise to be more careful in the future. The general then struck the right note with Obama. "Mr. President," he said, "you describe the mission, and we'll do whatever we need to carry it out." Though some of Obama's concerns were eased by this meeting, he still faced the general's urgent request for an additional 40,000 troops. Like Petraeus, Obama was not a fan of "history by analogy," but he could not contain a rising anxiety, which he shared with Biden, Donilon, and Emanuel, that the United States might be getting into another Vietnam-like mess. Fresh from their reading of the Goldstein book, they were especially sensitive to Vietnam comparisons.

Jones, irritated by McChrystal's public put-down of Biden, unintentional or not, complained to Gates and Mullen. "It is a firing offense," he warned. "You've simply got to stop this . . . or the president is going to have to fire somebody." When Obama next met with Gates and Mullen, he let them know that he did not appreciate the military's trying to box him into a troop increase. "It will never happen again," Mullen assured Obama. "It was not intentional."[98]

Yet with each meeting of the Afghanistan review, the gap between Obama and the military widened, the degree of distrust deepened.

Donilon, perhaps more than any other Obama adviser, was especially concerned about the widening gap. What he took away from the Goldstein book was that a president and his military advisers could be examining the same problem, based on the same intelligence, and yet reach different conclusions. That was the problem in Vietnam and now appeared to be the problem in Afghanistan. Every military plan of action, in Donilon's view, had to be subjected to rigorous process and review. Clarity was the essential ingredient. Otherwise, the president was likely to be blindsided. He could think he had just ordered the military to obliterate target "A" only to find out later that the military thought he meant target "B," or the military chose to ignore or misunderstand his order. "How many civilian decisionmakers have thought," Donilon asked, "that they have given a set of instructions to the military only to find out months or years later that in fact [the instructions] had been taken in an uncontemplated direction? . . . If you don't provide absolute clarity on the key questions . . . they're going to do what they think is best and go in the direction they believe they should go in."[99]

Another issue, central to any long-term solution to the Afghan War, was the formation of a future Kabul government. Would it be run only by Karzai and his cohorts, or would it be a coalition government, comprising Karzai, the Taliban, the Northern Alliance, and other groups? Up until this policy review, the Obama administration had rarely focused on this very tricky question, but now, as dozens of policy options were being considered, it inevitably came up for discussion. The U.S. approach to peace negotiations in Afghanistan, when and if these materialized, was simplistic: Karzai represented the legitimate government, and if the Taliban leaders wanted to talk peace, they would first have to put down their weapons, accept the constitution, and cut all ties to al Qaeda: in other words, stop being the Taliban. Not a very likely outcome, everyone agreed.

By October Gates was raising the possibility of the Taliban's being incorporated into a kind of coalition government in Kabul. The term "coalition government" was not used, but the idea was that the Taliban was part of the "political fabric"[100] of Afghanistan and could not be ignored in any negotiation to end the war. Was it possible to identify and separate moderates from extremists among the Taliban leaders, and bring the moderates into the government? Yes. In fact, the effort had already begun. Intermediaries, with the backing of the Karzai government, had met with Taliban representatives, but nothing had yet developed.[101] The Petraeus view was that fruitful negotiations could succeed only after the Taliban had been bloodied, a prospect in his mind still a year or more away. But everyone agreed that negotiations should be pursued.

Meanwhile, the Office of Management and Budget informed Obama that if he added the cost of shipping 40,000 additional troops to the cost of deployments and reconstruction projects already under way, the total for Afghanistan would be almost $1 trillion over the next ten years.[102] Once again Obama wondered whether he was about to be LBJ all over again—a president watching his domestic agenda go up in smoke on a foreign battlefield. "This is a 10-year, trillion dollar effort," he told an aide, "and does not match up with our interests."[103] Still, costs notwithstanding, Obama was resigned to continue the war.

For Obama, November 11 was a day of sorrow and fury. In the morning, to commemorate Veterans Day, he had gone to Arlington National Cemetery, where he delivered a speech honoring those who had died in service to their country. Afterward, he ventured into that part of the cemetery where, among fresh tombstones, he met the families of those recently killed in Afghanistan, killed on his shift. A few weeks earlier, on October 29, Obama had flown in the predawn darkness to Dover Air Force Base to witness the flag-draped caskets of eighteen Americans killed that week in Afghanistan. It was an emotional moment he was not to forget. "If I didn't think this was something worth doing," he later told his aides, "one trip to Dover would be enough to cause me to bring every soldier home. OK?"[104]

Obama then returned to the White House for another meeting on policy options. He had already reached a decision to send another 30,000 troops to Afghanistan—a figure that Gates had suggested in a late-October memo[105]—but he had not yet shared his decision with his senior advisers: in part, because that day he had another problem on his mind. He had just been told that two sensitive diplomatic cables from Ambassador Karl Eikenberry in Kabul to the National Security Council had been leaked, and he was livid and disappointed. "What I'm not going to tolerate is you talking to the press outside of this room," he told his advisers. "It's a disservice to the process, to the country and to the men and women of the military."[106]

Eikenberry, a general who had served in Afghanistan and in April had switched hats and become U.S. ambassador, had written in a November 6 cable that Karzai was "not an adequate strategic partner." In a successful counterinsurgency strategy, such a partner was considered essential. Karzai also "shun[ned] responsibility for any sovereign burden, whether defense, governance or development."[107] Petraeus agreed with Eikenberry, but he used stronger language, describing the Karzai regime to Obama as a "crime syndicate."[108] In another cable, written on November 9, Eikenberry had warned that Karzai's record was one of "inaction and grudging compliance." The ambassador questioned the need to send additional troops to Afghanistan unless the problem of terrorist sanctuaries in neighboring Pakistan could be addressed. In Eikenberry's view, "We will become more deeply engaged here with no way to extricate ourselves, short of allowing the country to descend again into lawlessness and chaos."[109]

While Eikenberry was bad-mouthing Karzai in diplomatic cables, the Afghan leader was preparing for his second inauguration as president. He won in a campaign marred by fraud, violence, and stuffed ballot boxes. No one seemed to take the election as a serious exercise in democracy, but from around the world came many leaders, including Secretary of State Clinton, to lend dignity to what many observers considered a "joke." Dressed in a version of Joseph's many-colored coat, Karzai took advantage of the artificial setting to promise a fight against corruption, which he called "a dangerous enemy of the state." He then said he wanted the Afghan army and police to take complete control of security in five years, meaning in 2014.[110] Karzai did not know at the time, nor did anyone else, that within a year 2014 would be proclaimed the year the United States would finally pull out of Afghanistan.

If, during this long policy review, Obama had to be reminded that his generals still felt the Vietnam War could have been won, *Newsweek* magazine ran a cover story on November 16 entitled "How We (Could Have) Won in Vietnam." It had the Pentagon's fingerprints all over it. The subtitle read: "For Obama & Afghanistan, the Surprising Lessons of a Long-Ago War." The cover photo showed dozens of people climbing up a ladder to the roof of a building near the U.S. embassy in Saigon, where a helicopter waited to fly them to safety. The story, written by Evan Thomas and John Barry, began with a quotation from a despairing President Johnson hunched over his desk, head in hand: "Doing what's right isn't the problem," Johnson was quoted as saying. "It is knowing what's right." In case anyone missed the Pentagon's message, as conveyed by *Newsweek,* it was there on the opening page. "Unraveling the mysteries of Vietnam," it read, "may prevent us from repeating its mistakes."[111]

By Thanksgiving 2009 even Obama recognized that his Afghan policy review had to come to an end. All the options had been examined, not once but dozens of times. On occasion, Obama would argue that he needed more options, but he knew there were no others that made sense. He had already ruled out an American withdrawal. He had also ruled out deposing Karzai; the

United States had done that in Vietnam with Diem, also with unsatisfactory results. And he did not want to be the president who presided over another American defeat. He felt trapped. What to do? On the one side, Gates, Mullen, and Petraeus were pressing him to go along with the McChrystal request for more troops, if not at the 40,000 level then at the 30,000 level. On the other side, Biden, Donilon, and Eikenberry were urging him to resist Pentagon pressure and settle for a small footprint in Afghanistan, supported by an enlarged training and building program, and a stepped-up antiterrorist operation in . neighboring Pakistan.

As one of Obama's advisers said: "The president is not steeped in military experience . . . of having to deal with these kinds of issues in a real way." The adviser chose not to be quoted when speaking about Obama. The president, he went on,

> did not really have kind of the depth of how do you face a bunch of generals in a room, who suddenly want to deploy a hell of a lot more troops. . . . It's a very intimidating experience for a younger president to basically tell them to go to hell. In Obama's case, the generals were making clear that this was the strategy that was needed in order to deal with it. And I think, for him, there were question marks. Is this truly the right way to do it? . . . So for many who might just simply have saluted and said, you know, politically I am in no position where I am going to tell the generals to go to hell. Instead he was willing to question and force them to face the issues that were involved here.

CIA director Panetta was quoted by Woodward as saying that "no Democratic president can go against military advice, especially if he has asked for it. So just do it. Do what they said."[112] But Obama felt that doing "what they said" got Johnson and the nation into the Vietnam mess, and he didn't want to be another LBJ; he thought he had made that clear.

By November 25 Obama finally made his decision: he told Jones, Donilon, and Emanuel that he was "inclined to go with the 30,000" troop increase, but he stressed that "this needs to be a plan about how we're going to hand it off and get out of Afghanistan. . . . I want to emphasize the speed with which we're doing things. Faster in. Faster out." He did not mean, he emphasized, the abandonment of Afghanistan; he meant that there would be a period of transition.[113] Obama imagined the plan to be rational and well considered, but it had the feel of a dreamy, unrealistic projection: the United States would increase the number of troops in Afghanistan while beginning the process of pulling them out, and, at the same time, train more and more Afghan troops and police to assume responsibility for their own security; and this would all happen by July 2011, a little more than two years after Obama began to implement his first review of Afghan policy. As he had said, he had only two years of the nation's patience.

But before Obama could broadcast his new Afghan policy to the nation and the world, he had to win the Pentagon's approval. Donilon, in explaining the uneasy relationship between Obama and the generals, returned to the Goldstein book to explain the need for the president always to be "absolutely clear from end to end on [his] instructions to the military." Obama agreed fully. He felt, in this case, that he needed what Donilon called "contractual clarity.[114]

Obama said: "We're not going to do this unless everybody literally signs on to it and looks me in the eye and tells me that they're for it. . . . I don't want anybody going out the day after and saying that they don't agree with this."[115] Secretary Clinton, always careful about her relations with Obama, emphasized: "One thing we didn't want—to have a decision made and then have somebody say, 'Oh, by the way.' No, come forward now or forever hold your peace."[116]

Donilon, the Washington lawyer, spent the next two days drafting "a seven-page, single-spaced set of instructions for the president that he would know word-by-word for himself and then word-by-word with the military leadership."[117] On November 27 Obama, also a lawyer, edited the "set of instructions." He thought they reflected what he and Gates had agreed to. But for the next two days Donilon and Mullen were again at war, arguing over every point. Couldn't the president accept McChrystal's 40,000 request? Couldn't we, shouldn't we, be launching a major counterinsurgency campaign? Shouldn't we drop the July 2011 timetable?

"I'm pissed," Obama said of all the questions. Donilon, thinking back to Vietnam, was astonished at the policy challenges the brass was hurling at the president, at the political power the brass was flaunting at the president's expense. Johnson had failed to give precise orders to the military, according to Goldstein, and Obama was now determined not to make the same mistake. He got copies of Donilon's memo and Gates's memo and, by himself, with pen and yellow-lined pad in hand, composed a "terms sheet,"[118] another way of describing a legal document of the sort used in a business transaction. No president had ever felt the need to draft a legal document defining his obligations to the military and theirs to him; this tactic showed how wide the gap was between them on American policy toward Afghanistan.

The Obama "Memorandum for the Principals," dated November 29, 2009, the day it was presented to his national security advisers, made it clear that U.S. policy in Afghanistan would not be a "fully resourced counterinsurgency or nation-building" project but rather, as Biden wished, a "narrower approach" limited to "disrupting, dismantling and eventually defeating al Qaeda and preventing al Qaeda's return to safe haven in Afghanistan or Pakistan." Then, to help McChrystal "set the conditions for accelerated transition to Afghan authorities," the United States would increase troop levels in Afghanistan by 30,000, to start arriving in the first half of 2010, and then, in July 2011, to begin a gradual drawdown of American forces "based on progress on the ground"—a bow to Gates, who disliked all timetables. As part of the transition, Afghan army and police would then begin to assume responsibility for their own security. In December 2010 the White House would run a check on the success of this transition. The total cost was estimated at $113 billion per year when the United States had peaked at roughly 100,000 troops in Afghanistan.[119]

Biden believed that "we're locked into Vietnam" if the new policy failed, prompting Obama to reply that "I'm not signing on to a failure. . . . If what I proposed is not working, I'm not going to be like these other presidents and stick to it based upon my ego or my politics—my political security."[120] What the president proposed—his six-page agreement—was handed out to Biden, Jones, and the Pentagon brass, all of whom read it carefully. Obama then stressed:

—There would be a 30,000 troop increase, plus an additional 10 percent if absolutely necessary.

—There would be no further troop increases; quite the contrary, come July 2011, there would begin a thinning out of American forces.

—At that time, a transition of authority from American forces to Afghan security would also begin, based on conditions on the ground.

—The United States would not become engaged in a broad program of counterinsurgency, or of nation building,[121] though the president must have known that was exactly what the United States was doing in Afghanistan.

Obama conceded that neither his political nor his military advisers were happy with his new Afghan policy, but he was convinced it was the right course for the nation. He looked around the room. "I'm not asking you to change what you believe," the president said. "But if you do not agree with me, say so now."

Silence followed.

"Tell me now," he repeated.

Gates signaled his agreement. Mullen followed, "Fully support, Sir." Petraeus added, "Ditto."[122]

Obama won. He had stared down the Pentagon. He had asserted his constitutional authority. But everyone knew that the battle between them had not ended.

The West Point Speech

"It's His War Now," shouted the cover of *Time* magazine on December 14, 2009, showing a photo of Obama, his back to the reader, reaching out to hundreds of West Point cadets. *Time* was somewhat late in its judgment. It had been Obama's war since he took the oath of office in January. Operationally, it had been his war since mid-February, when he ordered 17,000 troops to Afghanistan. Emotionally, it had been his war since he witnessed eighteen caskets returning from Afghanistan in October. And tactically, it had been his war since he decided, after another exhaustive review of Afghan policy, to "surge" even more troops into the war while also setting a controversial timetable for their withdrawal.

It was indeed his war. His policy was described by Joe Klein of *Time* as a "complex, slightly contradictory contraption."[123] Frank Rich of the *New York Times* was more stringent in his criticism. "Some circles of hell," he wrote, "can't be squared. What he's ended up with is a too-clever-by-half pushmi-pullyu holding action that lacks both a credible exit strategy and the commitment of its two most essential partners, a legitimate Afghan government and the American people."[124]

The cadets on the *Time* cover had just heard the president confirm what they already knew from the newspapers and the networks. Afghanistan was a war that would go on and on. Echoing the grim appraisal of the McChrystal report, Obama said that "the situation in Afghanistan has deteriorated" and "the status quo is not sustainable." The terrorists were on the march, plotting every minute of every day, even "as I speak." Therefore, the president explained, in his cool, unemotional style, that it was in "our vital national interest" to immediately send an additional 30,000 troops to Afghanistan, bringing the U.S. total there by mid-2010 to about 100,000. The troops were needed to "seize the initiative" from the Taliban and to step up the training of the Afghan army and police so that, by July 2011, American forces could begin a phased withdrawal, as the Afghans assumed greater responsibility for their own security. If he did not believe, Obama stressed, that the security and safety of the American people were "at stake in Afghanistan," he would "gladly order every single one of our troops home tomorrow."[125]

Earlier in the day, Obama had invited a group of reporters and columnists to lunch. Though time and again Obama had stubbornly rejected any analogy to Vietnam, he kept returning to that lost war for explanations of his current policy. He did so at times directly and at other times indirectly.

Indeed, when Obama asked his speechwriter, Ben Rhodes, to begin drafting his speech, he said he wanted it to emphasize the differences between Afghanistan, on the one hand, and Vietnam and Iraq, on the other. "We've had wrenching debates about these issues as a country," Obama recalled. "But we need to move beyond relitigating those debates."[126] And yet, even as he tried to put distance between himself and Vietnam, he felt the need to explain his take on Vietnam all over again.

One argument against escalation, Obama said, was that "this is Vietnam, and we should just abandon the field completely. I don't know anybody who has looked at this very carefully who thinks that we are going to be as effective as we need to be in targeting Al Qaeda and other extremists if we simply allow Afghanistan to collapse."[127]

In his speech, Obama argued that the comparison "depends on a false reading of history." Then, underlining the differences between Afghanistan and Vietnam, the president stressed that "unlike Vietnam," a phrase he repeated three times, the United States was now part of a "broad coalition of 43 nations." Also different, the United States was not facing a "broad-based popular insurgency." Finally, and most important, the United States was "viciously attacked from Afghanistan . . . and to abandon this area now . . . would . . . create an unacceptable risk of additional attacks on our homeland and our allies."[128]

Though Obama was a keen reader of history, he himself then engaged in a "false reading of history." First, the United States was part of a "coalition" during the Vietnam War, too, but not as "broad" a coalition as the one it was leading during the Afghan War. Still, in both wars, of all the foreign actors, it was the United States that made the major sacrifice in lives and treasure. Second, despite Obama's claim, the Taliban did in fact represent a "broad-based popular insurgency." Again, it might not have been as broadly based as the one in Vietnam, but within the context of Afghan society, it did have a broad base. Finally, and unmistakably, the United States was indeed attacked from Afghanistan, but it has also been the target of al Qaeda–inspired attacks from other places, in particular Yemen, without provoking a massive U.S. military response.

Though Obama would rarely admit it, LBJ was often on his mind, not as a model for emulation but as a warning against a dangerous policy of endless escalation. He stressed to his luncheon guests that his Afghan strategy was designed to be crystal clear and to offer the "best prospect of getting our troops home in some realistic time frame." He was thinking of his July 2011 time frame as one way of not getting sucked into an endless war. For political reasons, Obama wished to convey the impression that even though he was surging troops into Afghanistan, he was already planning for their withdrawal. Turning to *New York Times* columnist Thomas Friedman, who was sitting on his left, Obama tried to leave no doubt about his intention. "I'm interested in nation building here in the United States right now," he said.[129]

Unfortunately, for Obama's strategy to succeed, he would have to be both effective and lucky, and neither was assured. The United States was no longer the feared superpower of cold war days. Maybe, once upon a time, it could have snapped its fingers, and Pakistan would have opened its borders and allowed American Special Forces to crush the terrorist sanctuaries nestled in relative safety in the mountainous border regions. But no more. The United States could fire more drone missiles into these sanctuaries, more terrorist leaders could be killed, but the infiltration and the insurgency would still continue.

Obama, in his televised report to the nation, was speaking "the language of limits," to quote journalist Peter Beinart.[130] On March 27, when Obama reported on his first Afghan review, he spoke then much more confidently about "disrupt[ing], dismantl[ing], and defeat[ing] al Qaeda." Now, after his second review, he seemed to have lowered his horizons, speaking more about "revers[ing] the Taliban's momentum" than about "destroying" al Qaeda, more about military objectives than the broader goals of democracy, freedom, and women's rights.

It was not only Afghanistan that needed help; America needed help, too. The economy was in tatters, and "the days of providing a blank check are over," Obama said. "I refuse to set goals that go beyond our responsibility, our means or our interests."[131]

Obama recognized during his review of war options that if he was to achieve a stable and secure Afghanistan, he would have to do more than reverse the Taliban's momentum on the battlefield; he would also have to be flexible and imaginative and find a way to bring the Taliban into a broadened Kabul government, perhaps with Karzai, perhaps without him. Here the resemblance to Vietnam was painfully obvious. Once Nixon agreed in the early 1970s to allow North Vietnamese troops to remain in South Vietnam after a cease-fire, it was obvious, despite his denials, that he was agreeing to the establishment of a coalition government likely to be dominated and eventually run by the communists. History allows for no guarantees that what happened in one place would happen in another, but Obama knew that the lessons of Vietnam were, to a certain extent, applicable in Afghanistan.

"Evil Does Exist in the World"

After Obama's West Point speech, which set his war policy for Afghanistan, he had one other major address on his calendar for December 2009: his acceptance of the Nobel Peace Prize on the 10th in Oslo's City Hall. Because many people thought Obama did not deserve the prize, which seemed to be awarded more for his promise than for his performance, he wanted his words to sing with poetry, philosophy, religion, and the politics of war. "My accomplishments are slight," he acknowledged. But as president of the United States, he commanded two armies engaged in two wars, and every day he faced the "costs of armed conflict" and "the relationship between war and peace." Could peace ever replace war? Could a war ever be considered just? He came to Oslo with no glib answers but with an appeal for new thinking, which he did not really provide. Reluctantly, he stressed the "hard truth": "We will not eradicate violent conflict in our lifetimes."

Obama tried to justify his acceptance of a peace prize given his pursuit of a war in Afghanistan. "As a head of state sworn to protect and defend my nation," he said, " I face the world as it is, and cannot stand idle in the face of threats to the American people. For make no mistake: evil does exist in the world. A nonviolent movement could not have halted Hitler's armies. Negotiations cannot convince al Qaeda's leaders to lay down their arms. To say that force may sometimes be necessary is not a call to cynicism—it is a recognition of history; the imperfections of man and the limits of reason."[132]

10

"Good Enough"

I don't think you win this war. . . . This is the kind of fight we're in for the rest of our lives and probably our kids' lives.
—GENERAL DAVID PETRAEUS, quoted in Bob Woodward, *Obama's Wars*, 2010

I advise all those who place their trust in the Americans to learn the lesson of Vietnam.
—HASSAN NASRALLAH, Hezbollah, Al Jazeera interview, 2006

IN 2002 BARACK OBAMA sharply criticized President George W. Bush's plan to attack Iraq. He said such a war could lead to a "U.S. occupation of undetermined length, at undetermined cost, with undetermined consequences."[1] At the beginning of 2010, Obama might, in a reflective moment, have revisited his criticism of Bush. Now, as commander in chief for only one year, he had greatly expanded the size of the American army in Afghanistan. It would soon number 100,000 troops. He did not know how long they would be there, how much the war would cost, or what the consequences would be. Obama did not want to become a war president. He wanted out of Afghanistan, but he was stuck.

For years, the United States had underfunded and underresourced the war in Afghanistan. It was treated as an afterthought to the war in Iraq. Now, under Obama, with fresh resources and determination, the United States went on the offensive. Or tried to.

Stanley McChrystal was the top U.S. commander in Afghanistan. Counterinsurgency was his doctrine, and he pursued it with puritanical zeal. A soldier of keen intellect, he had studied David Kilcullen's theories about counterinsurgency. The Australian-born expert had discussed the importance of working in three areas—security, politics, and economics—to establish some sort

of control over a society, and eventually transfer that control to a central government.[2] It was a task bordering on the impossible in Afghanistan, where the
government of Hamid Karzai enjoyed only limited legitimacy, especially after
a presidential election described by many as a fraud.

McChrystal was an optimist. He reduced Kilcullen's complex strategy to
a simple formula: success in Afghanistan could be achieved by winning the
hearts and minds of the people, just as General Creighton Abrams had tried
to do in Vietnam. And how could this be done? By limiting civilian casualties
and respecting Afghan culture and religion, McChrystal believed, even if this
approach opened his own troops to greater danger. He cut back on close-in air
support for North Atlantic Treaty Organization (NATO) ground troops under
fire, restricted aggressive nighttime raids, and met frequently with local leaders, sitting on rugs in their tents, sipping tea, and listening to their complaints.
This careful, calibrated approach depended for its success on stretchable time
frames and deferrable deadlines, and here an old problem surfaced between
him and the president, and in a broader sense between the Pentagon and the
White House. The general thought in terms of years. Like David Petraeus, he
knew that a successful counterinsurgency strategy needed at least a decade or
more to plant roots and flower. Obama, preoccupied by an economic crisis at
home and worried about getting sucked into a Vietnam-style war in Afghanistan, thought more in terms of months, or a few years at most.

Marja and Then Kandahar—That Was the Plan

McChrystal's first target in early February 2010 was the Taliban stronghold of
Marja in Helmand Province, the center of opium traffic. The next target was
to be Kandahar, the heartland of the Taliban insurgency. These were the opening salvos in what was intended to be a decisive drive to break the Taliban's
momentum, build up the central government in Kabul, and move toward
transferring power and authority from the NATO coalition to the Afghan
army and police by Obama's target date of July 2011. That, at least, was the
general's plan.

At the time in southern Afghanistan stood a sizable force, under McChrystal's command, of 15,000 coalition troops.[3] His approach to the battle for
Marja was unconventional. Usually an invading army counts on surprise,
but in this case McChrystal deliberately chose to inform the Taliban of his
approaching assault. Operation Moshtarak (Dari for "together") was "due

to commence," the allies announced via a press release,[4] apparently believing that this announcement would have both psychological and practical benefits: namely, that the Taliban would panic and flee and maybe even surrender. At the same time, coalition forces would slowly move into the suburbs, set up forward positions, drop leaflets, begin talking to neighborhood mullahs, and prepare for the big attack on the city. NATO officers would assure local leaders that the people would receive compensation for any battle damage to their homes, farms, or businesses.[5]

There was never any doubt that McChrystal would win the battle for Marja, and within a few weeks NATO forces were indeed in control of the city, at least during the day. At night, control was contested. But in any counterinsurgency struggle, whether in Vietnam or Afghanistan, the end of the shooting was only a prelude to the real contest: who would end up running Marja, the old warlords or the Taliban? Would there be jobs for the people? Could residents walk the streets and marketplaces safely? These were questions demanding immediate answers. McChrystal had one answer. "We've got a government in a box, ready to roll in," he proudly told reporters.[6] In reality, he had a number of preselected officials, cleared by Karzai's government in Kabul, supposedly ready to run Marja.

Ten months later, columnist David Ignatius reported that while violence was down in Marja, there was still "more box than government," with many posts in the district government still unfilled. The Afghan army, supposedly taking over from the marines, was functioning at only half strength. Why? Because Afghan officers were pocketing the money set aside for recruiting.[7] This was hardly the changing of the guard that McChrystal had envisaged.

"You've got to have the governance part ready to go," said Brigadier General Frederick Hodges, one of the top American commanders in southern Afghanistan. "We talked about doing that in Marja, but didn't realize how hard it was to do." He added, "Ultimately, it's up to the Afghans to step forward."[8] And they didn't. General Hodges was echoing John Kennedy's judgment of his South Vietnamese allies in 1963. "In the final analysis, it is their war," the president told CBS's Walter Cronkite. "They are the ones who have to win it or lose it. We can help them, we can give them equipment, we can send our men out there as advisers, but they have to win it—the people of Viet-Nam—against the communists."[9]

McChrystal could not win in Marja, forty-seven years later, because he could not win the hearts and minds of the people. "When you go to protect people, the people have to want you to protect them," he explained. "It's a deliberative process. It takes time to convince people."[10] His military victory had bought him an opportunity to win a political victory and to institute a set of economic reforms, but, as it turned out, he could not pull it off. His opponent had at least one distinct advantage. The Taliban were, as Robert Gates had pointed out during Obama's policy review, part of the fabric of Afghan society. They spoke the language; they knew the customs, the streets, the bazaars. They were, good or bad, local people, known by and to other local people, and they were feared or trusted more than the soldiers of a foreign army, even an army willing to compensate for any unintended battlefield damage. Moreover, they were Karzai's enemy, and that brought them instant respectability among those Afghans embarrassed and disgusted by Karzai's chronically corrupt and pathetically ineffective government.

In April McChrystal accompanied Karzai to Kandahar for a regional meeting of over 1,000 tribal leaders. "Are you happy about this operation?" asked the Afghan president. He heard sounds of dissatisfaction. "No?" he continued. "Listen to me carefully. Until you're happy and satisfied, we will not conduct this operation."[11] Failing in Marja, McChrystal now had to postpone his planned attack on Kandahar for several months. Both were major setbacks.

As McChrystal's disillusionment with Karzai deepened, the Pentagon on April 28, 2010, sent its semiannual report to Congress on the situation in Afghanistan. There were improvements, according to the report, including data showing that 59 percent of the Afghan people now believed their government was moving "in the right direction."[12] But the overall situation in Afghanistan was judged to be only marginally better. Meaningful progress was not on the near horizon, and that frustrated Obama. The president's July 2011 target date remained more aspirational than real. Was there a better way?

McChrystal Rolling-Stoned and Out, Petraeus Extolled and In

On the list of presidential problems on June 22, none was more unexpected than a stunning story of insubordination, perpetrated by none other than the president's commanding general in Afghanistan. The story exploded in the June 25, 2010, issue of *Rolling Stone*. The eye-catching title was "The Runaway General," with the even more eye-catching subtitle, "Stanley McChrystal, Obama's top commander in Afghanistan, has seized control of the war by never taking his eye off the real enemy: The wimps in the White House." The reporter was Michael Hastings, who had been embedded with McChrystal and his staff for the better part of a month.

The thrust of the story, which circulated on the web days before publication, was that McChrystal was unhappy and restless under White House direction; and although many of the direct quotations came from his staff, enough of them came directly from McChrystal to force Obama to recall him immediately on June 22 and to fire him the following morning. McChrystal was quoted as saying he felt "betrayed" by the leak of critical comments made by Eikenberry about McChrystal's strategy, annoyed by a succession of Holbrooke e-mails ("Oh, not another e-mail from Holbrooke . . . I don't even want to open it."), and he also spoke disparagingly of Biden. Concerning two earlier meetings between McChrystal and Obama, Hastings wrote that McChrystal staffers described the president as "uncomfortable and intimidated" and "[not] very engaged." Anonymous McChrystal aides were quoted as calling General Jones a "clown," a French minister "f—— gay," and Senators McCain and Kerry "not very helpful."[13]

The article focused attention once again on the sour relationship between the White House and the Pentagon. McChrystal was clearly unimpressed by Obama's command of Afghan strategy, an attitude obviously absorbed by his staff and foolishly shared with a reporter. When Jones learned about McChrystal's indiscretions, he was baffled and angry. "This is pretty sensational stuff," he told Gates. Obama wanted "to see what in the world he [McChrystal] was thinking," press secretary Robert Gibbs told reporters. The president was furious.[14] Democrat David Obey of Wisconsin, chairman of the House Appropriations Committee, blasted McChrystal as one in a line of "reckless, renegade generals who haven't seemed to understand that their role is to implement policy, not design it."[15] Obey was a critic of both McChrystal and the Afghan War, which reminded him of Vietnam. Once he related to Obama a "terrible, gut-wrenching" story of a conversation between LBJ and Senator Richard Russell of Georgia, about the war in Vietnam with one saying to the other: "Well, we know this is damn near a fool's errand, but we don't have any choice."[16] Obey did not report Obama's response, but he left the impression that, in his view, we did have a choice in Afghanistan: learn from Vietnam; don't go any deeper into Afghanistan.

Even if the *Rolling Stone* article had been McChrystal's first and only run-in with the White House, he would still have been in deep trouble. Biden told ABC's Jake Tapper that before Obama fired McChrystal, he had Biden check with several top generals, and "every single one said he had to go."[17] McChrystal was the second general Obama fired in less than two years in office. This one was a Petraeus favorite. His flinty, hard-nosed approach to war had earned him the less-than-flattering sobriquet "Mullah McChrystal" in Kabul. He was impatient with criticism, disdainful of diplomacy, and he drove himself as mercilessly as he drove his subordinates. He cut back on alcohol, pizzas, and hamburgers at a NATO headquarters building and a major base, fueling angry criticism from soldiers who had been on dangerous patrols all day. "What next, no hot showers for anyone?" asked one soldier.[18]

Because McChrystal was commander not only of American troops in Afghanistan but also NATO forces, his dismissal had the potential for blowing apart Obama's strategy, so painfully put together during his 2009 review. Might this not encourage other restless NATO countries to pull out of Afghanistan? Canada and the Netherlands had already announced their intention to do so. McChrystal, never the romantic, understood the danger almost immediately. "I have compromised the mission," he confessed in an apology to Biden.[19]

Obama understood the danger too. June 2010 was proving to be the costliest month in terms of casualties for the United States and its coalition partners. Reports from Kabul were depressing. The Taliban fighters were advancing, and Karzai was becoming more ornery with each speech. Congress was mumbling about cutting back on America's commitment to Afghanistan rather than adding to it.

Other generals, Obama understood, could replace McChrystal, but there was only one who could instantly command respect and acceptance and start a new chapter in the Afghan story with barely a ripple of anxiety, and that was David Petraeus. At the beginning, Obama was suspicious of Petraeus, and a number of his aides worried that the general might seek the presidency in 2012. While Rahm Emanuel and others in the White House thought Petraeus was going to run, Jones disagreed. "I kept saying, 'I don't think so,'" recalled Jones, who saw Petraeus as "a patriot, a military man. . . . His motivation is very pure."[20] It took more than a year, but in time Obama shelved concerns about Petraeus's political intentions and came to appreciate the general's crisp intelligence and obvious dedication. Petraeus was a new, post-Vietnam kind of soldier.

Usually, Obama moved with regal deliberation. This time, he moved with impulsive speed. He invited Petraeus to join him in the Oval Office, and offered him the job. Petraeus accepted the new assignment. Obama needed him in Afghanistan, just as Bush had needed him in Iraq. Both presidents, to quote Bruce Riedel, "put all [their] bets down on the table on one guy—and it's the same guy."[21]

It was a demotion for Petraeus, who, as chief of Central Command, was technically McChrystal's boss, but the "hero of Iraq," as he was often called, saluted and, within a week, was on his way to Kabul, where he arrived on July 2. The following day, he met with President Karzai. On July 4 Petraeus took command. With a sense of drama reminiscent of Douglas MacArthur during World War II, Petraeus sounded like a general with no-nonsense grit and determination. "We are engaged in a tough fight," he told the assembled guests. "After years of war we have arrived at a critical moment." He added, speaking of the coalition forces, "We must demonstrate to the people and to the Taliban that Afghan and I.S.A.F. [International Security Assistance Force] forces are here to safeguard the Afghan people, and that we are in this to win."[22] The general was speaking of winning the war; and even though Obama had not used that word in a long time, he must have been pleased, at least privately, that Petraeus was in Kabul striking a note of optimism about a war that often seemed like a lost cause.

Six weeks later, in mid-August, Petraeus began his public defense of Obama's Afghan policy. He had toured Afghanistan, checked with his commanders, spoken with local leaders, most especially the problematic Karzai, and was eager to strike hard at the Taliban.

A brilliant briefer on a first-name basis with many reporters, Petraeus arranged a number of "exclusive" interviews with major news organizations: NBC's *Meet the Press,* the *New York Times,* and the *Washington Post.* Petraeus believed in a rainfall of briefings. Feed the beasts, meaning the reporters, his flacks would say. The general's reading of Vietnam (and Afghanistan) was that the American people, their representatives in Congress, and the media had to be brought into the loop; in wartime, they had to understand their government's policy and strategy. In the process, no lying—if at all possible—and no credibility gaps. Maybe, in this way, the White House would be believed, and the generals would be given the extra time they needed to fight the asymmetrical war of the day. It was an old-fashioned media blitz, orchestrated by the one person in the Obama administration who still commanded enough credibility to sell the Pentagon's case to the president and the president's policy to the public.

Petraeus made essentially the same points in all the interviews:

—"Conditions on the ground" will determine the rate of American troop withdrawal from Afghanistan starting in July 2011, as the president had promised. But while Obama had sounded firm, Petraeus left a little bit of wiggle room, suggesting that the withdrawal could be delayed or small-scale. "What the president very much wants from me . . . and what we talked about in the Oval Office," Petraeus said, "is the responsibility of a military commander on the ground to provide [his] best professional military advice, leave the politics to him. Certainly I'm aware of the context within which I offer that advice, but that just informs the advice, it doesn't drive it. The situation on the ground drives it."[23]

—Petraeus would resist any swift pullout of American troops. "Clearly the enemy is fighting back, sees this as a very pivotal moment, believes that all he has to do is outlast us through this fighting season," Petraeus said. "That is just not the case."[24]

—"The president didn't send me over here to seek a graceful exit," said Petraeus,[25] no doubt mindful of Kissinger's use of the phrase "decent interval" to describe the time between the withdrawal of American troops from Vietnam and the communist conquest of Vietnam.

NBC's David Gregory saved his will-you-run-for-president question for the end of his interview. "No way, no how," Petraeus told Gregory.[26] On NBC, the matter was dropped, for the moment. At the White House, Obama's political advisers still distrusted Petraeus. Better, they thought, for the general to be absorbed with war than with politics, and the war showed no signs of ending before the 2012 presidential campaign.

Although Petraeus tried to accentuate the positive, stressing that only in recent months had the war strategy finally been fine-tuned, resources delivered, and progress made, reporters and experts were not persuaded. They noted Taliban advances in different parts of the country, allied casualties rising rapidly, Karzai's government remaining corrupt and inefficient, and popular sentiment shifting toward the Taliban. "The coalition will not defeat this increasingly national insurgency," wrote Gilles Dorronsoro, an expert at the Carnegie Endowment for International Peace. "With America's European partners planning to leave over the next few years, the United States will be on its own, mired in a war with no clear exit strategy."[27]

Was the glass half-empty or half-full? Petraeus, aware of this gloomy forecast, still preferred to believe it was half-full. Now, at last, he had enough troops to resume the stalled offensive in and around Kandahar. He threw thousands of fresh American troops into the battle in Helmand and Kandahar provinces. Helicopter gunships, fighter jets, and bombers went into action. Because of the high rate of American casualties caused by improvised explosive devices (IEDs), balloon cameras and unmanned drones prowled the skies, searching for hidden IED booby traps and relentlessly attacking them.[28] In addition, Petraeus sent his Special Operations troops on controversial nighttime raids into villages and homes, resulting in the killing or capturing of more than 350 leaders of the insurgency. One official estimate put the number of such raids at 200 a month, six times the number eighteen months before.[29] One Taliban official admitted to a *Newsweek* reporter that the insurgency was losing good men, but he claimed they were being quickly replaced with other experienced men.[30] It seemed as if, in this latest American surge, Petraeus was holding nothing back. On November 19 the Pentagon went where it had never gone before in Afghanistan: it announced that it was sending fourteen Abrams tanks with accurate, sophisticated 120 mm guns to join what was still a guerrilla war in southern Afghanistan.[31] Soviet forces had also used tanks in their guerrilla war in Afghanistan and gotten nowhere. Now the United States was following a similar path. Clearly, Petraeus was changing America's war strategy from McChrystal's cautious, population-centric counterinsurgency to something more closely resembling Westmoreland's strategy of attrition: fight as aggressively as possible, kill as many Taliban as possible, and, as *Time* reporter Jason Motlagh put it, "rout the Taliban in their own backyard."[32] Petraeus wanted not only to break the Taliban's momentum, he wanted to weaken the Taliban so severely that they would have no option but to limp to the negotiating table and strike a deal with Karzai.

But Petraeus should have known better. According to his own counter-insurgency playbook, every victory on the battlefield had quickly to be followed up with better governance, economic reforms, and a legitimate central authority, or else the victory could well prove meaningless. What Petraeus observed was that after almost every battle, not enough happened. Sometimes nothing happened. Local leaders remained dependent on warlords and drug dealers. Reforms were only vaporous promises to be realized at some point in the future, if at all, and Kabul was still Kabul, the seat of corruption and ineffective governance. No matter how many military victories he secured in Afghanistan, Petraeus was still saddled with the continuing realities of an asymmetrical war in a backward country, led by a highly unreliable Karzai and made more complex by the presence of Taliban sanctuaries across the border in Pakistan. But it was not in his interest to emphasize any of this.

Equally important, Petraeus was under extraordinary pressure to produce results. He was the president's man, Obama's trump card; and if he couldn't produce results, nobody could. He could not ask for any more troops. Like his Pentagon colleagues, he had agreed to a "contractual" understanding with Obama that the additional 30,000 troops requested by McChrystal would do the job. But he could make a play for more time. By way of interviews with reporters, briefings for visiting congressional delegations, and a few well-placed leaks, Petraeus created the impression—partly real, partly hyped—that the United States was finally turning the corner in Afghanistan, that soon the Taliban might even agree to serious talks with Karzai, and that Obama's December report to the nation, promised the year before, would point to a genuine improvement in the American position in the Afghan War. That would buy the time that Petraeus needed. Clearly Petraeus was playing all of his cards. A shrewd judge of the president's political needs, Petraeus realized that Obama's clock was ticking with a new urgency, much more quickly than his own clock in Kabul, as one poll after another reported rising domestic discontent with the war and as Congress struggled with a weak economy and the burdensome costs of the war.

2014 Abruptly Replaces 2011 as Key Target Date

Another question for the general: what if the Taliban, like the North Vietnamese years before, learned to tolerate the intensified American attacks and still refused to negotiate with Karzai? Suppose the Taliban believed that if they could wait until July 2011, only another seven or eight months away, the Americans would begin to go home, just as Obama had announced in December 2009; and once they began to go home, they would never return. Was this not a formula for an eventual Taliban victory? The Americans, by late 2010, would be at war in Afghanistan for longer than the Soviet invaders, and the Taliban believed, much as Osama bin Laden did, that the Americans, addicted to TV reporting and commentary, could not stand the sight of their own blood being spilled in foreign lands, and, in any case, their reputation as world leader was "built on foundations of straw." For confirmation, the al Qaeda leader looked back to America's performance in "Vietnam, Beirut, Aden, and Somalia." "They left," he said of the Americans in Somalia, "after some resistance from powerless, poor, unarmed people whose only weapon is the belief in Allah the Almighty."[33]

Hassan Nasrallah, head of Lebanon's Hezbollah movement, echoed bin Laden's sentiments. "I cannot forget the sight of the American forces," he said, "leaving Vietnam in helicopters, which carried their officers and soldiers. . . . This is the sight I anticipate in our region. . . . I advise all those who place their trust in the Americans to learn the lesson of Vietnam . . . and to know that when the Americans lose this war—and lose it, they will, Allah willing—they will abandon them to their fate, just like they did to all those who placed their trust in them throughout history."[34]

Since the American defeat in Vietnam in 1975, it should not be surprising that just as presidents from Gerald Ford to Barack Obama have learned to live in the shadows of a lost war, so, too, have America's adversaries learned to exploit the defeat to advance their own strategic aims, assuming that a beaten America would be too weak to challenge them. In the mid-1970s, the Soviet Union and Cuba rang revolutionary alarms throughout Africa, and then in the late 1970s, Soviet forces invaded Afghanistan. In the Middle East, Islamic radicals, like Nasrallah, believed they could get away with attacking U.S. interests, even in one case murdering 241 marines in Beirut, because they thought the United States, after Vietnam, had been reduced to a paper tiger. In a number of key cases, though, the opponents miscalculated: in Afghanistan, the United States organized an unofficial, anticommunist alliance that ultimately defeated the Soviet army; and in the 1991 Persian Gulf War, the United States joined with allies to defeat the invading Iraqi army in Kuwait. The point was that the American loss in Vietnam produced opportunities for mischief and ripples of unpredictability in global diplomacy.

Petraeus, a student of history, as familiar with Lawrence of Arabia as with Tito's guerrilla triumphs in Yugoslavia, always rejected talk of "history by analogy" and therefore any comparison of Vietnam with Afghanistan. But having written his dissertation on the lessons of Vietnam, he could not escape the comparisons, especially when his enemy was drawing them. The North Vietnamese enjoyed sanctuaries in Cambodia; similarly the Taliban enjoyed sanctuaries in Pakistan. Moreover, Pakistan was a deeply troubled country, and it was nuclear-armed. What Petraeus desperately needed was more time, and inspiration came from a most unlikely source.

During his second inaugural address in November 2009, Karzai cockily forecast that within five years, meaning 2014, his armed forces would be in position to assume full control over all combat operations in Afghanistan. Most American generals did not share his optimism. Karzai, a Pashtun by birth, was playing to his many competing domestic audiences. He wanted to project the image of a powerful nationalist leader eager not only to display his army's might but also to encourage the withdrawal of foreign forces, which had always been the Taliban's number-one demand. At the time, Karzai's timetable was not taken seriously by foreign governments, and the Obama administration was deeply absorbed in an Afghan policy review of its own.

Officials waved him off: there goes Karzai again! Wikileaks cables showed that the Afghan ruler aroused bewilderment, amusement, and dismay among many foreign diplomats. When Karzai was first selected in 2001 to run and represent Afghanistan, he was a popular figure, especially among Americans, who admired his command of English and his love of Starbucks coffee. He was seen as dashing and optimistic, believing as late as 2006 that NATO could "complete the win . . . this year." However, when the insurgency spread, he became more anxious and frenetic. According to the secret cables, he was always seeing conspiracies, often blaming America for his many problems, and sometimes even threatening to join the Taliban as a way of expelling the foreigners and ending the war. "If I had to choose sides today," Karzai told Petraeus and Ambassador Eikenberry, "I'd choose the Taliban."[35] One Wikileaks cable from June 2008, referring to NATO secretary-general Jaap de Hoop Scheffer, said, "SecGen wondered aloud which Karzai would show up for the Afghan Donors Conference in Paris—the erratic Pashtun politician or the rational national leader."[36]

In late January 2010, the new 2014 Karzai timetable was on the agenda of a sixty-nation London conference on Afghanistan, but most of the diplomats were absorbed with a far more tantalizing timetable, announced by President Obama the month before: July 2011, when American forces would begin to pull out of Afghanistan, dependent on conditions on the ground.

Six months later, on July 20, a few weeks after Petraeus assumed his new duties in Afghanistan, representatives from dozens of nations convened in Kabul, where they discussed and endorsed Karzai's 2014 timetable, with qualifications. The final communiqué read: "The international community expressed its support for the president of Afghanistan's objective that the Afghan National Security Forces (ANSF) should lead and conduct military operations in all provinces by the end of 2014."[37] The qualifications related to conditions on the ground. According to Thomas Johnson, an adviser to the U.S. government, prospects were not good. He thought that almost no Afghan army units were able to function without international support.[38] In other words, 2014 as a goal was acceptable, even appealing to those NATO governments under popular pressure to get out of the war, but few considered it a realistic goal for an actual transition of security responsibilities from NATO to Afghan forces.

Only in the late summer of 2010, after Petraeus had begun grappling with insurgent realities, did Karzai's 2014 timetable begin to be taken seriously, not as a realistic goal for transition but rather as a crafty way of shifting the global spotlight from July 2011 to December 2014 or, put more colloquially, of kicking the can down the road. In briefings in Kabul and Washington, 2014 began to be mentioned much more frequently than July 2011, which was, after all, only months away. Thus 2014 was soon to become the timetable of choice.

By accepting 2014 as his goal, Obama also accepted Petraeus's formula for a very long and costly war. The president could have cut it short: the United States was in bad economic shape, and Petraeus (and his team of Pentagon and congressional backers) could have been wrong. But when a president presided over a long war, whether in Vietnam or Afghanistan, change required exceptional courage, which often proved to be in short supply. Obama still imagined himself capable of acting independently, on his own, but he could not confront Petraeus, not so long as Petraeus continued to maintain that he was making progress.

As preparations commenced for the NATO summit meeting in Lisbon in late November, U.S. diplomats began to express admiration for a final communiqué supporting the 2014 timetable for ending combat operations. Karzai's pronouncement had suddenly morphed into a formal NATO objective, primarily because it suited America's needs. Senior U.S. officials did not dismiss the July 2011 timetable; they simply downplayed its significance. Gates spoke of "fairly limited numbers" of troops likely to be withdrawn at that time and of a "thinning of our ranks."[39] Only Biden insisted, "It will not be a token" number.[40] If there were to be any withdrawal, it would likely be a small one, just enough to allow Obama to claim the American withdrawal had begun.

Afghanistan was always a war marked in diplomatic circles by unwelcome scoops and unexpected interviews. One such scoop/interview was published in the *Washington Post* on November 14. Karzai, the day before, had told reporter Joshua Partlow that he strongly disagreed with Petraeus's new and aggressive war strategy. Once again Karzai was asserting his own vision of an Afghan endgame. "The time has come to reduce military operations," the Afghan president said. "The time has come to reduce the presence of, you know, boots in Afghanistan . . . to reduce the intrusiveness into the daily Afghan life." Karzai objected specifically to nighttime raids by U.S. Special Operations Forces, which Petraeus considered his most effective tool for killing Taliban leaders. "The raids are a problem always," Karzai continued. "They have to go away. . . . The Afghan people don't like these raids." Karzai appealed for a smaller foreign footprint. "It's not desirable for the Afghan people either to have 100,000 or more foreign troops going around the country endlessly. . . . We'd like the Afghan countryside—villages, homes, towns—not to be so overwhelmed with the military presence. Life has to be seen [as] more normal."[41]

Petraeus, in a fury, dismissed Karzai's complaints, saying they could render Petraeus's position "untenable."[42]

Still, Karzai, defiant, unbowed, showed up at the Lisbon summit, which was devoted primarily to NATO policy on Afghanistan. Obama, irritated by the Afghan leader's comments, was in no mood for diplomatic niceties. He let Karzai know that he strongly supported Petraeus's use of nighttime raids to kill or capture Taliban commanders. "If we're ponying up billions of dollars," Obama told reporters at the summit, "to ensure that President Karzai can continue to build and develop his country, then he's got to also pay attention to our concerns as well . . . [H]e's got to understand that I've got a bunch of young men and women" who were "in a foreign country being shot at" and "need to protect themselves."[43] Despite Obama's sharp words, there was no sign in Lisbon that the United States was preparing to drop its support of Karzai.

The 2014 timetable was hedged, of course. Obama cautioned, "It is a goal to make sure that we are not still engaged in combat operations of the sort that we're involved with now." NATO secretary-general Anders Fogh Rasmussen put his emphasis on the conditionality of the timetable: "I don't foresee ISAF troops in a combat role beyond 2014, provided of course that the security situation allows us to move into a more supportive role." Mark Sedwill, who was NATO's top civilian in Kabul, relied on plain talk: "2014 is a goal," he said, "not a guarantee," and poor security in parts of the country could delay the transition. He predicted that Afghanistan could still face "eye-watering levels of violence by Western standards." One "senior European official" who heard Petraeus's upbeat briefing ("we have broken the Taliban's momentum") raised a rhetorical question. "Is it true, or not?" he asked. "I'm not so sure." He then added: "To many of us, it begins to have the ring of Vietnam," meaning military briefings that sounded confident and optimistic but were later proven to be inaccurate and misleading.[44]

Shortly after the Lisbon summit, twenty-three academics and experts on Afghanistan wrote the president urging that he change his policy. Military gains may suppress the insurgency but were unlikely to stop it, they warned. A better course was to open a direct negotiation with the Afghan Taliban based in Pakistan.[45]

If there was an Obama response to the experts, it was not disclosed. But the president, in any case, wanted to add a personal touch to his promised yearlong review of his Afghan policy. How better than by visiting the troops before Christmas? Late at night on December 2, in utter secrecy, befitting presidential travel in war zones, Obama left Washington and flew all the way to Bagram Air Base, not too far from Kabul, where he arrived on December 3. He could not see Karzai, reportedly because of bad weather, but he visited with wounded GIs, awarded medals, and delivered a rousing pep talk. "You're going on the offense," he told the troops. "[We're] tired of playing defense."[46] A week later, Gates followed in the president's footsteps and gave his blessings to the policy he helped formulate, pronouncing that he was "convinced that our strategy is working and that we would be able to achieve [our] key goals."[47] There was no doubt that in the presence of thousands of American troops in Helmand and Kandahar provinces, Afghan citizens were feeling more secure. No one knew what would happen when the Americans left, however. Thus the stage was set for the December report on Obama's war policy.

The report was an anticlimax. Though heralded for months as an important read on the president's Afghan policy, it had in fact been leaked, bits and pieces, for weeks; and when, finally, on December 16, 2010, the president appeared before cameras and reporters, he disclosed nothing that had not been known for some time. Most important, in Obama's view, there had been military progress in Helmand and Kandahar provinces, though the progress was fragile and reversible. A brake had been applied to the Taliban's momentum. Unfortunately, on two other fronts, there had not been similar progress: Karzai's government in Kabul remained corrupt and ineffective, and the terrorist safe havens in northwest Pakistan were still safe havens. Pakistan refused to take vigorous action against the terrorists, leaving White House officials to hint that the United States would now step up its drone attacks against the safe havens and even, when necessary, use Special Forces, perhaps even in cross-border operations.[48]

Obama emphasized military progress in his December report, ignoring the consensus judgment of the sixteen American intelligence agencies, which offered a far more pessimistic appraisal of the American effort in Afghanistan. In what are called National Intelligence Estimates, they concluded that there was only a limited chance of success unless the terrorist safe havens in Pakistan were shut down. According to the *New York Times,* "American military commanders say insurgents freely cross from Pakistan into Afghanistan to plant bombs and fight American troops and then return to Pakistan for rest and resupply."[49]

This difference of opinion between American intelligence and the American military was the same in Afghanistan as it was during the Vietnam War. The military, depending on casualty figures, produced optimistic reports for the president during Vietnam, and now in Afghanistan Petraeus and his team stressed military advances and Taliban defeats while the CIA and other intelligence-gatherers kept their eye on other crucial factors, such as continuing corruption in Karzai's government and Pakistan's unwillingness to take on the terrorist safe havens. The CIA was proved right in Vietnam, and may yet be proven right in Afghanistan. But for the moment, Obama was clearly listening to Petraeus.

Indeed, Obama was even grateful for public expressions of support from his military commanders. He was grateful, too, that the United States Army was an all-volunteer force. Otherwise, he was certain that many thousands of antiwar Americans would be demonstrating on college campuses and the Washington Mall by this time. But there were relatively few demands for an end to the war. One reason was that there was no draft, which played so vital a role in galvanizing antiwar sentiment during the Vietnam War. Obama knew he had only limited time to finish the job in Afghanistan and satisfy an American public that was increasingly unhappy and restless about the longest war in American history.

In time, depressing realities crowded into the Oval Office, perhaps none more depressing than the fact, now officially embroidered into NATO strategy, that the United States would be "on the offense," engaged in combat operations in Afghanistan, through at least 2014. And the United States would be "on the offense" when the American people, according to a Pew poll, were rapidly losing confidence in the war. Released on December 7, 2010, the poll showed that only 44 percent of the American people thought U.S. troops ought to remain in Afghanistan until some sort of stability was established. Six months earlier, the number had been 53 percent, a nine-point difference. And whereas 59 percent of the American people had thought the United States would "probably" or "definitely" succeed in Afghanistan, now the number was 49 percent, a steep ten-point drop.[50] The Afghan people were equally restless with the war, according to a poll conducted by the *Washington Post* and several other news organizations. In 2009, 61 percent had said they favored the American troop surge. A year later, the number was 49 percent, and falling. Finally, more than 70 percent said they favored a peace settlement with the Taliban.[51]

If Obama were reelected in 2012, that would mean that by 2014, the new target date, he would have been a war president going on six years, explaining to a tired, reluctant, and increasingly unhappy country why the United States must continue to fight in Afghanistan, especially when the Arab Middle East was in a period of unprecedented upheaval that demanded America's attention and resources. Though he considered himself a post-Vietnam president, he was, like his predecessors, stuck with the haunting legacy of a lost war.

If the war were entirely his to manage, he would probably long ago have set the United States on a slow, steady glide path out of Afghanistan. But, never having served in the military, being young and inexperienced in matters of war and peace, he could not stand up to the Pentagon brass, even though he projected an exceptionally cool front. Shortly after his inauguration, when Gates came knocking at his Oval Office door asking for more troops, Obama yielded; and a few months later, when McChrystal came knocking, trumpeting his approach with one leak after another, again Obama yielded, though after an agonizing review. And when he replaced McChrystal with Petraeus, he effectively yielded operational control of the war to a smart, shrewd, and popular general, who, he knew, could be an overnight political sensation with only a half nod of approval and then, given the sorry state of the nation, probably win the Republican presidential nomination and the White House in 2012. Obama had rolled the dice on Petraeus; his political fortunes were in the general's hands. Petraeus could ask for anything, and Obama would surely have to provide it, or else, as a Washington political pundit mischievously observed, the general could leave Kabul and head straight to Iowa for some presidential campaigning.

A reader of history, Obama knew that a Democratic president could not suffer another military defeat like the thoroughly humiliating American disaster in Vietnam. In 1949, when Democrat Harry Truman was in the White House and China collapsed to communism, Republicans were quick to raise the politically devastating question, "Who lost China?" It was a question they held over the heads of Democrats for decades. Were Obama to show signs of wobbling in Afghanistan or, worse, of abandoning the struggle against the Taliban and al Qaeda, "cutting and running," as it was put, what would stop his Republican opposition, dizzy from the success of their November 2010 election victories, from raising a modern version of the China question: "Who lost Afghanistan?" Their almost certain answer: "Obama."

Appearances in American politics are often as important as reality, and Obama knew he could be perceived as another Democrat who lost another war. To prevent that image from crystallizing in the public arena, Obama was ready to go along with another four years of war. Or maybe longer. Not happily, his aides quickly add. Even the 2014 timetable, after all, was conditions-based. Petraeus, when asked by George Stephanopoulos of ABC whether he was confident about a 2014 endgame, answered: "I think no commander ever is going to come out and say, 'I'm confident that we can do this.' . . . We have to do everything we can to improve the chances of that prospect." He added, "But again, I don't think there are any sure things in this kind of endeavor."[52] On another occasion, Petraeus said: "This is the kind of fight we're in for the rest of our lives and probably our kids' lives."[53]

Obama faced the extraordinary challenges of asymmetrical warfare. Could a modern state, fielding a conventional army, prevail over an insurgency of nationalist guerrillas motivated by medieval religious fervor? In other words, could the United States prevail in Afghanistan? Former President Jimmy Carter looked into his crystal ball and concluded, no. "Anybody who has ever invaded Afghanistan," he told an audience in Washington, D.C., "has come out a loser, and I have serious doubts that we will prevail."[54]

At the U.S. embassy in Kabul, senior American officials privately echo the Jones view. All the "elements of success are there," the general said, "if we can put it all together." Otherwise, look for a "good enough" end, good enough for Afghanistan and politically tolerable for America.[55] Or, as an embassy official put it, "A sense that things are moving forward, not backward may be the best we can hope for."

Vietnam was, in part, a guerrilla war, and the United States lost. Now the American experience in Vietnam seemed to be foreshadowing the possible outcome of the Afghan War: it could well be that the United States could lose that war too.

Why?

First, because Afghanistan was a polyglot mix of tribal traditions, deep religious beliefs, experimentation with modern democracy, ancient rivalries going back to Alexander the Great, modern rivalries involving Pakistan and India, and tantalizing economic prospects appealing to various countries including China and Japan. For all these reasons and more, Afghanistan was a tough nut to crack, even for the United States. Britain had tried, the Soviet Union had tried. Neither had succeeded.

Second, unless American officials were somehow able to solve the problem of Taliban and al Qaeda sanctuaries in the northwest corner of Pakistan, they would not be able to defeat or contain the insurgency in Afghanistan. One was indissolubly linked to the other. Lose a man in Afghanistan, there would always be another in the sanctuaries.

Third, because Afghanistan was such a difficult, time-consuming challenge, the American people, their congressional representatives, and the media, which play a major role in shaping public opinion, would all have to develop the patience of Job to wait out the Taliban; to lose hundreds, possibly thousands, of additional lives and spend billions, possibly trillions, of additional dollars in pursuit of a goal that was still murky and uncertain: all at a time when there were serious doubts in Washington about the capacity of the country to resolve its mounting economic and political problems, and when even the secretary of defense, in a farewell burst of candor, was raising questions about the wisdom of large-scale American interventions in the Middle East. "In my opinion," Gates told a West Point gathering of army officers, "any future defense secretary who advises the president to again send a big American land army into Asia or into the Middle East or Africa should have his head examined, as General MacArthur so delicately put it."[56] When the question arose in March 2011 about whether the United States would use ground troops to unseat Muammar Qaddafi from power in Libya, Gales unceremoniously quashed that option. "Not as long as I'm in this job," he told a congressional committee. The United States had just opened a third front in the Muslim world (after Iraq and Afghanistan), and Gates clearly wanted to contain the American involvement in this UN-sanctioned operation against Libya.[57]

Fourth, because the president, Obama or someone else, would have to have the skill and gumption to level with the American people about the cost and purpose of the war, balanced against the more urgent, demanding needs of the nation. In other words, could any president persuade America that another Vietnam-style war was worth it?

Finally, because the president, Obama or someone else, would have to be prepared to settle for a one-term presidency, so difficult would it be for any president to tell the whole truth about the U.S. effort in Afghanistan and still retain the nation's respect, popularity, and credibility and win reelection.

Obama was stuck, not because he did not want to extricate the United States from the Afghan War but because the mix of American politics and Afghan-Pakistan realities fought him every step of the way. He fancied himself post-Vietnam, but the war that was lost so many years before he assumed office still hovered over his presidency like Banquo's ghost—unwelcome, but unwilling to release its grip. With Obama or any of the other presidents from Ford on, Vietnam was rarely the only reason for a presidential decision about war or peace, but it was always there whenever the question arose about the possible use of American military power.

Up until Vietnam, the United States had been a nation of unlimited vision and capacity. No goal was considered beyond its reach. Even after the Tet offensive in South Vietnam in early 1968, the secretary of state, Dean Rusk, a public servant of towering integrity and dedication, pressed his right thumb down on his coffee table and, to make his point, kept pressing it down on the coffee table, until he said: "When the United States decides to do something, we do it." Seven years later, unimaginable to Rusk and many others of his generation, the United States departed from South Vietnam, a deeply humiliated superpower beaten by a "ragtag" army of communist guerrillas and troops. It lost its first war. Other nations had lost wars, but never the United States, and this lost war cast a long shadow over the Oval Office. Vietnam was a turning point for America, psychologically, politically, and militarily.

In the wake of that defeat, each president had his own way of dealing with the legacy of Vietnam. Ford, eager to prove that the United States still had its fighting spirit, sent massive firepower to liberate the merchant ship *Mayaguez*. Carter, seeking a bloodless presidency, came up short when faced with the Iranian hostage crisis and then sanctioned the creation of a bloody anti-Soviet alliance in Afghanistan. Reagan, persuaded that Americans had been "spooked" by the Vietnam War, refused to retaliate against Islamic radicals who had murdered 241 marines in Beirut, even though he enjoyed projecting a tough image. Bush I, the president perhaps most determined to battle the ghosts of Vietnam, sent a powerful force into the Persian Gulf to expel Saddam Hussein's army from Kuwait. Clinton, facing his own Vietnam-draft-era demons, withdrew from Somalia after Black Hawk Down and then used limited force in Bosnia and Kosovo but accomplished his purpose. Bush II, ready after 9/11 to wage war against al Qaeda in Afghanistan, instead went all-out in Iraq, determined to bury the inhibiting legacy of Vietnam.

Left in the rice paddies and impenetrable jungles of South Vietnam were more than America's vaunted self-confidence and its sense of idealism: 58,000 young Americans had paid the ultimate price there, and for what? As John Kerry asked after returning from military duty in Vietnam, "How do you ask a man to be the last man to die in Vietnam? How do you ask a man to be the last man to die for a mistake?" Updated, those questions might be, Who will be the last American to die for Karzai? Who will be the last American to die in Afghanistan?

Notes

Chapter One (Ford)

1. Gerald R. Ford, Remarks at Robert R. McCormick Tribune Foundation and U.S. Naval Institute Vietnam 1965–75 Symposium, Cantigny, Illinois, March 5, 1997, p. 8.

2. James Chace, *Acheson: The Secretary of State Who Created the American World* (New York: Simon and Schuster, 1998), p. 267.

3. Robert J. McMahon, *The Limits of Empire: The United States and Southeast Asia since World War II* (Columbia University Press, 1999), p. 47.

4. *Public Papers of the Presidents of the United States: Dwight D. Eisenhower* (Government Printing Office, 1960), p. 313.

5. Walter Isaacson, *Kissinger* (New York: Simon and Schuster, 1992), pp. 159–60.

6. Gerald R. Ford, *A Time to Heal* (New York: Harper and Row, 1979), p. 61.

7. Ibid., p. 46.

8. Ibid., p. 61.

9. Ibid., p. 64.

10. Ibid., p. 67.

11. Ford, Remarks, pp. 3–4.

12. Bob Woodward and Christine Parthemore, "No Point in Being Bitter," *Washington Post*, December 31, 2006.

13. Ford, Remarks, p. 5.

14. Ford, *A Time to Heal*, p. 74.

15. Ford, Remarks, p. 6.

16. Ford, *A Time to Heal*, p. 74.

17. Ibid., pp. 82–83.

18. Ibid., pp. 248–49.

19. Ibid., p. 249.

20. Ibid.

21. Ibid., p. 112.

22. Ibid., pp. 121–22.

23. Ibid., pp. 28–29.

24. Ibid., pp. 34–35.

25. Ibid., p. 30.

26. Ibid., pp. 37, 39, 41.

27. Henry Kissinger, *Years of Upheaval* (Boston: Little, Brown, 1982), p. 369.

28. National Intelligence Council, *Estimative Products on Vietnam 1948–1975* (GPO, April 2005), pp. 634–35.

29. David L. Anderson, *Shadow on the White House: Presidents and the Vietnam War 1945–1975* (University Press of Kansas, 1993), pp. 188–89.

30. Stanley Karnow, *Vietnam: A History* (New York: Viking Press, 1983), p. 664.

31. Richard Smyser, in an e-mail, October 28, 2010.

32. Ford, *A Time to Heal*, p. 250.

33. Karnow, *Vietnam: A History*, p. 666.

34. Ron Nessen, *It Sure Looks Different from the Inside* (Chicago: Playboy Press, 1978), pp. 95–96

35. Ron Nessen, author interview, January 17, 2009.

36. Nessen, *It Sure Looks Different from the Inside*, p. 98.

37. Nessen, interview.

38. Ford, *A Time to Heal*, p. 251.

39. Ibid., p. 253.

40. Ibid., p. 254.

41. Anderson, *Shadow on the White House*, p. 198.

42. Ibid., p. 196.

43. Ford, *A Time to Heal*, p. 255.

44. Nessen, *It Sure Looks Different from the Inside*, p. 98.

45. Ford, *A Time to Heal*, p. 256.

46. Karnow, *Vietnam: A History*, p. 667.

47. Ford, *A Time to Heal*, p. 256.

48. Karnow, *Vietnam: A History*, p. 668.

49. Nessen, *It Sure Looks Different from the Inside*, p. 112.

50. Donald Rumsfeld, author interview, October 6, 2009.

51. Ford, *A Time to Heal*, pp. 256–57.

Chapter Two (Ford and the Mayaguez)

1. Bob Woodward, author interview, November 15, 2007.

2. Gerald R. Ford, *A Time to Heal* (New York: Harper and Row, 1979), p. 275.

3. "Armed Forces: A Strong but Risky Show of Force," *Time* Magazine, May 26, 1975.

4. Ron Nessen, *It Sure Looks Different from the Inside* (Chicago: Playboy Press, 1978), p. 118.

5. Ford, *A Time to Heal*, p. 276

6. "Armed Forces: A Strong but Risky Show of Force."

7. Ibid.

8. Ibid.

9. Ford, *A Time to Heal*, p. 278.

10. See www.paperlessarchives.com/ss_mayaguez_.html.

11. Ford, *A Time to Heal*, p. 279.

12. Ibid., p. 280.

13. Lieutenant Colonel John F. Guilmartin Jr., "The *Mayaguez* Incident, 12–15 May 1975," *Air & Space Power Journal* (Spring 2005) (www.airpower.maxwell.af.mil/airchronicles/apj/apj05/spr05/vignette3.html).

14. Ford, *A Time to Heal*, p. 282.

15. Guilmartin, "The *Mayaguez* Incident."

16. Nessen, *It Sure Looks Different*, pp. 123–24.

17. Ford, *A Time to Heal*, p. 281.

18. Nessen, *It Sure Looks Different*, p. 124.

19. Ibid., pp. 124–25.

20. Ibid., pp. 125–26.

21. Ibid., p. 127.

22. Ibid., pp. 128–29.

23. Ibid., pp. 129–30.

24. "Armed Forces: A Strong but Risky Show of Force."

25. Ford, *A Time to Heal*, p. 284.

26. Ibid., p. 283.

27. "Armed Forces: A Strong but Risky Show of Force."

28. Ibid., p. 284.

29. Ibid., p. 285.

Chapter Three (Carter)

1. Morton Abramowitz, author interview, December 21, 2007.

2. James Wooten, *Dasher: The Roots and the Rising of Jimmy Carter* (New York: Summit Books, 1978), pp. 168–69.

3. Peter G. Bourne, *Jimmy Carter: A Comprehensive Biography from Plains to Postpresidency* (New York: Scribner, 1997), pp. 156–57.

4. Jody Powell, author interview, March 23, 2009.

5. Andrew J. Glass, author interview, April 21, 2009.

6. Jack Carter, Oral History, Jimmy Carter Library and Museum, June 25, 2003 (www.jimmycarterlibrary.gov).

7. Alec Russell, "Jack Carter Steps Out of His Father's Shadow at 58," December 12, 2005 (telegraph.co.uk).

8. Wooten, *Dasher*, p. 320.

9. *Governor Jimmy Carter: Addresses and Public Papers, 1971–1975*, pp. 134–35.

10. Jules Witcover, *Marathon: The Pursuit of the Presidency 1972–1976* (New York: Viking Press, 1977), p. 109.

11. Glass, interview, April 21, 2009.

12. PBS, *American Experience*, "Jimmy Carter" (pbs.org/wgbh/americanexperience/features/transcript/carter-transcript/).

13. Walter Mondale, author interview, May 20, 2009.

14. Kenneth E. Morris, *Jimmy Carter: American Moralist* (University of Georgia Press, 1996), pp. 220–21.

15. Gerald R. Ford, *A Time to Heal* (New York: Harper and Row, 1979), pp. 181–82.

16. Patrick Anderson, *Electing Jimmy Carter: The Campaign of 1976* (Louisiana State University Press, 1994), pp. 24–25.

17. Ford, *A Time to Heal,* pp. 415–16.

18. Witcover, *Marathon,* p. 614.

19. *Public Papers of the Presidents of the United States: Jimmy Carter* (GPO, 1977), p. 5.

20. Andrew Glass, "Carter Pardons Draft Dodgers Jan. 21, 1977," *Politico,* January 21, 2008 (www.politico.com).

21. "Vietnam and the Presidency: Interview with President Carter," March 11, 2006, J. F. Kennedy Presidential Library and Museum (www.jfklibrary.org).

22. Zbigniew Brzezinski, "Top Secret" memo to Carter, February 19, 1977. (Part of a series of memos from Brzezinski to Carter cited in this chapter.)

23. Brzezinski, memo, February 26, 1977.

24. Leslie H. Gelb, *Power Rules* (New York: HarperCollins Publishers, 2009), p. 56.

25. Ibid.

26. Brzezinski, memo, February 19, 1977.

27. Zbigniew Brzezinski, author interview, March 10, 2009.

28. Tom DeFrank, author interview, April 21, 2009.

29. Alexei Arbatov, author interview, April 10, 2009.

30. Vladimir Lukin, author interview, April 30, 2009.

31. Glass, interview, April 21, 2009.

32. Personal conversations with Menachem Begin.

33. "Nation: Ordeal in the Mountains," *Time* Magazine, October 2, 1978 (www.time.com).

34. Series of *New York Times* articles, September 4–30, 1978.

35. Sergei Rogov, author interview, May 2, 2009.

36. Ibid.

37. Brzezinski, memo, May 5, 1978.

38. Brzezinski, memo, February 26, 1977.

39. Edward Crankshaw, (London) *Sunday Times,* July 30, 1978.

40. Mondale, interview, May 20, 2009.

41. Brzezinski, memo, March 11, 1977.

42. Jimmy Carter, *Keeping Faith: Memoirs of a President* (New York: Bantam, 1982), pp. 189–90.

43. Brzezinski, memo, April 22, 1977.

44. Brzezinski, interview, March 10, 2009.

45. Brzezinski memo, April 21, 1978.

46. Jimmy Carter, letter, obtained from reliable source.

47. Brzezinski, interview, March 10, 2009.

48. Carter, *Keeping Faith,* pp. 195–99.

49. Ibid., pp. 202–05.

50. Brzezinski, memo, September 13, 1979.

51. Marvin Kalb, notes from Brzezinski briefing, November 7, 1978.

52. Ibid.

53. Carter, *Keeping Faith,* p. 438.

54. "BBC News, "Exiled Ayatollah Khomeini Returns to Iran," *On This Day,* February 1, 1979 (www.bbc.co.uk).

55. David Aaron, author interview, May 12, 2009.

56. Ibid.

57. Rosalynn Carter, *First Lady from Plains* (New York: Houghton Mifflin, 1984), p. 321.

58. Mondale, interview, May 20, 2009.

59. Ibid.

60. Mark Bowden, "The Desert One Debacle," *Atlantic* Online, May 2006 (theatlantic.com).

61. Aaron, interview, May 12, 2009.

62. Bowden, "Desert One Debacle."

63. Ibid.

64. Zbigniew Brzezinski, interview, *Le Nouvel Observateur,* January 15–21, 1998 (www.globalresearch.ca).

65. Robert M. Gates, *From the Shadows* (New York: Simon and Schuster, 1996), p. 131.

66. Ibid., p. 131.

67. Ibid., p. 132.

68. Ibid., pp. 144–45.

69. Ibid., p. 146.

70. Mondale, interview, May 20, 2009.

71. Rogov, interview, May 2, 2009.

72. Arbatov, interview, April 10, 2009.

73. Gates, *From the Shadows,* pp. 147–48.

74. Brzezinski, interview, March 10, 2009.

75. Deborah Kalb, Gerhard Peters, and John T. Woolley, eds., *State of the Union: Presidential Rhetoric from Woodrow Wilson to George W. Bush* (Washington: CQ Press, 2007), p. 799.

76. Anatoly Dobrynin, *In Confidence* (New York: Times Books, 1995), p. 445.

77. Ibid., pp. 443–48.

78. "Southwest Asia: Selling the Carter Doctrine," *Time* Magazine, February 18, 1980.

79. Gates, *From the Shadows,* p. 148.

80. Aaron, interview, May 12, 2009.

81. Brzezinski, memo, January 26, 1979.

Chapter Four (Reagan)

1. Robert McFarlane, author interview, April 13, 2009.

2. Theodore H. White, *America in Search of Itself: The Making of the President 1956–1980* (New York: Harper and Row, 1982), pp. 306–07.

3. Lou Cannon, *President Reagan: The Role of a Lifetime* (New York: Simon and Schuster, 1991), p. 335.

4. John Patrick Diggins, *Ronald Reagan: Fate, Freedom and the Making of History* (New York: W. W. Norton, 2007), pp. 147–48.

5. Kiron K. Skinner, Annelise Anderson, and Martin Anderson, eds., *Reagan: A Life in Letters* (New York: Free Press, 2003), p. 174.

6. Ibid., p. 36.

7. Elizabeth Drew, *Portrait of an Election: The 1980 Presidential Campaign* (New York: Simon and Schuster, 1981), p. 118.

8. Ronald Reagan, *An American Life* (New York: Simon and Schuster, 1990), p. 133.

9. Lou Cannon, *Governor Reagan: His Rise to Power* (New York: Public Affairs, 2003), p. 479.

10. Jack W. Germond and Jules Witcover, *Blue Smoke & Mirrors: How Reagan Won and Why Carter Lost the Election of 1980* (New York: Viking Press, 1981), p. 214.

11. Terence Hunt, "Reagan: No Regrets on Vietnam Statement," Associated Press, August 23, 1980.

12. Richard Perle, author interview, February 20, 2009.

13. Reagan, *An American Life*, p. 267.

14. Ibid., p. 266.

15. See http://whitehouse.gov/omb/budget/fy2005/pdf/hist.pdf.

16. Frank Carlucci, author interview, January 27, 2009.

17. James Webb, author interview, September 16, 2008.

18. Lawrence Wilkerson, author interview, February 20, 2009.

19. Milton Bearden, author interview, March 20, 2009.

20. Robert McFarlane, author interview, April 13, 2009.

21. Bearden, interview, March 20, 2009.

22. Morton Abramowitz, author interview, December 21, 2007.

23. Ronald Reagan, *The Reagan Diaries* (New York: HarperCollins, 2007), p. 169.

24. Reagan, *An American Life*, p. 449.

25. Robert C. McFarlane and Zofia Smardz, *Special Trust* (New York: Cadell and Davies, 1994), p. 263.

26. Ibid., p. 262.

27. Ibid.

28. Reagan, *An American Life*, pp. 450–51.

29. Ibid., p. 451.

30. Ibid., p. 452.

31. McFarlane and Smardz, *Special Trust*, p. 262.

32. George Shultz, author interview, July 1, 2009.

33. Thomas L. Friedman, "Beirut Death Toll at 161 Americans," *New York Times,* October 24, 1983.

34. Ibid.

35. Ibid.

36. "Follow the Flag," A&E Network, October 22, 1993.

37. William Perry, author interview, July 16, 2009.

38. Ibid.

39. McFarlane and Smardz, *Special Trust*, p. 206.

40. Ibid., pp. 208–09.

41. Ibid., pp. 209–10.

42. Reagan, *Reagan Diaries*, p. 100.

43. McFarlane and Smardz, *Special Trust*, p. 211.

44. Ibid., p. 211.

45. Ibid., pp. 211–12.

46. "Transcript of President Reagan's Speech on Sending Marines into Lebanon," *New York Times,* September 21, 1982.

47. Thomas L. Friedman, *From Beirut to Jerusalem* (New York: Anchor Books, 1990), pp. 194–97.

48. Ibid., pp. 194–97.

49. Reagan, *Reagan Diaries*, p. 137.

50. Ibid., p. 145.

51. McFarlane and Smardz, *Special Trust*, p. 250.

52. Ibid., pp. 250–51.

53. Thomas L. Friedman, *From Beirut to Jerusalem*, p. 252.

54. McFarlane and Smardz, *Special Trust*, p. 252.

55. Ibid., pp. 253–54.

56. Robert Timberg, *The Nightingale's Song* (New York: Simon and Schuster, 1995), p. 330.

57. Reagan, *An American Life*, p. 466.

58. Ibid., p. 462.

59. Robert McFarlane, author interview, April 22, 2010.

60. Timberg, *The Nightingale's Song*, p. 285.

61. McFarlane and Smardz, *Special Trust*, p. 267.

62. Ibid., p. 270.

63. James Lyons, "Grim Anniversary," *Washington Times*, October 19, 2008.

64. Ibid.

65. McFarlane and Smardz, *Special Trust*, p. 270.

66. McFarlane, interview, April 13, 2009.

67. Reagan, *Reagan Diaries*, pp. 191–92.

68. Shultz, interview, July 1, 2009.

69. Reagan, *Reagan Diaries*, pp. 194–95.

70. "Follow the Flag."

71. John W. Vessey Jr., author interview, July 2, 2009.

72. "Follow the Flag."

73. David Brooks, "The Uncertainty Factor," *New York Times*, April 13, 2004.

74. Reagan, *Reagan Diaries*, p. 197.

75. McFarlane and Smardz, *Special Trust,* p. 270.

76. "Follow the Flag."

77. McFarlane, interview, April 13, 2009.

78. Ibid.

79. Ibid.

80. McFarlane and Smardz, *Special Trust*, p. 271.

81. McFarlane, interview, April 13, 2009.

82. Shultz, interview, July 1, 2009.

83. Reagan, *Reagan Diaries*, p. 198.

84. McFarlane and Smardz, *Special Trust*, p. 273.

85. Reagan, *Reagan Diaries*, p. 214.

86. "Most of U.S. Forces to Board Ships within 30 Days, President Says," *New York Times*, February 16, 1984.

87. Robert McFarlane, "From Beirut to 9/11," *New York Times*, October 23, 2008.

88. Reagan, *An American Life*, p. 465.

89. Abramowitz, interview, December 21, 2007.

90. Reagan, *An American Life*, p. 465.

91. Ibid., p. 466.

92. Friedman, *From Beirut to Jerusalem*, p. 205.

93. Reagan, *An American Life*, p. 466.

94. Steve Coll, *Ghost Wars* (New York: Penguin, 2004), p. 147.

95. Bearden, interview, March 20, 2009.

96. Adam Curtis, "The Power of Nightmares," BBC, October 27, 2004 (www.want toknow.info/war/power_of_nightmares_transcript_2).

97. Bearden, interview, March 20, 2009.

98. Coll, *Ghost Wars*, pp. 180–84.

99. Alexei Arbatov, author interview, April 10, 2009.

100. Alexander Lyakhovsky, *Tragedy and Valor of Afghan,* translated by Svetlana Savranskaya (Moscow: Iskon, 1995), appendix II.

Chapter Five (Bush I)

1. Jonathan Wolman, "Baby Boomers Will Understand," Associated Press, August 19, 1988.

2. Jules Witcover, *Crapshoot: Rolling the Dice on the Vice Presidency* (New York: Crown, 1992), p. 42.

3. Charles Black, author interview, August 13, 2009.

4. Witcover, *Crapshoot*, p. 42.

5. See excerpts from Colin L. Powell, "U.S. Forces: Challenges Ahead," *Foreign Affairs*, Winter 1992 (www.pbs.org/wgbh/pages/frontline/shows/military/force/powell.html).

6. "Talking Global: Diplomacy in a Dangerous World," *Nikkei Weekly*, March 26, 2007.

7. Powell, *My American Journey*, p. 207.

8. Caspar W. Weinberger, "The Uses of Military Power," speech at the National Press Club, November 28, 1984, *Frontline*, WGBH Educational Foundation (www.pbs.org/wgbh/pages/frontline/shows/military/force/weinberger.html).

9. Ronald Reagan, *An American Life* (New York: Simon and Schuster, 1990), p. 466.

10. Weinberger, "The Uses of Military Power."

11. Frank Carlucci, author interview, January 27, 2009.

12. Colin Powell, author interview, November 13, 2008.

13. Weinberger, "The Uses of Military Power."

14. Powell, "U.S. Forces: Challenges Ahead."

15. Powell, *My American Journey*, p. 148.

16. Lawrence Wilkerson, author interview, February 20, 2009.

17. Herbert S. Parmet, *George Bush: The Life of a Lone Star Yankee* (New Brunswick, N.J.: Transaction, 2001), p. 116.

18. Timothy Naftali, *George H. W. Bush* (New York: Times Books, 2007), p. 17.

19. George Bush, *All the Best, George Bush: My Life in Letters and Other Writings* (New York: Scribner, 1999), pp. 111–13.

20. Ibid., p. 127.

21. Marvin Kalb, "Nine Ways to Elect a President," *New York Times*, May 5, 2007.

22. "Voters Now Give Bush Edge over Dukakis, a Poll Shows," Associated Press, August 22, 1988 (www.nytimes.com).

23. Dan Quayle, *Standing Firm* (New York: HarperCollins, 1994), p. 18.

24. Parmet, *George Bush*, p. 346.

25. Witcover, *Crapshoot*, p. 341.

26. Elizabeth Drew, *Election Journal: Political Events of 1987–88* (New York: William Morrow, 1989), p. 249.

27. Black, interview, August 13, 2009.

28. Quayle, *Standing Firm*, p. 30.

29. "Enough on the Guard, More on Quayle," Editorial, *New York Times*, August 24, 1988.

30. Quayle, *Standing Firm*, p. 11.

31. Witcover, *Crapshoot*, p. 361.

32. Michael Isikoff and Joe Pichirallo, "Allegations Called 'Lies' by Quayle," *Washington Post*, August 24, 1988.

33. Robert Dvorchak, "Quayle's Biography Inflates State Job; Quayle Concedes Error," Associated Press, August 27, 1988.

34. Tim Ahern, "Quayle Eulogized Head of Draft, Spoke on Vietnam," Associated Press, August 23, 1988.

35. Bob Woodward and David S. Broder, *The Man Who Would Be President: Dan Quayle* (New York: Simon and Schuster, 1992), p. 194.

36. Parmet, *George Bush*, p. 349.

37. Robert M. Gates, *From the Shadows: The Ultimate Insider's Story of Five Presidents and How They Won the Cold War* (New York: Simon and Schuster, 1996), p. 483.

38. Bill Kristol, author interview, August 24, 2009.

39. Gates, *From the Shadows*, p. 486.

40. Ibid., p. 487.

41. Mikhail Gorbachev, interview, PBS *Frontline* oral history series on Persian Gulf War (www.pbs.org/wgbh/pages/frontline/gulf /oral).

42. Brent Scowcroft, interview, PBS *Frontline* oral history series on Persian Gulf War.

43. "Confrontation in the Gulf," *New York Times*, September 23, 1990.

44. Colin Powell interview, PBS *Frontline* oral history series on Persian Gulf War.

45. Ibid.

46. General Norman Schwarzkopf and Powell interviews, PBS *Frontline* oral history series on Persian Gulf War.

47. Scowcroft, interview, PBS *Frontline*.

48. Parmet, *George Bush,* p. 450.

49. Scowcroft, interview, PBS *Frontline.*

50. Parmet, *George Bush*, p. 456.

51. Scowcroft, interview PBS *Frontline.*

52. Powell, interview, PBS *Frontline.*

53. Ibid.

54. Ibid.

55. Powell, interview, November 13, 2008.

56. Powell, interview, PBS *Frontline.*

57. Ibid.

58. Schwarzkopf, interview, PBS *Frontline.*

59. James A. Baker III, *The Politics of Diplomacy, Revolution, War and Peace, 1989–1992* (New York: G. P. Putnam's Sons, 1995), p. 2.

60. Ibid., p. 3.

61. Ibid., p. 5.

62. Ibid., p. 6.

63. Ibid., p. 10.

64. Ibid., p. 11.

65. Ibid., pp. 11–12.

66. Ibid., p. 13.

67. Ibid., p. 13.

68. Ibid., p. 14.

69. Ibid., p. 14.

70. Ibid., p. 14.

71. Ibid., p. 15.

72. Ibid., p. 15.

73. Ibid., p. 16.

74. George Bush and Brent Scowcroft, *A World Transformed* (New York: Vintage Books, 1998), p. 326.

75. Baker, *The Politics of Diplomacy*, p. 16.

76. Powell, interview, PBS *Frontline.*

77. Ibid.

78. Ibid.

79. Ibid.

80. Ibid.

81. Powell, *My American Journey*, p. 488.

82. Bush and Scowcroft, *A World Transformed*, p. 394.

83. Ibid., p. 354.

84. Powell, interview, PBS *Frontline.*

85. Ibid.

86. Ibid.

87. Michael R. Gordon, "Mideast Tensions: Bush Sends New Units to Gulf to Provide 'Offensive Option,'" *New York Times*, November 9, 1990.

88. Bush and Scowcroft, *A World Transformed*, p. 396.

89. Ibid., p. 396.

90. Ibid., p. 397.

91. Ibid., p. 398.

92. Baker, *The Politics of Diplomacy*, pp. 325–27.

93. Bush and Scowcroft, *A World Transformed*, p. 418.

94. Ibid., p. 408.

95. Ibid., pp. 434–35.

96. Baker, *The Politics of Diplomacy*, p. 355.

97. Bush and Scowcroft, *A World Transformed*, pp. 441–42.

98. Baker, *The Politics of Diplomacy*, pp. 359–64.

99. Ibid.

100. Ibid.

101. Bush and Scowcroft, *A World Transformed*, pp. 445–46.

102. Powell, interview, PBS *Frontline*.

103. Ibid.

104. Ibid.

105. Former President George H. W. Bush and members of his inner circle discuss the first Gulf War, NBC News, January 21, 2011 (www6.lexisnexis.com/publisher/End User?Action=UserDisplayFullDocument&orgId=574&topicId=100007221&docId=l:1344119973&start=31).

106. Powell, interview, PBS *Frontline*.

107. Ibid.

108. George Bush, Remarks to the American Legislative Exchange Council, Washington, D.C., March 1, 1991 (http://bushlibrary.tamu.edu/research/public_papers.php?id=2754&year=1991&month=3).

109. George Bush, radio address to United States Armed Forces stationed in the Persian Gulf Region, March 2, 1991, broadcast over Armed Forces Radio Network (http://bushlibrary.tamu.edu/research/public_papers.php?id=2758&year=1991&month=3).

110. Powell, interview, PBS *Frontline*.

Chapter Six (Clinton)

1. Bill Clinton, *My Life* (New York: Alfred A. Knopf, 2004), p. 104.

2. Taylor Branch, *The Clinton Tapes* (New York: Simon and Schuster, 2009), p. 632.

3. David E. Sanger, "Clinton in Vietnam: The American Missing," *New York Times*, November 19, 2000.

4. Rajiv Chandrasekaran, "Clinton Faces War's Open Wounds," *Washington Post*, November 19, 2000.

5. Sanger, "Clinton in Vietnam."

6. Clinton, *My Life*, p. 931.

7. Branch, *The Clinton Tapes*, p. 568.

8. David E. Sanger, "Clinton in Hanoi, Intent on Forging New Relationship," *New York Times*, November 17, 2000.

9. Hillary Rodham Clinton, *Living History* (New York: Simon and Schuster, 2003), p. 240.

10. Sanger, "Clinton in Hanoi."

11. Madeleine Albright, author interview, September 17, 2009.

12. Anthony Lake, author interview, February 8, 2008.

13. Strobe Talbott, author interview, December 4, 2007.

14. William Cohen, author interview, September 21, 2009.

15. Sandy Berger, author interview, December 14, 2007.

16. Clinton, *My Life*, p. 94.

17. David Maraniss, *First in His Class* (New York: Touchstone, 1995), p. 106.

18. Clinton, *My Life*, p. 120.

19. Ibid., p. 104.

20. Maraniss, *First in His Class*, pp. 118–19.

21. Clinton, *My Life*, p. 134.

22. Ibid., p. 144.

23. Ibid., p. 147.

24. Ibid., p. 151.

25. Maraniss, *First in His Class*, p. 165.

26. Ibid., p. 171.

27. Clinton, *My Life*, p. 155.

28. Ibid., p. 157.

29. Ibid., p. 158; Maraniss, *First in His Class*, p. 180.

30. Clinton, *My Life*, pp. 169–70; Maraniss, *First in His Class*, pp. 211–13.

31. Maraniss, *First in His Class*, p. 190.

32. Clinton, *My Life*, p. 159.

33. Ibid., p. 159.

34. See www.pbs.org/wgbh/pages/frontline/shows/clinton/etc/draftletter.html.

35. Colin L. Powell with Joseph E. Persico, *My American Journey* (New York: Random House, 1995), pp. 581–82.

36. Clinton, *My Life*, p. 173.

37. Ibid., p. 341.

38. David Halberstam, *War in a Time of Peace: Bush, Clinton and the Generals* (New York: Simon and Schuster, 2001), p. 19.

39. Dan Balz, "Clinton, Kerrey: A New Set of Questions," *Washington Post*, January 18, 1992.

40. George Stephanopoulos, *All Too Human: A Political Education* (Boston: Little, Brown, 1999), pp. 70–71.

41. Elizabeth Kolbert, "A Trap for Candidates," *New York Times*, February 9, 1992.

42. Mary Matalin and James Carville, *All's Fair: Love, War, and Running for President* (New York: Random House, 1994), p. 99.

43. Jeffrey H. Birnbaum, "Clinton Received a Vietnam Draft Deferment for an ROTC Program That He Never Joined," *Wall Street Journal*, February 6, 1992.

44. Stephanopoulos, *All Too Human*, p. 74; Matalin and Carville, *All's Fair*, p. 135.

45. Stephanopoulos, *All Too Human*, p. 74.

46. Matalin and Carville, *All's Fair*, p. 137.

47. Ibid., p. 138.

48. ABC News, *Nightline*, transcript, February 12, 1992.

49. Jack Germond and Jules Witcover, *Mad as Hell: Revolt at the Ballot Box, 1992* (New York: Warner Books, 1993), p. 205.

50. Stephanopoulos, *All Too Human*, p. 77.

51. Clinton, *My Life*, p. 427.

52. Monica Crowley, *Nixon in Winter* (New York: Random House, 1998), p. 260.

53. Clinton, *My Life*, p. 445.

54. Berger, interview, December 14, 2007.

55. Cohen, interview, September 21, 2009.

56. Berger, interview, December 14, 2007.

57. Ibid.

58. Leon Fuerth, author interview, June 26, 2008.

59. Albright, interview, September 17, 2009.

60. Richard Cohen, "It's Not Another Vietnam," *Washington Post*, December 1, 1992.

61. Raymond Bonner, "Buy Up the Somalis' Guns," *New York Times*, December 2, 1992.

62. George J. Church, "Somalia: Anatomy of a Disaster," *Time* Magazine, October 18, 1993.

63. Albright, interview, September 17, 2009.

64. Church, "Somalia: Anatomy of a Disaster."

65. Halberstam, *War in a Time of Peace*, p. 261.

66. Cohen, interview, September 21, 2009.

67. William Perry, author interview, July 16, 2009.

68. John F. Harris, *The Survivor: Bill Clinton in the White House* (New York: Random House, 2005), p. 122.

69. Elizabeth Drew, *On the Edge: The Clinton Presidency* (New York: Simon and Schuster, 1994), p. 328.

70. Church, "Somalia: Anatomy of a Disaster."

71. Perry, interview, July 16, 2009.

72. Berger, interview, December 14, 2007.

73. Michael Dobbs, "Despite Risks, Intervention Boosts Clinton," *Washington Post*, October 14, 1996.

74. Madeleine Albright, *Madam Secretary: A Memoir* (New York: Hyperion, 2003), p. 145.

75. Powell, *My American Journey*, pp. 586, 588.

76. Halberstam, *War in a Time of Peace*, p. 265.

77. Talbott, interview, December 4, 2007.

78. Morton Abramowitz, author interview, December 21, 2007.

79. Perry, interview, July 16, 2009.

80. Richard A. Clarke, *Against All Enemies* (New York: Simon and Schuster, 2004), p. 88.

81. Ibid., p. 41.

82. Albright, *Madam Secretary*, p. 177.

83. Ibid., p. 182.

84. Michael Dobbs, *Madeleine Albright: A Twentieth-Century Odyssey* (New York: Henry Holt, 1999), p. 359.

85. Albright, *Madam Secretary*, p. 180.

86. Warren Christopher, *Chances of a Lifetime: A Memoir* (New York: Scribner, 2001), p. 252.

87. Halberstam, *War in a Time of Peace*, p. 32.

88. Clinton, *Living History,* pp. 169–70.

89. Clinton, *My Life*, pp. 512–13.

90. Richard Holbrooke, *To End a War* (New York: Random House, 1998), pp. 92–93.

91. Donald Rumsfeld, author interview, October 6, 2009.

92. David Maraniss, "First and Last," *Washington Post* Magazine, October 27, 1996.

93. Martin Walker, "Dole Woos War Generation," (Manchester) *Guardian,* August 16, 1996.

94. Ron Marsico, "Veterans Split on Candidates' War Records," (Newark) *Star-Ledger,* May 28, 1996.

95. Katharine Q. Seelye, "Dole Makes Appeal to Patriotism in Texas," *New York Times,* June 30, 1996.

96. Stephanopoulos, *All Too Human*, p. 415.

97. Michael Dobbs, "Fewer Doubts about Clinton as Commander," *Washington Post,* September 6, 1996.

98. Eric Black, "Dole's Resume Doesn't Appear to Help," (Minneapolis) *Star-Tribune,* October 20, 1996.

99. Maraniss, "First and Last."

100. Richard Benedetto, "Is Dole's Heroism a Political Liability?" *Denver Post*, May 27, 1996.

101. Cohen, interview, September 21, 2009.

102. Ibid.

103. Albright, interview, September 17, 2009.

104. Halberstam, *War in a Time of Peace*, p. 398.

105. Clinton, *My Life*, pp. 850–51.

106. Halberstam, *War in a Time of Peace*, pp. 423–25.

107. Albright, *Madam Secretary*, p. 408.

108. Cohen, interview, September 21, 2009.

109. Berger, interview, December 14, 2007.

110. Ibid.

111. Albright, interview, September 17, 2009.

112. Berger, interview, December 14, 2007.

113. Ibid.; Albright, interview, September 17, 2009.

114. Clinton, *My Life*, p. 851.

Chapter Seven (Bush II)

1. Bob Woodward, *Bush at War* (New York: Simon and Schuster, 2002), p. 38.

2. Donald Rumsfeld, author interview, October 6, 2009.

3. Frank Bruni, "Succeeding, from the Ruling Class, Meet the Next President," *New York Times*, March 12, 2000.

4. Bill Minutaglio, *First Son: George W. Bush and the Bush Family Dynasty* (New York: Three Rivers Press, 1999; afterword, 2001), p. 115.

5. Jacob Weisberg, *The Bush Tragedy* (New York: Random House, 2008), p. xx.

6. George W. Bush, *A Charge to Keep* (New York: William Morrow, 1999), p. 50.

7. Minutaglio, *First Son*, pp. 115–16.

8. Bush, *A Charge to Keep*, p. 50.

9. Ibid., pp. 50–51.

10. George Lardner Jr. and Lois Romano, "At Height of Vietnam, Graduate Picks Guard," *Washington Post*, July 28, 1999.

11. James Moore and Wayne Slater, *Bush's Brain: How Karl Rove Made George W. Bush Presidential* (Hoboken, N.J.: John Wiley & Sons, 2003), pp. 306–07.

12. Richard Serrano, "Bush Treated Well in Guard," *Los Angeles Times*, July 4, 1999.

13. Lardner and Romano, "At Height of Vietnam, Graduate Picks Guard."

14. Minutaglio, *First Son*, p. 125.

15. Bush, *A Charge to Keep*, p. 55.

16. Ibid., p. 55.

17. Ann Richards, author interview, April 20, 1998.

18. Moore and Slater, *Bush's Brain*, p. 303.

19. Ibid., p. 303.

20. David Maraniss and Ellen Nakashima, *The Prince of Tennessee* (New York: Touchstone, 2000), p. 91.

21. Bill Turque, *Inventing Al Gore* (New York: Houghton Mifflin, 2000), p. 59.

22. Maraniss and Nakashima, *The Prince of Tennessee*, p. 102.

23. Kyle Longley, *Senator Albert Gore, Sr.* (Louisiana State University Press, 2004), pp. 220–21.

24. David Maraniss and Ellen Nakashima, "Gore: To Serve or Not to Serve," *Washington Post*, December 29, 1999.

25. Turque, *Inventing Al Gore*, p. 73.

26. Brigitte Greenberg, "Gore to Stress Vietnam Service," Associated Press Online, August 22, 2000.

27. Turque, *Inventing Al Gore*, p. 85.

28. Elaine Kamarck, "Bill and Al's Excellent Adventure," Harvard University, Kennedy School of Government, March 2006.

29. Roger Simon, *Divided We Stand* (New York: Crown, 2001), p. 77.

30. Charles Krauthammer, "Heroism of Vietnam Endurance Sets McCain Apart," *Deseret News*, March 12, 2000.

31. David Woo, "Interest in McCain Candidacy Tests Vietnam Era Attitudes," Newhouse News Service, February 3, 2000.

32. Allen G. Breed, "Bush, McCain Bid for 'Military' Vote," Associated Press Online, February 6, 2000; Richard L. Berke, "Big Turnout Seen for South Carolina Primary," *New York Times*, February 19, 2000.

33. Breed, "Bush, McCain Bid for 'Military' Vote."

34. Marc Lacey, "Five Senators Rebuke Bush for Criticism of McCain," *New York Times*, February 5, 2000.

35. R. G. Ratcliffe and Greg McDonald, "Veterans Group Attacks McCain's Voting Record," *Houston Chronicle*, February 4, 2000.

36. Simon, *Divided We Stand*, p. 99.

37. See http://transcripts.cnn.com/TRANSCRIPTS/0002/15/lkl.00.html.

38. Berke, "Big Turnout Seen for South Carolina Primary."

39. Paul Alexander, *Man of the People: The Life of John McCain* (Hoboken, N.J.: John Wiley & Sons, 2003), p. 263.

40. Lou Dubose, Jan Reid, and Carl M. Cannon, *Boy Genius* (New York: Public Affairs, 2003), p. 142.

41. C. W. Nevins, Marc Sandalow, and John Wildermuth, "McCain Criticized for Slur," *San Francisco Chronicle,* February 18, 2000.

42. Rajiv Chandrasekaran, "In Vietnam, McCain Finds Unlikely Allies," *Washington Post,* February 28, 2000.

43. Claudia Smith Brinson, "There Are No Monolithic Voting Blocs," (Columbia, S.C.) *State,* February 26, 2000.

44. Walter V. Robinson, "1-Year Gap in Bush's Guard Duty," *Boston Globe,* May 23, 2000.

45. Walter V. Robinson, "Bush Defends Guard Record," *Boston Globe,* May 24, 2000.

46. Walter V. Robinson, "Questions Remain on Bush's Service as Guard Pilot," *Boston Globe,* October 31, 2000.

47. Walter V. Robinson, "Kerrey Blasts Bush on Service," *Boston Globe,* November 1, 2000.

48. Scott Shepard, "Gore Emphasizes War Record in Speech to American Legion," Cox News Service, September 8, 1999.

49. Curtis Wilkie, "Gore's Letters from Vietnam Era Reveal He Struggled with Decision to Enlist," *Boston Globe,* October 2, 1999.

50. Laurence McQuillan, "Gore Turned Down Guard Offer in '69," *USA Today,* November 12, 1999.

51. Laurence McQuillan, "Vietnam Still Vivid, Visceral for Al Gore," *USA Today,* November 12, 1999.

52. Scott Shepard, "Gore's Vietnam Days Loom Large in Foreign Policy Views," Cox News Service, May 28, 2000.

53. Sandra Sobieraj, "Army Days Loom Large in Gore's Campaign," Associated Press, May 29, 2000.

54. Frank Bruni, "Bush Questions Gore's Fitness for Commander in Chief," *New York Times,* May 31, 2000.

55. George C. Wilson, "Cheney Believes Gorbachev Sincere," *Washington Post,* April 5, 1989.

56. Richard Sisk with Kenneth R. Bazinet, "Dems Blast GOP Pair's Viet Record," (New York) *Daily News,* August 1, 2000.

57. Walter V. Robinson, "Republican Ticket Lets a Military Connection Slip," *Boston Globe,* July 28, 2000.

58. Joseph Lieberman, author interview, July 21, 2007.

59. "Transcript of Debate between Vice President Gore and Governor Bush," *New York Times,* October 4, 2000.

60. "Exchanges between the Candidates in the Third Presidential Debate," *New York Times,* October 18, 2000.

61. "Democrats Launch Attack on Bush," *St. Louis Post-Dispatch,* November 4, 2000.

62. Stephen Hadley, author interview, October 12, 2009.

63. Dick Cheney, author interview, January 14, 2010.

64. "Former President George H. W. Bush and Members of His War Council Meet 20 Years after Start of First Gulf War," transcripts, NBC News, January 20, 2011 (www6.lexisnexis.com/publisher/EndUser?Action=UserDisplayFullDocument&orgId=574&topicId=100007221&docId=l:1344036036&start=34).

65. Condoleezza Rice, author interview, February 24, 2010.

66. Rumsfeld, interview, October 6, 2009.

67. Douglas Feith, author interview, December 22, 2009.

68. Cheney, interview, January 14, 2010.

69. Woodward, *Bush at War*, p. 209.

70. Ibid., p. 88.

71. Ibid., p. 168

72. Ibid., p. 168.

73. Ibid., p. 176.

74. Ibid., p. 95.

75. Ibid., p. 282.

76. Ibid., p. 95.

77. Ibid., p. 282.

78. Cheney, interview, January 14, 2010.

79. Ibid.

80. Feith, interview, December 22, 2009.

81. Woodward, *Bush at War*, p. 88.

82. Feith, interview, December 22, 2009.

83. Rumsfeld, interview, October 6, 2009.

84. Susan B. Glasser, "The Battle of Tora Bora," *Washington Post, Outlook,* December 20, 2009.

85. "A Nation Challenged: Excerpts from the Presidential Remarks on the War on Terrorism," *New York Times,* October 12, 2001.

86. "This Is a Time of Testing," *Washington Post,* October 12, 2001.

87. George W. Bush, *Decision Points* (New York: Crown, 2010), p. 199.

88. R. W. Apple Jr., "A Military Quagmire Remembered: Afghanistan as Vietnam," *New York Times,* October 31, 2001.

89. William Kristol, "The Wrong Strategy," *Washington Post,* October 30, 2001.

90. Charles Krauthammer, "Not Enough Might," *Washington Post,* October 30, 2001.

91. Joyce Howard Price, "Support Grows for U.S. Troops on Ground," *Washington Times,* October 29, 2001.

92. Woodward, *Bush at War*, pp. 256–57.

93. Rice, interview, February 24, 2010.

94. Douglas J. Feith, *War and Decision* (New York: HarperCollins, 2008), pp. 332–34.

95. Feith, interview, December 22, 2009.

96. William Cohen, author interview, September 21, 2009.

97. "Former President George H. W. Bush and Members of His War Council Meet 20 Years after Start of First Gulf War."

98. Bradley Graham, "Rumsfeld Tells of Regrets," *Washington Post,* February 3, 2011.

99. Dexter Filkins, "The Army You Have," *New York Times Book Review,* October 25, 2009.

100. Ibid.

101. Andrew J. Bacevich, "The Petraeus Doctrine," *Atlantic,* October 2008.

102. Ibid.

103. James Webb, "Down and Dirty: The War in Iraq Turns Ugly," *New York Times,* March 30, 2003.

104. R. W. Apple Jr., "Bush Peril: Shifting Sands and Fickle Opinion," *New York Times,* March 30, 2003.

105. Gary Anderson, "Saddam's Greater Game," *Washington Post,* April 2, 2003.

106. Feith, interview, December 22, 2009.

107. Filkins, "The Army You Have."

108. David Cloud and Greg Jaffe, *The Fourth Star: Four Generals and the Epic Struggle for the Future of the United States Army* (New York: Crown, 2009), p. 172.

109. Hadley, interview, October 12, 2009.

110. Bush, *Decision Points,* p. 367.

Chapter Eight (Swift Boat Campaign)

1. John Kerry, Testimony, "Proposals Relating to the War in Southeast Asia," Senate Committee on Foreign Relations, April 22, 1971 (www.c-span.org/vote2004/jkerry testimony.asp).

2. Ibid.

3. Douglas Brinkley, *Tour of Duty: John Kerry and the Vietnam War* (New York: William Morrow, 2004), pp. 14–15.

4. Michael Kranish, "With Antiwar Role, High Visibility," *Boston Globe,* June 17, 2003.

5. Joe Klein, "The Long War of John Kerry," *New Yorker,* December 2, 2002.

6. Michael Dobbs, "After Decades, Renewed War on an Old Conflict," *Washington Post,* August 28, 2004.

7. Brinkley, *Tour of Duty,* p. 403.

8. Ibid., p. 404.

9. Steve Hayes, author interview, September 13, 2006.

10. Brinkley, *Tour of Duty,* p. 177; Roy Hoffmann, author interview, August 18, 2005.

11. Joe Ponder, author interview, October 10, 2005.

12. William Franke, author interview, December 20, 2005.

13. Cameron Kerry, author interview, December 15, 2005.

14. *Hannity & Colmes,* transcript, Fox News, August 4, 2004.

15. Survey, University of Pennsylvania, Annenberg Public Policy Center (www.annenbergpublicpolicycenter.org/Downloads/Political_Communication/naes/2004_03_swiftboat-ad_08-20_pr.pdf).

16. Leroy Sievers, author interview, September 21, 2005.

17. Lois Romano and Jim VandeHei, "Kerry Says Group Is a Front for Bush," *Washington Post,* August 20, 2004.

18. Ibid.

19. Kate Zernike and Jim Rutenberg, "Friendly Fire: The Birth of an Attack on Kerry," *New York Times,* August 20, 2004.

20. John Kerry, author interview, December 14, 2005.

21. Peter S. Canellos, "Weighing Defeat, Kerry Sees Lessons to Guide Future," *Boston Globe,* February 6, 2005.

22. John Kerry, "Vietnam Then Was Worlds Apart from 'Apocalypse Now,'" *Boston Herald-American,* October 14, 1979.

23. John Kerry, Senate Floor Speech, *Congressional Record* (March 27, 1986), pp. 6421–23.

24. Roy Hoffmann, author interview, August 18, 2005.

25. John F. O'Neill and Jerome R. Corsi, *Unfit for Command: Swift Boat Veterans Speak Out against John Kerry* (Washington: Regnery, 2004), pp. 47–48.

26. Bill Zaladonis, author interview, May 9, 2006.

27. *Meet the Press,* NBC News, January 30, 2005.

28. Michael Kranish, "Kerry Disputes Allegation on Cambodia," *Boston Globe,* August 18, 2004.

29. *Meet the Press,* January 30, 2005.

30. David Stone, author interview, September 28, 2005.

31. Kerry, interview, December 14, 2005.

32. Hoffmann, interview, August 18, 2005.

33. Kate Zernike, "Kerry Pressing Swift Boat Case Long after Loss," *New York Times,* May 28, 2006.

34. *NewsHour* Online, PBS, August 19, 2004 (www.pbs.org/newshour/bb/politics/july-dec04/vietnam_8-19.html).

35. Ron Brinson, "Schachte Ready to Re-engage in Kerry Purple Heart Dispute," (Charleston, S.C.) *Post and Courier,* May 4, 2006.

36. Michael Kranish, "Retired Rear Admiral Contends Kerry Wound Not from Enemy Fire," *Boston Globe,* August 28, 2004.

37. "Purple Heart News," *National Review,* August 28, 2004.

38. Stephen Braun, "The Race to the White House: Kerry's Own War over Vietnam," *Los Angeles Times,* July 5, 2004.

39. Michael Kranish, "Heroism, and Growing Concern about War," *Boston Globe,* June 16, 2003.

40. Brinkley, *Tour of Duty,* pp. 144–45, 460.

41. David Halberstam, author interview, May 2, 2006.

42. William Schachte, e-mail, April 18, 2006.

43. "Purple Heart News."

44. Brinkley, *Tour of Duty,* pp. 145–47.

45. Ibid., p. 148.

46. Kranish, "Retired Rear Admiral Contends Kerry Wound Not from Enemy Fire."

47. Bill Zaladonis and Pat Runyon, author interview, April 9, 2006.

48. Kranish, "Retired Rear Admiral Contends Kerry Wound Not from Enemy Fire."

49. Zaladonis and Runyon, interview, April 9, 2006.

50. James Zumwalt, e-mail, January 3, 2006.

51. O'Neill and Corsi, *Unfit for Command*, pp. 36–37.

52. Braun, "The Race to the White House."

53. Kranish, "Heroism, and Growing Concern about War."

54. David Thorne, author interview, September 28, 2005.

55. Kerry, interview, December 14, 2005.

56. O'Neill and Corsi, *Unfit for Command*, p. 36.

57. Zaladonis, interview, April 9, 2006.

58. Kate Zernike, "Veterans Long to Reclaim the Name 'Swift Boat,'" *New York Times*, June 30, 2008.

Chapter Nine (Obama)

Special note: The chapter title is taken from a statement made by Obama and reported in John Harwood, "Obama Rejects Afghanistan-Vietnam Comparison," *New York Times*, September 15, 2009.

1. Peter Baker, "For Obama, Steep Learning Curve as Chief in War," *New York Times*, August 28, 2010.

2. Robert M. Gates, "Helping Others Defend Themselves: The Future of U.S. Security Assistance," *Foreign Affairs*, May/June 2010.

3. Admiral Mike Mullen, "Chairman's Corner: Three Principles for Use of Military," American Forces Press Service, March 5, 2010.

4. Michael Hirsh, "Obama's Bad Cop," *Newsweek*, April 23, 2010.

5. Jeffrey T. Kuhner, "Obama's Vietnam?" *Washington Times*, January 25, 2009.

6. John Barry and Evan Thomas, "Obama's Vietnam," *Newsweek*, February 9, 2009

7. Mark Landler, "Post-Holbrooke Question: 'What Now?'" *New York Times*, December 14, 2010.

8. James Steinberg, author interview, April 7, 2010.

9. Ibid.

10. Chuck Hagel, author interview, April 20, 2010.

11. Barack Obama, *The Audacity of Hope* (New York: Three Rivers Press, 2006), p. 36.

12. Richard Wolffe, *Renegade: The Making of a President* (New York: Crown, 2009), p. 241.

13. David Remnick, *The Bridge: The Life and Rise of Barack Obama* (New York: Knopf, 2010), pp. 344–45.

14. Ibid., p. 345.

15. Ibid., pp. 345–47.

16. David Mendell, *Obama: From Promise to Power* (New York: Amistad, 2007), p. 177.

17. James W. Ceaser, Andrew E. Busch, and John J. Pitney Jr., *Epic Journey: The 2008 Elections and American Politics* (Lanham, Md.: Rowman and Littlefield, 2009), p. 39.

18. David Plouffe, *The Audacity to Win* (New York: Viking, 2009), pp. 104–05.

19. Jack Reed, author interview, May 7, 2010.

20. Glenn Kessler, "Hagel Defends Criticisms of Iraq Policy," *Washington Post*, November 16, 2005.

21. Carlotta Gall and Jeff Zeleny, "In Kabul, Obama Calls Afghan Front 'Central' to War on Terror," *New York Times*, July 20, 2008.

22. Reed, interview, May 7, 2010.

23. Ibid.

24. Ibid.

25. Ibid.

26. Ted Barrett, "GOP Senator: Bush Plan Could Match Vietnam Blunder," CNN, January 11, 2007.

27. "Hagel Criticizes 'Arrogant' Bush White House," CNN, November 29, 2007.

28. Hagel, interview, April 20, 2010.

29. Reed, interview, May 7, 2010.

30. Matt Bai, "The McCain Doctrines," *New York Times Magazine*, May 18, 2008.

31. Obama's speech to the Veterans of Foreign Wars (www.clipsandcomment. com/2008/08/19/full-text-obama-speech-to-vfw-national-convention/).

32. John Heilemann and Mark Halperin, *Game Change* (New York: HarperCollins, 2010), pp. 301–02.

33. Dan Balz and Haynes Johnson, *The Battle for America 2008* (New York: Viking, 2009), p. 265.

34. Heilemann and Halperin, *Game Change*, p. 318.

35. Ceaser and others, *Epic Journey*, p. 149.

36. Evan Thomas, *A Long Time Coming* (New York: Public Affairs) p. 141.

37. Scott Shane, "Obama and '60s Bomber: A Look into Crossed Paths," *New York Times*, October 4, 2008.

38. Balz and Johnson, *The Battle for America*, p. 361.

39. Plouffe, *The Audacity to Win*, p. 354.

40. Bruce Riedel, author interview, April 15, 2010.

41. Bob Woodward, *Obama's Wars* (New York: Simon and Schuster, 2010), p. 110.

42. Elisabeth Bumiller, "Major Push Is Needed to Save Afghanistan, General Says," *New York Times*, January 9, 2009.

43. Helene Cooper, "Obama's War," *New York Times*, January 25, 2009.

44. Army Staff Sergeant Michael J. Carden, "Petraeus Discusses Way Ahead for Afghanistan," American Forces Press Service, January 9, 2009.

45. Ann Scott Tyson, "Gates Predicts 'Slog' in Afghanistan," *Washington Post*, January 28, 2009.

46. Riedel, interview, April 15, 2010.

47. James Jones, author interview, January 6, 2011.

48. Jones, interview, April 23, 2010.

49. Thomas Donilon, author interview, May 11, 2010.

50. Jones, interview, April 23, 2010.

51. Riedel, interview, April 15, 2010.

52. White House, Office of the Press Secretary, February 17, 2009 (www.whitehouse. gov/the_press_office/Statement-by-the-President-on-Afghanistan/).

53. Ann Scott Tyson, "'Sustained' Push Seen in Afghanistan," *Washington Post*, February 19, 2009.

54. Riedel, interview, April 15, 2010.

55. Ibid.

56. Ibid.

57. Ibid.

58. "President Obama's Remarks on New Strategy for Afghanistan and Pakistan," *New York Times*, March 27, 2009.

59. Ann Scott Tyson, "Afghan Effort Is Mullen's Top Focus," *Washington Post*, May 5, 2009.

60. Ann Scott Tyson, "Military Wants More Troops for Afghan War," *Washington Post*, April 2, 2009.

61. Bob Woodward, "Key in Afghanistan—Economy, Not Military," *Washington Post*, July 1, 2009.

62. Ibid.

63. Helene Cooper and Eric Schmitt, "Obama Afghanistan Plan Narrows U.S. War Goals," *New York Times*, March 28, 2009.

64. Rajiv Chandrasekaran, "Pentagon Worries Led to Command Change," *Washington Post*, August 17, 2009.

65. Ibid.

66. Ibid.

67. Ann Scott Tyson, "Top U.S. Commander in Afghanistan Is Fired," *Washington Post*, May 12, 2009.

68. Elisabeth Bumiller and Mark Mazzetti, "General Steps from Shadow," *New York Times*, May 13, 2009.

69. Ann Scott Tyson, "New Approach to Afghanistan Likely," *Washington Post*, June 3, 2009.

70. See www.newsweek.com/2008/10/24/what-vietnam-teaches-us.html.

71. Richard Holbrooke, author interview, December 17, 2009.

72. Ibid.

73. Stanley Karnow, *Vietnam: A History* (New York: Viking Press, 1983).

74. Ibid.

75. Stanley Karnow, author interview, October 21, 2010.

76. Slobodan Lekic, "U.S. Looks to Vietnam for Afghanistan Tips," *Lawrence Journal-World*, August 7, 2009.

77. Gordon M. Goldstein, *Lessons in Disaster: McGeorge Bundy and the Path to the War in Vietnam* (New York: Times Books, 2008).

78. Donilon, interview, May 11, 2010.

79. Holbrooke, interview, December 17, 2009.

80. Richard Holbrooke, "The Doves Were Right," *New York Times Book Review*, November 30, 2008.

81. Donilon, interview, May 11, 2010.

82. Bui Diem, "Reflections on the Vietnam War," in *Looking Back on the Vietnam War*, edited by William Head and Lawrence E. Grinter (Westport, Conn.: Praeger, 1993), p. 243.

83. Bui Diem, author interview, October 21, 2010.

84. Dean Rusk, author interview, 1977.

85. Goldstein, *Lessons in Disaster*, p. 186.

86. Lewis Sorley, *A Better War: The Unexamined Victories and Final Tragedy of America's Last Years in Vietnam* (Orlando, Fla.: Harcourt, 1999).

87. Peter Spiegel and Jonathan Weisman, "Behind Afghan War Debate, A Battle of Two Books Rages," *Wall Street Journal,* October 7, 2009.

88. David Barno, e-mail, October 29, 2010.

89. David Barno, address to Meeting of the American Political Science Association, Washington, D.C., September 3, 2010.

90. Peter Baker, "LBJ All the Way," *New York Times,* August 23, 2009.

91. Garry Wills, "Obama's Legacy: Afghanistan," *New York Review of Books,* July 27, 2010 (www.nybooks.com/blogs/nyrblog/2010/jul/27/obamas-legacy-afghanistan).

92. Bob Woodward, "Top U.S. Commander for Afghan War Calls Next 12 Months Decisive," *Washington Post,* September 21, 2009.

93. Woodward, *Obama's Wars,* p. 192.

94. Ibid., p. 175.

95. Leon Panetta, author interview, April 9, 2010.

96. Mark Landler and Jeff Zeleny, "Ambassador's Views Show Sharp Afghanistan Divide," *New York Times,* November 13, 2009.

97. Stanley McChrystal, interview, *60 Minutes,* CBS News, September 27, 2009 (/www.cbsnews.com/stories/2009/09/24/60minutes/main5335445_page4.shtml?tag=contentMain;contentBody).

98. Woodward, *Obama's Wars,* pp. 192–97.

99. Donilon, interview, May 11, 2010.

100. Woodward, *Obama's Wars,* p. 219.

101. Dexter Filkins, "U.S. Pullout a Condition in Afghan Peace Talks," *New York Times,* May 20, 2009.

102. Woodward, *Obama's Wars,* p. 251.

103. Peter Baker, "How Obama Came to Plan for 'Surge' in Afghanistan," *New York Times,* December 5, 2009.

104. Baker, "For Obama, Steep Learning Curve as Chief in War."

105. Woodward, *Obama's Wars,* p. 260.

106. Baker, "How Obama Came to Plan for 'Surge' in Afghanistan."

107. Eric Schmitt, "U.S. Envoy's Cables Show Worries on Afghan Plans," *New York Times,* January 25, 2010.

108. Baker, "How Obama Came to Plan for 'Surge' in Afghanistan."

109. Schmitt, "U.S. Envoy's Cables Show Worries on Afghan Plans."

110. Adam Gabbatt and Matthew Weaver, "Hamid Karzai Sets Afghan Security Target in Inauguration Speech," *Guardian* (U.K.), November 19, 2009.

111. Evan Thomas and John Barry, "How We (Could Have) Won in Vietnam," *Newsweek,* November 16, 2009.

112. Woodward, *Obama's Wars,* photo 22.

113. Ibid., pp. 301–02.

114. Donilon, interview, May 11, 2010.

115. Woodward, *Obama's Wars,* pp. 305.

116. Baker, "How Obama Came to Plan for 'Surge' in Afghanistan."

117. Donilon, interview, May 11, 2010.

118. Woodward, *Obama's Wars,* pp. 311–14.

119. Ibid., pp. 385–90.

120. Ibid., p. 324.

121. Ibid., pp. 324–29, 385–90.

122. Baker, "How Obama Came to Plan for 'Surge' in Afghanistan."

123. Joe Klein, "In the Arena," *Time* Magazine, December 14, 2009.

124. Frank Rich, "Obama's Logic Is No Match for Afghanistan," *New York Times*, December 5, 2009.

125. White House, Office of the Press Secretary, "Remarks by the President in Address to the Nation on the Way Forward in Afghanistan and Pakistan," December 1, 2009.

126. Woodward, *Obama's Wars*, p. 306.

127. Marc Ambinder, "Lunch with the President: The Politics of Obama's War Plan," *Atlantic*, December 1, 2009.

128. White House, "Remarks by the President," December 1, 2009.

129. Ambinder, "Lunch with the President."

130. Peter Beinart, "Shrinking the War on Terrorism," *Time* Magazine, December 14, 2009.

131. White House, "Remarks by the President," December 1, 2009.

132. White House, Office of the Press Secretary, "Remarks by the President at the Acceptance of the Nobel Peace Prize," Oslo, Norway, December 10, 2009.

Chapter Ten ("Good Enough")

1. Barack Obama, Illinois state senator, "Remarks against Going to War with Iraq," October 2, 2002 (www.barackobama.com).

2. David J. Kilcullen, "Three Pillars of Counterinsurgency," remarks delivered at the U.S. Government Counterinsurgency Conference, Washington, D.C., September 28, 2006 (www.au.af.mil/au/awc/awcgate/uscoin/3pillars_of_counterinsurgency.pdf).

3. "Operation Marjah," *Foreign Policy*, February 17, 2010 (www.foreignpolicy.com/articles/2010/02/17/operation_marjah?page=0,0).

4. Michael M. Phillips, "U.S. Announces Helmand Offensive," *Wall Street Journal*, February 3, 2010.

5. Tony Perry and Laura King, "Marines Focus on Civilian Safety in Afghanistan," *Los Angeles Times*, February 9, 2010.

6. Dexter Filkins, "Afghan Offensive Is New War Model," *New York Times*, February 12, 2010.

7. David Ignatius, "Progress in Afghanistan, with Caveats," *Washington Post*, December 17, 2010.

8. Karen DeYoung and Craig Whitlock, "Kandahar Offensive Will Take Months Longer than Planned," *Washington Post*, June 11, 2010.

9. President John F. Kennedy, interview with Walter Cronkite, CBS, September 2, 1963 (www.mtholyoke.edu/acad/intrel/kentv.htm).

10. DeYoung and Whitlock, "Kandahar Offensive Will Take Months Longer."

11. Ibid.

12. Alissa J. Rubin, "U.S. Report on Afghan War Finds Few Gains in 6 Months," *New York Times*, April 29, 2010.

13. Michael Hastings, "The Runaway General," *Rolling Stone,* June 22, 2010 (www.rollingstone.com/politics/news/the-runaway-general-20100622).

14. Bob Woodward, *Obama's Wars* (New York: Simon and Schuster, 2010), pp. 372–73.

15. Brian Montopoli, "Top Democrat David Obey Calls for 'Dangerous' McChrystal to Be Relieved of Command," CBS News, June 22, 2010 (www.cbsnews.com/8301-503544_162-20008453-503544.html).

16. Sheryl Gay Stolberg, "Legislator Sees Echoes of Vietnam in Afghan War," *New York Times,* December 13, 2009.

17. "Biden Responds to McChrystal Jibe," ABC News, July 18, 2010 (http://blogs.abcnews.com/politicalpunch/2010/07/biden-responds-to-mcchrystal-jibe.html).

18. Laura King, "A Hard-Driving, Unyielding Commander," *Los Angeles Times,* June 22, 2010.

19. Woodward, *Obama's Wars,* p. 372.

20. James Jones, author interview, January 6, 2011.

21. Peter Baker, "For Obama, Steep Learning Curve as Chief in War," *New York Times,* August 29, 2010.

22. Dexter Filkins, "Petraeus Takes Command of Afghan Mission," *New York Times,* July 4, 2010.

23. *Meet the Press,* NBC, transcript for August 15, 2010 (www.msnbc.msn.com/id/38686033/ns/meet_the_press-transcripts/).

24. Dexter Filkins, "Petraeus Opposes a Rapid Pullout in Afghanistan," *New York Times,* August 15, 2010.

25. Ibid.

26. *Meet the Press,* transcript for August 15, 2010.

27. Gilles Dorronsoro, "Afghanistan Will Only Get Worse," *International Herald Tribune,* September 14, 2010.

28. Jason Motlagh, "The Afghan War: Why the Kandahar Campaign Matters," *Time Magazine,* October 18, 2010.

29. Joshua Partlow, "Karzai Wants U.S. to Reduce Military Operations in Afghanistan," *Washington Post,* November 14, 2010.

30. Ron Moreau, "The Taliban Call a Time-Out," *Newsweek,* November 27, 2010.

31. Rajiv Chandrasekaran, "U.S. Deploying Heavily Armed Battle Tanks for First Time in Afghan War," *Washington Post,* November 19, 2010; Jim Garamone, "U.S. Tanks En Route to Southwestern Afghanistan," American Forces Press Service, November 19, 2010.

32. Motlagh, "The Afghan War."

33. James S. Robbins, "An Old, Old Story: Misreading Tet, Again," *World Affairs,* September/October 2010.

34. Ibid.

35. Rajiv Chandrasekaran, "As U.S. Assesses Afghan War, Karzai a Question Mark," *Washington Post,* December 13, 2010.

36. Helene Cooper and Carlotta Gall, "Cables Offer Shifting Portrait of Karzai," *New York Times,* December 2, 2010.

37. "Draft Communique Sets 2014 as Target for Afghan Military to Lead," *New York Times,* July 20, 2010.

38. "Conference Endorses Afghan Goal for Security Handover," BBC News, July 20, 2010 (www.bbc.co.uk/news/world-south-asia-10687527).

39. *This Week*, ABC, August 1, 2010 (http://abcnews.go.com/ThisWeek/week-transcript-pelosi-gates/story?id=11298444&page=3).

40. *Meet the Press*, NBC, December 19, 2010 (www.msnbc.msn.com/id/40720643/).

41. Partlow, "Karzai Wants U.S. to Reduce Military Operations in Afghanistan."

42. Joshua Partlow and Karen DeYoung, "Petraeus Warns Afghans about Karzai's Criticism of U.S. War Strategy," *Washington Post*, November 15, 2010.

43. Steven Erlanger and Jackie Calmes, "NATO Sees Long-Term Role after Afghan Combat," *New York Times*, November 20, 2010.

44. Ibid.

45. Arnaud de Borchgrave, "Vietnam Syndrome?" December 13, 2010 (www.upi.com/Top_News/Analysis/de-Borchgrave/2010/12/13/Commentary-Vietnam-syndrome/UPI-83661292245020/).

46. Peter Baker, "Obama Pays Visit to Afghanistan," *New York Times*, December 3, 2010; Carol E. Lee, "Barack Obama, in Afghanistan, Tells Troops They're 'On the Offensive,'" *Politico*, December 3, 2010 (www.politico.com/news/stories/1210/45923.html).

47. David Alexander, "Gates Says Afghanistan Strategy on Right Track," Reuters, December 8, 2010 (www.reuters.com/article/idUSTRE6B753420101208).

48. Helene Cooper and David E. Sanger, "Obama Cites Afghan Gains as Report Says Exit Is on Track," *New York Times*, December 16, 2010.

49. Elisabeth Bumiller, "Intelligence Reports Offer Dim View of Afghan War," *New York Times*, December 14, 2010.

50. Poll on Afghanistan War, Pew Research Center for the People and the Press, December 7, 2010 (http://pewresearch.org/pubs/1822/poll-bush-tax-cuts-start-treaty-boehner-pelosi-afghanistan-korea).

51. Eugene Robinson, "A War's Cycle to Nowhere," *Washington Post*, December 17, 2010.

52. General David Petraeus, interview with George Stephanopoulos, ABC News, December 6, 2010 (http://blogs.abcnews.com/george/2010/12/cxclusive-gen petraeus-not-sure-victory-in-afghanistan-by-2014.html).

53. Woodward, *Obama's Wars*, photo 17.

54. Amy Rhodin, "Carter: U.S., Obama Will Likely Lose the War in Afghanistan," *GW Hatchet*, December 6, 2010 (http://uwire.com/2010/12/06/carter-u-s-obama-will-likely-lose-the-war-in-afghanistan/).

55. James Jones, author interview, January 6, 2011.

56. Thom Shanker, "Gates Ratchets Up His Campaign of Candor," *New York Times*, March 4, 2011 (www.nytimes.com/2011/03/05/world/05/gates.html).

57. Elisabeth Bumiller and Thom Shanker, "2 Cabinet Officials Say U.S. Isn't Likely to Arm Libyans," *New York Times*, March 31, 2011, p. 1.

Index to Quotations

Index